A
POST-SYMBOLIST
BIBLIOGRAPHY

compiled by

Henry Krawitz

The Scarecrow Press, Inc.
Metuchen, N.J.   1973

Library of Congress Cataloging in Publication Data

Krawitz, Henry.
  A post-symbolist bibliography.

  1. Literature, Modern--20th century--Bibliography.
2. Symbolism in literature--Bibliography. I. Title.
Z6520.S9K7   016.809'04   73-1181
ISBN 0-8108-0594-4

1755804

To My Parents

PREFACE

The idea for A Post-Symbolist Bibliography was first suggested to me by Haskell M. Block, professor of comparative literature at Brooklyn College and the Graduate School and University Center (CUNY). It was under his able direction that the present project was originally begun. I owe him a special debt of gratitude for having introduced me to this fascinating period of literary history.

I also wish to express my sincere thanks to the reference librarians of the Paul Klapper Library at Queens College. Mrs. Olive James was especially helpful in solving numerous bibliographic complexities. I am grateful to her for suggesting publication of the original manuscript. Mr. Wendell Daniel, head of the reference division, provided me with much expert advice and technical assistance. The combined efforts of both these individuals helped to make this scholarly project a reality.

A university appointment enabled me to concentrate all my energies upon the difficult task of researching and organizing the data for the bibliography. I therefore wish to express my gratitude to the Graduate Division of the City University of New York for its continued support in this endeavor.

Lastly, for any errors which may appear in the present compilation, I alone am responsible. If the bibliography succeeds in making the field of post-Symbolist criticism more accessible, my efforts have been amply rewarded.

H. K.

July 1972
The Graduate School and University Center
The City University of New York

v

CONTENTS

INTRODUCTION

Although much attention has been devoted to a study of the Symbolist movement proper, relatively little effort has been directed towards an investigation of the subsequent development of Symbolist aesthetics. With few exceptions*, the serious student of this influential literary movement lacks the tools with which to undertake an intensive investigation of the post-Symbolist period.

The present bibliography is intended to fill this need. In addition to providing selected bibliographies on individual writers, poets, and dramatists, the compilation approaches the field of post-Symbolist studies on three additional levels. The first section includes books and articles which purport to deal with the subject from a supranational perspective; many of the works listed in this section are concerned with questions of theory and definition of the movement. The second section, as the heading implies, is primarily national in scope. The third section is reserved for studies involving two or more literary figures; the question of influence is specifically dealt with in this latter category.

The bibliography is comparative in nature, with special emphasis upon recent criticism (1950-1970) written in English, French, German, Spanish, and Italian. Attention has also been given to books and articles (written in English) which deal with other national literatures (e. g., Russian). Strict alphabetical order has been observed in all sections of the bibliography. For the sake of conciseness, common abbreviations have been employed wherever possible. Anonymous studies are acknowledged as such. Joint ventures are headed "Essays by various hands." Where earlier editions of a book are known, the date has been placed within parentheses--e. g., 1969(1950)--following the main entry.

---

*The following book-length studies should be mentioned: C. M. Bowra, The Heritage of Symbolism; Kenneth Cornell, The Post-Symbolist Period; Michel Décaudin, La Crise des Valeurs Symbolistes; and Bernard Weinberg, The Limits of Symbolism.

A POST-SYMBOLIST BIBLIOGRAPHY

INTERNATIONAL STUDIES

1. Alonso, Amado, and Raimundo Lida. "El concepto lingüístico de Impresionismo," El Impresionismo en el Lenguaje, Buenos Aires: 1936, pp. 121-251.
2. Angers, Pierre. "Situation du symbolisme," Nouv. Rev. Canadienne, I, 6 (févr.-mars 1952), 10-20.
3. Anon. "Impressionnisme et symbolisme dans la litt. et dans les arts," Cah. de l'Assoc. Intern'l des Etudes Françaises, XII (juin 1960), 103-87.
4. _____. "Hermétisme et poésie," Cah. Assoc. Intern'l des Etudes Françaises, XV (mars 1963), 7-161.
5. Aubéry, Pierre. "The anarchism of the literati of the symbolist period," French Review, XLII, 1 (Oct. 1968), 39-47.
6. _____. "L'Anarchisme des littérateurs au temps du Symbolisme," Le Mouvement Social, no. 69 (Oct.-Déc. 1969), 21-34.
7. _____. Pour une Lecture Ouvrière de la Litt. Paris: (1969) (incl. Symbolism, Mallarmé).
8. Balakian, Anna. The Symbolist Movement: A Critical Appraisal. N.Y.: 1967. (Stud. in Lang & Lit, 11) (bibliogr., pp. 199-203).
9. _____. El Movimiento Simbolista: Juicio Crítico, trad. José-Miguel Velloso. Madrid: 1969. (Col. Punto Omega.)
10. _____. "Le caractère intern'l du symbolisme," Actes du 5ième Congrès de l'Assoc. Intern'l de Litt. Comparée (1969), 293-9. (In English: Mosaic, II, 4 (Summer 1969), 1-8.)
11. Bally, Charles, et al. El Impresionismo en el Lenguaje. Buenos Aires: 1936. (Col. de Estudios Estilísticas, II.)
12. Barea, José A. "Las modernas tendencias de vanguardia," Sustancia, II, 6 (Marzo 1941), 254-61.

(Symbolism/Surrealism.)

13. Barre, André. Bibliographie de la Poésie Symboliste.
    Paris: 1911. (Cf. article, same title, in Revue
    Palladienne, no. 15, 2e dizaine, no. 5 (juin-juill.
    1951), cah. 1 & 2; no. 16, 2e diz., no. 6 (oct.-
    nov. 1951), cah. 3; nos. 19-20, 2e diz., nos. 9-
    10 (1952), cah. 4.)

14. _____. Le Symbolisme. Essai Historique....
    Genève: 1970. (Slatkine Reprints.)

15. Barrère, J. -B. Le Regard d'Orphée ou de Fantômes
    et de Poésie. Cambridge, Eng.: 1956.

16. Battisti, Eugenio. "Simbolo ed arte figurativa, " Rev.
    di Estetica (Univ. Padova), VII (1962), 185-97.

17. Beach, Joseph W. Obsessive Images: Symbolism in
    Poetry of the 1930's and 1940's, ed. W. van
    O'Connor. Minneapolis: 1960.

18. Beatty, R. C. "The heritage of symbolism in mod.
    poetry, " Yale Review, XXXVI (Mar. 1947), 467-77.

19. Beebe, Maurice, ed. Literary Symbolism: An Introd.
    to the Interpr. of Lit. San Francisco: 1961.

20. Bell, S. M., and W. M. L. "The Nineteenth Century, "
    (Post-Romantic), The Year's Work in Mod.
    Lang. Studies (Cambridge), XXXI (1969), 139-56.

21. Benamou, Michel, et al. "Symposium on lit. impres-
    sionism, " Yearbook of Comp. & Gen'l Lit.,
    XVII (1968), 40-68.

22. Berefelt, Gunnar. "On symbol and allegory, " Journ.
    of Aesthetics and Art Crit., XXVIII (1969), 201-
    12.

23. Bersier, Jean-Eugène. Contre l'Impressionnisme
    (suivi de) Pour l'Impressionnisme par Jean-
    Dominique Rey. Paris: 1969. (Coll. Pour ou
    Contre, 17.)

24. Block, Haskell M. "Surrealism and mod. poetry.
    Outline of an approach, " Journ. of Aesthetics
    and Art Crit., XVIII (1959/60), 174-82.

25. _____. "The alleged parallel of metaphysical and
    symbolist poetry, " Comp. Lit. Studies, IV (1967),
    145-59.

26. _____. "Interpr. Symbolist poetry, " Comp.
    Lit. Studies, VII (1970), 489-503.

27. Bonneau, G. "Symbolisme poétique et symbolisme
    théâtral, " Mélanges Critiques. Ankara: 1956,
    pp. 127-36.

28. Borel, Jacques. "D'Une expérience de l'impuissance, "
    (Symbolisme, Surrealisme) Cah. du Sud, LVIII
    (1964), 270-87.

29. Boucher, M. "Uber das Esoterische in der Lyrik, "
    Unterscheidung u. Bewahrung. Berlin: 1961,
    pp. 31-40.
30. Bousono, Carlos. "Die Suggestion i.d. mod. Lyrik.
    Mod. Lyrik u. Romantik: Suggestion gegen
    Grosssprecherei, " Wort in der Zeit (Wien), XI,
    10 (1965), 15-24.
31. Bowra, C. M. The Heritage of Symbolism. London:
    1959 (older ed. 1943). (Incl.: Valéry, Rilke,
    George, Blok, and Yeats) [Paperback ed., N.Y.:
    Schocken Books, 1961.]
32. _____. Das Erbe d. Symbolismus, trans. Ernst
    Sander. Wien: 1948. (Earlier ed., Hamburg:
    1947.)
33. _____. The Creative Experiment. London: 1949.
34. _____. "Poetry in Europe, 1900-1950, "
    Diogenes (Winter 1953), 8-24.
35. _____. Inspiration and Poetry. London: 1955.
36. Boyé, Maurice-Pierre. "Autres visages du symbolisme:
    les petits revues qui surgirent et ressucitèrent
    dès l'année qui suivit l'armistice de 1918, " Rolet,
    no. 565 (15 août 1956), 4; no. 566 (1 sept. 1956),
    4.
37. Brémond, Henri. La Poésie Pure. Paris: 1926.
38. Brumm, U. "Symbolism and the novel, " Partisan Re-
    view, XXV (1958), 329-42.
39. Brun, M. "L'hermétisme dans la poésie, " Afrique,
    CCLXVIII (1958), 26-31.
40. Buccellato, M. "Il linguaggio e la filos. delle forme
    simboliche, " Riv. Crit. di Storia della Filos.,
    X (1955), 58-68.
41. Burke, K. "Symbol and association, " Hudson Review,
    IX (1956/7), 212-25.
42. Caillois, Roger. "Obscurité, voyance et images
    poétiques, " Médicine de France, no. 21 (1951).
43. Caminade, Pierre. Image et Métaphore. Un Problème
    de Poétique Contemp. Paris: 1970. (Etudes
    Supér., série rouge, 36.)
44. Carmody, Francis. "Le décadisme, " Cah. Assoc. In-
    tern'l Etudes Françaises, no. 12 (juin 1960),
    121-31.
45. Cary, Joseph B., Jr. "The theory and practice of the
    vague. A study in a mode of 19th cen. poetry, "
    Diss. Abstr., XXVII (1966/7), 1362A (N.Y.U.).
46. Cassou, Jean, et al. Les Sources du XXe Siècle.
    Paris: 1961.

47. Cattaui, Georges. "L'ésotérisme des poètes, " Critique, no. 113 (oct. 1956), 819-35.

48. Cazamian, Louis. Symbolisme et Poésie. Neuchâtel: 1947.

49. Champigny, Robert. "Trois définitions du symbolisme, " Comp. Lit. Studies, IV (1967), 127-33.

50. Charpentier, John. Le Symbolisme. Paris: 1927.

51. Chiari, Joseph. "Symbolism and reality, " Realism and Imagination. London: 1960, pp. 109-24.

52. Chicoteau, Marcel. Studies in Symbolist Psychology: Mind-Spirit-Morals-Men. Cardiff: 1940 (2d ed. Sydney: 1958).

53. Christophe, Lucien. "Ombres et lumières du symbolisme, " Revue Générale Belge, XCIII, no. 3 (mars 1957), 28-40.

54. Clémeur, Marcel. Alchimie et Chimie Poétiques. Essai. Bruxelles: 1970.

55. Cocteau, Jean. "Poetry and invisibility, " (trans. Jean Stewart) London Magazine, IV, 1 (Jan. 1957), 29-44.

56. Cohen, John M. Poetry of This Age: 1908-'58. London: 1960.

57. Cohn, Robert G. "The Assault on Symbolism, " Comp. Lit. Studies, V, 1 (March 1968), 69-75.

58. Cook, Harold E. "The musicality of poetry, " Bucknell Review, IX (1961), 303-17.

59. Cornell, Kenneth. The Symbolist Movement. New Haven: 1951. (Bibliog., pp. 207-9.)

60. _____, ed. "Symbol and symbolism, " Yale French Studies, IX (1952), 165 pp. (Allegory and dream intuition in poetry.)

61. Crastre, Victor. Poésie et Mystique. Neuchâtel: 1967.

62. Cunningham, James V. Tradition and Poetic Structure. Denver: 1960.

63. Debidour, V.-H. "Poésie et silence, " Bull. des Lettres, XIII, 125 (15 févr. 1951), 49-54.

64. Décaudin, Michel. "La poésie en 1914, " Mercure de France, no. 1158 (févr. 1960), 248-58.

65. _____. "Poésie impressionniste et poésie symboliste (1870-1900), " Cah. Assoc. Intern'l. Etudes Françaises, XII (juin 1960), 133-42.

66. _____. "Pré-symbolisme, symbolisme, post-symbolisme, " Problèmes de Périodisation dans l'Histoire Litt.: Colloque Intern'l Organisé par la Section d'Etudes Romanes de l'Univ. Charles de Prague. (29 nov. -1 déc. 1966). Praha: 1968, pp. 41-6. (Also in: Romanistica Pragensia,

V, 1968, 41-6.)

67. Deguy, Michel. "Usages poétiques du symbole, " Cah. Intern'aux de Symbolisme, XIII (1967), 3-18.

68. Delbouille, Paul. Poésie et Sonorités. La Critique Contemp. Devant le Pouvoir Suggestif des Sons. Paris: 1961.

69. Denat, Antoine. "Les deux poétiques: poétique du langage, poétique de la transcendance, " Vu des Antipodes. Synthèses Critiques. Paris: 1969, pp. 122-38. (Orig.: Austral. Journ. French Studies (Melbourne), V (1968), 3-17.)

70. Dinar, André. La Croisade Symboliste. Paris: 1943.

71. Dresse, Paul. "La sacrilisation du silence ou une idée-force en poésie, " Points et Contrepoints, LX (mars 1962), 1-6.

72. _____. "Que fut le symbolisme?" Audace (Bruxelles), XVI, 1 (1970), 3-7.

73. Dubois, Jacques, et al. "Rhétorique généralisée, " Cah. Intern'aux de Symbolisme, XV/XVI (1967/ 8), 103-15.

74. Dupont, Louis. "Pour ou contre l'obscurité en poésie, " Vie et Langage, XVII (1968), 638-42.

75. Durgnat, Raymond. "Symbolism and the underground, " Hudson Review, XXII, 3 (Autumn 1969), 457-68.

76. Eco, Umberto. "L'oeuvre ouverte et la poétique de l'indétermination, " Nouvelle Revue Française, (juillet 1960), 117-24; (août 1960), 313-20.

77. Edeline, Fr. "L'expression indirecte en poésie, " Courrier du Centre Intern'l d'Etudes Poétiques, XXXVII/XXXVIII (janv. 1962), 7-25.

78. Eluard, Paul, ed. Poésie Involontaire et Poésie Intentionnelle. Poésie 42. Paris: 1963 (1942).

79. Essays by var. hands. "Symbol and Symbolism." Yale French Studies, IX (1952), 165 pp. (Incl. Fowlie, Wallace. "Legacy of symbolism, " 20 6; Frye, Northrop. "Three meanings of symbolism, " 11-19; Pucciani, Oreste F. "The univ. lang. of symbolism, " 27-35; Steiner, Herbert. "A note on symbolism, " 36-9.)

80. _____. "Surrealismo e Simbolismo, " Archivio di Filos., no. 3 (1965), 1-141. (num. spec.).

81. _____. "The Symbolist Movement, " Comp. Lit. Stud., IV, 1/2 (1967), 226 pp. (Special issue) (introd. by Haskell M. Block, pp. 1-3.)

82. _____. "Symposium in literary impressionism, " Yearbook of Comp. & Gen'l Lit., XVII (1968), 40-68.

83. Etiemble, René. "La poésie: expérience mystique ou plaisir musculaire?" Les Temps Modernes, VI, 68 (juin 1951), 2231-9; VII, 69 (juillet 1951), 147-54.

84. Flora, F. Dal Romanticismo al Futurismo. Piacenza: 1922.

85. Fox, E. Inman. "La poesía 'socia' y la trad. simbolista, " Torre, LXIV (1969), 47-62.

86. Gaunt, William. The Aesthetic Adventure. London: 1945.

87. Gengoux, J. "Le symbolisme et les symbolismes, " Les Lettres Romanes, V, 1 (1 févr. 1951), 3-37.

88. Ghil, René. Les Dates et les Oeuvres: Symbolisme et Poésie Scientifique. Paris: 1923.

89. Gibbs, B. J. "Impressionism as a lit. movement, " Mod. Lang. Journ., XXXVI (1952), 175-83.

90. Gihoul, R. P. Luc-Henri. "Poésie et mystique, " Revue d'Esthétique, IX, 2 (avril-juin 1956), 117-54.

91. Gille, Valère. "Du symbolisme (esquisse), " Bull. de l'Acad. Royale de Langue et de Litt. Françaises, XIX (1940), 21-37.

92. Girard, Marcel. "Naturalisme et symbolisme, " Cah. l'Assoc. Intern'l des Etudes Françaises, no. 6 (juillet 1954), 97-106.

93. Gourmont, Rémy de. Le Livre des Masques. Portraits Symbolistes. Paris: 1963 (reprint).

94. _____. Promenades Littéraires. T. III: Le Symbolisme. Paris: 1963 (reprint).

95. Gresset, Michel. "Voyeur et voyant. Essai sur les données et le mécanisme de l'imag. symboliste, " Nouv. Rev. Française, XIV, 167 (nov. 1966), 809-26.

96. Grimm, Reinhold. "Macht über die Zeichen. Zur Frage des Symbols in mod. Dichtg, " Pädagogische Provinz (Frankf. a. M.), XII (1958), 407-13.

97. Grojnowski, Daniel. "Vue d'ensemble: le symbolisme, " Critique, 16 année, XXI, 213 (févr. 1965), 178-85.

98. Gros, Bernard. "Le Symbolisme: la litt. comme accomplissement de la vie, " La Litt.: Du Symbolisme au Nouveau Roman. Paris: 1970, pp. 490-519. (Dictionnaire du Savoir Moderne.)

99. Guérard, Albert L. Art for Art's Sake. Boston: 1936. (Paperback edn., N. Y.: Schocken Books, 1963).

100. Guimbretière, André. "Symbole et langage dans

l'expér. poétique, " Cah. Intern'aux de Symbolisme, no. 6 (1964), 49-67.

101. Guiraud, Pierre. Index du Vocab. du Symbolisme. Paris: 1953.

102. _____ . "La symbolique du temps lyrique, " Essais de Stylistique. Paris: 1969, pp. 173-89. (Initiation à la Linguistique, B, 1).

103. Hagopian, John V. "Symbol and metaphor in the transform. of reality into art, " Comp. Lit., XX (1968), 45-55.

104. Hamann, Richard. Der Impressionismus in Leben u. Kunst. Marburg: 1923.

105. _____ , & Jost Hermand. Impressionismus. Berlin: 1960.

106. Haraucourt, Edmond. Mémoires des Jours et des Gens. Paris: 1946.

107. Hayes, Charles. "Symbol and allegory. A problem in lit. theory, " German Review, XLIV (1969), 273-88.

108. Hayward, John F. "Mimesis and symbol in the arts, " Chicago Review, XV, 1 (1961), 93-106.

109. Henel, Heinrich. "Erlebnis-dichtg u. Symbolismus, " Zur Lyrik-Diskussion, ed. R. Grimm. Darmstadt: 1966, pp. 218-54. (Orig. in: Dt. Vjschr., XXXII (1958), 71-98.)

110. Hinderer, Walter. "Theory, conception, and interpr. of the symbol, " Persp. in Lit. Symbolism, ed. Joseph Strelka. Univ. Park/London: 1968, pp. 83-127.

111. Honig, Edwin. Dark Conceit: The Making of Allegory. Providence, R.I.: 1959.

112. Hough, Graham. Image and Experience: Studies in a Lit. Revolution. London: 1960. (Paperback edn. Lincoln, Nebr.: Bison Books, 1962.)

113. Howe, Irving. "The idea of the Modern, " Lit. Modernism. Greenwich, Conn.: 1967, pp. 11-40.

114. Hull, R. F. C. "Poetry and symbolism, " New English Weekly, XXIII, 3 (May 6, 1943), 23-4.

115. Isaacs, Jacob. The Background of Mod. Poetry. N.Y.: 1952. (Paperback edn. N.Y.: Dutton, 1958).

116. Ivanov, Vjačeslav. "Symbolism, " (trans. Thomas E. Bird) Russian Review, XXV, 1 (Jan. 1966), 24-34.

117. Jackson, Holbrook. The Eighteen Nineties: A Review of Art and Ideas at the Close of the Nineteenth

              Cen. N. Y. : 1922.
118. Jean, Georges. "Cette voix étrange (obscurité), " Vie
              et Langage, XVI (1967), 401-5.
119. Johansen, Sven. Le Symbolisme. Copenhague: 1945.
120. Jouffroy, Alain. "Cerner l'incernable, " Lettres
              Nouvelles, III, 27 (mai 1955), 710-20.
121. Joussain, André. "La poésie clandestine, " Ecrits de
              Paris, (nov. 1953), 84-94.
122. Kahn, Gustave. Symbolistes et Décadents. Paris:
              1902.
123. _____. Les Origines du Symbolisme. Paris: 1936.
124. Kamerbeek, J. , Jr. "Op zoek naar een definite van
              het symbolisme, " Levende Talen (Groningen),
              CCLXIV-LXXIII (1970), 767-77.
125. Kayser, W. "Der europ. Symbolismus. Versuch. e.
              Einführung, " Die Vortragsreise. Studien z. Lit.
              Bern: 1958, pp. 287-304.
126. Kennick, W. E. "Art and the ineffable, " Journ. of
              Philosophy, LVIII (1961), 309-20.
127. Kermode, Frank. Romantic Image. London: 1957.
              (Paperback edn. N. Y. : Vintage, 1964).
128. Klemperer, V. "La poésie pure, " Vor 33 ... nach
              45. (Ges. Aufsätze.) Berlin: 1956, pp. 121-
              39. (Also in: Neuphil. Monatsschr. , (1930),
              233-56.)
129. Knights, L. C. & B. Cottle, eds. Colston Research
              Society: Metaphor and Symbol. Proceed. of the
              12th Symposium. Univ. of Bristol, March 28th-
              31st, 1960. London: 1960. (Colston Papers,
              12.)
130. Kronegger, M. E. "Impressionist tendencies in lyr.
              prose, 19th and 20th cen. , " Rev. Litt. Comparée,
              XLIII (1969), 528-44.
131. Kugel, James L. The Techniques of Strangeness in
              Symbolist Poetry. New Haven/London: 1971.
132. Lambert, Marcel. "Le symbole poétique, " Dialogue
              (Montréal), II, 2 (sept. 1963), 144-54.
133. Landsberger, F. Impressionismus u. Expressionis-
              mus. Leipzig: 1919.
134. Lang, Wilhelm. "Zeichen, Symbol, Chiffre, " Dt.
              unterricht, XX, 4 (1968), 12-27.
135. Langbaum, Robert. The Mod. Spirit: Essays on the
              Continuity of 19th and 20th Cen. Lit. N. Y. :
              1970.
136. Lavaud, Guy. "Retour au symbolisme, " Acropole, II,
              8 (août-sept. 1950), 2-5.
137. Legris, Renée, and Pierre Pagé. Le Symbole, Carre-

four Interdisciplinaire. Montréal: 1969. (Recherches en Symbolique, 1.)

138. Lehmann, Andrew G. "Un aspect de la critique symboliste: signification et ambiguité dans les beaux-arts," Cah. Assoc. Intern'l des Etudes Françaises, XII (juin 1960), 161-74.

139. Lehmann, Winfred P. "The stony idiom of the brain: symbolic manipulation of lang. in lit.," Lit. Symbolism, ed. Helmut Rehder. Austin: 1965, pp. 11-30.

140. Lejeune, Claire. "Du désir à la parole," Cah. Intern'x de Symbolisme, XV/XVI (1967/8), 29-52.

141. Leonhard, K. "Das Problem d. Form u. d. orphische Dasein: e. Vers. z. Deutung d. Seinserlebnisses in neuerer Dichtg u. Malerei," Lit. Revue, III (1948), 259-69.

142. Lescure, Jean. "Du calcul des improbabilités," Cah. Intern'x de Symbolisme, VI (1964), 69-87.

143. Lesdain, P. "Sur la tombe du Symbolisme," Synthèses, XVIII, 209 (oct. 1963), 397-412.

144. Lethève, Jacques. Impressionnistes et Symbolistes Devant la Presse. Paris: 1959. (Bibliogr., pp. 285-96.)

145. Levin, Harry. Symbolism and Fiction. Charlottesville: 1956.

146. Linze, G. "Poésie obscure," Lettres 55 (janv.-févr. 1957), 26-8.

147. Lote, G. "La poétique du symbolisme: poésie et musique; la synesthésie," Rev. des Cours et Conférences, XXXV (1934), 109-26.

148. Louisgrand, Jean. "De l'expression à la suggestion: l'alexandrin," De Lucrèce à Camus: Litt. et Philos. comme Réflex. sur l'Homme. Paris: 1970, pp. 193-208. (Essais et Critiques, 10.)

149. Luzi, M. "La strada del Simbolismo," Paragone, CXVIII (Ott. 1959), 3-18.

150. _____. L'Idea Simbolista. Roma: 1959.

151. Maier, Rudolph N. "Das Symbolische d. Gedichts u. d. Erziehg. d. Symbol. Sinns," Wirkendes Wort, VI (1955/6), 41-53.)

152. Maritain, Jacques. Art et Scolastique: Frontières de la Poésie. Paris: 1935. (English version: Art and Scholasticism, and the Frontiers of Poetry, trans. Joseph W. Evans. N.Y.: 1962.)

153. Martin, Wallace. "The sources of the Imagist aesthetic," PMLA, LXXXV (1970), 196-204. (Negates

infl. of Symbolism.)
154. Martino, Pierre. Parnasse et Symbolisme. Paris:
      1923. (Later ed. 1967) (Coll. U2, 11.)
155. _____ . "Rapports de la litt. et les arts plastiques;
      Parnasse et Symbolisme, " Actes du 5ième Congrès
      Intern'l des Langues et Litt. Modernes. Les
      Langues et Litt. Modernes dans leurs Relations
      avec les Beaux-Arts. Florence: 1955, pp. 399-
      410.
156. Martins, W. Introd. ao Estudo do Simbolismo. Curi-
      tiba: 1953. (Letras, Univ. do Paraná, 1.)
157. Mayer, Hans. "Sprechen u. Verstummen d. Dichter, "
      Das Geschehen u. d. Schweigen: Aspekte der Lit.
      Frankfurt: 1969, pp. 11-34.
158. Mayoux, J. J. "At the sources of symbolism, " Criti-
      cism, I (1959), 279-97.
159. Mazel, Henri. Aux Beaux Temps du Symbolisme,
      1890-1895. Paris: 1943.
160. Menard, René. "Essai sur l'expér. poétique, " Cah.
      Intern'x de Symbolisme, XIV (1967), 39-51.
161. Menemencioglu, Melâhat. "L'automatisme psychique
      dans le poème hermétique, " Cah. Assoc. Intern'l
      des Etudes Françaises, XV (mars 1963), 141-9.
162. Mercier, Alain. Les Sources Esotériques et Occultes
      de la Poésie Symboliste, I. Paris: 1969.
163. Michailow, A. "Symbol, Allegorie, Gleichnis, " Kunst
      u. Lit., XV (1967), 254-60; 360-70.
164. Michaud, Guy. La Doctrine Symboliste, Documents.
      Paris; 1947.
165. _____ . Message Poétique du Symbolisme. Paris:
      1947. (4 Tomes) (later ed. 1951) (bibliogr.,
      pp. 669-79.)
166. _____ . "Symbolique et symbolisme, " Cah. Assoc.
      Intern'l des Etudes Françaises, no. 6 (juillet
      1954), 75-95.
167. Michell, Joyce. Symbolism in Music and Poetry
      (thesis) Univ. Penn.: 1944. (Richard Wagner--
      esp.)
168. Millepierres, François. "Vocabulaire poétique, "
      Vie et Langage, no. 154 (janv. 1965), 10-19.
169. Mitchell, Bonner. "Equivocal 'engagement' in the
      1890's, " Romance Notes, III, 1 (Autumn 1961),
      1-5.
170. Mitterand, Henri. "De l'écriture artiste au style
      décadent, " Wiss. Ztschr. d. Humboldt-Univ. z.
      Berlin, Gesell. u. Sprachwiss. Reihe, XVIII, 4
      (1969), 617-24. (Repr. in: Romanische Philol.
      Heute. Festschrift R. Schober, ed. W. Zyla.

Berlin: 1969, pp. 617-23.)
171. Moles, A. "Poésie expérimentale, poétique et art permutationnel, " Arguments. Cah. de Discussion, VI, 27/8 (3e et 4e trim. 1962), 93-7.
172. Moncy, Agnes T. "The Formative Aspects of Symbols in Theory and Poetic Practice, " Diss. Abstr., XXIX (1968), 610A/11A (Texas).
173. Moore, A. K. "The case for poetic obscurity, " Neophilologus, XLVIII, 4 (Dec. 1964), 322-40.
174. Moreau, Pierre. "Symbole, symbolique, symbolisme, " Cah. Assoc. Intern'l des Etudes Françaises, VI (1954), 123-9.
175. _____. "De la symbolique religieuse à la poésie symboliste, " Comp. Lit. Stud., IV (1967), 5-16.
176. Morrissette, Bruce A. Les Aspects Fondamentaux de l'Esthétique Symboliste. (diss.) Clermont-Ferrand: 1933.
177. Mounin, Georges. La Communic. Poétique. Paris: 1969. (Coll. "Les Essais, " 145) (reviewed: "Hermetic Habits, " TLS, no. 3520 (Aug. 14, 1969), p. 898.)
178. Muner, Mario. Per il Riordinamento Sistematico degli Studi su Simbolismo, Decadentismo, Ermetismo. Cremona: 1957.
179. Nelli, René. "Le temps imaginaire et ses structures dans l'oeuvre poétique, " Cah. Intern'x de Symbolisme, XIV (1967), 53-67.
180. Olson, E. A. "A dialogue on symbolism, " Critics and Criticism, ed. R. S. Crane. Chicago: 1952, pp. 567-94.
181. Oppert, K. "Der Reiz d. Ungesagten in d. Lyrik, " Wirk. Wort, VI (1955/6), 76-82.
182. Ortigues, E. Le Discours et le Symbole. Paris: 1962.
183. Padhye, Prabhakar. "Symbol into sign into symbol, " Indian Writing Today, II (Oct. -Dec. 1967), 57-61.
184. Pasa, A. "Poesia e poetiche, I: La stagione della poesia pura, " Poesia e Critica I, 1 (Guigno 1961), 107-35.
185. Périgord, Monique. "Valeur esthétique du secret, " Rev. d'Esthétique, XIV (1961), 137-67.
186. Pillet, Roger A. "The practice of symbolism, " Diss. Abstr., XV (1955), 1857 (Northwestern).
187. Podraza-Kwiatkowska, Maria. "Symbolistyczna koncepcja poezji, " Pamiętnik Literacki (Warsaw), LXI, 4 (1970), 91-138.

188. Press, John. The Chequer'd Shade: Reflections on Obscurity in Poetry. New York: 1963. (Oxford Paperbacks, 54.)

189. Rayan, Krishna. "Metaphor and suggestion," Malahat Review, II (1967), 50-64.

190. _____. "When meaning is suggested," Malahat Review, VII (1968), 77-89.

191. Raynaud, Ernest. La Mêlée Symboliste. 3 Tomes. Paris: 1918-22.

192. _____. "Le Symbolisme et les Cafés Littéraires," Mercure de France, CCLXVIII (1 juin 1936), 282-93.

193. Richard, Noël. A l'Aube du Symbolisme: Hydropathes, Fumistes, et Décadents. Paris: 1961.

194. _____. Le Mouvement Décadent. Dandys, Esthètes et Quintessents. Paris: 1968. (Bibliogr., pp. 265-70.)

195. Rieder, Heinz. "Die Geburt der Moderne in der Lit. d. Jh. wende," Osterr. in Geschichte u. Lit. (Wien), XIII (1969), 462-70.

196. Robichez, Jacques. Le Symbolisme au Théatre. Paris: 1957. (Covers years 1890-1899; studies use of symbolism by Ibsen and Maeterlinck.)

197. Rolland de Renéville, André. "La poésie et l'hermétisme," La Rev. du Caire, XII, 123 (oct. 1949), 203-7.

198. Rousset, Lucien. "L'age héroique du symbolisme," Confluences, n.s., no. 2 (août 1941), 157-66; no. 3 (sept. 1941), 299-310.

199. Ruf, Gaudenz. Wege der Spätromantik: Dichter. Verhaltensweisen in der Krise des Lyrischen. Bonn: 1969. (AKML, 83.)

200. Ruprecht, Erich, and Dieter Bänsch, eds. Literar. Manifeste d. Jh. wende (1890-1910). Stuttgart: 1970. (Vol. 42 in ser.).

201. Sabatier, Robert. "Poésie consciente, poésie spontanée," Rev. du Caire, XVIII, 185 (nov. 1955), 277-83.

202. Sainz de Robles, F. C. Los Movimentos Lit.: Hist., Interpr. Crit. Madrid: 1957.

203. Schmidt, Albert-Marie. La Litt. Symboliste (1870-1900). Paris: 1967. (Coll. Que sais-je, 82) (earlier ed. 1942).

204. Senior, John. "The occult in 19th cen. symbolist lit.," Diss. Abstr., XVII (1957), 1769/70 (Columbia) (publ. in book form as: The Way Down and Out: the Occult in Symbolist Lit. Ithaca, N.Y.: 1959; Bibliog., pp. 207-13.)

205. Siciliano, Ital. "Poésie pure et poésie engagée, " Actes du 4îême Congrès Intern'l d'Hist. Litt. Mod. Paris: 1950, pp. 177-89. (Etudes de litt. étrangère et comparée, 22.)

206. Slochower, Harry. "Symbolism and the creative process, " American Imago, XXII (1965), 112-27.

207. Sojcher, Jacques. "Une pensée dépossédante, " Cah. Intern'x de Symbolisme, XV/XVI (1967/8), 71-91.

208. Spender, Stephen. "Symbolist Poetry, " Britain Today, no. 87 (July 1943), 26. (Review article.)

209. Spire, André. Plaisir Poétique et Plaisir Musculaire. Essai sur l'Evol. des Techniques Poétiques. New York: 1949. (Bibliogr., pp. 524-44.)

210. Starkie, Enid. "L'esthétique des symbolistes, " Cah. Assoc. Intern'l des Etudes Françaises, no. 6 (juillet 1954), 131-8.

211. Stepun, Fedor. "Das Wesen des Symbolismus, " Orbis Scriptus: Festschrift D. Tschizewskij...., ed. D. Gerhardt et al. Mchn: 1966, pp. 805-10.

212. Stinglhamber, Louis. "Le sentiment de l'infini dans la poésie moderne, " Bull. Assoc. Guillaume Budé, IV, 1 (mars 1956), 119-32. (Symbolistes et Surréalistes.)

213. Strelka, Joseph. "Comparative Crit. and Lit. Symbolism, " Persp. in Lit. Symbolism, ed. J. Strelka. Univ. Park/London: 1968, pp. 1-28. (Yearbook of Comp. Crit. 1) (trans. from the German by Alice Kennington.)

214. _____. "Esoterische Symbolik in d. Lit., " Lit. u. Kritik, XLV (1970), 278-88.

215. Symbolism. Romanic Review (special issue), XLVI, 3 (Oct. 1955) (incl. Anna Balakian, "Stud. in French Symbolism, 1945-55, " pp. 223-30; Olga Ragusa, "French Symbolism in Italy, " pp. 231-5).

216. _____. Le Mouvement Symboliste (Catalogue d'Exposition) Bruxelles: 1957. (31 janv.-3 mars 1957).

217. Symons, Arthur. The Symbolist Movement in Lit. London: 1899. (Later ed. New York: 1958.) [Latter includes essay by Richard Ellmann, "Introd., " pp. vii-xvi.]

218. _____. "Impressionistic writing, " Dramatis Personae. Indianapolis: 1923, pp. 343-50.

219. Tielroy, J. "Van l'art pour l'art tot poésie pure, " Verkenningen in het Land d. Lit. Groningen: 1954, pp. 270-98.

220. Tindall, William Y. The Literary Symbol. New
      York: 1955. [Paperback edn., Bloomington,
      Ind.: Midland Books, 1958.]
221. Tonelli, Giorgio. Aspetti della Lirica Tedesca, 1895-
      1960. Palermo: 1963.
222. Torre, Guillermo de. Lit. Europ. de Vanguardia.
      Madrid: 1923. (1925).
223. _____. Hist. de las Lit. de Vanguardia. Madrid:
      1965.
224. Trahard, Pierre. "L'éternelle recherche," Le
      Mystère Poétique. Paris: 1970. (Orig. publ.
      1940.)
225. Uitti, Karl D. The Concept of Self in the Symbolist
      Novel. 's-Gravenhage: 1961.
226. Van Roosbroeck, Gustave L. The Legend of the
      Decadents. N.Y.: 1927.
227. Vigée, Claude. "La théorie du symbole," La Table
      Ronde, no. 108 (déc. 1956), 58-70.
228. _____. "Genèse de la sensibilité poétique moderne,"
      Preuves, X, 108 (févr. 1960), 14-31.
229. _____. "Métamorphoses de la poésie moderne,"
      Cah. du Sud, XLVII, 356 (juin-juillet 1960), 89-
      119. (Also in: Révolte et Louanges. Paris:
      1962, pp. 9-43.)
230. _____. "L'invention poétique et l'automatisme
      mental," Mod. Lang. Notes, LXXV, 2 (Feb.
      1960), 143-54.
231. Vortriede, Werner. "Die Entstehung des Symbols in
      d. Dichtg," Dt. Rundschau, LXXXVIII (1962),
      744-9.
232. Vossler, K. "Poesía simbólica y neosimbolista,"
      Rev. Cubana, XV (1941), 5-45.
233. Warren, R. P. "Pure and impure poetry,"
      Critiques and Essays in Criticism, 1920-'48.
      New York: 1949, pp. 85-104.
234. Weinberg, Bernard. "Les limites de l'hermétisme,
      ou hermétisme et intelligibilité," Cah. Assoc.
      Intern'l des Etudes Françaises, XV (mars 1963),
      151-61. (Repr. in English in the author's The
      Limits of Symbolism.... Chicago: 1966,
      pp. 420-30.)
235. Weisstein, Ulrich. "A bibliogr. of crit. writings
      concerned with lit. impressionism," Yearbook of
      Comp. & Gen'l Lit., XVII (1968), 69-72.
236. Wellek, René. "The term and concept of Symbolism
      in lit. history," Discriminations: Further Con-
      cepts of Crit., VI. N.Y.: 1970, pp. 90-121.

(Repr. in New Lit. Hist., I (1969/70), 249-70; also repr. in Actes du 5ième Congrès de l'Assoc. Intern'l de Litt. Comparée (1969), 275-92.)

237. West, Rebecca. "The post-symbolists," Time & Tide, XXIV, 14 (April 1943), 272-3. (Review article.)

238. Wheelwright, P. The Burning Fountain: A Study in the Lang. of Symbolism. Bloomington: 1954.

239. _____. "The archetypal symbol," Persp. in Lit. Symbolism, ed. Joseph Strelka. Univ. Park/London: 1968, pp. 214-43. (Yearbook of Comp. Crit.)

240. Whitehead, Alfred North. Symbolism: Its Meaning and Effect. N.Y.: 1927.

241. Wilson, Colin. Poetry and Mysticism. London: 1970.

242. Wilson, Edmund. Axël's Castle: A Study in the Imaginative Lit. of 1870-1930. New York: 1931. [Paperback edn., N.Y.: Scribner Library, 1960 (SL, 12).]

243. Wyczynski, Paul. "Symbolisme et creation poétique," Poésie et Symbole. Montréal: 1965, pp. 235-52. (Also incl.: "Perspectives du symbolisme," pp. 17-79.)

NATIONAL STUDIES

244. Achury Valenzuela, Darío. "Dos momentos de la poesía venezolana, " Bol. Cultural (Câmara Municipal do Porto), X, 8 (1967), 91-9. (Generation of 1910 and exile poets.)
245. Aderaldo Castelo, J. "Apontamentos para a hist. do simbolismo no Brasil, " Rev. da Univ. de São Paolo, (1950), 111-21.
246. Alberti, Rafael. La Poesía Popular en la Lírica Española Contemp. Jena/Leipzig: 1933.
247. Albrecht, H. Tendéncias in la Lit. Alemana desde el Naturalismo hasta Nuestros Dias. Vol. I: Del Naturalismo al Neorromanticismo. Tucumán: Univ. Nac. de Tucumán, 1954. (German writers comp. with French, Russian writers et al.)
248. Alonso, Dámaso. Poetas Españoles Contemp., 3rd rev. edn. Madrid: 1965 (1952).
249. _____. "Una gener. poética, 1920-1936, " Fin, 2a época, I (1948), 193-220. (Repr. in Poetas Españoles Contemp., pp. 167-92.)
250. _____. Poesía Española: Ensayo de Métodos y Límites Estilísticos, 5th edn. Madrid: 1966
251. Alvarez, A. The Shaping Spirit: Stud. in Mod. English and Amer. Poets. London: 1958.
252. Anceschi, L. Le Poetiche del Novecento in Italia. Milano: 1962.
253. Antonielli, S. Aspetti e Figure del Novecento. Parma: 1955.
254. Apollonio, M. Ermetismo. Padova: 1945.
255. Arbour, Roméo. Henri Bergson et les Lettres Françaises. Paris: 1955. (Symbolism, Surrealism, Valéry, et al.)
256. Asmus, V. "Filos. i estetika russkogo simvolizma, " Literaturnoe Nasledstvo (Moscow), XXVII-VIII (1937), 1-53.
257. Atal, G. "Turkish and French Symbolism, Ahmet Hashim, " Diss. Abstr., XXIII (1962/3), 4351/2 (Indiana).
258. Aub, M. La Poesía Española Contemp. México: 1954.

26

259. Aubery, Pierre. "The anarchism of the literati of
the symbolist period, " French Review, XLII
(1968), 38-47.
260. Balakian, Anna. The Lit. Origins of Surrealism: A
New Mysticism in French Poetry. N.Y.: 1947.
(Paperback edn. N.Y.: Gotham Library, 1966.)
261. Balaşov, Nikolai. "Simbolismul francez, " Studii şi
Cercetări de Isotorie Lit. şi Folclor, X (1961),
317-44.
262. Barre, André. Le Symbolisme. Essai Historique
sur le Mouvement Symboliste en France de 1885
à 1900, Suivi d'une Bibliogr. de la Poésie Symboliste. Paris: 1911. (Later ed.: N.Y.:
1968; 2 vols.; Essays in Lit. & Crit., 8.)
263. Bastide, Roger. A Poesia Afro-Brasileira. São
Paolo: 1943.
264. Bastos, C. Tavares. O Simbolismo no Brasil e Out-
ros Escritos. Rio de Janeiro: 1969.
265. Bayley, John. The Romantic Survival: A Study in
Poetic Evol. London: 1969 (1957).
266. Belchior, Maria de Lourdes. "Verlaine e o simbolismo em Portugal, " Brotéria, XC (1970), 305-19.
267. Bell, A. F. G. Contemp. Spanish Lit., 3rd edn.
N.Y.: 1933. (Earl. edn. London: 1926.)
268. Berdyaev, N. The Russian Idea. London: 1947.
269. _____. Dream and Reality. London: 1950. (Russian symbolism.)
270. Bernardini, Ada P. Simbolisti e Decadenti. Roma:
1935.
271. Berry, R. M. "The French Symbolist Poets in Germany:
Criticism and Translations, 1870-1914. " (Diss.)
Harvard: 1944. (See: Harvard Univ. Summaries of
Theses ... 1943-45. Cambridge: 1947, pp. 504-8.)
272. Bertrán, P., and S. J. Juan Bautista. "Caravana de
poetas a Belén. Del Simbolismo hasta nuestros
dias: España, Francia, Italia, " Razón y Fe,
XLVIII, 137 (Enero-Junio 1948), 12-36. (Incl.
Samain, Péguy, Ghéon, Marie Noël.)
273. Beyette, Thomas K. "Symbolism and Victorian Lit., "
Diss. Abstr. Intern'l, XXX (1970), 5440A (Austin,
Texas).
274. Bhattacharya, Lokenath. "French infl. in contemp.
Bengali poetry, " Indian Lit. VIII, 1 (1965), 90-
107. (Baudelaire to Valéry.)
275. Bianchi, Ruggero. La Poetica dell'Imagismo. Milano:
1965/6.

28 A Post-Symbolist Bibliography

276. Bianquis, Geneviève. La Poésie Autrichienne de Hofmannsthal à Rilke. Paris: 1926.
277. Bidle, Kenneth E. "Impressionism in Am. Lit. to the year 1900, " Diss. Abstr., XXX (1969), 715A/ 16A (No. Ill.).
278. Bigongiari, Piero. Poesia Francese del Novecento. Firenze: (1968).
279. Binni, Walter. La Poetíca del Decadentismo, 3rd edn. Firenze: 1961.
280. Biordi, Raffaello. La Poesia del Silenzio. Roma: 1959.
281. Bleyhl, Werner. Die französ Lit. im Spiegel d. engl. Kritik von 1900 bis 1910. (Diss.) Tüb.: 1967.
282. Block, Haskell M. "The impact of French Symbolism on mod. Amer. poetry, " The Shaken Realist: Essays in Mod. Lit. in Honor of Frederick J. Hoffmann, ed. Melvin Friedman & John B. Vickery. Baton Rouge, La.: 1970, pp. 165-217.
283. Bloom, Harold. "First and last Romantics, " Studies in Romanticism (Boston Univ.), IX (1970), 225-32.
284. Boase, Alan M. The Poetry of France: An Anth. with Introd. & Notes. London: 1969. (Vol. 6: 1900-1965.)
285. Bojtár, E. "Le problème des tendances dans la poésie est-européenne entre les deux guerres, " Studia Slavica Academiae Scientiarum Hungaricae, XIV (1968), 67-73.
286. Bonnefoy, Yves. "Symbolism, " Concise Encyclop. of Engl. and Am. Poets and Poetry, eds. Stephen Spender and Donald Hall. London: 1963, pp. 323-6. [Trans. Stephen Spender.]
287. Böschenstein, Bernhard. "Wirkungen d. französ. Symbolismus auf d. dt. Lyrik d. Jhwende, " Euphorion, LVIII, 4 (1964), 375-95. (Esp. George) (also in: Studien z. Dichtg d. Absoluten. Zürich: 1968, pp. 127-49.)
288. Boucher, Maurice. "Uber d. Esoterische in d. Lyrik, " Unterscheidung u. Bewahrung: Festschrift f. H. Kunisch.... Berlin: 1961, pp. 31-40. (German poetry.)
289. Braet, Herman. L'Accueil Fait au Symbolisme en Belgique, 1885-1900. Bruxelles: 1967. (Subtitle: Contrib. à l'Etude du Mouvement et de la Critique Symbolistes) (bibliogr., pp. 177-95.)
290. Brandt, P. A. D. dt. Dichtg am Ende d. 19 Jhs. im Spiegel d. Kritik. (Diss.) Leipzig: 1932.

291. Brodin, Pierre. Les Ecrivains Françaises de l'Entre-
     Deux-Guerres. Montréal: 1942. (Incl. Valéry)
     (bibliogr., pp. 377-89) (2nd ed. 1943) (bibliogr.,
     pp. 351-62.)
292. Brösel, K. Veranschaulichung im Realismus, Im-
     pressionismus u. Frühexpressionismus. München:
     1928.
293. Brotherston, Gordon. "The literatures of Spanish-
     speaking America: A survey of styles and ten-
     dencies, " Style, III (1969), 1-16.
294. Brumm, Ursula. "Der neue Symbolismus in Ameri-
     ka, " Neue dt. Hefte, XLVII (1958), 244-50.
295. Buckley, Jerome H. The Victorian Temper. Cam-
     bridge, Mass.: 1951. (Paperback edn. N. Y.:
     Vintage, 1964.)
296. Burdett, Osbert. The Beardsley Period: An Essay
     in Perspec. London: 1925.
297. Burns, C. A. "The 19th cen. (post-romantic) (1961), "
     Year's Work in Mod. Lang. Studies, XXIII (1963),
     105-20. (French bibliogr.)
298. Burnshaw, Stanley. "The three revolutions of mod.
     poetry, " Sewanee Review, LXX (1962), 418-50.
     (American?).
299. Cano, José L. De Machado a Bousoño. Notas sobre
     Poesía Española Contemp. Madrid: 1955.
300. _____. Poesía del Siglo XX: de Unamuno a Blas
     de Otero. Madrid: 1960.
301. Cansinos-Asséns, Rafael. Poetas y Prosistas del
     Novecientos, España y América. Madrid: 1919.
302. Cantwell, William R. "The Friedrichshagener Dich-
     terkreis: A study of change and continuity in the
     German lit. of the 'Jhwende, ' " Diss. Abstr.,
     XXVIII (1967), 668A (Wisconsin).
303. Carco, Francis. Les Derniers Etats de la Poésie.
     Paris: 1920.
304. Carden, Poe. "Parnassianism, Symbolism, Decaden-
     tism--and Spanish-American Modernism, " His-
     pania (Univ. of Conn.), XLIII (1960), 545-51.
305. Carvalho, J. G. Herculano de. "Simbolo e conheci-
     mento simbólico, " Rumo, XII (1968), 301-10.
     (Portugal).
306. Cary, Joseph B., Jr. "Italian poetry under the sign
     of Hermes, " Cesare Barbieri Courier, VIII, 1
     (1966), 8-14.
307. Cassou, Jean. Panorama de la Litt. Espagnole Con-
     temp. Paris: 1929.

308. Castillo, Homero, ed. Estudios Crit. sobre el Modernismo. Madrid: 1968.
309. Castro, E. M. de. L'Influence du Symbolisme Français dans la Poésie Portugaise Contemporaine. Paris: 1923.
310. Cazamian, Louis. Symbolisme et Poésie, l'Exemple Anglais. Paris: 1947.
311. Černov, Viktor. "Modernizm v russkoj poezii, " Vestnik Europy (Dec. 1910), 123.
312. Cernuda, Luis. Estudios sobre Poesía Española Contemp. Madrid: 1957.
313. Chabás, J. Lit. Española Contemp. (1898-1950). La Habana: 1952.
314. Chalsma, Howard W. "Russian Acmeism: its history, doctrine and poetry, " Diss. Abstr., XXVIII (1968), 3633A (Univ. of Wash.).
315. Charlesworth, Barbara. Dark Passages: The Decadent Consciousness in Victorian Lit. Madison, Wisc.: 1965.
316. Chisholm, A. R. "La fortune du symbolisme français en Australie, " Mercure de France, CCCVII, 1033 (1 sept. 1949), 112-16.
317. Christophe, Lucien. "Ombres et lumières du symbolisme, " Rev. Générale Belge, XCIII, 3 (mars 1957), 28-40. (Symbolist poetry in Belgium.)
318. Cirre, José F. Forma y Espíritu de una Lírica Española (1920-'35)...., 2nd edn. Madrid: 1966 (earl. edn. Méjico: 1950).
319. Clark, J. G. "Impressionist Criticism in France. Its debt to the past and its value for the present, " Lit. Hist. and Lit. Crit. New York: 1965, pp. 237-8. (Summary of a conference.)
320. _____. "Les notions d'origine, d'influence et de cosmopolitisme chez les critiques impressionnistes français, " Actes du IVe Congrès de l'Assoc. Intern'l de Litt. Comp. La Haye/Paris: 1966, pp. 1296-1303.
321. Clémeur, Marcel. "De l'hermétisme, " Nouv. Rev. Wallonne, XIV (1964/5), 229-40. (Belgian poetry.)
322. Closs, August. "Substance and symbol in poetry, " Medusa's Mirror. Studies in German Lit. London: 1957, pp. 8-42. (Also contains: "German poetry after 1945, " pp. 213-21.)
323. _____, ed. Reality and Creative Vision in German Lyrical Poetry. London: 1963. (Contains: S. S. Prawer, "Reflections on the numinous and the

324. uncanny in German poetry, " pp. 153-72.)
_____. "Concealment and revelation in mod. German lyric poetry, " Reality and Creative Vision in German Lyric Poetry, ed. A. Closs. London: 1963, pp. 211-34.
325. Clothier, Peter Dean. "Magicians of insecurity. Contemp. French poets on poetry, " Diss. Abstr., XXX (1969/70), 3452A/53A (Iowa '69 diss.).
326. Clouard, Henri. La Poésie Française Mod., des Romantiques à Nos Jours. Paris: 1924.
327. _____. "La poésie du parnasse au surréalisme, " Neuf Siècles de Litt. Française. Paris: 1958, pp. 589-672.
328. Coellen, L. Neuromantik. Jena: 1906.
329. Coffman, Stanley K., Jr. Imagism: A Chapter for the Hist. of Mod. Poetry. Norman, Okla.: 1951.
330. Coghlan, Brian. "The turn of the century, " Periods in German Lit., ed. James M. Ritchie. London: 1966, pp. 229-54.
331. Cohen, J. M. Poetry of this Age, 1908-1958. Philad.: 1962 (English and Amer. lit.).
332. Cornell, Kenneth. The Post-Symbolist Period. French Poetic Currents, 1900 to 1920. New Haven/Paris: 1958. (Bibliogr., pp. 171-4.) [Yale Romanic Studies, second series, No. VI] [reprint: Hamden, Conn: 1970 (Archon).]
333. Correa, Gustavo. "El simbolismo del mar en la poesía española del siglo XX, " Rev. Hisp. Moderna, XXXII (1966), 62-86.
334. _____. "Temporality and commitment in Span. poetry after 1936. " Ventures (Magaz. Yale Grad. School), X, 1 (1970), 33-6.
335. Cortes, Manuel M. "Tendencies and stylistic schools in Spain, " Style, III (1969), 134-54.
336. Craig, G. Dundar. The Modernist Trend in Spanish-American Poetry. Berkeley: 1934.
337. Cruickshank, John, ed. French Lit. and its Background. Vol. 5: The Late Nineteenth Century. N.Y./London: 1969.
338. Darge, Elisabeth. Lebensbejahung in d. dt. Dichtg um 1900. Breslav: 1934.
339. Davidson, Donald, ed. British Poetry of the Eighteen-Nineties. N.Y.: 1937.
340. Davy, Charles. "Symbols and Signs, " Words in the Mind. Exploring Some Effects of Poetry, English and French. London: 1965. (Esthetics, existentialism, symbolism etc.).

341. Deac, Augustin, and Teodor Pintean. Poezii Munici-
      toreşti Revol. din România: 1872-1944. Bucha-
      rest: 1970.
342. De Bella, Nino. Dagli Scapigliati agli Ermetici.
      Roma: 1965.
343. Debicki, Andrew P. Estudios sobre Poesía Española
      Contemp.: La Generac. de 1924-5. Madrid:
      1968.
344. Décaudin, Michel. "Poêtes belges et français devant
      l'idéalisme français, " Les Flandres dans les
      Mouvements Romantique et Symboliste. Actes
      du IIe Congrès Nat'l de la Soc. française de Litt.
      Comp. Paris: 1958, pp. 95-102.
345. _____. La Crise des Valeurs Symbolistes et la
      Poésie Française (1895-1914). (Thèse) Univ. de
      Paris, Lettres: 1958, 4 vols. (Summary in:
      Annales de l'Univ. de Paris, XXIX, 2 (avril-
      juin 1959), 331-2.)
346. _____. "Le mouvement poétique de 1895 à 1914, "
      L'Inform. Litt., XII, 5 (nov.-déc. 1960), 199-
      203. (Incl. Romains, Verhaeren, Larbaud,
      Apollinaire, Claudel, Fargue, Perse.)
347. _____. La Crise des Valeurs Symbolistes: Vingt
      Ans de Poésie Française, 1895-1914. Toulouse:
      1960. (Bibliogr., pp. 507-11) (Coll. Universitas)
      (reviewed: Leroy C. Breunig, Romanic Review,
      LI, 4 (Dec. 1960), 302-4.)
348. _____. "Etudes sur la poésie française contempo-
      raine, I: Les traditionnalistes, " L'Inform. Litt.,
      XIV (1962), 197-203.
349. Decker, H. W. Pure Poetry, 1925-1930: Theory
      and Debate in France. Berkeley/Los Angeles:
      1962. (Univ. of Calif. Publ. in Mod. Philol.,
      64.)
350. Dehennin, Elsa. La Résurgence de Góngora et la
      Génération Poétique de 1927. Paris: 1962.
351. Delbouille, Paul. Poésie et Sonorités: La Critique
      Contemporaine Devant le Pouvoir Suggestif des
      Sons. Paris: 1961. (Bibliothèque de la Fac.
      de Philos. et Lettres de l'Univ. de Liège, fasc.
      CLXIII.) (French).
352. DeMichelis, Euralio. "Delle trad. in ispecie dai
      simbolisti francesi, " Studi in Onore di Vittorio
      Lugli e Diego Valeri. Venezia: 1962, pp. 325-
      32.
353. Dérieux, H. La Poésie Française Contemp., 1885-
      1935, 3rd edn. Paris: 1935.

354. De Robertis, Giuseppe. Scrittori del Novecento. Firenze: 1940.
355. Díaz, Janet W. "Main currents in 20th cen. Spanish poetry," Romance Notes (Univ. No. Carol.), IX (1968), 194-200.
356. Díez-Canedo, Enrique. Estudios de Poesía Española Contemp. México: 1965.
357. Dieckmann, Liselotte. "Symbols of isolation in some late 19th cen. poets," Studies in German Lang. & Lit. in Memory of Fred. O. Nolte...., ed. E. Hofacker & L. Dieckmann. St. Louis: 1963, pp. 133-48.
358. Digeon, Claude. La Crise Allemande de la Pensée Française, 1890-1914. Paris: 1959. (Bibl., pp. 543-52.)
359. Donchin, Georgette. "French infl. on Russian Symbolist versification," Slav. & East Europ. Review, XXXIII, 80 (Dec. 1954), 161-88.
360. _____. "A Russian Symbolist Journal and its Links with France," Rev. Litt. Comp., XXX (1956), 405-19.
361. _____. The Infl. of French Symbolism on Russian Poetry. 's-Gravenhage: 1958. (Bibl., pp. 216-33.)
362. Dornis, Jean. La Sensibilité dans la Poésie Française, 1885-1912. Paris: 1912.
363. Driver, Sam. "Acmeism," Slavic & East Europ. Journ., XII, 2 (1968), 141-56.
364. Duhamel, Georges. Les Poètes et la Poésie, 1912-1913. Paris: 1914.
365. Dupouy, Auguste. La Poésie de la Mer dans la Litt. Française. Paris: 1947. (Symbolism, Loti, Richepin.)
366. Duthié, Enid L. L'Influence du Symbolisme Français dans le Renouveau Poétique de l'Allemagne: 'les Blätter für die Kunst' de 1892 à 1900. Paris: 1933.
367. Duwe, Wilhelm. Dt. Dichtung des 20. Jh.: Vom Naturalismus z. Surrealismus. 2 Bde. Zürich: 1962.
368. _____. Ausdrucksformen dt. Dichtg vom Naturalismus bis z. Gegenwart: Eine Stilgeschichte d. Moderne. Berlin: 1965.
369. Eguía Ruiz, C. "La crisis del simbolismo lit. en España," Literaturas y Literatos..., prim. ser. Madrid: 1914, pp. 433-56.

370. Eimermacher, K., ed. Lit. Manifesty, ot Simvolizma
      K Oktyabruy, vol. I. Munich: 1969. (Slav.
      Propyläen, no. 64.)
371. Engelberg, Edward, ed. The Symbolist Poem: The
      Develop. of the English Trad. N. Y. : 1967.
      (Dutton paperback, D194.) (Incl. "Introd. , " pp.
      17-46; Symbolist criticism, pp. 289-345; bibliog. ,
      pp. 348-50.)
372. Erlich, Victor. "Russian poets in search of a poetics,"
      Comp. Lit. , no. 4 (1952).
373. _____. Russian Formalism: History--Doctrine.
      's. -Gravenhage: 1955. (Slav. Print. and Re-
      print. , 4.)
374. _____. "Images of the poet and of poetry in Slavic
      romanticism and neo-romanticism, " American
      Contrib. to the Fifth Intern'l Congress of Slavists.
      Hague: 1963, II, pp. 79-113. (Blok & Briusov)
      (Sofia, Sept. 1963).
375. Essays by var. hands. Les Lettres Françaises et la
      Trad. Hermétique. Paris: 1947. (Les Cah.
      d'Hermês, no. 1) (incl. : Rimbaud, Lautréamont,
      Péladan.)
376. Evans, Benjamin I. English Poetry in the Later Nine-
      teenth Century. London: 1933.
377. Falk, Walter. "Impressionismus u. Expressionismus, "
      Expression. als Lit. Ges. Studien, ed. W. Rothe.
      Bern/München: 1969, pp. 69-86.
378. Falqui, Enrico. Novecento Letterario, II. Firenze:
      1960 (1954).
379. Farinelli, Giuseppe. Storia e Poesia dei Crepuscolari.
      Milano: 1969.
380. Farmer, Albert J. Le Mouvement Esthétique et
      'Décadent' en Angleterre (1873-1900). Paris:
      1931.
381. Farrell, R. B. "Problems of periods and movements,"
      Periods in German Lit. , ed. James M. Ritchie.
      London: 1966, pp. 3-14.
382. Faurie, Marie-Josèphe. Le Modernisme Hispano-
      Américain et ses Sources Françaises. Paris:
      1966.
383. Fehr, A. J. A. De Franse Symbolisten en de Muziek
      .... Groningen: 1961.
384. Feidelson, Charles, Jr. Symbolism and American Lit.
      Chicago: 1953.
385. Feldman, David. La Revue Symboliste 'La Plume'
      (1889-'99) (thèse) Univ. de Paris: 1954.
386. Filon, A. "Le symbolisme anglais et l'art français, "

1755804

Journ. des Débats, XXII, 2 (1899).

387. Flora, F. La Poesia Ermetica. Bari: 1936.

388. Florian-Parmentier. Hist. Contemp. des Lettres Françaises de 1885 à 1914. Paris: 1914.

389. Fontainas, André. Dans la Lignée de Baudelaire. Paris: 1930.

390. _____, and N. Berberova. Le Symbolisme. Débats au Studio Franco-Russe. Paris: 1931.

391. Fort, Paul, and Louis Mandin. Hist. de la Poésie Française Depuis 1850. Paris: 1926.

392. Forti, Marco. Le Proposte della Poesia. Milano: 1963.

393. Frank, Heinz-Georg. Wechselwirk. dt. -französ. Einflüsse in symbolist. Dichtg. (diss.) Univ. of Manitoba (Winnipeg): 1967.

394. Frattini, Alberto. Poesia Nuova in Italia: Tra Ermetismo e Neoavanguardia. Milano: 1968. (Earl. edn. Roma: 1966).

395. Gale, Robert L. "Symbolism in Am. Lit., " Annali Instituto Universitario Orientale, Napoli, Sezione Germanica, II (1959), 167-86.

396. Gargiulo, A. Lett. Italiana del Novecente. Firenze: 1940.

397. Gatto, E. Lo. La Poesia Russa della Rivoluzione. Roma: 1923.

398. Gaudefroy-Demombynes, J. "L'infl. de la poésie française sur la poésie symboliste, " Rev. Univ. Laval, III, 8 (avril 1949), 658-71.

399. Gentil, P. le. "Le cinquantenaire du symbolisme et le Portugal, " Bull. des Etudes Portugaises, IV (1937).

400. Gianessi, Ferdinando. Gli Ermetici, 2nd edn. Milano: 1963.

401. Gibaudan, René. La Lyre Mystérieuse. Paris: 1965. (Coll. Alternance.)

402. Gilman, Margaret. The Idea of Poetry in France. Cambridge, Mass.: 1958.

403. Gofman, M., and R. Gofman. Les Symbolistes Russes. Paris: n. d. (Cf. M. & R. Hofmann.)

404. Goldstücker, Eduard. "Zum Profil d. Prager dt., Dichtg um 1900, " Philol. Pragensia, V (1962), 130-5.

405. González Muela, Joaquin, and J. M. Rozas. La Generac. Poética de 1927. Estudio, Antol. y Documentacion. Madrid: 1966.

406. González Ruiz, N. La Lit. Española del Siglo XX. Madrid: 1941.

36   A Post-Symbolist Bibliography

407. Gourmont, Rémy de. <u>Promenades Litt., 7 série.</u>
Paris: 1905-27.
408. Graaf, Daniël A. de. "Le mouvement 'Van Nu En
Straks' dans le cadre du symbolisme, " <u>Les</u>
<u>Flandres dans les Mouvements Romantique et</u>
<u>Symboliste.</u> <u>Actes du IIe Congrès nat'l de la</u> Soc.
<u>Française de Litt.</u> Comparée. Paris: 1958,
pp. 110-16.
409. _____. "Trefpunten tussen het Franse symbolisme
en de Duitse Romantiek, " <u>De Vlaamse Gids,</u>
XLVI, 8 (July 1962), 533-54.
410. Gray, Ronald. <u>The German Trad. in Lit.</u> (1871-1945).
Cambridge: 1966. (Incl. Rilke & Hofmannsthal.)
411. Grimm, Reinhold. "Zur Vorgesch. d. Begriffs
'Neuromantik, ' " <u>Das Nachleben d. Romantik in</u>
<u>d. mod. dt. Lit.,</u> ed. W. Paulsen. Heidel.:
1969, pp. 32-50.
412. Gsteiger, Manfred. "Französ. Lyrik zw. Gestern u.
Morgen, " <u>Lit. d. Ubergangs.</u> Bern: 1963,
pp. 36-48. (Also incl.: "Poesie u. Poetik d.
Gegenwart, " pp. 128-36.)
413. Guglielminetti, M. <u>Struttura e Sintassi del Romanzo</u>
<u>Italiano.</u> Milano: 1964.
414. Guiette, Robert, ed. <u>Poètes Français de Belgique.</u>
<u>De Verhaeren au Surréalisme.</u> Bruxelles/Paris:
1948.
415. _____. "Poètes symbolistes et langue poétique, "
<u>Les Flandres dans les Mouvements Romantique</u>
<u>et Symboliste.</u> <u>Actes du IIe Congrès Nat'l de la</u>
<u>Soc. Française de Litt. Comp.</u> Paris: 1958,
pp. 87-94.
416. Guillén, Jorge. <u>Language and Poetry: Some Poets</u>
<u>of Spain.</u> Cambridge, Mass.: 1961.
417. Gullón, Ricardo. <u>Direcciones del Modernismo.</u> Madrid: 1963.
418. Gurevich, L. "German romanticism and the symbolism of our days, " <u>Russkaya Mysl,</u> IV (1914).
419. Guth, Paul. <u>Hist. de la Litt. Française.</u> T. II:
<u>Des Orages Romantiques à la Grande Guerre.</u>
Paris: 1967. (Symbolism.)
420. Haas, Willy. "Vom Jugendstil z. Expressionismus, "
<u>Gestalten: Essays z. Lit. u. Gesellschaft.</u>
Berlin/Frankf. a. M. /Wien: 1962, pp. 56-65.
421. Hagelstange, R. "Dt. Lyrik nach Rilke, " <u>Dt. Akad.</u>
<u>f. Sprache u. Dichtg. Darmstadt Jahrb.,</u>
(1954), 63-80.

422. Hamann, Richard. Der Impressionismus in Leben u. Kunst, 2nd edn. Marburg: 1923 (Earlier edn. Köln: 1907.)
423. _____, and Jost Hermand. Impressionismus. Berlin: 1960. (Dt. Kunst u. Kultur von d. Gründerzeit bis z. Expressionismus, 3.)
424. Hatzfeld, H. Der französ. Symbolismus. Mchn: 1923.
425. Hatzfeld, Helmut. "Pure Poetry, " Trends and Styles in 20th Cen. French Lit. Washington: 1966, pp. 217-32.
426. Haumant, E. La Culture Française en Russie (1700-1900). Paris: 1910. (1913).
427. Henríquez-Ureña, Max. "Las infl. francesas en la poesía hispanoamer. , " Rev. Iberoamer. , II, 4 (Nov. 1940), 401-15.
428. Henríquez-Ureña, P. Literary Currents in Hispanic America. Harvard U. P.: 1945.
429. Hermand, Jost. "Der 'neuromant.' Seelenvagabund, " Das Nachleben d. Romantik...., ed. W. Paulsen. Heidel.: 1969, pp. 95-115.
430. Heyen, William. "Toward the still point: the imagist aesthetic, " Ball State Univ. Forum, IX, i (1968), 44-8. (American).
431. Hippius, Z. "Notes sur la litt. russe de notre temps, " Mercure de France, LXXI (1908), 71-9.
432. Hoffman, Daniel G. , ed. Am. Poetry and Poetics: Poems and Crit. Documents from the Puritans to Robert Frost. Garden City, N. Y.: 1962.
433. Hoffman, Frederick J. " 'Symbolisme' and mod. poetry in the U. S. , " Comp. Lit. Studies, IV (1967), 193-9.
434. Holthusen, Johannes. Studien z. Asthetik u. Poetik d. russischen Symbolismus. Gött.: 1957.
435. Hösle, J. Die dt. Lit. im Spiegel französ. Ztschr. von 1900-'14. (Diss.) Tüb.: 1954. (Cf. also: "Französ. lit. Ztschr. d. Jh. wende in ihrem allg, Verhält. z. dt. Schrifttum, " Rev. Litt. Comp. , XXX (1956), 552-64.)
436. _____. "Die dt. erzählende u. lyrische Dichtg d. Jh. wende im Spiegel französ. Ztschr. von 1900-1914, " Forschungsprobleme d. vergl. Lit. geschichte, II (1958), 135-53.
437. Hughs, Glenn. Imagism and the Imagists. Oxford/ Stanford, Calif.: 1931.
438. Hyman, Stanley E. Poetry and Criticism: Four Revol. in Lit. Taste. New York: 1961. (Mod. Engl. Poetry.)
439. Ilie, Paul. The Surrealist Mode in Spanish Lit.: An

Interpr. of Mod. Trends from Post-Romant. to
the Spanish Vanguard. Ann Arbor: 1968.

440. Isaacs, Jacob. The Background of Mod. Poetry.
N.Y.: 1952. (French symbolism and Anglo-
American Imagism.)

441. Ishikawa, T. Etude sur la Litt. Impress. au Japon.
Paris: 1910.

442. Itterbeek, Eugene van. "Van Symbolisme tot objekti-
visme, " Dietsche Warande en Belfort, CVI (1961),
591-600. (France).

443. Ivanov, Vjačeslav. "Zavety simvolizma, " Apollon,
VIII (1910).

444. Jackson, A. B. La Revue Blanche (1889-1903). Ori-
gine, Influence, Bibliographie. Paris: 1960.
(Bibliog., pp. 152-312) (Bibliothèque des Lettres
Modernes.)

445. Jaensch, E. R. "Uber impressionistisches Sehen u.
impress. Weltansicht, " Ztschr. f. Sinnesphysiolo-
gie, LIV (1923).

446. Jiménez, José O. "Medio siglo de poesía española
(1917-'67)," Hispania, L (1967), 931-46.

447. Johansen, Sven. Le Symbolisme: Etude sur le Style
des Symbolistes Français, tr. Hélène Laurent-
Lund. Copenhague: 1945. (Bibliog., pp. 365-
72.)

448. John, S. B. & H. R. Kedward. "Lit. and Ideology,
1880-1914, " French Lit. and its Bkgd., ed. John
Cruickshank. Oxford: 1969, pp. 173-97.

449. Johnson, E. D. H. The Alien Vision of Victorian
Poetry. Princeton, N.J.: 1952.

450. Jones, A. R. "Imagism: a unity of gesture, " Am.
Poetry, ed. John R. Brown et al. London:
1965, pp. 115-33. (Stratford-upon-Avon Studies,
7.)

451. Jones, P. Mansell. The Bkgd of Mod. French Poetry. Essays & Interviews. Cambridge: 1951.
(Bibliog., pp. 183-90.) (Reprint: 1968.)

452. Josipovici, G. D. "The birth of the modern, 1885-
1914, " French Lit. and its Background, ed. John
Cruickshank. London: 1969, pp. 1-20. (Oxford
Paperbacks, 184.)

453. Kahn, Gustave. Symbolistes et Décadents. Paris:
1902.

454. Karátson, André. Le Symbolisme en Hongrie. L'Infl.
des Poétiques Françaises sur la Poésie Hongroise
dans le Premier Quart du XXe Siècle. Paris:
1969. (Publ. de la Fac. des Lettres et Sciences

Hum. de Paris-Sorbonne. Série Recherches, 40)
(bibliog., pp. 473-84.)

455. Kaufmann, Hans. "Zur Situat. d. dt. Lit. um d. Jh.
wende, " Krisen u. Wandlungen d. dt. Lit. von
Wedekind bis Feuchtwanger. Fünfzehn Vorlesung-
en, 2nd edn. Berlin: 1969 (1966), pp. 19-46.

456. Kaun, Alexander S. "Russian poetic trends on the eve
of and on the morning after 1917, " Slavonic Yearbook, XX (Am. Series, I) (1941), 55-85.

457. _____. Soviet Poets and Poetry. Freeport, N.Y.:
1968 (1943). (Essay Index reprint series.)

458. Kayser, Wolfgang J. Gedichte d. französ. Symbolismus
in dt. Ubers. Tüb.: 1955. (Dt. Texte, 2.)

459. Kies, Albert. "L'Image de la Flandre chez quelques
ecrivains belges de l'époque symboliste, " Les
Flandres dans les Mouvements Romantique et
Symboliste. Actes du IIe Congrès Nat'l de la
Soc. Française de Litt. Comp. Paris: 1958,
pp. 103-9.

460. Killy, Walter, ed. 20. Jh.: 1880-1930. Mchn: 1966.
(Die dt. Lit., Texte u. Zeugnisse, VII.)

461. Kimmich, Anne. Krit. Auseinandersetzung mit dem
Begriff Neuromantik in d. Lit.gesch. Schreibung.
(Diss.) Tüb.: 1936.

462. Klemperer, V. "Entstehung u. Eigenart d. französ
Neuromantik, " Jahrb. f. Philol., II (1927), 143-72.

463. _____. Mod. französ. Lyrik: Dekandenz, Symbolismus, Neuromantik. Studie u. Komment. Texte.
Berlin: 1957, pp. 1-88.

464. Klotz, Volker. "Jugendstil in d. Lyrik, " Kurze
Komment. z. Stücken u. Gedichten. Darmstadt:
1962, pp. 51-60. (Hessische Beiträge z. dt.
Lit., 10.)

465. Kluckhohn, P. "Die Wende vom 19.z.20 Jh. in d. dt.
Dichtg, " Dt. Vjschr., XXIX (1955), 1-19.

466. Koch, J. K. "The recep. and infl. of mod. Am.
poetry in France (1918-'50), " Diss. Abstr., XX
(1959/60), 4660 (Columbia).

467. Kotzin, Michael. "Pre-Raphaelitism, Ruskinism, and
French Symbolism, " Art Journ., XXV, 4 (Summer
1966), 347-50.

468. Kushner, Eva. Le Mythe d'Orphée dans la Litt. Française Contemp. Paris: 1961. (Bibliog., pp.
351-9) (symbolism in poetry.)

469. Laffranque, Marie. "Aux sources de la poésie espagnole contemp.: la querelle du créationnisme, "
Bull. Hispanique, LXIV bis (1962), 479-97.

(Pub. sep. as book: Bordeaux: 1962.)

470. Lanson, Gustave. "L'Epoque symboliste et l'avant-
guerre, " Histoire de la Litt. Française. (Re-
maniée et compl. pour la période 1850-1950 par
Paul Tuffrau.) Paris: 1952, pp. 1211-1337.

471. Lauterbach, U. H. Bang: Studien z. dänischen Impressionismus. Breslau: 1937.

472. Lawler, James R. The Lang. of French Symbolism.
Princeton/London: 1969.

473. Leavis, Frank R. New Bearings in English Poetry.
London: 1950.

474. LeHir, Yves. Esthétique et Structure du Vers Français d'après les Théoriciens du XVIe Siècle à
Nos Jours. Paris: 1956.

475. Lehmann, Andrew G. The Symbolist Aesthetic in
France, 1885-95. Oxford/New York: 1950.
(2nd ed. 1968.)

476. Lemaître, Georges E. From Cubism to Surrealism
in French Lit. Cambridge, Mass.: 1941.

477. Lethève, Jacques. Impressionnistes et Symbolistes
Devant la Presse. Paris: 1959.

478. Levin, Harry. "The poetics of French symbolism, "
Romanic Review, XLVI, 3 (Oct. 1955), 161-3.

479. _____. The Power of Blackness: Hawthorne, Poe,
Melville. N.Y.: 1958. (Symbolism in Amer.
Lit.)

480. Lewisohn, Ludwig. The Poets of Mod. France. Port
Wash., N.Y.: 1970. (Bibliog., pp. 163-91)
(orig. publ. 1918.)

481. Linden, Walther, ed. Eindrucks-u. Symbolkunst.
Leipzig: 1940. (Vom Naturalismus zur neven
Volksdichtung, Band 2.)

482. Lirondelle, André. "La poésie russe de l'art pour
l'art et sa destinée, " Rev. des Etudes Slaves, I
(1921).

483. Lombardo, Agostino. Realismo e Simbolismo: Saggi
di Lett. Amer. Contemp. Roma: 1957. (Biblioteca di Studi Amer., 3.)

484. Lorenz, E. Der metaphor. Kosmos d. mod. Spanis-
chen Lyrik (1936-1956). Hamburg: 1961.

485. Losereit, Sigrid. Die Suche nach d. verlorenen Eden
in d. Lyrik d. französ. Symbolisten. Zur Trad.
eines mythischen 'thème.' (Diss.) Heidel.: 1969.

486. Lossky, N. O. "Philos. ideas of poet-Symbolists, "
Hist. of Russian Philosophy. N.Y.: 1951, pp.
335-45.

487. Máchal, J. O Symbolismu v Lit. Polské a Ruské.

Praha: 1935.
488. MacIntyre, C. F., trans. French Symbolist Poetry.
Berkeley/Los Angeles: 1958. (Notes, pp. 115-
47) (bibliog., pp. 148-50.)
489. Macrí, O. Caratteri e Figure della Poesia Italiana
Contemp. Firenze: 1956.
490. _____. Proceso Contro el Hermetismo, trans.
Arroita-Jaurégui. Santandar: La Isla de los
Ratones, 1963.
491. _____. Realtà del Simbolo: Poeti e Critici del
Novecento Italiano. Firenze: 1968.
492. Mähl, Hans-Joachim. "Die Mystik d. Worte. Zum
Sprachproblem in d. mod. dt. Dichtg.," Wirk.
Wort, XIII (1963), 289-303.
493. [No entry.]

494. Manzini, G. Ritratti e Pretesti. Milano: 1960.
495. Martin, Wallace and Ian Fletcher. A Catalogue of the
Imagist Poets. N.Y.: 1966. (Incl.: W. Mar-
tin, "The Forgotten School of 1909 and the Origins of Imagism," pp. 7-38; I. Fletcher, "Some
Anticipations of Imagism," pp. 39-53.)
496. Maslenikov, Oleg A. The Frenzied Poets: A. Biely
and the Russian Symbolists. Berkeley: 1952.
(Bibliog., pp. 225-30.)
497. _____. "Russian symbolists: the mirror theme
and allied motifs," Russian Review, XVI, 1
(1957), 42-52.
498. Mathews, A. J. La Wallonie, 1886-92: the Symbolist Movement in Belgium. N.Y.: 1947.
499. Matlaw, R. E. "The manifesto of Russian Symbolism,"
Slav. & East Europ. Journ., XV, 3 (Fall 1957),
177-91.
500. Matthiessen, F. O. "Amer. poetry, 1920-'40," Sewanee Review, LV (1947), 24-55.
501. Megroz, R. L. Mod. English Poetry, 1882-1932.
London: 1933.
502. Mehring, F. "Naturalismus u. Neuromantik,"
Meisterwerke dt. Lit. kritik, hrsg. Hans Mayer.
2 Bde. Berlin: 1956, II, 1, pp. 932-5. (Also
in: Aufs. z. dt. Lit. von Hebbel bis Schweichel.
Berlin: 1961, pp. 227-9.) (Orig. in: Die neue
Zeit, XXVI (1907/8), II, 961-3.)
503. Melis, Antonio. "Bilanco degli studi sul modernismo
ispanoamer.," Lavori Ispanistici, serie 2. Firenze: Univ. deli Studi di Firenze, Fac. de

Magis., 1st Ispanico, 1970, pp. 259-312.

504. Mendes Campos, Mario. "Fund. del Modernismo His-panoamer.," Univ. Pontificia Bolivariana, XXX (1968), 204-13.

505. Mercier, Alain. Les Sources Esotériques et Occultes de la Poésie Symboliste (1870-1914). Tome I: Le Symbolisme Français. Paris: 1969. (Bib-liog., pp. 271-81.)

506. Michaud, Guy. "Le thème du miroir dans le symbo-lisme français," Cah. de l'Assoc. Intern'l des Etudes Françaises, XI (mai 1959), 199-216.

507. Mickiewicz, Denis. "Apollo and modernist poetics," Russian Lit. Tri-Quarterly, no. 1 (Fall 1971), 226-61.

508. Milazzo, E. Sintesi di Lett. Spagnola Contemp. Roma: 1958.

509. Minder, Robert. "Dt. u. französ. Lit. Inneres Reich u. Einbürgerung d. Dichters," Acht Essays z. dt. Lit. Frankf. a. M.: 1969, pp. 28-58. (Fischer Bücherei, 983.)

510. Mirsky, D. S. (Svjatopolk). Contemp. Russian Lit., 1881-1925. London: 1929 (1926).

511. Mohrenschildt, D. S. von. "The Russian Symbolist movement," PMLA, LIII, 4 (1938).

512. Moore, Harry T. "French poetry betw. the wars," 20th Cen. French Lit. to W. W. II. Carbondale: 1966, pp. 150-77.

513. Morawska, Ludmila. "Stylistyka statystyczna (na marginesie prac. P. Guiraud)," (La stylistique statistique, en marge des travaux de p. Guiraud), Kwartalnik Neofilolgiczny, VI, 1 (1959), 51-3. (French Symbolist poetry.)

514. Moreh, Shmuel. "The infl. of Western poetry (and partic. T. S. Eliot) on mod. Arabic poetry," Asian and African Studies, V (1969), 1-50.

515. Morris, C. B. A Generation of Spanish Poets (1920-'36). London: 1969. (Incl. "Bio-Bibliog. Index.")

516. Morrissette, Bruce A. "Early English and Am. cri-tics of French symbolism," Studies in Hon. of F. W. Shipley (Wash. Univ.) St. Louis: 1942.

517. Moser, Ruth. L'Impressionnisme Français: Peinture, Litt., Musique. Genève/Lille: 1952.

518. Mucci, Renato. "Parnassiani e simbolisti in Italiano," Idea, VI, 4 (24 Genn. 1954), 2.

519. Müller-Freienfels, R. "Der Neuromantik," Literari-sches Echo, XV

520. Munson, Gorham B., and Ann Stanford. "Poetry: 1900 to the 1930's," Am. Lit. Scholarship: an Annual (1968), ed. Albert J. Robbins. Durham, N.C.: 1970, pp. 228-44.

521. Muricy, Andrade. Panorama do Movimento Simbolista Brasileiro, 3 vols. Rio de Janeiro: 1951/2.

522. Naremore, James. "The Imagists and the French 'generation of 1900,' " Contemp. Lit. (Madison, Wisc.), XI (1970), 354-74.

523. Neely, Robert T. "Endymion in France: A brief survey of French symbolist poetry," Les Mardis. St. Mallarmé and the Artists of his Circle (Exhib. Catal.) Univ. Kansas Museum of Art: 1966. (Bibliog., p. 49) (Publ. of the Museum of Art 61.)

524. Noth, Ernst Erich. "German Poetry after Rilke," Forum (Houston), III, vii (1961), 16-19.

525. Noulet, E. "El Hermetismo en la poesía francesa moderna," Filos. y Letras, I (Jan.-March 1941), 69-101.

526. _____. "L'Hermétisme dans la Poésie Française Moderne," Etudes Litt. Mexique: 1944, pp. 11-76.

527. _____. "Le sillage symboliste," Hist. Illus. Lettres Françaises Belg. Bruxelles: 1958, pp. 467-74. (Belgian symbolist poetry.)

528. van Nuffel, Roberto O. J. "Polémique belges autour du symbolisme," Comp. Lit. Studies, IV (1967), 91-102.

529. Orsini, V. Ermetismo: 2nd edn. Pescara: 1956.

530. Ortega y Gasset, José. El Novecentismo. Buenos Aires: 1916.

531. Pagnini, Marcello. "Imagism," Studi Americani (Roma), II (1965), 181-95.

532. _____. "Strutt. semantica del grande Simbolismo Americano," Il Simbolismo nella Lett. Nord-Americana, ed. Mario Praz. Firenze: 1965, pp. 29-52.

533. Palmer, H. E. Post-Victorian Poetry. London: 1938.

534. Panayotopoulos, J. M. "Le symbolisme et les poètes lyriques néo-grecs," Hellénisme Contemporain, (mars 1954), 99-111.

535. Pancrazi, P. Scrittori Italiani del Novecento. Bari: 1934.

536. _____. Scrittori d'Oggi, I. Bari: 1946.

537. Panizza, O. Die dt. Symbolisten. Gegenwart(?): 1895.

538. Pasolini, P. P. Passione e Ideologia. Milano: 1960.

539. Patnode, Jack. "English and Am. Lit. Relations in the 1890's: the Cosmop. Impressionists, " Diss. Abstr., XXIX (1969), 2721A (Minn.).

540. Pauls, E. "Romantik u. Neuromantik, " Ztschr. f. d. dt. Unterr., XXXII (1918), 129-146.

541. Pellegrini, Carlo. "Il paesaggio interiore nei poeti simbolisti francesi, " Studi in Onore di V. Lugli e D. Valeri. Venezia: 1962, pp. 701-13. (Repr. in: Lett. e Storia nell' Ottocento Francese e Altri Saggi. Roma: 1967, pp. 201-14.)

542. Petriconi, H. Die spanische Lit. der Gegenwart seit 1870. Wiesbaden: 1926. (Bibliog., pp. 191-5.)

543. Petrucciano, Mario. La Poetica dell'Ermetismo Italiano. Torino: 1955.

544. _____. "La crisi dell'ermetismo nella poesia del dopo guerra, " Cultura e Scuola, I, 3 (1962), 18-24.

545. Picard, M. Das Ende d. Impressionismus, 2nd edn. Erlenbach-Zürich: 1920 (1916).

546. Piccioni, Leone. Lett. Leopardiana e Altri Saggi. Firenze: 1952.

547. _____. Sui Contemporanei. Milano: 1956.

548. _____. Lavagna Bianca. Firenze: 1964.

549. Picco, F. "Simbolismo francese e simbolismo italiano, " Nuova Antologia (Roma), CCXLVII (Maggio-Giugno 1926), 82-91.

550. Piccoli, R. Poesia e Vita Spirituale. Saggi sulla Lett. e la Civiltà Inglese e Americana e sui Loro Rapporti con l'Italia. Bari: 1934.

551. Pinto, V. de S. Crisis in English Poetry, 1880-1940. London: 1951.

552. Poggioli, Renato. The Poets of Russia, 1890-1930. Cambridge, Mass.: 1960. [Reviewed by Gleb Struve, Russian Review, XX, 1 (Jan. 1961), 79.]

553. _____. "Simbolismo russo e occid., " Lett. Modern, XI (1961), 586-602.

554. Ponomareff, C. V. "The Image Seekers: an analysis of Imaginist [sic?] poetic theory, 1919-24, " Slav. & East Europ. Journ., XII (1968), 275-96. (Russian).

555. Pouilliart, Raymond. Le Romantisme. vol. III: (1869-1896). Paris: 1968. (Coll. Litt. Française.) (Symbolism).

556. Pozzi, G. La Poesia Italiana del Novecento: Da Gozzano Agli Ermetici. Torino: 1967(1965).

557. Pratt, William, ed. The Imagist Poem: Mod. Poetry in Miniature. N.Y.: 1963.

558. Prochnik, P. "German studies: Lit., 1880 to the present day, " Year's Work in Mod. Lang. Studies, XXX (for 1968), 556-76.
559. Ragusa, Olga. "French symbolism in Italy, " Romanic Review, XLVI (1955), 231-5.
560. Raitt, A. W. "French studies: the 19th cen. (postromantic), " Year's Work in Mod. Lang. Studies, XXVII (1965), 117-31 (bibliog.).
561. Raiziss, Sona. La Poésie Américaine Moderniste, 1910-40. Paris: 1948.
562. Rall, Dietrich. Die Zeitgenössische Spanische Lit. im Spiegel französ. Ztschr. von 1898 bis 1928. (Diss.) Tüb: 1968.
563. Ramsey, Warren. "Uses of the Visible: Am. Imagism, French Symbolism, " Comp. Lit. Stud., IV (1967), 177-91.
564. Randall, A. W. G. "French symbolism and mod. German poetry, " Anglo-French Review, III, 4 (1920), 314-20.
565. Ransom, J. C. "Symbolism: Amer. style, " New Republic, II, 11 (1953), 18-20.
566. Rapsilber, E. Recherches sur les Rapports Artistiques Franco-Allemands de la Fin du XIXe Siècle à la Première Guerre Mondiale. (Thèse) Univ. Paris: 1961.
567. Rasch, Wolfdietrich. "Aufbruch z. mod. Dichtg. Dt. u. europ. Lit. um d. Jh. wende, " Universitas, XXI (1966), 517-26.
568. Ravegnani, G. Uomini Visti, III. Milano: 1955.
569. Rexroth, K. "L'Influence de la poésie française sur la poésie américaine, " Europe, CCCLVIII-IX (févr.-mars 1959), 43-66.
570. Richter, Elise. "Impressionismus, expressionismus u. Grammatik, " Ztschr. f. romanische Philologie, XLVII, (1927), 349-71.
571. Rimanelli, Giose. "Still on Italian hermeticism, " Italica, XLIII (1966), 285-99.
572. Roinard, P. N., V. E. Michelet, and G. Apollinaire. La Poésie Symboliste. Paris: 1909.
573. Romano, Salvatore F. Poetica dell'Ermetismo. Firenze: 1942. (Biblioteca del Leonardo, 21.)
574. Rose, William J. "The poets of young Poland, 1890-1903, " Slavonic Yearbook, Amer. Series, I (1941), 185ff.
575. Rosenberg, Harold. "French silence and Am. poetry, " Encounter, III, 5 (Nov. 1954), 17-20.

576. Rosenhaupt, H. W. Der dt. Dichter um d. Jh.wende
      u. seine Ausgelöstheit von d. Gesellschaft.
      Bern/Leipzig: 1939.
577. Rousselot, Jean. "Orphées belges, " (la poésie) Les
      Nouv. Litt., 2189 (4 sept. 1969), 4.
578. Roy, Ross G. "A bibliog. of French symbolism in
      Engl. lang. publ. to 1910 (Mallarmé-Rimbaud-
      Verlaine)" Rev. Litt. Comp., XXXIV, 4 (oct.-
      déc. 1960), 645-60.
579. Rubio, D. Symbolism & Classicism in Mod. Lit. In-
      trod. to the Study of Symbolism in Span. Am.
      Lit. Philadelphia: 1923.
580. Rudler, Madeleine G. Parnassiens, Symbolistes et
      Décadents. Paris: 1938.
581. Russi, Antonio. Gli Anni della Antialienazione: Dall'-
      Ermetismo al Neo-Realismo. Milano: 1967.
582. Rutten, M. "Le symbolisme français et le renouveau
      de la poésie belge d'expression néerlandaise, "
      Etudes Germaniques, XVII, 3 (juillet-sept. 1962),
      328-43. (Incl. Morice, Régnier, Verhaeren.)
583. Sabaneeff, Leonid. "Relig. and mystical trends in
      Russia at the turn-of-the-century, " Russian Re-
      view, XXIV, 4 (Oct. 1965), 354-68.
584. Salinas, Pedro. Lit. Española Siglo XX, 2nd rev.
      edn. México: 1949.
585. _____. Ensayos de Lit. Hispánica, 3rd edn. Ma-
      drid: 1967.
586. Sanguinetti, Edoardo. Tra Liberty e Crepuscolarismo.
      Milano: 1961.
587. _____. Poeti e Poetiche del Primo Novecento.
      Torino: 1966.
588. Santos Torroella, R. Medio Siglo de Publ. de Poesía
      en España. Cat. de Revistas. Segovia/Madrid:
      1952.
589. Sauro, Antoine. La Lingua Poetica in Francia dal
      Romanticismo al Simbolismo. Bari: 1954.
      (Bibliog., pp. 403-18.)
590. Scarpati, Claudio. "Sulle orig. dell'ermetismo criti-
      co, " Vita e Pensiero, LI (1968), 354-63.
591. Schmid, E. "Französ. Romantizismus u. dt. Neuro-
      mantik, " Das neue Leben, (1926).
592. Schneider, Marcel. "Fantastique symboliste et déca-
      dent (1884-1912), " La Litt. Fantastique en France.
      Paris: 1964. (Bibliog., pp. 417-20) (also dis-
      cusses Valéry.)
593. Scholnick, Robert J. "The Children of the Night: the
      Situation for Poetry in the Am. 1890's, " Diss.

Abstr., XXX (1969), 1574A (Brandeis).
594. Schonthal, Aviva H. "The symbolist poetics in the
'Mercure de France' (1890-1905), " Diss. Abstr.,
XVII (1957), 1768/9. (Columbia).
595. Seaman, David W. "French concrete poetry: the develop. of a poetic form, from its origins to the
present day, " Diss. Abstr., XXXI, 5 (Nov. 1970),
2402A (Bklyn). (Incl. Laforgue, Mallarmé,
Apollinaire, Surrealism.)
596. Secchi, Giovanni. "L'involuzione dei poeti ermetici, "
Nuova Corrente, no. 15 (1959), 21-34.
597. Séché, Alphonse. Les Caractères de la Poésie Contemp. Paris: 1913.
598. Seillière, E. Morales et Religions Nouvelles en Allemagne. Paris: 1927 (Impressionismus).
599. _____. Le Néoromantisme en Allemagne. Paris:
1931.
600. Seroni, A. Ragioni Critiche. Firenze: 1944.
601. Shattuck, Roger. The Banquet Years: The Origins
of the Avant-Garde in France--1885 to W.W.I.
N.Y.: 1968 (bibliog., pp. 365-81) (rev. ed.
London: 1969).
602. _____. "How poetry got its teeth: Paris, 1857
and after, " Western Review, XXIII (1958-9), 175-86.
602a. Silveira, Tasso da. "A poesia simbolista em Portugal, "
Ocidente (Lisbon), XXVI (July 1945), 150-8.
603. Simon, J. "Les poètes américains et leurs introd.
français, " Langues Modernes, XLII (1948).
604. Slonim, Marc. Mod. Russian Lit. from Chekhov to
the Present. N.Y.: 1953.
605. _____. "After the symbolists, " From Chekhov
to the Revol.: Russian Lit. 1900-17. N.Y.:
1962, pp. 211-33.
606. _____, and George Reavey. Anth. de la Litt.
Soviétique, 1918-'34. Paris: 1935.
607. Sommavilla, Guido. "Simbolismo conciliatore, "
Letture, XIV (1959), 563-70.
608. Sommerhalder, Hugo. Zum Begriff d. literar. Impressionismus. Zürich: 1961.
609. Sorensen, Bengt A. Symbol u. Symbolismus in d.
ästhet. Theorien d. 18 Jh. u. d. dt. Romantik.
Kopenhagen: 1963. (Orig. diss. Aarhus.)
610. Spitzer, Leo. "Le innov. sintatt. del simbolismo
francese, " Marcel Proust e Altri Saggi di Lett.
Francese Moderna. Torino: 1959.
611. Stahl, E. L. "The genesis of Symbolist theories in
Germany, " Mod. Lang. Review, XLI (1946), 306-17.

48 A Post-Symbolist Bibliography

612. Starkie, Enid. From Gautier to Eliot: the Infl. of France on Engl. Lit, 1851-1939. London: 1960.
613. Steinhauser, H. D. dt. Dichtg, 1880-1933. N.Y.: 1941.
614. Strakhovsky, Leonid I. "The silver age of Russian poetry: symbolism and acmeism, " Canadian Slavonic Papers, IV (1959), 61-87.
615. Strémooukhoff, D. "Echos du symbolisme français dans le symbolisme russe, " Autour du Symbolisme, ed. P. G. Castex. Lille/Paris: 1955, pp. 297-9.
616. Stroka, Anna. "Der Impressionismus d. dt. Lit.: ein Forschungsbericht, " Germanica Wratislaviensia (Wroclaw), X (1966), 141-61.
617. Struve, Gleb. Twenty-Five Years of Soviet Russian Lit. London: 1944 (1929).
618. _____. Soviet Russian Lit. (1917-1950). Okla.: 1951.
619. Subrahmanian, Krishnaswami. "The theory of 'suggestion' in Sanskrit poetics, English Romanticism, and French Symbolism, " Diss. Abstr. Intern'l, XXX (1969/70), 4957A (Ind.).
620. Taboada, Juan M. Diez. "El germanismo y la renov. de la lírica española en el siglo XIX, " Filologia Moderna, II, 5 (1961), 21-55.
621. [No entry.]

622. Taupin, René. L'Infl. du Symbolisme Français sur la Poésie Américaine de 1910 à 1920. Paris: 1929.
623. Tedesco, Natale. La Condizione Crepuscolare: Saggi sulla Poesia Italiana del Novecento. Firenze: 1970.
624. Temple, Ruth Z. The Critic's Alchemy: A Study of the Introd. of French Symbolism into England. N.Y.: 1953. (Bibliog., pp. 304-21) (later ed. New Haven: 1962) (Columbia Univ. thesis).
625. Tentori, Francesco. "Ermetismo Ispanoamer., " Approdo, L (1970), 49-51.
626. Thon, Luise. "Die Sprache d. dt. Impressionismus, " Wortkunst (Mchn) (1928).
627. Tindall, William Y. Forces in Mod. Brit. Lit., 1885-1946. N.Y.: 1947. (Rev. paperback edn. N.Y.: Vintage, 1956.)
628. TittaRosa, G. Poesia Italiana del Novecento. Siena: 1953.

629. Torrente Ballester, G. Lit. Española Contemp. (1898-1936). Madrid: 1949.

630. Tosi, Guy. "Aperçus sur les infl. litt. françaises en Italie dans le dernier tiers du XIXᵉ Siècle, " Rivista di lett. mod. e. comparate, XIX (1966), 165-70.

631. Unbegaun, B. O. Russian Versification. N. Y. /Oxford: 1956.

632. Valbuena Prat, Angel. La Poesia Espanõla Contemp. Madrid: 1930.

633. Valentinov, Nikolay. Two Years with the Symbolists, ed. Gleb Struve. Stanford, Calif.: 1969. (Russian).

634. Valeri, D. Il Simbolismo Francese da Nerval a De Regnier. Padova: 1954.

635. Vandercammen, E. "Du Parnasse au Symbole (la poésie en Belgique), " Hist. Illus. Lettres Françaises Belgiques. Bruxelles: 1958, pp. 532-6.

636. Videla, Gloria. El Ultraísmo: Estudio sobre Movimientos Poéticos de Vanguardia en España. Madrid: 1963.

637. Vigée, Claude. "Vers une descrip. méthodique du symbole dans notre litt., " Les Artistes de la Faim. Paris: 1960, pp. 161-4. (Also incl.: "Genèse de la sensibilité poétique moderne, " pp. 13-60.)

638. Vines, Sherard. Movements in Mod. English Poetry. Oxford: 1927.

639. Visan, Tancrède de. L'Attitude du Lyrisme Contemporain. Paris: 1911.

640. _____. "Essai sur le Symbolisme (préface), " Paysages Introspectifs. Paris: 1904.

641. Vivanco, Luis F. Introd. a la Poesía Española Contemp. Madrid: 1957.

642. Vortriede, Werner. Novalis u. d. franzӧs. Symbolisten. Zur Entstehungsgeschichte d. dicht. Symbols. Stutt: 1963. (Sprache u. Lit., 8.)

643. Vossler, K. Ital. Lit. d. Gegenwart von d. Romantik z. Futurismus. Heidel: 1914.

644. Wautier, André. "La trad. symboliste chez les poètes français de Wallonie, " Culture Française, no. 5 (4ᵉ trim. 1962), 10-43.

645. Weidlé, Wladimir. "Peterburgskaia poetika, " Sobranie Sochinenii, IV, (?), v-xxxvi. (On Acmeism.)

646. Wenguérow, Z. "Lettres russes: le symbolisme en France et en Russie, & c, " Mercure de France (Nov. 1890).

647. West, James. Russian Symbolists. A Study of V.
     Ivanov and of the Russian Symbolist Aesthetic.
     London: 1970. (Reviewed by George Ivask,
     Russian Review, XXXI, 2 (April 1972), 192-3.)
648. Whitney, A. H. "Synaesthesia in 20th cen. Hungarian
     poetry, " Slav. & East Europ. Review, XXX, 75
     (1952), 444-65.
649. Wiegner, Kathleen. "French Symbolism in England:
     1890-1900, " Wisconsin Studies in Lit., VI (1969),
     50-7.
650. Wien, A. Die Seele d. Zeit um d. Jh. wende. Leipzig:
     1921. (Impressionismus).
651. Wiley, Paul L., and Harold Orel, eds. British Poe-
     try, 1880-1920: Edwardian Voices. N. Y.: 1969.
652. Wunberg, Gotthart. "Utopie u. fin de siècle: z. dt.
     Lit. kritik vor d. Jh. wende, " Dt. Vierteljahrss.,
     XLIII (1969), 685-706.
653. Xirau, Ramón. "Introd. to contemp. Span. -Amer.
     poetry, " Mundus Artium (Ohio Univ.), III, 1
     (1969), 13-27.
654. Zardoya, Concha. Poesía Española Contemp.: Es-
     tudios Temáticos y Estilísticos. Madrid: 1961.
655. _____. Poesía Española del '98 y del '27: Es-
     tudios Temáticos y Estilísticos. Madrid: 1968.
656. Zerega-Fombona, A. Le Symbolisme Français et la
     Poésie Espagnole Moderne. Paris: 1920.
657. _____. El Simbolismo Francés y la
     Mod. Poesía Española. Venezuela: 1922.
658. Ziolkowski, Theodore. "Das Nachleben d. Romantik
     in d. mod. dt. Lit. Methodolog. Uberlegungen, "
     Das Nachleben d. Romantik...., ed. W. Paulsen.
     Heidel: 1969, pp. 15-31.
659. Zirmunskij, Viktor M. "Preodolevshie simvolizm, "
     Russkaia Mysl, no. 12 (1916), 25-56. (Repr.
     with addenda in Voprosy Teorii Literatury.
     Hague: 1962, pp. 278-336). (Differentiates
     betw. Symbolism and Acmeism.)
660. Zukovsky, Louis. "Amer. poetry, 1920-'30, " Sym-
     posium, (Jan. 1931), 60-84.

COMPARATIVE STUDIES

661. Abrams, H. M. "Coleridge, Baudelaire, and modernist poetics," Immanente Asthetik, ed. W. Iser. Mchn: 1966.
662. Abril, Xavier. Dos Estudios: I. Vallejo y Mallarmé. II. Vigencia de Vallejo. Buenos Aires: 1965 (1960).
663. Accaputo, Nino. L'Estetica di Baudelaire e le sue Fonti Germaniche. Torino: 1961.
664. Adams, Hazard. Blake and Yeats: The Contrary Vision. Ithaca, N.Y.: 1955.
665. Adlard, John. Stenbock, Yeats, and the Nineties, with an hitherto unpubl. essay by A. Symons and a bibliog. by T. Smith. London: 1969.
666. Adorno, Th. W. "George u. Hofmannsthal," Prismen. Kulturkritik u. Gesellschaft. Bln/Frankf. a. M.: 1955, pp. 232-82. (Later ed. 1963, pp. 190-231; G u. H. zum Briefwechsel, 1891-1906.)
667. Adriani, B. Baudelaire u. George. 1939.
668. Adt, W. Das Verhältnis George u. s. Kreises zu Hölderlin (diss.) Frankfurt: 1934.
669. Aguirre, A. M. "Relac. amistosas entre R. Darío y J. R. Jiménez," Quad. Ibero-Amer., XXXVII (1969), 42-6.
670. Albrecht, Hellmuth F. G. "'Fin de siècle' y 'décadence' y superación en H. v. Hofmannsthal, R. M. Rilke, y St. George," Humanitas (Rev. de la Fac. de Filos. y Letras de la Univ. Nac. de Tucumán), VII, 2 (1959), 99-130.
671. Alewyn, Richard. "H. u. St. George," Uber H. v. H. Gött: 1963/4, pp. 292-7. (Also incl. "H. u. s. Zeit," pp. 5-13; "H's Wandlungen," pp. 161-79.)
672. Alexander, Ian W. "Valéry and Yeats: the rehabilitation of time," Scottish Periodical, I, 1 (Summer 1947), 77-106.
673. Allemann, Beda, ed. Ars Poetica. Texte von Dichtern d. 20 Jh. z. Poetik. Darmstadt: 1966. (George, H. v. H., Musil, Benn.)

51

674. Allinger, Erich. George u. Hofmannsthal (Diss.).
        Wien: 1950.
675. Alvar, Manuel. "R. Darío y Musset (a propósito de
        'El Clavicordio de la Abuela'), " Studia Philologica:
        Homenaje Ofrecido a Dámaso Alonso..., 2 vols.
        Madrid: 1960, I, pp. 79-85.
676. Andelson, Robert V. "The concept of creativity in
        the thought of Rilke and Berdyaev, " Personalist,
        XLIII (1962), 226-32.
677. Angioletti, G. B. L'Anatra alla Normanna. Milano:
        1957. (Incl. Rimbaud, Mallarmé, Valéry et al.)
678. Annekov, George. "The poets and the revolution--
        Blok, Mayakovsky, Esenin, " Russian Review,
        XXVI, 2 (1967), 129-43. (Trans. W. Todd III.)
679. Anon. "The poet as symbolist: towards a remade
        experience, " Times Lit. Suppl., no. 2065 (Aug.
        30, 1941), 418, 421. (Mallarmé and Moréas.)
680. Aspetsberger, Friedbert. "Wiener Dichtg d. Jh.
        wende. Beobachtg zu Schnitzlers u. Hofmannsthals
        Kunstformen, " Studi Germaniche, VIII (1970),
        410-51.
681. Austin, Lloyd J. L'Univers Poétique de Baudelaire:
        Symbolisme et Symbolique. Paris: 1956.
682. _____. "Les moyens du mystère chez Mallarmé
        et chez Valéry, " Cah. Assoc. Intern'l des Etudes
        Françaises, XV (mars 1963), 103-17.
683. _____. "New light on Brennan and Mallarmé, "
        Austral. Journ. French Studies (Melbourne), VI
        (1969), 154-62.
684. Bachler, K. "Drei grosse 'B, ' " (Broch, Brecht,
        Benn) Schweiz. Rds., LIV (1954/5), 678-83.
685. Bailey, J. "Blok and Heine: an episode from the
        hist. of Russian 'dol'niki', " Slav. & East Europ.
        Journ., XIII, 1 (Spring 1969), 1-22.
686. Balseiro, José A. "Presencia de Wagner y casi
        ausencia de Debussy en R. Darío, " Abside, XXXI
        (1967), 174-89.
687. Bark, Joachim. Der Wuppertaler Dichterkreis: Un-
        tersuch. zum Poeta Minor im 19. Jh. Bonn:
        1969. (AKML, 86.)
688. Barnes, T. R. "Yeats, Synge, Ibsen, and Strindberg, "
        Scrutiny, V, 3 (Dec. 1936), 257-62.
689. Bays, Gwendolyn. The Orphic Vision: Seer Poets
        from Novalis to Rimbaud. Lincoln, Nebr.: 1964.
        (Bibliog., pp. 289-91) (incl. essay "A confusion
        of ways, " (Mallarmé, Morice, Rimbaud), pp. 3-
        30.)

690. Beery, Judith A. "The relev. of Baudelaire to T. S. Eliot's 'The Waste Land,' " Susquehanna Univ. Studies, VII (1966), 283-302.

691. Behrmann, Alfred. "Der Tod d. Orpheus in zwei mod. Gedichten. Rilke, Sonnette an Orpheus I, 26 ('22); Benn, 'Orpheus' Tod' ('46), " Dt. unterr., XVII, 4 (1965), 82-9.

692. Bémol, Maurice. Variations sur Valéry. Tome II: V confronté à Dante, Pétrarque, Goethe, Maurice de Guérin, Sainte-Beuve, Rilke. Paris: 1960. (Earlier ed. Saarebruck: 1952.)

693. Benamou, Michel. "J. Laforgue and W. Stevens, " Romanic Review, L (1959), 107-17.

694. _____. "Wallace Stevens and Apollinaire, " Comp. Lit., XX (1968), 289-300.

695. _____. "Recent French poetics and the spirit of Mallarmé, " Contemp. Lit. (Madison, Wisc.), XI, 2 (Spring 1970), 217-25.

696. Benda, Julien. La France Byzantine ou le Triomphe de la Litt. Pure: Mallarmé, Gide, Valéry ... les Surréalistes; Essai d'une Psychologie Orig. du Littérateur. Paris: 1945 [later edn. 1970].

697. Berge, André. "Rilke et Proust, " Cah. du Mois, nos. 23/4 (1926), 54-6. (Collected in Reconnaissance à Rilke. Paris: 1926.) (Also incl. "Le poète de l'enfance, " by Tividar Raith.)

698. Berger, Y. "Deux poètes devant la trahison de langage (Bonnefoy & P. Emmanuel), " Preuves, IX, 104 (oct. 1959), 75-8.

699. Bernard, Suzanne. Le Poème en Prose de Baudelaire Jusqu'à nos Jours. Paris: 1959. (Bibl., pp. 775-97.)

700. Berne-Joffroy, André. "Destin de la rhétorique: Stendhal, Valéry, Paulhan, " Cah. du Sud, 37ᵉ année, XXXI, 300 (1ᵉʳ sem. 1950), 272-98.

701. Bertholf, R. J. "The vast ventriloquism: Wordsworth and W. Stevens, " Diss. Abstr., XXIX (1969), 3605A (Ore.).

702. Bertocci, Angelo P. From Symbolism to Baudelaire. Carbondale: 1964. (Bibl., pp. 215-18) (incl. Mallarmé, Rimbaud, Valéry, Verlaine.)

703. Betz, Maurice. "Valéry et Rilke, " Cah. du Sud, XXXIII, 276/8 (1946), 212-16.

704. Beyerhaus, G. "R. M. R. u. P. Valéry: e. Dichterfreundschaft, " Sammlung (Gött.), I (1945/6), 460-9.

705. Birtwell, Lorna R.   "From Blok and Bely: transl.,"
      Russian Review, II, 1 (Autumn 1942), 102ff.
      (Incl. biogr. sketches.)
706. Blanchot, Maurice.   La Part du Feu.   Paris: 1949.
      (Mallarmé, Rimbaud, Valéry, Lautréamont, Char,
      Surrealism.)
707. Blissett, William.   "Pater and Eliot, " Univ. Toronto
      Quarterly, XXII, 3 (April 1953), 261-8.
708. Block, H. M. and H. Salinger, eds.   The Creative
      Vision. N. Y. /London: 1960.   (Incl. transl.
      from Valéry.)
709. _____. Mallarmé and the Symbolist Drama.   De-
      troit: 1963.

710. Bloom, Harold.   " 'The Central Man':   Emerson,
      Whitman, W. Stevens, " Massachusetts Review,
      VII (Winter 1966).
711. Bocelli, Arnaldo.   "Da Baudelaire ai surrealisti, " La
      Nuova Europa, II, 45 (Nov. 11, 1945), 7-8.
712. Boisdeffre, Pierre de.   "Un siècle de poésie fran-
      çaise: de Baudelaire à Y. Bonnefoy, " Arts-
      Loisirs, no. 66 (28 déc. 1966-3 janv. 1967),
      26-9.
713. Bolle, Louis.   Les Lettres et l'Absolu: Valéry-
      Sartre-Proust.   Genève: 1959.
714. Bollier, E. P.   "La poésie pure: the silent debate
      betw. T. S. Eliot and P. Valéry, " South Central
      Bull., XXVIII, 3 (Oct. 1968), 75.   (Abstract).
715. _____. "La poésie pure: The ghostly dialogue
      betw. T. S. Eliot and P. Valéry, " Forum (Hous-
      ton), VIII, i (1970), 54-9.
716. Bondy, L. J.   "The legacy of Baudelaire, " Univ.
      Toronto Quart., XIV (July 1945), 414-30.
717. Bonnet, Henri.   De Malherbe à Sartre.   Essai sur
      les Progrès de la Conscience Esthétique.   Paris:
      1964.   (Incl.:   "Le Symbolisme, " pp. 96-107;
      "Après M. Proust: poésie pure et roman pur, "
      pp. 119-22 (on Valéry).)
718. Bordeaux, Henry.   "Les poètes au commencement du
      siècle.   Souvenirs sur M. Maeterlinck, F.
      Jammes, C. Guérin, A. de Noailles, " Rev. des
      Deux Mondes, no. 21 (1er nov. 1952), 20-35.
719. Bordier, Roger.   "Whitman et Lorca, " Europe, 483/4
      (1969), 188-91.
720. Borel, Pierre.   "Mallarmé et Valéry, " Autour de
      Montaigne: Etudes Litt.   Neuchâtel: 1945, pp.
      73-6.

721. Bornstein, George. Yeats and Shelley. Chicago: 1970.

722. Bosquet, Alain. "La poésie est aussi dans la clarté: Y. Bonnefoy et R. Sabatier, " Combat, no. 6635 (21 oct. 1965), 7.

723. Boucher, Maurice. "Rilke et George, " Etudes Germaniques, VII, 2/3 (avril-sept. 1952), 117-22.

724. Breugelmans, R. "St. George and O. Wilde: a confrontation, " Proceed. Pacific Northwest Confer. For. Lang., XV (1964), 40-59.

725. _____. "Alienation, the destiny of mod. lit. ? O. Wilde and St. George, " Mosaic, II, i (1968), 18-28.

726. _____. "The reconcil. of opposites in the mythopoesis of Wilde, George, and Hofmannsthal," Proceedings: Pacific Northwest Confer. on Foreign Langs., 21st Annual Meeting (April 3-4, 1970), Vol. 21, ed. Ralph W. Baldner. Victoria, B.C.: 1970, pp. 248-54.

727. Brissoni, Armando. Due Saggi di Poesia: Ungaretti e Foscolo. Padova: 1969.

728. Brooks, Cleanth, Jr. The Hidden God: Studies in Hemingway, Faulkner, Yeats, Eliot, and Warren. New Haven: 1963.

729. Brückler, S. H. v. H. u. M. Maeterlinck (diss.). Würzburg: 1953.

730. Brumleve, Sister Barbara. "Whitman and Stevens: From an organic to a process metaphor, " Diss. Abstr. Intern'l, XXX (1970), 3450A/51A (St. Louis).

731. Brunius, August. "Yeats och Moore, " Var Tid Arsbok Utgiven av Samfundet De Nio 1923. Stockholm: 1923, pp. 75-95.

732. Bucher, Jean-Marie F. "A crit. apprec. of Valéry's infl. on Rilke, " Diss. Abstr., XXVIII (1967), 1389A (Brown).

733. Bunn, James H. "The Palace of Art: A Study of Form in the Retrosp. Poems about the Creative Process, " Diss. Abstr. Intern'l, XXX (1970), 4400A (Emory). (Incl. Yeats and Stevens.)

734. Burch, Francis F. Tristan Corbière: L'Originalité des "Amours Jaunes" et leur infl. sur T. S. Eliot. Paris: 1970.

735. Burger, Hilde. "H. v. H. --M. Maeterlinck: zwei unveröffentl. Briefe, " Neue Rundschau, LXXIII (1962), 314-19.

736. Burne, Glenn S. "Rémy de Gourmont and the aesthe-
     tics of symbolism, " Comp. Lit. Studies, IV
     (1967), 161-75.
737. Burnshaw, Stanley. "The three revol. of mod. poe-
     try, " Varieties of Lit. Experience. N. Y.: 1962,
     pp. 137-69. (Also in: Sewanee Review, LXX, 3
     (Summer 1962), 418-50.) (Incl. Rimbaud, Mal-
     larmé, Perse, Breton.)
738. Buxó, José P. Ungaretti Trad. de Góngora. Un Es-
     tudio de Lit. Comparada. Maracaibo, Venez. :
     Univ. del Zulia, Fac. de Human. y Educ., 1968.
739. Cambon, Glauco. "Nothingness as catalyst: an analy-
     sis of 3 poems by Ungaretti, Rilke, and Stevens, "
     Comp. Lit. Studies, (special advance issue)
     (1963), 91-9.
740. Campos, C. L. "Symbolism and Mallarmé, " French
     Lit. and its Background, ed. John Cruickshank.
     London: 1969, pp. 132-53.
741. Caretti, Laura. "Eliot come Pécuchet, " Studi Ameri-
     cani (Roma), XIV (1968), 247-64.
742. Carey, Sister M. C. "Baudelaire's infl. on
     'The Waste Land, ' " Renascence, XIV (1962),
     185-92, 198.
743. Carré, J. M. "Maeterlinck et les litt. étrangères, "
     Rev. Litt. Comp., VI (1926), 449-501.
744. Carvalho, J. de M. "R. Darío e Eça de Queiroz, "
     O Estado de São Paolo, supl. lit. (May 10, 1969),
     p. 1.
745. Cary, Meredith. "Yeats and Moore--an autobiog.
     conflict, " Eire (St. Paul), IV, 3 (1969), 94-109.
746. Cassou, Jean. Trois Poètes: Rilke, Milosz, Ma-
     chado. Paris: 1954.
747. Castay, Marcel. Trois Voix Perdues: J. Giraudoux,
     P. Valéry, Léon-Paul Fargue. Paris: 1949.
748. Casteras, Raymonde de. Avant le Chat Noir: les
     Hydropathes. présenté de Maurice Donnay.
     Paris: 1945. (Symbolists.)
749. Castex, Pierre-Georges, ed. Autour du Symbolisme:
     Villiers-Mallarmé-Verlaine-Rimbaud. Lille /
     Paris: 1955. (Incl. : Jacques-Henry Bornecque,
     "Rêves et réalités du symbolisme, " pp. 5-23;
     M. Décaudin, "L'Ermitage, 1890-96, " pp. 275-
     83; ibid., "Le symbolisme en 1885/6 d'après la
     corresp. inédit d'Edouard Dujardin, " pp. 271-3).
750. Cattaui, Georges. Trois Poètes: Hopkins, Yeats,
     Eliot. Paris: 1947.
751. Chast, Denyse. "Eugenio de Castro et St. Mallarmé, "

Rev. Litt. Comp., XXI, 2 (avril-juin 1947), 243-53. (Introd. of symbolism to Portugal.)

752. Chastel, Guy. "J.-K. Huysmans et les poètes," Rolet, n.s., no. 553 (15 sept. 1955), 4. (Incl. Laforgue, Mallarmé, Valéry, Verlaine.)

753. Chiari, Joseph. Contemp. French Poetry. N.Y.: 1952. (Bibl., pp. 175-80; incl. Valéry, Supervielle, Claudel, Perse, Michaux, Surrealism; another ed. Manchester: 1952; "P. Valéry," pp. 13-44.)

754. _____. Symbolisme from Poe to Mallarmé: the Growth of a Myth. Foreword by T. S. Eliot. London: 1956. (Bibl., pp. 188-92.)

755. Chica-Salas, Susana. "Synge y Garcia-Lorca: aprox. de dos mundos poéticas," Rev. Hisp. Moderna, XXVII (1961), 128-37.

756. Chisholm, A. R. "Three architects of pessimism: Leopardi, Baudelaire, Valéry," Meanjin, XIII, 4 (Summer 1954), 551-8.

757. _____. "Towards an analytical crit. of poetry," AUMLA, no. 22 (Nov. 1964), 164-77. (Heredia, Mallarmé, Valéry.)

758. _____. "The role of consciousness in the poetry of Mallarmé and Valéry," Comp. Lit. Studies, IV (1967), 81-9.

759. Ciplijauskaité, Biruté. La Soledad y la Poesía Española Contemporanea. Madrid: 1962. (Incl. Jiménez and Guillén.)

760. _____. "J. Guillén y P. Valéry, al despertar," Insula, XVIII (Dic. 1963), ccv, 1, 14. (Repr. in Papeles de Son Armadans (Mallorca), XXXIII, 99 (Junio 1964), 267-94. (Compares 'Cántico' with 'Charmes.')

761. Clancier, G.-E. De Rimbaud au Surréalisme. Panorama Critique. Verviers: 1959. (Earlier ed. Paris: 1953.)

762. Clive, H. P. "O. Wilde's first meeting with Mallarmé," French Studies (Oxford), XXIV (1970), 145-9.

763. Cobb, Carl W. "F. G. Lorca and J. R. Jiménez: the question of infl.," Tennessee Stud. in Lit., XV (1970), 177-88.

764. Coeuroy, André. "Le déclin: Rolland, Barrès, Claudel, Valéry, Gide," R. Wagner et l'Esprit Romantique. Paris: 1965, pp. 318-39.

765. Cohen, Gustave. Ceux Que J'ai Connus. Montréal: 1946. (Incl. Maeterlinck and Valéry.)

766. Cohn, Robert G. "Proust and Mallarmé," French
     Studies (Oxford), XXIV (1970), 262-75.
767. Collet, G.-P. "Edouard Dujardin et le symbolisme,"
     South Central Bull., XX, 1 (Feb. 1960), 18.
     (Abstract; incl. Mallarmé.)
768. Cook, Albert. "Mod. verse. Diffusion as a princi-
     ple of composition," Kenyon Review, XXI, 2
     (Spring 1959), 199-220. (Reverdy, Mallarmé,
     Valéry.)
769. Cordiè, Carlo. Due Epigoni del Simbolismo Francese:
     A. Samain e Louis le Cardonnel (con lett. e
     docum. inediti). Arona/Milano: 1951.
770. Cornell, J. G. "Apolog. pro exegetice," Journ.
     Australas. Univ. Lang. & Lit. Assoc., no. 10
     (May 1959), 21-7. (Mallarmé-Valéry.)
771. Cornell, Kenneth. "French symbolism," Contemp.
     Lit., IX, 1 (Winter 1968), 136-9. (Valéry, Mal-
     larmé, Rimbaud, St.-Jean Perse.)
772. Cornwell, E. F. The Still Point: Theme and Varia-
     tions in the Writings of T. S. Eliot, Coleridge,
     Yeats, Henry James, Virginia Woolf, and D. H.
     Lawrence. New Brunswick, N.J.: 1962.
773. Cortázar, Julio. "Para una poética," La Torre, II,
     7 (Julio-Sett. 1954), 121-38. (Rimbaud and
     Valéry.)
774. Costa, John. "Aesthetics behind the poems of C.
     Baudelaire and R. M. Rilke on autumn," Culture,
     XXVII (1966), 350-5.
775. Costaz, G. "Lugné-Poë et le théâtre symboliste belge
     à la fin du XIXe siècle," Audace (Bruxelles),
     XVI, 1 (1970), 130-5.
776. Cox, C. B. and A. E. Dyson. Mod. Poetry: Studies
     in Practical Criticism. London: 1963. (Essays
     on specific poems by Yeats, Eliot et al.)
777. Cronin, Anthony. "A question of modernity," X, A
     Quart. Rev., I (1960), 283-92. (The 'lit. revol.'
     of the past 50 years: Pound, T. S. Eliot, Yeats
     and Joyce.)
778. _____. A Question of Modernity. London: 1966.
     (Eliot and Yeats.)
779. Curtius, Ernst R. M. Proust y P. Valéry. Buenos
     Aires: c. 1941.
780. _____. "George, Hofmannsthal u. Calderon,"
     Krit. Essays z. europ. Lit. Bern: 1950,
     pp. 172-201. (Also in: Essais sur la Litt.
     Européenne, trad. Claude David. Paris: 1954,
     pp. 163-91.)

781. Dallot, René. Ricordi Italiani: D'Annunzio, Valéry. Con uno studio su Giulio Grassi, trad. di L. Gasparini e A. Pittoni. Trieste: 1960.
782. David, Claude. "Quelques études récentes sur Rilke et sur George, " Etudes Germaniques, XVII (1962), 441-9.
783. Davie, Donald. "Pound and Eliot: a distinction, " Eliot in Perspective: A Symposium, ed. Graham Martin. London/N.Y.: 1970, pp. 62-82.
784. Davray, Henry D. "L'Infl. de Laforgue et de Péguy sur T. S. Eliot, " Mercure de France (15 Juillet 1937), 421-3.
785. Décaudin, Michel. "Maeterlinck et le symbolisme, " Europe, 399-400 (juill. -août 1962), 105-14.
786. _____. "L'Avant-garde autour d'Apollinaire, " L'Information Littéraire, XXI (1969), 116-23.
787. Decker, H. W. Pure Poetry, 1925-30. Theory and Debate in France. Berkeley/Los Angeles: 1962. (Henri Brémond & Paul Valéry.) (Univ. Calif. Publ. Mod. Philol., 64.)
788. _____. "Baudelaire and the valéryan concept of pure poetry, " Symposium, XIX, 2 (Summer 1965), 155-61.
789. Dédéyan, Charles. Le Cosmopolitisme Litt. de Charles Du Bos. Tome II: La Maturité de Ch. du Bos (1914-'27). Paris: 1966. (Symbolism, Mallarmé, Valéry.)
790. _____. Le Nouveau Mal du Siècle: de Baudelaire à nos Jours. Tome I: Du Postromantisme au Symbolisme, 1840-'89. Paris: 1968.
791. Delsemme, P. Teodor de Wyzewa et le Cosmop. Litt. en France à l'Epoque du Symbolisme. Bruxelles: 1967. [69] (Univ. Libre de Bruxelles; travaux de la fac. de philos. et lettres, 34.)
792. Demetz, Peter. "Engl. Spiegelungen R. M. Rilkes, " Orbis Litt., XI (1956), 18-30. (St. Spender, W. H. Auden, S. Keyes.)
793. Denat, Antoine. "Towards an ontology of the poem (from Valéry to Ponge), " AUMLA, no. 6 (May 1957), 14-19.
794. Desmond, Shaw. "Dunsany, Yeats, and Shaw: Trinity of Magic, " Bookman (N. Y.), LVIII, 3 (Nov. 1923), 260-6.
795. Dettmering, Peter. Dichtg u. Psychoanalyse: Th. Mann, R. M. Rilke, R. Wagner. München: 1969.
796. Devoto, Daniel. "G. Lorca y Darío, " Asomante, XXIII, ii (1967), 22-31.

797. Díaz-Plaja, Guillermo. "J. R. Jiménez y R. Darío, "
      Clavileño, VII (Nov. -Dic. 1956).
798. Dietrich, M. "Maeterlinck u. Hofmannsthal, " Europ.
      Dramat. im 19. Jh. Graz: 1961, pp. 514-54.
799. Diez del Corral, Luis. La Función del Mito Clásico
      en la Lit. Contemp. Madrid: 1957. (Incl. Mal-
      larmé, Valéry, Symbolism.)
800. Dollot, René. "Un précurseur de l'unité italienne:
      l'aieul de P. Valéry: Giulio Grassi, 1793-1874, "
      Rev. des Etudes Italiennes, n. s. (1931/2).
801. Dragonetti, Roger. Aux Frontières du Langage
      Poétique. Etudes sur Dante, Mallarmé, Valéry.
      Ghent: 1961. (Univ. de Gant. Fac. de Philos.
      et Lettres.) (Romanica Gandensia, 9.) (Incl. :
      comment on Valéry. "Les larmes ou
      l'impuissance du langage. ")
802. Drieu la Rochelle, Pierre. Sur les Ecrivains. Es-
      sais Critiques. Paris: 1964. (Includes: "L'au-
      tre face du symbolisme, " pp. 232-41; "Naturalisme
      et symbolisme, " pp. 224-32; "Lecture de Valéry,"
      pp. 258-60.)
803. Dubu, Jean. "Valéry et Courbet: origine de 'La
      Fileuse, ' " Rev. d'Hist. Litt. de la France, LXV,
      2 (avril-juin 1965), 239-43.
804. Durzak, Manfred. "Die Kunsttheoretische Ausgangs-
      position St. Georges: Zur Wirkung Edgar Allan
      Poes, " Arcadia, IV (1969), 164-78.
805. Duthie, Enid L. "Some references to the French
      symbolist movement in the corresp. of St. George
      and H. v. H. , " Comp. Lit. Studies, IX (1943),
      15-18.
806. El-Azma, Nazeer. "The Tammūzī movement and the
      infl. of T. S. Eliot on Badr Shākir al-Sayyāb, "
      Journ. Amer. Oriental Society, LXXXVIII (1968),
      671-8.
807. Eliot, T. S. From Poe to Valéry. N.Y. : 1948.
      (Cf. Hudson Review, II, 3 (Autumn 1949), 327-
      42.)
808. El Kayem, Henri. "Rencontres avec trois poètes:
      Schehadé, Jouve, Bonnefoy, " Rev. du Caire,
      XVIII, 178 (mars 1955), 87-110.
809. Ellmann, Richard. "Yeats and Eliot, " Encounter,
      XXV, 1 (1965), 53-5.
810. _____ . Eminent Domain: Yeats Among Wilde,
      Joyce, Pound, Eliot, and Auden. N.Y. : 1967.
      [1970].

811. Enright, D. J. "Reluctant admiration. A note on
     Auden and Rilke, " The Apothecary's Shop: Es-
     says on Lit. London: 1957, pp. 187-205.
812. Epting, Karl. "Die dt-französ. geistige Begegnung, "
     Zeitwende, XL (1969), 298-306. (Incl. St. George,
     Rilke, Goethe & France, Mme de Staël, R.
     Rolland.)
813. Eschmann, E. W. "Valéry u. Rilke (Fragmente e.
     Vergleiches), " Neue Schweizer Rundschau, N. F.,
     XVI, 3 (Juli 1948), 179-87.
814. Essays by var. hands. "Les langues et litt. mod.
     dans leurs relat. avec les beaux arts, " Actes du
     Vième Congrès Intern'l des Langues et Litt.
     Modernes. Florence: 1955. (Incl. symbolism,
     Mallarmé, Valéry, Proust).
815. _____. M. Maeterlinck in Dtland. Eine Ausstell.
     aus Anl. d. 100 Geb. d. Dichters. Zusammen
     gestellt von d. Dt. Akad. f. Sprache u. Dichtg.
     Darmstadt: 1962.
816. _____. "Poètes maudits et décadents, " L'Esprit
     Créateur (Lawrence, Kan.), IX, 1 (Spring 1969).
     (Special issue. Incl. Nouveau, Rimbaud, Ver-
     laine, Mallarmé, Corbière, et al.).
817. Evans, Arthur R., Jr. On Four Modern Humanists:
     Hofmannsthal, Gundolf, Curtius, Kantorowicz.
     Princeton, N. J.: 1970. (Princeton Essays in
     Europ. & Compar. Lit.)
818. Evans, Calvin H. "Hofmannsthals' 'kleine Dramen' as
     seen in the focus of Maeterlinck's 'Static Drama,' "
     Diss. Abstr., XX (1959), 1785. (Oregon).
819. Evans, David W. "T. S. Eliot, Charles Williams,
     and the sense of the occult, " Accent (A Quart.
     of New Lit.), XIV (1954).
820. Eykman, Christoph. Die Funktion d. Hässlichen in d.
     Lyrik Georg Heyms, Georg Trakls u. G. Benns.
     Zur Krise d. Wirklichkeitserfahrung im dt. Ex-
     pressionismus. Bonn: 1965. (Later ed. 1969;
     also diss: Bonn.)
821. Fagundo Guerra, Ana M. "The infl. of Emily Dickin-
     son on J. R. Jiménez' poetry, " Diss. Abstr.,
     XXIX (1968), 258A (Univ. Wash.).
822. Falk, Walter. Leid u. Verwandlung: Rilke, Kafka,
     Trakl u. d. Epochenstil d. Impressionismus u.
     Expressionismus. Salzburg: 1961. (Trakl-
     Studien, 6.)
823. Fein, J. M. "Eugénio de Castro and the reaction to
     symbolism in Portugal, " Mod. Lang. Journ.,

XXXVI (1952), 268-71.

824.   . "Eugénio de Castro and the introd. of Modernismo to Spain, " PMLA, LXXII (1958), 556-61.

825. Fernandez, Ramon. "De Descartes à Valéry, " La Nouv. Rev. Française, année 29, vol. LV, no. 331 (1er Sept. 1941), 359-66.

826. Feshbach, S. "W. Stevens and Erik Satie: a source for 'The Comedian as the Letter C, ' " Texas Stud. in Lit. & Lang., XI (1969), 811-18.

827. Field, Andrew. "Mikhail Kuzmin: notes on decadent's prose, " Russian Review, XXII, 3 (July 1963), 289-300.

828. Fields, Kenneth W. "The rhetoric of artifice: Ezra Pound, T. S. Eliot, Wallace Stevens, Walter Conrad Arensberg, Donald Evans, Mina Loy, and Yvor Winters, " Diss. Abstr., XXVIII (1968), 4627A (Stanford).

829. Filipuzzi, Carla. H. v. H. u. G. d'Annunzio. Verwandtes u. Trennendes. (Diss.) Wien: 1965.

830. Fiser, Eméric. Le Symbole Littéraire: Essai sur la Signification du Symbole chez Wagner, Baudelaire, Mallarmé, Bergson et Proust. Paris: 1943. (Bibliog., pp. 213-23.)

831. Fogelquist, Donald F. The Liter. Collabor. and Personal Corresp. of R. Darío and J. R. Jiménez. Coral Gables, Florida: 1956.

832. Fontainas, André. "De Mallarmé à P. Valéry: Lettres et souvenirs inédits, " Rev. de France, V (1927), 327-45.

833. Forster, Leonard W. The Poet's Tongues: Multilingualism in Lit. New York: 1970. (Study of poetry written in languages other than the poet's native tongue. Incl. George, Rilke, T. S. Eliot.)

834. Fortassier, P. "L'expression indirecte du réel et sa théorie chez Valéry, La Fontaine, Musset, " L'Information Littéraire, XX, 1 (janv. -févr. 1968), 7-17.

835. Fowlie, Wallace. A Guide to Contemp. French Lit. from Valéry to Sartre. N.Y.: 1957.

836.   . "Baudelaire and Eliot: Interpreters of their Age, " Sewanee Review, LXXIV, 1 (Jan. - March 1966), 293-309.

837. Francavilla, Francesco. Il Simbolismo, con 12 Tavole Fuori Testo. Milano: 1944. (Maeterlinck and Valéry.)

838. Frandon, Ida-Marie. "Jeux du relatif et de l'absolu: positivisme et métaphysique dans notre litt, " L'Inform. Litt., XII, 3 (mai-juin 1960), 97-105. (Incl. Rimbaud, Valéry, Mallarmé.)

839. Fraser, G. S. "W. B. Yeats and T. S. Eliot, " T. S. Eliot: A Symposium for His Seventieth Birthday, ed. Neville Braybrooke. N.Y.: 1958, pp. 196-216.

840. _____. "Complexity, allusiveness, irony, obscurity in mod. poetry, " The Mod. Writer and his World. Harmondsworth, Middlesex: 1964, pp. 31-49. (Incl. Mallarmé and Rimbaud.)

841. Freedman, Ralph. "Symbol as terminus: some notes on symbolist narrative, " Comp. Lit. Studies, IV (1967), 135-43. (Incl. Gide and Mallarmé.)

842. _____. "Wallace Stevens and R. M. Rilke: two versions of a poetic, " The Poet as Critic, ed. Frederick P. W. McDowell. Evanston, Ill.: 1967, pp. 60-80.

843. Frey, John Andrew. Motif Symbolism in the Disciples of Mallarmé (thesis). Washington: 1957. (Catholic Univ. of America) (Studies in Rom. Lang. & Lit., 55) (Bibliog., pp. 148-55).

844. Freymuth, Günther. "Georg Simmel u. St. George, " Neue dt. Hefte, CXXVII (1970), 41-50.

845. Friedrich, Hugo. Die Struktur d. mod. Lyrik von Baudelaire bis z. Gegenwart. Hamburg: 1960.

846. Fromilhague, René. "Hugo et Valéry: la dialectique ombre-lumière, " Bull. de la Soc. Toulousaine d'Etudes Classiques, (avril 1962).

847. _____. "P. Valéry, émule de Malherbe? La richesse des rimes, " Mélanges d'Hist. Litt. (XVIe-XVIIe siècle) Offerts à R. Lebègue.... Paris: 1969, pp. 363-9.

848. _____. "P. Valéry: inspir. méditerr., " Quad. Francesi, a Cura di E. Giudici, Vol. I. Napoli: Ist. Univ. Orientale, Sem. di Francese, 1970, pp. 621-6. (Camus).

849. Fuchs, Albert. "G. Benn, Henri Matisse, Asphodèles. Versuch e. Interpretation, " Acta Germanica, III (1968), 233-9.

850. Fullwood, Daphne. "The infl. on W. B. Yeats of some French poets, " The Southern Review, VI (1970), 356-79. (Mallarmé, Verlaine, Claudel.)

851. _____. "Balzac and Yeats, " Southern Review, V (1969), 935-49.

852. Fumet, Stanislas. "Symbolisme contemporain, "
      Polarité du Symbole. Paris: 1960, pp. 135-48.
      (Etudes Carmélitaines) (incl. Mallarmé and Rim-
      baud).
853. Gaède, Edouard. Le Rêve chez Nietzsche et Valéry
      (thèse). Paris: 1962.
854. Gallejo Morell, Antonio. "Cuando Federico (García
      Lorca) leyó a Machado, " Estafeta Literaria (15
      Nov. 1944).
855. Gallup, Donald C. "T. S. Eliot and Ezra Pound:
      Collaborators in Letters, " Atlantic Monthly,
      (Jan. 1970), 49-62. [Also repr. in Poetry Aus-
      tralia, XXXII (1970), 58-80.]
856. Gaughan, Gerald C. "W. Stevens and St. Mallarmé:
      a comparative study in poetic theory, " Diss.
      Abstr., XXVII (1967), 3453A (Northwestern).
857. Gaulupeau, Serge. "Rilke, lecteur de Maurice de
      Guérin, " Etudes Germaniques, XXV (1970), 25-
      40.
858. Gavelle, Robert. "Callot, A. Bertrand, Baudelaire,
      Mallarmé et Valéry, " Rev. d'Hist. Litt. de la
      France, XL (1933), 101-2.
859. Geen, Renée. "Valéry and Diderot, " Romance Notes,
      VII, 1 (Autumn 1965), 5-8.
860. _____. "Valéry et Swedenborg, " French Studies,
      XX, 1 (1966), 25-32.
861. Gershman, Herbert S. "Valéry, Breton and Eluard
      on Poetry, " French Review, XXXVIII (1965), 332-
      6.
862. _____. "Valéry and Breton, " Yale French Stud.,
      no. 44 (1970), 199-206.
863. Gheorghe, Ion. "Le mythe de la création par la
      musique chez P. Valéry et Lucien Blaga, " Rev.
      des Sciences Humaines, CXXXIV (Avril-Juin
      1969), 275-82.
864. Ghyka, Matila. "Of some French writers and their
      key words, " Life and Letters Today, XL, 79
      (March 1944), 162-7. (Incl. Mallarmé and
      Valéry.)
865. Gibson, Robert D., ed. Mod. French Poets on Poe-
      try, An Anthology. N.Y.: 1961 (incl. Mal-
      larmé, Verlaine, Rimbaud, Valéry.)
866. Gicovate, Bernardo. Julio Herrera y Reissig: a
      symbolist poet. (diss.) Harvard: 1952.
867. _____. "The poetry of Julio Herrera y Reissig
      and French symbolism, " PMLA, LXVIII, 5 (Dec.
      1953), 935-42.

868. _____. Julio Herrera y Reissig and the Symbolists.
Berkeley: 1957. (French infl. on Uruguay poetry.)
869. _____. "De R. Darío a C. Vallejo: una constante
poética, " Torre, XIII (1965), xlix, 27-44.
870. Girolamo, Nicola di. Teodor de Wyzewa dal Simbolismo al Trad., 1885-1887. Bologna: 1969.
(Mallarmé, Rimbaud, Verlaine.)
871. Glasser, Marvin. "The early poetry of Tennyson and
Yeats: a comparative study, " Diss. Abstr.,
XXIV (1964), 4174 (N. Y. U.).
872. Glauser, Alfred. Le Poème-Symbole de Scève à
Valéry. Paris: 1967.
873. Glur, G. Kunstlehre u. Kunstanschauung d. George-
kreises u. die Aesthetik O. Wildes. Bern: 1957.
874. Goff, Penrith. "H. v. Hofmannsthal and Walter Pater, " Comp. Lit. Studies, VII (1970), 1-11.
875. Goffin, Robert. Entrer en Poésie. Pour mieux com-
prendre Apollinaire, Verlaine, Mallarmé, Valéry,
Bataille, Maeterlinck, Claudel, Cendrars, Cocteau,
Eluard, Ganzo, Follain, Fombeure et les Surréalistes. Gand: 1948.
876. _____. Mallarmé Vivant. Paris: 1955(6). (Incl.
Valéry.)
877. _____. Fil d'Ariane pour la Poésie. Paris: 1964.
(Incl. Valéry, Mallarmé, Rimbaud.)
878. Goldgar, H. " 'Axël' de Villiers de l'Isle-Adam et
'The Shadowy Waters' de W. B. Yeats, " Rev. de
Litt. Comparée, XXIV (1950),
879. González Muela, Joaquin. El Lenguaje Poético de la
Generación Guillén-Lorca. Madrid: 1954.
880. _____. "Poesía y amistad: J. Guillén y Pedro
Salinas, " Bull. Hisp. Studies (Liverpool), XXXV
(1958).
881. Goodman, John F. "A. Symons and French Symbolism. The Critical Theory, " Diss. Abstr., XXX
(1969/70), 5408A (Wisc. '69).
882. Goth, Maja. "The myth of Narcissus in the works of
Rilke and of Valéry, " Wisconsin Studies in Contemp. Lit., VII, 1 (Winter/Spring 1966), 12-20.
883. Gothot-Mersch, Claudine. "Apollinaire et le symbolisme: 'Le Larron, ' " Rev. d'Hist. Litt. de la
France, LXVII, 3 (juillet-sept. 1967), 590-600.
884. Graaf, Daniël A. de. "Quelques aspects du cercle
des Zutistes, " Rev. des Langues Vivantes, XXVII,
6 (1961), 482-5. (Incl. Art Nouveau, Rimbaud,
Verlaine.)

885. Greene, E. J. H. "Jules Laforgue et T. S. Eliot, "
      Rev. de Litt. Comparée, XXII (juillet-sept. 1948),
      363-97.
886. Greenhut, Morris. "Sources of obscurity in mod. poe-
      try: the examples of Eliot, Stevens, and Tate, "
      Centennial Review of Arts and Science (Mich.
      State), VII (1963), 171-90.
887. Gregh, Fernand. Portrait de la poésie moderne de
      Rimbaud à P. Valéry. Paris: 1939.
888. Grimm, Reinhold. "Zur Wirkungsgesch. M. Maeter-
      lincks in dt. sprach. Lit. " Rev. de Litt. Com-
      parée, XXXIII (1959), 535-44.
889. Grosclaude, Pierre. "L'assonance interne dans le
      vers français, " Français Moderne, XIX, 3 (juil-
      let 1951), 175-80. (Incl. Valéry, Mallarmé,
      Verlaine.)
890. Grossman, L. Ot Pushkina do Bloka: Etiudy i Por-
      trety. Moscow: 1926.
891. Gsteiger, Manfred. "Arzt u. Dichter. Bemerkgn zu
      Benn u. Carossa, " Schweiz. Rds., LXI (1962),
      148-57.
892. _____. " 'Die Blumen des Bösen.' George als
      Übersetzer Baudelaires, " Lit. d. Übergangs. Es-
      says. Bern/Mchn: 1963, pp. 49-91.
893. Guerrero Ruiz, Juan. "A J. Guillén de J. Guerrero
      Ruiz (sobre J. R. Jiménez), " Alicante, (Julio
      1933).
894. Guiette, Robert. "P. Claudel et la langue poétique, "
      Romanica Gandensia, VIII (1960), 131-5.
895. _____. "Un cas de symbiose dans le symbolisme
      en France, " Comp. Lit. Studies, IV (1967), 103-
      7. (A. Symons).
896. Guimbretière, André. "Symbole et langage dans
      l'expérience poétique, " Cah. Intern'x de Symbo-
      lisme, VI (1964), 49-67. (Incl. Aragon, Bache-
      lard, Bonnefoy, Joë Bosquet, Breton, Emmanuel,
      & Claire Lejeune.)
897. Gullón, Ricardo. "Simbolismo en la poesía de A. Macha-
      do, " Clavileño, IV, 22 (Julio-Agosto 1953), 44-50.
898. _____, ed. Monumento de Amor: Cartas de Z.
      Camprubí y J. R. Jiménez. Univ. de Puerto
      Rico: 1959. (Ed. de la Torre.)
899. _____. Cartas de A. Machado a J. R. Jiménez.
      San Juan, Puerto Rico: 1959. (Ed. de la Torre,
      Univ. de Puerto Rico, serie B, num. I.)
900. _____. "Mágicos lagos de A. Machado: Machado
      y Juan Ramón, " Papeles de Son Armadans (Mal-

lorca), XXIV (1962), 26-61.

901. _____ . Relac. entre A. Machado y J. R. Jiménez.
Pisa: 1964.

902. Gundolf, Elisabeth. "Meine Begegnungen mit R. M.
Rilke u. St. George," Castrum Peregrini, LXIX
(1965), 34-51 (also in book form with add. essays: Amsterdam: 1965).

903. Günther, W. "Uber d. absolute Poesie: zur geistigen
Struktur neuerer Dichtg, " Dt. Vjschr., XXIII
(1949), 1-32; XXIV (1950), 146-7. (Incl. Mallarmé, Rimbaud, Valéry) (also in: Weltinnenraum,
2 Aufl. Bln: 1952, pp. 255-84; Zur Lyrik-Diskussion. Darmst.: 1966, pp. 1-45.)

904. Halbeisen, Hiltrud. Das Selbstverständnis d. Dichters:
R. M. R. u. St. George (diss.). Bonn: 1952.

905. Halévy, D. "De Mallarmé à P. Valéry," Revue Universelle, I (1920), 281-8.

906. Hamburger, Michael. The Truth of Poetry. Tensions
in Mod. Poetry from Baudelaire to the 1960's.
London: 1969. (Bonnefoy, Mallarmé, Rimbaud,
Valéry, et al.)

907. Hannum, Hunter G. "George and Benn: the autumnal
vision," PMLA, LXXVIII (1963), 271-9.

908. Hardy, John E. The Curious Frame: Seven Poems
in Text and Context. Notre Dame, Indiana: 1962.
(Incl. Baudelaire's 'Rêve parisien'; Rilke's 'Sonnette an Orpheus,' I, 20; and Yeats' 'A Prayer
for my Daughter.')

909. Harrison, John. The Reactionaries: Yeats, Lewis,
Pound, Eliot, Lawrence: A Study of the Anti-
Democratic Intelligentsia. New York: 1967.

910. Hartmann, Geoffrey H. The Unmediated Vision: An
Interpr. of Wordsworth, Hopkins, Rilke, and
Valéry. New Haven, Conn.: 1954.

911. Hartung, C. V. "Browning and Impressionism," Diss.
Abstr., XIV (1954), 358 (Stanford).

912. Hassan, Ihab H. "French symbolism and mod. British
poetry, with Yeats, Eliot and Edith Sitwell as in-
dices," Diss. Abstr., XIII (1953), 232-3.

913. _____ . "Edith Sitwell and the symbolist trad.,"
Comp. Lit., VII, 3 (Summer 1955), 240-51.
(Incl. Rimbaud, Verlaine, Mallarmé, Cocteau,
Laforgue, Corbière, Ghil, Régnier.)

914. Haüsermann, Hans W. "W. B. Yeats' idea of Shelley,"
The Mint, ed. Geoffrey Grigson. London: 1946,
pp. 179-94.

915. _____. "W. B. Yeats' criticism of Ezra Pound, "
      English Studies, XXIX, 4 (August 1948), 97-109.
916. Hays, Hoffman R. "Laforgue and W. Stevens, " Ro-
      manic Review, XXV (1934), 242-8.
917. Heller, Erich. "Als der Dichter Yeats zum ersten
      Mal Nietzsche las, " Sprach u. Politik. Festgabe
      für D. Sternberger..., ed. Carl-Joachim Fried-
      rich and Benno Reifenberg. Heidelberg: 1968,
      pp. 116-31.
918. _____. "Yeats and Nietzsche: reflex. on a poet's
      marginal notes, " Encounter, XXXIII (Dec. 1969),
      64-72.
919. Heller, P. "Eisgekühlter Expressionismus, " Merkur,
      IX (1955), 1095-1100. (Benn, Brecht, Jünger.)
920. Hellman, H. "Baudelaire and Michel de Ghelderode, "
      Rev. de Litt. Comparée, XLII (1968), 427-8.
921. Henriot, Emile. De Lamartine à Valéry. Lyon:
      1946. (Incl. Verlaine, Rimbaud, Mallarmé, La-
      forgue, Moréas, H. de Régnier.)
922. Hérain, F. Les Grands Ecrivains Critiques d'Art.
      Paris: 1943. (Incl. Valéry and Zola.)
923. Hermann, F. St. George u. H. v. H. Dichtg u.
      Briefwechsel. Zürich: 1947.
924. Heybey, Wolfgang. "Der Mensch vor d. Zukunft.
      Eine Vergl. Betrachtg. von Gedichten G. Benns
      u. B. Brechts, " Pädagogische Provinz (Frankf.
      a. M), XV (1961), 337-49.
925. Hidden, Norman. "Walter Pater: aesthetic standards
      or impressionism?" Unisa English Studies, II
      (1968), 13-18.
926. Highet, Gilbert. "The symbolist poets and James
      Joyce, " The Classical Trad.: Greek and Roman
      Infl. on West. Lit. N. Y.: 1949, pp. 501-9.
      (Incl. Mallarmé and Valéry.)
927. Hillebrand, Bruno. Artistik u. Auftrag. Zur Kunst-
      theorie von Benn u. Nietzsche. Mchn: 1966.
928. Hines, Thomas J. " 'The outlines of being and its
      expressings': Husserl, Heidegger, and the later
      poetry of W. Stevens, " Diss. Abstr. Intern'l,
      XXXI (1970), 1278A/79A (Ore.).
929. Hirsch, Rudolf. "Edmund Husserl u. H. v. Hofmanns-
      thal, " On Four Modern Humanists: Hofmannsthal,
      Gundolf, Curtius, Kantorowicz. Princeton, N.J.:
      1970, pp. 108-15.
930. Hobsbaum, Philip. "Eliot, Whitman, and Amer.
      trad. , " Journ. Amer. Stud. , III (1969), 239-64.
931. Höck, Wilhelm. " 'Vorüberlied u. Dennochlied. ' Dt.

Lyrik zw. Heissenbüttel u. Benn, " Hochland, LVI
(1963/4), 119-36.

932. Hoffman, Daniel G. Barbarous Knowledge: Myth in
the Poetry of Yeats, Graves, and Muir. London:
1970.

933. Hoffmann, Peter. "Claus Graf Stauffenberg u. St.
George: Der Weg zur Tat, " Jahrb. d. dt.
Schiller-Gesellschaft, XII (1968), 520-42.

934. Holthusen, H. E. "Das Schöne u. d. Wahre in d.
Poesie. Zur Theorie d. Dichterischen bei Eliot
u. Benn, " Das Schöne u. d. Wahre. Neue Studien
z. mod. Lit. Mchn: 1958, pp. 5-37. (Also in:
Merkur, XI (1957), 305-30.)

935. Howarth, Herbert. "Eliot and Hofmannsthal, " South
Atlantic Quarterly, LIX (1960), 500-9.

936. Hubert, Claire M. H. "The still point in the turning
world: a comparison of the myths of G. de Nerval and W. B. Yeats, " Diss. Abstr., XXVI
(1965), 1042/3 (Emory).

937. Hughs, D. J. "Coleridge and Valéry. An essay in
mod. poetics, " Diss. Abstr., XIX, 7 (Jan. 1959),
1758 (Brown).

938. Hux, Samuel. "Irony in 'The Aspern Papers': the
unreliable symbolist, " Ball State Univ. Forum,
X (1969), i, 60-5. (James).

939. Ibel, Rudolf. Mensch der Mitte: George, Carossa,
Weinheber. Hamburg: 1962.

940. Ilie, Paul. "Verlaine and Machado: the aesthetic
role of time, " Comp. Lit., XIV (1963), 261-5.

941. Ireson, J. C., ed. "Towards a theory of the symbolist theatre, " Stud. in French Lit. pres. to H.
W. Lawton.... N. Y./Manchester, England:
1968, pp. 135-56. (Incl. Kahn, Mallarmé, Mockel.)

942. Iskandar, Fayez. "Yeats and Cocteau: two anti-
romanticists, " Cairo Stud. in English, ed. Magdi
Wahba. Cairo: Univ. Cairo, 1963-6, pp. 119-35.

943. Ivanov, Georgii. "Blok i Gumilev, " Vozrozhdenie, VI
(1949), 113-26.

944. Ivanov-Razumnik, R. V. A. Blok--A. Bely. Chicago: 1968. (Photog. reissues, Russian Lang.
Specialties). (Orig. Petersburg: 1919.)

945. Jaén, D. T. "Walt Whitman: tema literario, " Torre,
LX (1968), 77-100. (Lorca).

946. Jain, Sushil K. "Indian elements in the poetry of W.
B. Yeats, with special ref. to Yeats' relat. with
Chatterji and Tagore, " Comp. Lit. Studies, VII

(1970), 82-96.
947. Jaloux, Edmond. "Deux poêtes: P. Valéry et L.-P.
      Fargue, " Rev. Hebdomadaire, X (1931), 548-61.
948. _____. Les Saisons Litt., 1896-1903. Fribourg:
      1942. (Incl. symbolism, Mallarmé, Gide.)
      (Later ed. Paris: 1947.)
949. _____. Visages Français. Paris: 1954. (Incl.
      Rimbaud, Lautréamont, symbolism.)
950. Jameson, Grace E. "Mysticism in A. E. and in
      Yeats in relat. to Oriental and Amer. thought,"
      Ohio Univ. Abstr. of Doctors' Diss., no. 9
      (1932), 144-51.
951. Jancke, O. "Totengespräch mit Th. Mann, G. Benn
      u. B. Brecht," Neue dt. Hefte, IV (1957/8),
      225-32.
952. Jans, Adrien. Entretiens Poétiques. Tome I. La
      poésie à la recherche de son âme: Ch. Baude-
      laire, R. M. Rilke, Patrice de la Tour du Pin.
      Bruxelles: 1943.
953. Jareño, Ernesto. " 'El Caballero de Olmedo,' García
      Lorca y Albert Camus," Papeles de Son Arma-
      dans (Mallorca), LVIII (1970), 219-42. (Lope de
      Vega).
954. Jaszi, Andrew O. "In the realm of beauty and an-
      guish: some remarks on the poetry of aestheti-
      cism," Chicago Review, XV, 2 (1961), 57-70.
      (Incl. George, Hofmannsthal, Rilke.)
955. Jens, W. "Der Mensch u. d. Dinge. Die Revol. d.
      dt. Prosa," Statt e. Lit. geschichte, 2 Aufl.
      Pfullingen: 1958, pp. 59-85. (Incl. Hofmanns-
      thal, Rilke, Musil, Kafka, Heym.)
956. Johansen, Sven. "D'un symbolisme ésotérique, ...
      dont parle Hermès Trismégiste en son Pimandre,"
      Orbis Litterarum, XXV (1970), 281-5. (Apolli-
      naire).
957. Jones, James L. "Keats and the last Romantics:
      Hopkins and Yeats," Diss. Abstr. Intern'l, XXX
      (1969), 2530A (Tulane).
958. Jones, P. Mansell. "Whitman and the symbolists,"
      French Stud., II (Jan. 1948), 54-67.
959. _____. "Baudelaire, Verlaine, and Verhaeren,"
      Mod. Lang. Review, XXI (1965), [cf. Mansell,
      J. P.--errata.]
960. Jones, Rhys S. "The infl. of A. Poe on P. Valéry
      prior to 1900," Comp. Lit. Stud., nos. 21/2
      (1946), 10-15.
961. _____. "Poincaré and Valéry: a note on the

'symbol' in science and art, " Mod. Lang. Review,
XLII, 4 (Oct. 1947), 485-88.

962. _____ . "The selection and usage of symbols by
Mallarmé and Valéry, " Trivium, I (1966), 44-55.

963. _____ . "Mallarmé and Valéry: imitation or con-
tinuation?" Gallica: Essays pres. to J. H.
Thomas.... Cardiff: 1969, pp. 201-17.

964. Jong, Martien J. De. " 'Dichters en der Schoonheid
zonen': A. Verwey en St. George, " Spiegel der
Letteren, IX (1966), 272-80.

965. Julien, Hershey. "Virginia Woolf: post-impressionist
novelist, " Diss. Abstr., XXIX (1969), 4490A (N.
M.)

966. Kaiser, Helmut. "Die idealogische Entwicklung G.
Benns u. Ernst Jüngers. Eine Untersuch. z.
Weltanschaulichen Dekadenz d. dt. Bourgeosie, "
Wissenschaftl. Ztschr. d. Humboldt-Univ. z.
Berlin, (Gesellschafts-u. sprachwissenschaftl.
Reihe), IX (1959/60), 510-11.

967. _____ . Mythos, Rausch u. Reaktion: Der Weg G.
Benns u. Ernst Jüngers. Berlin: 1962.

968. Kaufmann, Hans. "Zwei Lyriker: R. M. Rilke u.
St. George, " Krisen u. Wandlungen d. dt. Lit....
Berlin: 1969, pp. 122-55.

969. Kermode, Frank. "A Babylonish dialect, " Continuities.
N. Y.: 1968, pp. 67-77. (Yeats and Eliot).

970. Kies, Albert. "Baudelaire et Valéry, " Lettres Romanes, X, 1 (1 févr. 1956), 51-63. (Also in:
Etudes baudelairiennes. Paris: 1967, pp. 81-
95.)

971. _____ . "Baudelaire et les poètes français de Belgique, " Journées Baudelaire. Actes du Colloque
Namur-Bruxelles, 10-13 Oct. 1967. Bruxelles:
1968, pp. 21-31.

972. Killy, Walter. "Der Tränen nächtige Bilder. Trakl
u. Benn, " Wandlungen des lyr. Bildes. Gött:
1956, pp. 95-114. (Later ed. 1967, pp. 116-35.)

973. King, S. K. "Eliot, Yeats and Shakespeare, " Theoria
5. Pietermaritzburg: Univ. of Natal, 1953,
pp. 113-19.

974. Klemperer, V. "Morgenstern u. d. Symbolismus, "
Ztschr. f. dt. Unterricht, XLII, 1 (1928), 39-55.

975. Klossowska, Baladine. "La rencontre de deux poètes:
Rilke et Valéry (lettre de P. Valéry à Rilke,
déc. 1921), " Neue schwciz. Rundschau, N. F.,
XVI, 7 (Nov. 1948), 427-9.

976.   Kobayashi, Makoto.   "Die metaphorischen Formen bei
       R. M. Rilke u. G. Benn: Versuch e. Phänomeno-
       logie d. Bildersprache, " Doitsu Bungaku, XL
       (1968), 92-104.

977.   Kobylinskij, L.   Russkie Simvolisty: Konstantin
       Bal'mont, Valerij Brjusov, Andrej Belyi. Mos-
       cow: 1910.

978.   Kohlschmidt, Werner.   "Hofmannsthals 'Ein Traum
       von grosser Magie' u. Rilkes 'Der Magier, ' "
       Entzweite Welt. Studien z. Menschenbild in d.
       neueren Dichtg. Gladbeck: 1953, pp. 69-76.

979.   Kosutitch, Vl. R.   "Le parnasse et le symbolisme chez
       les Serbes: les infl. sur Milan Rakić, " Annales
       de la Fac. de Philol. de l'Univ. de Belgrade, II
       (1962), 295-310.

980.   Kronegger, M. E.   "(James) Joyce's debt to E. A.
       Poe and the French symbolists, " Rev. de Litt.
       Comparée, XXXIX 2 (avril-juin 1965), 243-54.
       (Incl. Mallarmé and Huysmans.)

981.   Küchler, W.   "Inspiration u. Kunstwille, " (Anmerk. z.
       Lyrik von V. Hugo, Ch. Baudelaire, St. Mal-
       larmé, P. Valéry) Anzeiger d. phil. -hist. Kl. d.
       Osterr. Akad. d. Wiss., LI (   ), 292-306.

982.   _____. "Weltgefühl u. Formtrieb--Mallarmé u.
       Valéry, " Actes du Vième Congrès Intern'l des
       Langues et Litt. Mod. Florence: 1955, pp. 497-
       504.

983.   Kugel, James L.   The Techniques of Strangeness in
       Symbolist Poetry. New Haven/London: 1971
       (incl. Nerval, Rimbaud, Mallarmé, Brjusov, Blok,
       Mandelstam, W. Stevens, Hart Crane).

984.   Kuhn, H.   "Zur mod. Dichtersprache, " Wort u. Wahr-
       heit, IX (1954), 348-59. (Th. Mann, Rilke,
       Kafka, Benn).

985.   Kuhn, Reinhard C.   "Vielé-Griffin and the symbolist
       movement, " Diss. Abstr., XVIII, 1 (Jan. 1958),
       233 (Princeton).

986.   Kumar, Jitendra.   "Consciousness and its correlates:
       Eliot and Husserl, " Philosophy and Phenomenolog-
       ical Research, XXVIII (1968), 332-52. (Cf. "La
       conscienza e i suoi correlati: Eliot e Husserl, "
       Verri, XXXI (1969), 37-59.)

987.   _____. "Poesia e percezione: Eliot e Merleau-
       Ponti, " Verri, XXXI (1969), 60-82.

988.   Laboulle, M. J. J.   "T. S. Eliot and some French
       poets, " Rev. Litt. Comparée, XVI (Avril-Juin
       1936), 389-99.

989. Labry, Raoul. "A. Blok et Nietzsche," Revue des Etudes Slaves, XXVII (1951), 201-8.
990. Lachmann, E. "Hofmannsthal u. George," Stimmen d. Zeit, CLVIII (1955/6), 182-7.
991. Lacôte, René. "T. S. Eliot, Jean de Boschère, St. Mallarmé, Charles Cros, Saint-Denys Garneau-- Poésie de poche," Les Lettres Françaises, no. 1309 (19-25 Nov. 1969), 10.
992. Lalou, René. "E. Poe et la France," L'Education Nationale, no. 4 (26 janv. 1950), 7-8.
993. Lang, Liselotte. Der Zyklus bei George u. Rilke. (Diss.) Erlangen: 1948.
994. Lang, Renée. "Ein fruchtbringendes Miss- verständnis: Rilke u. Valéry," Symposium, XIII, 1 (Spring 1959), 51-62.
995. _____. Rilke, Gide et Valéry. Boulogne-sur- Seine/Paris: 1953. (Les Editions de la Revue Prétexte.)
996. _____, ed. Rilke, Gide e Valéry nel Carteggio Inedito. Firenze: 1960.
997. Lange, V. "Forms of contemp. German poetry," Monatshefte f. d. dt. Unterr., XLVI (1954), 171- 80. (Incl. Rilke, Hofmannsthal, George, Trakl, Benn.)
998. Lapisardi, F. S. "The same enemy: notes on cer- tain similar. betw. Yeats and Strindberg," Modern Drama, XII (1969), 146-54.
999. Larrea, Juan. "C. Vallejo frente a A. Breton," Rev. de la Univ. Nac. de Córdoba, X (1969), 799-858.
1000. Laurette, Pierre. Le thème de l'arbre chez P. Valéry et R. M. Rilke. (Diss.) Univ. des Saar- landes. Saarbrücken: 1962.
1001. _____. "La notion d'influence chez Valéry et Goethe," Actes du IVe Congrès de l'Assoc. In- tern'l de Litt. Comparée, (Fribourg: 1964) Hague: 1966, II, pp. 1043-8. (Also incl.: Georges Pistorius. "Le problème d'infl. selon P. Valéry," pp. 1036-42 (Mallarmé and Gide).)
1002. Lausberg, Heinrich. "Vertonung zweier französ. Gedichte: M. Maeterlinck "Chanson'; P. Valéry 'Les Grenades,' " Serta Rómanica. Festschr. G. Rohlfs, ed. R. Baehr & K. Wais. Tüb: 1968, pp. 269-89.
1003. Lawler, James R. "T. S. Eliot et P. Valéry," Mercure de France, CCCXXXVIII, 1169 (janv. 1961), 76-101.

1004. _____. "A symbolist dialogue (Valéry-Claudel), "
Essays in French Lit., IV (Nov. 1967), 80-105.
(Cf. "Valéry et Claudel: un dialogue symboliste,"
Nouv. Rev. Française, XVI, 32 (sept. 1968),
239-61.)

1005. _____. "Magic and movement in Claudel and
Valéry, " The Language of French Symbolism.
Princeton, N.J./London: 1969, pp. 112-45.

1006. Lázaro Carreter, Fernando. "J. R., A Machado y G.
Lorca, " Insula, XII, 128-9 (Julio-Agosto 1957), 1,
5, 21. (Variant listing: Carreter, Fernando Lázaro)

1007. L. C. "Encontro de dois poetas: R. Darío e Alberto O. de Castro, " Bol. de Acad. Portug. de
Ex-Libros, XIII (1968), 52-5.

1008. Lebois, A. Les tendances du symbolisme à travers
l'oeuvre d'Elémir Bourges. Paris: 1952.

1009. _____. "T. S. Eliot, les Imagistes et Jean de
Boschère, " Rev. Litt. Comparée, XXVI (1952),
365-79.

1010. Lednicki, Waclaw A. "Mickiewicz, Dostoevsky, and
Blok, " Bull. Polish Instit. of Arts and Sciences
in America, I (1942), 74-6. (Summary of lecture
given May 14, 1942.)

1011. Legrand, Jacques. "Rilke, trad. de Valéry, " Allemagne d'Aujourd'hui, (Sept.-Oct. 1968), 50-6.

1012. Lehmann, A. G. "Two indefinables: symbolism and
impressionism, " Listener, XLV, 1161 (May 31,
1951), 869-70; 885. (Incl. Mallarmé and Rimbaud.)

1013. Lehmann, Peter L. "Uber Jean-Paul--von George
her, " Dt. Beitr. z. geist. Uberliefg., V (1965),
185-201.

1014. Lehnert, Herbert. George, Hofmannsthal u. Rilke.
Ihr Selbstverständnis als Dichter (diss.). Kiel:
1952.

1015. Lehrmann, G. De Marinetti à Maiakovski: Destins
d'un Mouvement Litt. Occidental en Russie. Fribourg: 1942.

1016. LeLouët, Jean. "Discipline et divin en poésie, "
Médicine de France, no. 173 (juin 1966).
(Incl. Valéry et Mallarmé.)

1017. Lemaître, H. La Poésie depuis Baudelaire. Paris:
1965. (Coll. 'U, ' série Lettres Françaises.)

1018. Lentricchia, Frank R., Jr. "The poetics of will:
W. Stevens, W. B. Yeats, and the theoretic in-
heritance, " Diss. Abstr., XXVII (1966), 1373A
(Duke).

1019. _____. "Four types of 19th cen. poetic," Journ. of Aesth. & Art. Crit., XXVI (1967/8), 351-66. (Incl. Zola, Mallarmé, Valéry.)

1020. _____. The Gaiety of Language: An Essay on the Radical Poetics of W. B. Yeats and Wallace Stevens. Berkeley: 1968. (Persp. in Crit., 19.)

1021. Levi, Albert W. "Three," The Hidden Harmony: Essays in Honor of Philip Wheelwright, ed. Oliver Johnson et al. N.Y.: 1966, pp. 73-91. (Incl. Stevens, Pound, T. S. Eliot.)

1022. Lewis, Hanna B. "Hofmannsthal and Browning," Comp. Lit., XIX (1967), 142-59.

1023. Liedholm, Alfred. "A. Beardsley: Symbolisms mästare under 90-talet," Grafiskt Forum, LXXII (1967), 538-40.

1024. Lienhardt, R. G. "Hopkins and Yeats," Scrutiny, XI, 3 (Spring 1943), 220-4. (Review of Menon's The Develop. of W. B. Yeats.)

1025. Little, Roger. "T. S. Eliot and Saint-John Perse," Arlington Quarterly, II, 2 (1969), 5-17.

1026. Lohner, E. "G. Benn u. T. S. Eliot," Neue dt. Hefte, III (1956/7), 100-7.

1027. Lorenzo-Rivero, Luis. "Afinidades poéticas de J. Guillén con Fray Luis de León," Cuad. Hispanoamer., CCXXX (1969), 421-36.

1028. Lövgren, Sven. The Genesis of Modernism: Seurat, Gauguin, Van Gogh, and French Symbolism in the 1880's. Stockholm: 1959.

1029. Lucas, F. L. The Drama of Chekhov, Synge, Yeats and Pirandello. London: 1963.

1030. Lücke, Theodor. "Die Morgendämmerung löst die Ungeheuer auf: Ch. Baudelaire, P. Valéry, Edouard (sic Eluard)," Aufbau, IV, 1 (Jan. 1948), 470-3.

1031. Lucques, Claire. Le Poids du Monde: Rilke et Sorge. Paris: 1962.

1032. Lükemann, Ingo. "G. Benns 'Einsamer nie...' u. St. Georges 'Es lacht in dem steigenden Jahr dir': Eine vergl. Gedichtsinterp.," Lit. in Wissenschaft u. Unterr. (Kiel), I (1968), 282-7.

1033. Lund, Mary G. "The androgynous moment: Woolf and Eliot," Renascence, XII (1960), 74-8.

1034. Luzi, Mario. "Mallarmé e la poesia moderna," La Rassegna d'Italia (Sett. 1949), 899-909.

1035. Mackey, William F. "Yeats' debt to Ronsard on a carpe diem theme," Comp. Lit. Studies, XIX (1946), 4-7. ('When You Are Old').

1036.   Maione, Italo. Trittico Neoromantico: George, Hof-
        mannsthal, Rilke. Messina: 1950. (Biblioteca
        di Cultura Contemp., 28.)
1037.   Malone, David H. "Notes on Archibald MacLeish
        and the French symbolists," South Atlantic Bull.,
        XIX, 3 (Jan. 1954), 9. (Abstract) (incl. Laforgue
        and Rimbaud.)
1038.   Mansell, J. P. "Whitman and the origins of the
        'vers libre,' " French Studies, II, 2 (April 1948),
        129-39. (Cf. Jones, P. Mansell.)
1039.   Marissel, André. "De Rimbaud aux poètes d'aujourd'-
        hui, " Revue Socialiste, n. s., no. 110 (oct. 1957),
        339-45. (Incl. Rimbaud et Alain Bosquet.)
1040.   Marks, Emerson R. "Pragmatic poetics: Dryden to
        Valéry, " Bucknell Review, X (1962), 213-23.
1041.   Martin, P. W. Experiment in Depth. A Study of
        the Work of Jung, Eliot and Toynbee. London:
        1955.
1042.   Martín-Crosa, Ricardo. "Notas de urgencia para una
        poesía de lo absoluto, " Cuad. Hispanoamer., LXI
        (1965), 103-9. (Guillén & Jiménez.)
1043.   Martz, Louis L. The Poem of the Mind: Essays on
        Poetry, English and American. N. Y.: 1966.
        (Incl. Eliot and Stevens.)
1044.   Maslenikov, Oleg. "Ruskin, Bely and the Solov'yovs,"
        Slav. & East Europ. Review, XXXV, 84 (Dec.
        1956), 15-24.
1045.   Mason, Eudo C. "Rilke u. St. George, " Gestaltung,
        Umgestaltung. Leipzig: 1957, pp. 249-78.
        (Also in: Exzentr. Bahnen. Stud. zum Dichter-
        bewusstsein d. Neuzeit. Gött: 1963, pp. 205-
        49.)
1046.   Matoré, Georges. "A propos du vocab. des couleurs,"
        Annales de l'Univ. de Paris, XXVIII, 2 (avril-
        juin 1958), 137-50. (Incl. Proust, Zola, Sartre,
        symbolism.)
1047.   Mattenklott, Gert. Bilderdienst. Asthet. Opposition
        bei Beardsley u. George. München: 1970.
1048.   Matthews, W. K. "The bkgd and poetry of Gustav
        Suits: a study in Estonian symbolism, " Amer.
        Slav. & East Europ. Review, IX, 2 (1950), 116-27.
1049.   Matthiessen, F. O. "Yeats and four Amer. poets, "
        Yale Review, XXIII, 3 (March 1934), 611-17.
        (Review of The Coll. Poems, 1933.)
1050.   McKulik, Benjamin M. "Archibald MacLeish and the
        French Symbolist trad., " Diss. Abstr., XXX
        (1969/70), 3950A. (South Carolina).

1051. McLaren, James C. "Criticism and creativity: po-
      etic themes in Mallarmé and Valéry, " L'Esprit
      Créateur, IV (1964), 222-7.
1052. Melchiori, Giorgio. "Eliot and Apollinaire, " Notes
      and Queries, XI (1964), 385-6.
1053. _____. "Yeats and Dante, " English Miscellany,
      XIX (1968), 153-79.
1054. Melone, Thomas. "Architecture du monde: Chinua
      Achebe et W. B. Yeats, " Conch (A Biafran Journ.
      of Lit. and Cult. Analysis), II, 1 (1970), 44-52.
1055. Mercanton, Jacques. "Rilke et Valéry, " Poètes de
      l'Univers. Paris: 1947, pp. 190-208.
1056. Mercier, Alain. "Charles Henry et l'esthétique sym-
      boliste, " Rev. des Sciences Humaines (Lille),
      XXXV, 138 (Avril-Juin 1970), 251-72.
1057. Mester, L. "Die Seele i. d. Bewegg: Deutg. d.
      Figuren 'Puppe', 'Tänzerin' u. 'Engel' bei H. v.
      Kleist, P. Valéry u. R. M. Rilke, " Sammlung
      (Göttingen), VIII (1953), 238-52.
1058. Metzger-Hirt, Erika. "Das Klopstock-Bild st.
      Georges u. s. Kreises, " PMLA, LXXIX (1964),
      289-96.
1059. Meylan, Pierre. Les Ecrivains et la Musique.
      Tome II: Les Modernes Français. Etudes de
      musique et de litt. comparées. Lausanne: 1951.
      (Incl. Mallarmé et Valéry.)
1060. Michell, Joyce. Symbolism in Music and Poetry
      (Diss.) Philad.: 1944. (Misnomer; deals with
      Richard Wagner.)
1061. Mikhail, E. H. "French infl. on Synge, " Rev. de
      Litt. Comparée, XLII (1968), 429-31.
1062. Miller, J. Hillis. Poets of Reality: Six Twentieth-
      Century Writers. Cambridge, Mass.: 1966
      (incl. Yeats, Eliot, Stevens).
1063. Milon, F. J. Proust, Valéry et le plaisir de la
      lecture. Paris: 1938.
1064. Milward, Peter S. J. "Sacramental symbolism in
      Hopkins and Eliot, " Renascence, XX (1968), 104-
      11.
1065. Mirabent, F. "Dos poetas y la estética, " Rev. de
      Ideas Estéticas, I (1943), 97-102. (Valéry and
      Claudel.)
1066. Mockel, Albert. Esthétique du symbolisme. Pré-
      cédés d'une étude sur A. Mockel par Michel
      Otten. Bruxelles: 1962. (Acad. royale de lan-
      gue et de litt. françaises.) (Bibliog. des écrits
      d'esthétique et de critique d'Albert Mockel,

pp. 55-64.
1067. Modern, R. E. "St. George y H. v. Hofmannsthal:
       relac. de un desencuentro, " Torre, LXII (1968),
       49-68.
1068. Monahan, Michael. "Yeats and Synge, " Nova Hibernia.
       N. Y.: 1914, pp. 13-37.
1069. Mondor, Henri. "Verlaine et Valéry, " Arts et Let-
       tres, no. 2 (avril 1946), 98-107.
1070. _____. "P. Valéry et les 'Cahiers d'André Wal-
       ter, ' " Nef, XXIII (oct. 1946), 3-32.
1071. _____. "P. Valéry et 'A Rebours, ' " Rev. de
       Paris, LIV, 3 (mars 1947), 3-18.
1072. _____. "Le premier entretien Mallarmé-Valéry, "
       Cah. du Sud, nos. 276/8 (1946), 49-64.
1073. _____. L'Heureuse rencontre de Valéry et Mal-
       larmé. Lausanne: 1948.
1074. _____. "Filiations poétiques, " Résonances, no. 5,
       4e trim. (1951),   . (Possible infl. of Leconte
       de Lisle on Rimbaud and Valéry.)
1075. _____. "P. Valéry et Rimbaud, " Rev. de Paris,
       LXIV, 2 (févr. 1957), 3-23.
1076. Monférier, Jacques. "Symbolisme et anarchie, " Rev.
       d'Hist. Litt... LXV 2 (avril-juin 1965), 233-8.
       (Incl. Saint-Pol Roux, Mallarmé, Barrès, 'La
       Revue Blanche, ' 'Les Entretiens Politiques et
       Litt. ')
1077. Monteiro, A. C. "Teoria da impersonalidada: Fer-
       nando Pessoa e T. S. Eliot, " O Tempo e o Modo,
       LXVIII (1969), 204-9.
1078. Montgomery, Marion. "Emotion recoll. in tranquill-
       ity: Wordsworth's legacy to Eliot, Joyce, and
       Hemingway, " Southern Review, VI (1970), 710-21.
1079. Moore, John Rees. "Artifices for eternity: Joyce
       and Yeats, " Eire (St. Paul), III, 4 (1968), 66-73.
1080. Morawska, Ludmila. L'adjectif qualificatif
       dans la langue des symbolistes français: Rim-
       baud, Mallarmé, Valéry. Poznan: 1964. (Univ.
       im Adama Mickiewicza w Posnaniu.)
1081. Morice, Louis. "Le drame de la poésie mod., "
       Rev. Univ. Laval, VII, 7 (mars 1953), 582-97.
       (Rimbaud).
1082. Morier, Henri. Le rythme du vers libre symboliste
       étudié chez Verhaeren, H. de Régnier, Vielé-
       Griffin, et ses relations avec le sens. Genève:
       1943. (In 3 vols.)
1083. Morris, C. B. " 'Vision' and 'mirada' in the poetry
       of Salinas, Guillén, and Dámaso Alonso, " Bull.

Hisp. Stud., XXXVIII (1961), 103-12.

1084. Morrissette, Bruce A. "T. S. Eliot and G. Apollinaire," Comp. Lit., V (Summer 1953), 262-8.

1085. Morse, Samuel F. "W. Stevens, Bergson, Pater,"
The Act of the Mind: Essays on the Poetry of
W. Stevens..., ed. Roy H. Pearce and J. Hillis
Miller. Baltimore: 1965, pp. 48-92.

1086. Mossop, D. J. "Poe's theory of pure poetry,"
Durham Univ. Journ., XLVIII, 2 (new series,
vol. XVII, 2) (March 1956), 60-7. (Incl. Mallarmé and Valéry.)

1087. _____. The origins of the idea of 'pure poetry'
(inaug. lect.). Durham: 1964. (Incl. Mallarmé
and Valéry.)

1088. Mouton, Jean. "Edouard Manet entre Baudelaire et
Valéry," Le Français dans le Monde, no. 35
(sept. 1965), 22-6.

1089. Mulertt, W. "Verlaines Bezieh. zu Dtschld," Archiv
für d. Stud. d. neueren Sprachen, CLXXXV
(1948), 62-74.

1090. Musgrove, Sydney. T. S. Eliot and Walt Whitman.
Wellington, New Zealand: 1952.

1091. deNardis, L. "Simbolismo minore: Maeterlinck,"
Annali della Fac. di Filos. e Lett. dell'Univ.
Statale di Milano, XVI (1963), 103-10.

1092. Nash, John R. "Jarry, Reverdy, and Artaud: the
abrupt path," Diss. Abstr., XXVIII, 7 (Jan. 1968),
2691A.

1093. Nattier-Natanson, E. "Les amitiés de Valéry. Sa
jeunesse: J. K. Huysmans, Pierre Louys et
Mallarmé," Rev. Nationale, XXXII, 323 (sept.
1960), 239-41.

1094. Nicolas, Henry. Mallarmé et le Symbolisme. Au-
teurs et Oeuvres. Paris: 1963 (éd. Classiques
Larousse.)

1095. Nicoletti, Gianni. "Max Nordau e i primi critici del
'Simbolismo' in Italia," Studi Francesi, no. 9
(Sett.-Dic. 1959), 433-8.

1096. Niebuhr, Walter. Das Problem d. Einsamkeit im
Werke von H. v. Hofmannsthal u. St. George
(diss.). Kiel: 1949.

1097. Nitsche, Roland. "Zur Typologie der Einsamkeit:
Nietzsche, Rilke, Benn, Schönweise," Forum
(Wien), VII (1961), 328-31.

1098. Nivat, Georges. "A. Blok et A. Belyj: Etude de
la Corresp. des Deux Poètes," Rev. des Etudes
Slaves, XLV (1966), 145-64.

1099. Noltenius, Rainer. Hofmannsthal, Schröder, Schnitz-
      ler: Möglichkeiten u. Grenzen des mod. Aphoris-
      mus. Stuttgart: 1969. (GA, 30.)
1100. Nott, Kathleen. "The writer and semantics: lit. as
      lang., concept, and meaning, " Intern'l P. E. N.,
      XIV, 2 (1963), 42-8. (Incl. Bonnefoy and Valéry.)
1101. Noulet, Emilie. Etudes Littéraires. Mexique: 1944.
      (Incl. "L'hermétisme dans la poésie française";
      "L'infl. d'E. Poe sur la poésie française"; "Ex-
      égèse de trois sonnets de St. Mallarmé.")
1102. _____. Suites: Mallarméennes, rimbaldiennes,
      valéryennes. Paris 1964.
1103. O'Connor, Frank. "Two friends: Yeats and A. E., "
      Yale Review, n. s., XXIX, 1 (Sept. 1939), 60-88.
1104. Oechler, W. F. "The reception of E. Verhaeren in
      Germany, " Mod. Lang. Notes, LXII (1947), 226-
      34. (Some unpubl. letters of St. Zweig.)
1105. O'Faoláin, Sean. "A. E. and W. B., " Virginia
      Quart. Rev., XV, 1 (Winter 1939), 41-57.
1106. Oliver, Antonio. "La amistad entre J. R. Jiménez
      y A. Machado, " Rev. de Archivos, Bibliotecas y
      Museos, LXIX (1961), 871-8.
1107. Oliveros-Delgado, Rafael. "Darío y Nervo: su culto
      por Francia, " Abside, XXXIV (1970), 35-44.
1108. Onís, Carlos M. de. "El Surrealismo y cuatro poe-
      tas de la generación de 1927, " Diss. Abstr. In-
      tern'l, XXXI (1970), 1793A (N. M.). (Incl. Lorca,
      Alberti, Cernuda, and Aleixandre.)
1109. Oswald, Jean. "Baudelaire, en passant par Valéry, "
      Les Pharaons, no. 2 (Hiver 1970), 60-3.
1110. Owen, Claude R. "Darío and Heine, " Susquehanna
      Univ. Stud. (Selingsgrove, Pa.), VIII (1970), 329-
      49.
1111. Palleske, S. O. Maeterlinck en Allemagne. Paris:
      1938.
1112. Parkin, Andrew. " 'Scraps of an ancient voice in
      me not mine....': Similar. in the plays of Yeats
      and Beckett, " Ariel (A Review of Intern'l English
      Lit.), I, 3 (1970), 49-58.
1113. Parks, Lloyd C. "The infl. of Villiers de l'Isle-
      Adam on W. B. Yeats, " Diss. Abstr., XX (1960),
      2784/5 (Wash.).
1114. Patri, Aimé. "Livres sur la poésie, " L'Arche, III,
      27 (Mai 1947), 177-82. (Rimbaud, Mallarmé,
      Symbolism.)
1115. Pattinson, John P. "A study of British poetic criti-
      cism betw. 1930 and 1965 as exemplified in the

critics of Yeats, Pound, and Eliot, " Diss. Abstr.
Intern'l, XXX (1970), 4460A/61A (N. Y. U.).

1116. Pavel, Germaine. "Deux poètes du sommeil: Proust
et Valéry, " Bull. de la Soc. des Amis de M.
Proust et des Amis de Combray, no. 10 (1960),
211-23 (part 1); no. 11 (1961), 399-410 (part 2).

1117. Paxton, N. "St. Mallarmé u. St. George, " Mod.
Languages (London), XLV, 3 (Sept. 1964), 102-4.

1118. Peralta, Jaime. "España en tres poetas hispanoamericanos: Neruda, Guillén y Vallejo, " Atenea,
XLV, 170 (1968), 37-49.

1119. Perl, W. H. "L. v. Andrian, ein vergessener Dichter d. Symbolismus, Freund Georges u. Hofmannsthals, " Philobiblon, II (1958), 303-9.

1120. Perrin, Henri. "Entre Parnasse et Symbolisme:
Ephraim Mikhaël (autour d'une corresp.), " Rev.
d'Hist. Litt. de la France, LVI, 1 (janv.-mars
1956), 96-107.

1121. Peyre, Henri. "Laforgue among the Symbolists, "
Laforgue: Essays on a Poet's Life and Work,
ed. Warren Ramsay. Carbondale & Edwardsville,
Ill.: 1969, pp. 39-51. (Cross-currents. Mod.
Critiques.)

1122. Pia, Pascal, ed. Album Zutique. Paris: 1962.

1123. Plätz, H. "Rilke u. Baudelaire, " Das Wort in der
Zeit (Regensburg), V (1937/8), 435-8.

1124. Poggenburg, Raymond P. "Baudelaire and Stevens:
l'esthétique du mal, " South Atlantic Bull., XXIII
(1968), iv, 14-18.

1125. Poggioli, Renato. "Italian Lit. Chronicles. I: Poetry, 1944-1947, " Italica, XXV, 1 (March 1948),
52-6. (Incl. Ungaretti, Montale, Quasimodo,
Luzi.)

1126. Poizat, Alfred. Le Symbolisme de Baudelaire à
Claudel. Paris: 1919.

1127. Polansćak, Antun. "Effort et style, " Studia Romani-
ca et Anglica Zagrabiensia, nos. 15/16 (1963),
115-23. (Proust, Valéry.)

1128. Pommier, Jean. La Mystique de Baudelaire. Paris:
1932.

1129. _____. "Etude de quelques textes poétiques de
Nerval à Valéry, " Annuaire du Collège de France,
(1961).

1130. Ponge, Francis. "Le monde muet est notre seul
patrie, " Arts, no. 365 (26 juin-2 juillet 1952),
1 & 8.

1131. Porché, Fr. Poètes Français Depuis Verlaine.

Paris: 1924.
1132. Porter, Katherine Anne. "From the notebooks of K.
A. Porter--Yeats, Joyce, Eliot, Pound," Southern
Review, I (1965), 570-3.
1133. Postic, Marcel. Maeterlinck et le Symbolisme.
Paris: 1970.
1134. Pradal-Rodríguez, G. "La técnica poética y el caso
Góngora-Mallarmé," Comp. Lit., II, 3 (Summer
1950), 269-80.
1135. Praz, Mario. "T. S. Eliot and Dante," Southern
Review, II, 3 (Winter 1937), 525-48. (On 'Ash
Wednesday'). (Repr. in The Scottish Review, I,
2 (Summer 1948), 30-51; also in: Leonard Unger,
ed. T. S. Eliot: A Sel. Critique. N. Y. /To-
ronto: 1966, pp. 296ff.)
1136. Previtali Morrow, Giovanni. " 'Don Segundo Sombra'
y los simbolistas franceses," Cuad. Hispanoamer.,
LXXIX (1969), 222-31. (Corbière, Laforgue,
Mallarmé). (Repr. in La Estafeta Literaria,
núm. 419 (1 Mayo 1969), 4-6.)
1137. Proudfit, Sharon L. "The fact and the vision: Virginia Woolf and Roger Fry's post-impressionist
aesthetic," Diss. Abstr., XXVIII (1968), 5066A
(Mich.).
1138. Quennell, Peter. Baudelaire and the Symbolists:
Five Essays. London: 1954 (1929). (Incl. Villiers, Laforgue, Corbière, Rimbaud, Mallarmé.)
[Later edn. Port Wash., N. Y.: 1970.]
1139. Raaphorst, Madeleine. "P. Valéry et Voltaire,"
South-Central Bull., XXVI, 1 (March 1966), 16.
(Abstract.) (Cf. "P. Valéry and Voltaire," French
Review, XL, 4 (Feb. 1967), 487-94.)
1140. Ragusa, Olga. Mallarmé in Italy. N. Y.: 1957.
1141. _____. "Vittorio Pica, first champion of French
symbolism in Italy," Italica, XXXV, 4 (Dec.
1958), 255-61.
1142. Raimondi, Giuseppe. "Rimbaud & Compagnia," Il
Mondo, II, 51 (23 Dic. 1950), 9.
1143. Raitt, A. W. Villiers de l'Isle-Adam et le Mouvement Symboliste. Paris: 1965. (Incl. Poe,
Baudelaire, Wagner, Mallarmé, Verlaine, Gourmont, Dujardin.)
1144. Ramsey, Warren. Jules Laforgue and the Ironic In-
heritance. N. Y.: 1953, pp. 192-4, 197-204.
(Discusses Eliot's French sources.)
1145. Ray, Mohit K. "T. S. Eliot and Irving Babbitt: a
question of crit. infl.," Univ. Rajasthan Stud. in

English, No. 4, ed. R. K. Kaul et al. Jaipur: 1969, pp. 97-102.

1146. Raymond, Marcel. De Baudelaire au Surréalisme. Paris: 1952. (Cf.: From Baudelaire to Surrealism. N. Y.: 1949)--(Documents of Mod. Art Series, 10.) (London ed. 1957 incl. "A Reader's Guide" (bibliog.), comp. by B. Karpel, pp. 368-412.)

1147. Read, Herbert. "The poet and his Muse (E. A. Poe and P. Valéry)," British Journ. of Aesthetics, IV, 2 (April 1964), 99-108.

1148. Rebay, Luciano. "Three early poems of G. Ungaretti: a study of Apollinaire's infl.," Contemp. Lit., IX (1968), 451-72.

1149. Reboul, Olivier. "La création en art: artiste et artisan; Alain, Bergson et Valéry," L'Homme et Ses Passions d'Après Alain. Tome 2: La Sagesse. Paris: 1968, pp. 69-74.

1150. Rees, Garnet. "A French infl. on T. S. Eliot: Rémy de Gourmont," Rev. de Litt. Comparée, XVI, 4 (Oct. -Déc. 1936), 764-7.

1151. Rees, T. R. "T. S. Eliot, Rémy de Gourmont, and dissociation of sensibility," Stud. in Comp. Lit., ed. Waldo F. McNeir. Baton Rouge: 1962, pp. 186-98. (La. State Univ. Stud., Humanities Series, no. 11.)

1152. _____. "T. S. Eliot's early poetry as an extension of the symbolist technique of Jules Laforgue," Forum (Houston), VIII, 1 (1970), 46-52.

1153. Reeve, F. D. "Dobroljubov and Brujusov: Symbolist extremists," Slav. & East Europ. Journ., VIII (1964), 292-301.

1154. Régnier, Henri de. "Par Valéry vers Mallarmé: proses datées," Mercure de France, (1925), 31-41. (Cf. Rev. de France, IV (1923), 642-9.)

1155. Reiss, Hans. "Trad. in mod. poetry: T. S. Eliot and R. M. Rilke, a comparison," Proceed. IVth Congress Intern'l Comp. Lit. Assoc., ed. François Jost. (Fribourg: 1964) Hague: 1966, II, pp. 1122-7.

1156. Remenyi, Joseph. "Endre Ady, Hungary's apocalyptic poet (1877-1919)," Slav. & East Europ. Review, XXII, 58 (1944), 84.

1157. Rest, Jaime. "La crisis contemp. y el espíritu en el testimonio de dos poetas: T. S. Eliot y P. Valéry," Imago Mundi, III, 11-12 (Marzo-Junio 1956), 134-82.

1158. Reuter, Eva. Die Schwermut als e. Grundstimmung d. mod. Dichtg i. d. Werken von Rilke, Trakl u. H. v. Hofmannsthal (diss.). Innsbruck: 1949.

1159. Rewald, John. "Symbolists and anarchists from Mallarmé to Redon, 1886-1890, " Post-Impressionism: from Van Gogh to Gauguin. N. Y.: 1962, pp. 147-84. (2nd ed.)

1160. Reynaud, L. La Crise de Notre Litt. Des Romantiques à Proust et P. Valéry. Paris: 1930.

1161. Rice, P. B. "A modern poet's technique: G. Apollinaire, " Symposium, II (Oct. 1931), 468-83. (Incl. T. S. Eliot.)

1162. Richard, J. -P. Poésie et Profondeur. Paris: 1956. (Incl. Verlaine et Valéry.)

1163. Richthofen, Erich von. "Vigny als philosophischdichterischer Wegbereiter des Symbolismus, " Romanische Forsch., LXIII, 1/2 (1951), 124-8. (Incl. Rimbaud, Mallarmé, Valéry.)

1164. Rickman, H. P. "Das Vergängliche u. die Dichtg. Eine vergl. Studie von Gedankengängen in Rilke u. Eliot, " Sammlung, XII (1957), 178-96. (Cf. "Poetry and the ephemeral. Rilke's and Eliot's conceptions of the poet's task, " German Life & Letters, XII (1958/9), 174-85.)

1165. Riddel, Joseph N. "Walt Whitman and Wallace Stevens: functions of a Literatus, " W. Stevens: A Coll. of Crit. Essays, ed. Marie Borroff. Englewood Cliffs, N. J.: 1963, pp. 30-42.

1166. Ritscher, Hans. "Lyrik d. Gegenwart auf d. Oberstufe. Benn, Eich., " Dtschunterr., XII, 3 (1960), 13-33.

1167. Robichez, Jacques. "Le symbolisme au théâtre: Lugné-Poë et les débuts de l'Oeuvre, " L'Inform. Litt., VII, 4 (sept. -oct. 1955), 143-9. (Cf. Le Symbolisme au Théâtre. Paris: 1957. Covers years 1890-'99; studies use of symbolism by Ibsen and Maeterlinck.)

1168. Robinet de Cléry, A. "Rilke et P. Valéry, " Annales du Centre Universitaire Méditerr. de Nice, III (1948/50), 160f. (Résumé).

1169. Rolland de Renéville, André. "Les inédits de Mallarmé et de Valéry, " Nef, IV, 27 (févr. 1947), 120-4.

1170. _____. "De Baudelaire à la poésie contemporaine," Rev. du Caire, XIV, 145 (déc. 1951), 54-7.

1171. Romane, Jacques. "De Nerval et Rimbaud à Claudel," Rev. Nouv., XI, 11 (15 nov. 1955), 443-9.

1172.   Rose, Alan.   "The impersonal premise in Wordsworth,
        Keats, Yeats, and Eliot, " Diss. Abstr. Intern'l,
        XXX (1969), 2547A/48A (Brandeis).
1173.   Rose, Marilyn G.   "The kindred vistas of W. B. and
        Jack B. Yeats, " Eire (St. Paul), V, 1 (1970), 67-
        79.
1174.   Rose, William.   "A letter from W. B. Yeats on
        Rilke, " German Life & Letters, XV (1961), 68-70.
1175.   Rousselot, Jean.   "La civilisation de l'écrit est-elle
        morte?   Flaubert, Wilde, Valéry, Durrell à la
        recherche d'un nouveau style, " Mort ou Survie du
        Langage.   Paris: 1969, pp. 261-3.
1176.   Sagnes, Guy.   "L'Ennui dans la litt. française de
        Flaubert à Laforgue (1848-1884), " L'Inform. Litt.,
        XXII (1970), 103-8.
1177.   Sakell, Venice P.   "Baudelaire in Germany.   The
        crit. recep., 1900-'57, " Diss. Abstr., XXVI
        (1965), 3351.   (N. Carol.)
1178.   Salgado, Maria A.   " 'Teatro de ensueño': colab.
        modernista de J. R. Jiménez y G. Martinez
        Sierra, " Hispanófila (Madrid), XXXVIII (1970),
        49-58.
1179.   Sarrazin, Bernard.   "A propos de quelques pages de
        Bachelard--pierres et pierreries: l'expérience
        symbolique de J.-K. Huysmans, " Rev. des
        Sciences Humaines, CXXXIII (1969), 93-115.
1180.   Sarykin, D. M.   "Blok i Strindberg, " Vestnik Lenin-
        gradskogo Univ., serija Istorii, Jazyka i Lit.,
        XVIII, 1 (1963), 82-91.
1181.   Savage, Catherine H.   "Gide's criticism of symbo-
        lism, " Mod. Lang. Review, LXI (1966), 601-9.
1182.   Scarfe, Francis.   "Eliot and Nineteenth-Cen. French
        Poetry, " Eliot in Perspective: A Symposium, ed.
        Graham Martin.   London/N.Y.: 1970, pp. 45-
        61.
1183.   Schleiner, Louise.   "The angel and the necessary
        angel: formalist readings of Rilke and Stevens, "
        Lit. in Wissenschaft u. Unterricht (Kiel), II
        (1969), 215-37.
1184.   Schmidt, Albert-Marie.   "L'Itinéraire symboliste de
        Claudel, " La Table Ronde, no. 88 (avril 1955),
        24-6.
1185.   Schmitz, Victor A.   "Das Ethische d. Kunst bei
        George u. Rilke, " Dt. Beitrr. z. geist. Uber-
        liefg, VI (1970), 98-119.
1186.   Schneidau, Herbert N.   "Pound and Yeats: the ques-
        tion of symbolism, " Journ. of Engl. Lit. Hist.,

XXXII (1965), 220-37.

1187. Schorske, Carl E. "Schnitzler u. Hofmannsthal: Politik u. Psyche im Wien des 'fin de siècle, " Wort u. Wahrheit, XVII (1962), 367-81.

1188. Schuhmann, Klaus. "Lyrikprobleme d. Jh. mitte in theoret. Sicht: (Die Theorie d. Gedichts im Alterswerk Johannes R. Bechers u. G. Benns), " Weimarer Beiträge, V (1966), 81-99.

1189. Schulman, Ivan A., and Manuel P. González. Martí, Darío y el Modernismo. Con un pról. de Cintio Vitier. Madrid: 1969.

1190. Schultz, Hartwig. Vom Rhythmus der mod. Lyrik. Parallele Versstruk. bei Holz, George, Rilke, Brecht u. d. Expressionisten München: 1970. (Lit. als Kunst) (Bibliog., pp. 158-60).

1191. Schwarz, Egon. Hofmannsthal u. Calderón. 's-Gravenhage: 1962. (Also: Cambridge, Mass.: 1963.)

1192. Scott, N. A. Rehearsals of Discomposure. Alienation and Reconciliation in Mod. Lit.: Franz Kafka, Ignacio Silone, D. H. Lawrence, T. S. Eliot. London: 1952.

1193. Seidler, Herbert. "Die künstlerischen Voraussetzungen f. d. österr. Lyrik d. 20. Jh., " Osterr. in Geschichte u. Lit. (Wien), XIII (1969), 81-94. (Incl. Rilke and Hofmannsthal.)

1194. Semaan, Khalil I. H. "T. S. Eliot's infl. on Arabic poetry and theater, " Comp. Lit. Stud., VI (1969), 472-89.

1195. Serra-Lima, Federico. "R. Darío y Gérard de Nerval, " Rev. Hisp. Moderna, XXXII (1966), 25-32.

1196. Sewell, Elizabeth. "Wordsworth and Rilke, " The Orphic Voice: Poetry and Nat. Hist. New Haven: 1960, pp. 276-405. (Also: London.)

1197. Shalvey, Thomas J. S. J. "Valéry and Frost: two views of subjective reality, " Renascence, XI, 4 (Summer 1959), 185-8.

1198. Shaw, Priscilla W. "P. Valéry: the world in the mind, " Rilke, Valéry and Yeats: the Domain of the Self. New Brunswick, N.J.: 1964, pp. 107-174.

1199. Sheehan, Donald G. "The poetics of infl.: a study of T. S. Eliot's uses of Dante, " Diss. Abstr. Intern'l, XXX (1969), 2043A/44A (Wisc.).

1200. Sheets, Jane M. "Landscape in the poetry of R. M. Rilke and A. Machado, " Diss. Abstr., XXVI

(1966), 6725 (Indiana).

1201. Sheppard, R. W. "Rilke's 'Duineser Elegien': a crit. apprec. in the light of Eliot's 'Four Quartets,' " German Life & Letters, XX (1967), 205-17.

1202. Shmiefsky, Marvel. "Yeats and Browning: the shock of recognition, " Stud. in English Lit., 1500-1900, X (1970), 701-21.

1203. Simons, Hi. "W. Stevens and Mallarmé, " Mod. Philol., XLIII, 4 (May 1946), 235-59.

1204. Singer, Kurt. "Der Streit der Dichter: Gedanken zum Briefwechsel zw. George u. Hofmannsthal, " Castrum Peregrini, LX (1963), 5-28.

1205. Slonim, Marc. "Blok and the symbolists, " From Chekhov to the Revol.: Russian Lit., 1900-'17. N. Y.: 1962, pp. 184-210. (Also incl. "After the symbolists, " pp. 211-33.)

1206. Smith, A. J. M. "The poetic process: of the making of poems, " Centennial Review of Arts and Sciences, VIII, 4 (Fall 1964), 353-70. (Incl. Rimbaud and Valéry.)

1207. Smith, Rowland. "(Roy) Campbell and his French sources, " Comp. Lit., XXII (1970), 1-18. (Baudelaire, Rimbaud, Valéry).

1208. Sonoda, Muneto. "Der Weg von Nietzsche zu Benn. Zum Verständnis d. Begriffs 'Ausdruck,' " Forschgsberr. z. Germanistik, VIII (1966), 16-29. (In Japanese, with short summary in German.)

1209. Sorrento, Luigi. Dal Parnaso al Simbolismo, con Particolare Studio sulla Poesia di Sully Prudhomme e di Francis Jammes. Con brevi note di critica e di bibliografia. Milano: 1952.

1210. Souday, P. Proust, Gide, P. Valéry. Paris: 1927. (3 vols.)

1211. Soulairol, Jean. "Mallarmé, Valéry et Hegel, " Horizons (Nantes), no. 2 (1945), 69-71.

1212. Spender, Stephen. "Rilke and the angels; Eliot and the Shrines, " Sewanee Review, LXI (1953), 557-81.

1213. Spilka, Mark. "Was D. H. Lawrence a symbolist?" Accent, XV (1955), 49-60.

1214. Spire, André. "Baudelaire, esthéticien et précurseur du symbolisme, " Europe, 456/7 (avril-mai 1967), 79-99.

1215. Stahl, E. L. "The genesis of symbolist theories in Germany, " Mod. Lang. Rev., XLI (1946), 306-19. (Incl. Herder & Goethe.)

1216. Staiger, Emil. "Himmel u. Strom. Zu Gedichter
Goethes, Platens u. Benns," Jahrb. d. freien dt.
Hochstifts. Tübingen: 1968, pp. 237-56.
1217. Stallworthy, Jon. "W. B. Yeats and Wilfred Owen,"
Critical Quarterly, XI (1969), 199-214.
1218. Staub, Hans. Laterna Magica: Studien z. Problem
d. Innerlichkeit in d. Lit. Zurich: 1960. (Incl.
Jean-Paul, Nerval, Proust, Rilke) (Diss. -
Zürich: 1959).
1219. Stead, C. K. The New Poetic: Yeats to Eliot. N. Y.:
1966.
1220. Steiner, H. "A note on 'symbolism,' " Yale French
Studies, IX (1952), 36-9. (Infl. upon George and
Hofmannsthal.)
1221. _____ . Begegnungen mit Dichtern. Tüb: 1963.
(Incl. George, Hofmannsthal, Valéry, Saint-Jean
Perse, Rilke, Borchardt.)
1222. Stephenson, William C. "The meditative poetry of
Wordsworth and W. Stevens," Diss. Abstr. Intern'l, XXX (1968), 2552A. (Minn.).
1223. Stergiopoulos, Kostas. Apo Ton Symbolismo Sti Nea
Poiisi. Athina: 1967. (Incl. Vaphopoulos,
Geralis, Dimakis, Varvitsiltis, Themelis.)
1224. Stevenson, W. H. "Yeats and Blake: the use of
symbols," W. B. Yeats, 1865-1965: Centenary
Essays on the Art of W. B. Yeats. ed. D. E.
S. Maxwell and S. B. Bushrui. Ibadan: 1965,
pp. 219-25.
1225. Stewart, Nancy. "Symbolism in the theatre from
1890 to 1900," South Atlantic Bull., IV, 3 (Dec.
1938), 5 (abstract). (Incl. Paul Fort and Lugné-
Poë.)
1226. Stonier, G. W. "Books in gen'l," New Statesman
and Nation, XXIV, 601 (Aug. 29, 1942), 143.
(On infl. of Poe upon Rimbaud, Verlaine, Mallarmé, Maeterlinck, Valéry.)
1227. Stormon, E. J., S. J. "Some notes on T. S. Eliot
and Jules Laforgue," Essays in French Lit., (Univ.
of West. Australia), no. 2 (1965), 103-14.
1228. Strachan, W. J. Apollinaire to Aragon: thirty mod.
French poets. London: 1948.
1229. Strakhovsky, Leonid I. Craftsmen of the Word:
Three Poets of Modern Russia: Gumilyov, Akhmatova, Mandelstam. Cambridge, Mass.: 1949.
1230. Strauss, Walter A. "The reconcil. of opposites in
orphic poetry: Rilke and Mallarmé," Centennial
Review, X (1966), 214-36.

1231. Strelka, Joseph. Rilke, Benn, Schönweise u. d. Ent-
       wicklung d. mod. Lyrik. Wien: 1960. (Incl.
       "R. M. R., der Symboliker des Seinsganzen, "
       pp. 5-52; "G. Benn, der Hyperboliker des Per-
       spektivismus, " pp. 53-93.)
1232. Struve, Gleb. "Blok and Gumilyov, " Slav. & East
       Europ. Review, XXV, 64 (1946), 176-83.
1233. Stults, Taylor. "George Kennan: Russian specialist
       of the 1890's, " Russian Review, XXIX, 3 (1970),
       275-85.
1234. Stump, Jeanne A. "Varieties of symbolism, " Les
       Mardis. St. Mallarmé and the Artists of his
       Circle (exhib. cat.) Lawrence, Kansas: 1966,
       pp. 33-48. (Incl. Huysmans and Péladan.)
1235. Suckling, Norman. "Towards a better poetic. The
       contrib. of the post-symbolists, " French Studies,
       III, 3 (July 1949), 233-44.
1236. Sugar, L. de. Baudelaire et R. M. Rilke. Paris:
       1954. (Subtitle: Etude d'Infl. et d'Affinités
       Spirituelles.)
1237. Swanson, Roy A. "Valéry, Camus and Pindar, "
       Mosaic, I, 4 (July 1968), 5-17.
1238. Swigger, Ronald T. "The life of the world: a com-
       parison of Stevens and Rilke, " Diss. Abstr.,
       XXVIII (1968), 3687A (Indiana).
1239. Symons, Arthur. Figures of Several Centuries. Lon-
       don: 1916. (Incl. Poe, Rosetti, Swinburne, Baude-
       laire, Mallarmé, Verlaine, Rimbaud, et al.)
1240. Taumann, Léon. Valéry ou le Mal de l'Art. Paris:
       1969. (Cf. "Le langage de l'art, " AUMLA, no.
       10 (May 1959), 142-51. --Incl. Proust and Valéry.)
1241. Taupin, René. L'Infl. du Symbolisme Français sur
       la Poésie Américaine de 1910 à 1920. Paris:
       1929, pp. 225-32. (On T. S. Eliot's French
       infl.)
1242. _____ . "The example of Rémy de Gourmont, "
       Criterion, X, 41 (July 1931), 614-25 (Eliot).
1243. _____ . "French symbolism and the English lan-
       guage, " Comp. Lit., V, 4 (Fall 1953), 310-22.
       (Incl. Mallarmé, Schwob, Verlaine, Rimbaud.)
1244. Theall, Donald F. Communic. theories in mod.
       poetry: Yeats, Pound, Eliot, Joyce. (Diss.)
       Univ. Toronto: 1955.
1245. Theile, Wolfgang. "Die Beziehung. René Ghils zu
       V. Brjusov u. d. Ztschr. 'Vesy': ein Beitr. z.
       Verständn. d. französ. Symbolismus in Russland, "
       Arcadia, I (1966), 174-84.

1246. Thiele, Herbert. "Drei Gedichte über den Dichter: Hinweise für e. Unterrichtseinheit in der Oberprima," Der Dtschunterricht, XIV, 3 (1962), 38-46. (Hofmannsthal, George, Rilke).

1247. Tindall, William Y. "James Joyce and the hermetic trad.," Journ. Hist. of Ideas, XV, 1 (Jan. 1954), 23-39.

1248. Toesca, E. B. "L'Indicateur Italien di Mr. Valéry," Nuova Antologia, num. 481 (1961), 219-32. (Antoine-Claude Pasquin, 1789-1847.)

1249. Torre, Guillermo de. El Fiel de la Balanza. Madrid: 1961. (Incl. Lorca, Guillén, Jiménez.)

1250. Torrens, J. S. "T. S. Eliot and the contrib. of Dante towards a poetics of sensibility," Diss. Abstr., XXIX (1968), 916A/917A (Mich.).

1251. Tosi, Guy. "La tentation symboliste chez d'Annunzio, (1890-3)," Autour du Symbolisme, ed. P. G. Castex. Lille/Paris: 1955, pp. 285-96.

1252. _____. Gabriele D'Annunzio et Paul Valéry. Firenze: 1960. (Biblioteca degli eruditi e dei bibliofili, 47.)

1253. Truc, Gonzague. "Valéry, Mallarmé et le style artiste," L'Ecole, (31 mai 1958).

1254. Tsukimura, Reiko. "The lang. of symbolism in Yeats and Hagiwara," Diss. Abstr., XXVIII (1968), 3689A (Indiana).

1255. Tucker, Cynthia G. "Studies in Sonnet Lit.," Diss. Abstr., XXVIII (1968), 2659A/60A (Iowa) (incl. Rilke & Baudelaire).

1256. Turnell, G. M. "Baudelaire, the symbolists, and Mr. T. S. Eliot," Cambridge Review, LI (1930).

1257. Turnell, Martin. "A school of poetry," Sewanee Review, LXII, 4 (Oct.-Dec. 1954), 672-83. (Incl. Mallarmé, Rimbaud, Laforgue.)

1258. Turquet-Milnes, G. The Infl. of Baudelaire on France and England. London: 1913.

1259. Unger, Leonard. "Laforgue, Conrad, and Eliot," T. S. Eliot: Moments and Patterns, 3rd edn. Minneapolis, Minn.: 1966, pp. 103-56.

1260. _____, ed. Seven Mod. Am. Poets: An Introd. Minneapolis: 1967. (Incl. Stevens and Eliot.)

1261. Valéry, Paul. Situation de Baudelaire. Paris: 1924. (Cf. "Uber Ch. Baudelaire," trans. A. Brücher, Die neue Rundschau, XLI (1930), 245-60.) ("Baudelaire," Rev. de France, V (1924), 217-35.)

1262.   . Fragments sur Mallarmé. Paris: 1924.
(Cf. Ecrits Divers sur St. Mallarmé. Paris:
1951.) (Lettre sur Mallarmé adressée à J.
Boyère. Paris: 1928.) (Cf. same in Rev. de
Paris, II (1927), 481-91.)

1263.   . Discours à l'Inaug. du Monument E. Ver-
haeren. Paris: 1929. (Cf. "Hommage à E.
Verhaeren," Chroniques des Lettres Françaises,
VI (1928), 1, 16.)

1264.   . "St. Mallarmé," Conférencia, I (1933),
441-53. (Concl: Nouv. Rev. Française, II (1933),
845-53.)

1265.   . "Mallarmé," Neue Rundschau,
(1936), 382-97.

1266.   . "Svedenborg," Nouv. Rev. Frçse, I (1936),
825-44.

1267.   . Cuatro Maestros Franceses: Stendhal,
Baudelaire, Verlaine, Mallarmé. Bogotá:
(1944). (Trans. from vol. 2 of Variété.)

1268.   . Vues. Paris: 1949. (Incl. Mallarmé.)
1269.   . "Sometimes I said to St. Mallarmé,"
Kenyon Review, XXVII, 1 (Winter 1965), 94-112.
(Trans. M. Cowley.)

1270. Vallin, G. "Erreur et poésie," Temps Modernes,
no. 26 (nov. 1947), 824-43. (Incl. Rilke and
Rimbaud.)

1271. Vanwelkenhuyzen, Gustave. Vocations Litt. Camille
Lemonnier, Georges Eekhoud, Emile Verhaeren,
Georges Rodenbach, Maurice Maeterlinck. Ge-
nève: 1959.

1272. Vigée, Claude. "Metamorphoses of mod. poetry,"
Comp. Lit., VII, 2 (Spring 1955), 97-120.

1273.   . "Les artistes de la faim," La Table
Ronde, (avril 1957), 43-64 (also in: Comp. Lit.,
IX (1957), 97-117.) (L'ascétisme dans la litt.:
Baudelaire, Lautréamont, Mallarmé, Kafka, T.
S. Eliot.)

1274. Virtanen, R. "The irradiations of 'Eurêka.' Valéry's
reflect. on Poe's cosmology," Tennessee Stud. in
Lit., VII (1962), 17-25.

1275.   . "Allusions to Poe's poetic theory in
Valéry's 'Cahiers,'" Poetic Theory--Poetic Practice. Papers of the Midwest Mod. Lang. Assoc.,
pres. at the annual meeting for 1968, ed. Robert
Scholes. Iowa City: 1969, pp. 113-20.

1276. Vitti, Mario S. "Eliot tra Valéry e Masters," Idea,
IV, 32 (10 Agosto 1952), 4.

1277. Vivier, Robert. "Albert Mockel et le symbolisme, " Marche Romane, XVIe année, tome XVI, no. 3 (3e trim. 1966), 87-92.

1278. Voellmy, Jean. Aspects du silence dans la poésie mod. Une étude sur Verlaine, Mallarmé, Valéry, Rimbaud, Claudel, René Char, et Francis Ponge. (Thèse) Zürich: 1952.

1279. Vogel, Lucy. "Blok in the Land of Dante, " Russian Review, XXVI, 3 (1967), 251-63.

1280. _____. "A Symbolist's Inferno: Blok and Dante, " Russian Review, XXIX, 1 (1970), 38-51.

1281. Vordtriede, Werner. The concep. of the poet in the works of St. Mallarmé and St. George. (Diss.) Evanston: 1944. (Also in: Novalis u. d. französ. Symbolisten and Northwestern Univ. Summ. of Doct. Diss., XII (1947), 48-50 (abstract).

1282. _____. "The mirror as symbol and theme in the works of St. Mallarmé and St. George, " Mod. Lang. Forum, XXXII (1947), 13-24.

1283. _____. Novalis u. d. französ. Symbolisten. Zur Entstehungsgeschichte d. dicht. Symbols. Stutt: 1963. (Sprache u. Lit., 8.) (Incl. Gide, Laforgue, Maeterlinck, Rodenbach, Villiers.)

1284. Wais, K. "D. H. Lawrence, Valéry, Rilke in ihrer Auseinandersetzung mit d. bild. Künsten, " Germanisch-Romanische Monatsschr., N. F., II, 4 (Okt. 1952), 301-24.

1285. _____. "Maeterlinck, initiateur des poètes allemands, " Synthèses, 195 (août 1962), 129-49.

1286. Wais, Karin. Studien z. Rilkes Valéry-Übertragungen. (Diss.) Tüb.: 1967.

1287. Waldrop, Rosmarie. " 'Monsieur Teste' and 'Der Ptolemäer': abstractness in the fiction of Valéry and Benn, " East-West Review (Japan), I (1965), 317-27.

1288. Walzer, Pierre Olivier. La Révolution des Sept: Lautréamont, Mallarmé, Rimbaud, Corbière, Cros, Nouveau, Laforgue. Neuchâtel: 1970. (Incl. seven portraits.)

1289. Ward, David E. "Il culto dell'impersonalità: Eliot, Sant' Agostino e Flaubert, " Verri, XXXI (1969), 83-95.

1290. Waters, Leonard. Coleridge and Eliot: a compar. study of their theories of poetic composition. (Diss.) Univ. Michigan: 1948.

1291. Weatherhead, A. K. "Baudelaire in Eliot's 'Ash Wednesday IV, ' " English Lang. Notes, II (1965), 288-9.

1292. Weber, Jean-Paul. Génèse de l'Oeuvre Poétique.
      Paris: 1960. (Coll. Bibl. des Idées) (incl.
      Baudelaire, Mallarmé, Verlaine, Valéry).
1293. Weevers, Theodoor. "Albert Verwey and St.
      George: their conflicting affinities, " German Life & Let-
      ters, XXII (1969), 79-89.
1294. Weigand, E. "Rilke and Eliot: the articulation of
      the mystic experience. A discussion centering
      on the 'Eighth Duino Elegy' and 'Burnt Norton, ' "
      Germanic Review, XXX (1955), 198-210.
1295. Weinberg, Bernard. The Limits of Symbolism:
      Studies of Five Mod. French Poets. Chicago:
      1966. (Incl. Baudelaire, Rimbaud, Mallarmé,
      Valéry, Perse.)
1296. Weinberg, Kerry. T. S. Eliot and Ch. Baudelaire.
      Hague/Paris: 1969. (Studies in Gen'l & Comp.
      Lit., vol. V.)
1297. Weinberg, Kurt. Henri Heine, 'romantique défroqué'
      héraut du symbolisme français. Paris/New Ha-
      ven: 1954. (Bibliog., pp. 283-93.)
1298. Weindling, S. "St. George als Ubersetzer Baude-
      laires, " Diss. Abstr., XIII (1953), 235/6 (Penn.).
1299. Weisgerber, Jean. "Présence d'E. Poe dans la
      poésie moderne, " Synthèses, III, 7 (1948), 78-90.
1300. Wellershoff, Dieter. Der Gleichgültige. Versuche
      über Hemingway, Camus, Benn u. Beckett.
      Köln/Berlin: 1963.
1301. West, William C. "Concepts of reality in the poetic
      drama of W. B. Yeats, W. H. Auden, and T. S.
      Eliot, " Diss. Abstr., XXV (1965), 6120/21 (Stan-
      ford).
1302. Whitfield, J. H. "Pirandello e T. S. Eliot: identità
      e contrasti, " Le Parole e le Idee (Napoli), IV
      (1962), 5-30.
1303. Willard, Nancy M. "An experiment in objectivity:
      the poetic theory and practice of W. C. Williams
      and R. M. Rilke, " Diss. Abstr., XXIV (1963),
      2045/6 (Mich.).
1304. _____. "A poetry of things: Williams, Rilke,
      Ponge, " Comp. Lit., XVII (1965), 311-24.
1305. _____. Testimony of Invisible Man: W. C. Wil-
      liams, Francis Ponge, R. M. Rilke, Pablo Ne-
      ruda. Columbia, Mo.: 1970.
1306. Wilson, Clotilde. "Rilke and Corção, " Luso-Brazil-
      ian Review, VII, 1 (1970), 74-80.
1307. Wilson, E. M. "Studies in mod. Span. poetry: I.
      Guillén and Quevedo on death, " Atlante, I (1953),

237-8. ("Postscript," Atlante, II, 4 (1954).)
1308. Wilson, Edmund. "Proust and Yeats," New Republic,
LII, 670 (Oct. 5, 1927), 176-177a.
1309. _____. "W. Stevens and E. E. Cummings," The
Shores of Light. London: 1952, pp. 49-56.
1310. _____. "Symbolism," Axël's Castle. A Study in
the Imag. Lit. of 1870-1930. London: 1961.
(Fontana Library 539L) (incl. Mallarmé, Zola,
Valéry).
1311. Wilson, F. A. A. "Yeats and G. Hauptmann,"
Southern Review (Australian Journ. Lit. Stud.),
no. 1 (1963), 69-73.
1312. Winters, Yvor. On Mod. Poets. N.Y.: 1959.
(Incl. Stevens & Eliot.)
1313. Witschel, Günter. Rausch u. Rauschgift bei Baudelaire, Huxley, Benn u. Burroughs. Bonn: 1968.
1314. Witt, Marion W. "A note on Yeats and Symons,"
Notes & Queries, VII (1960), 467-9.
1315. Wood, Frank. "Rilke and Eliot: Trad. & Poetry,"
Germ. Rev., XXVII (1952), 246-59.
1316. Wook, S. "Internal space in Eastern and Western
poetry: Rilke, Naong, Hwang Jini," Phoenix
(Korea Univ.), XI (1967), 32-9.
1317. Wright, George. The Poet in the Poem: the Personae of Eliot, Yeats and Pound. Berkeley:
1960. (Persp. in Crit., 4.)
1318. Wyczynski, Paul. Poésie et Symbole: Perspectives
du Symbolisme-Emile Nelligan-Saint-Denys Gar-
neau-Anne Hebert-Le Langage des Arbres. Montréal: 1965. (Canadian poets.)
1319. Wyss, Tobias. Dialog u. Stille. Max Jacob, G.
Ungaretti, Fernando Pessoa. Zürich: 1969.
(Orig.: Diss. Zürich.)
1320. Xirau, Ramón. "Lectura a 'Cántico,' " Cuad.
Americanos, CXXI, 2 (1962), 248-57.
(Guillén and Valéry).
1321. Yeargers, Marilyn M. "Poesis: the theme of poe-
try-making in the poetry of W. Stevens and P.
Valéry," Diss. Abstr. Intern'l, XXXI (1970),
1298A (Mich. State).
1322. Y. L. "The poet's virginity," Dublin Mag., XXIII,
4 (Oct.-Dec. 1948), 39-47. (Incl. Valéry and
Ponge.)
1323. Young, Howard T. The Victorious Expression: A
Study of Four Contemp. Spanish Poets: Unamuno,
Machado, Jiménez, Lorca. Madison: 1964.

1324.   Young, Raymond A.   "Benavente, Martínez Sierra y
        R. Darío: una comparacion, " Duquesne Hispanic
        Review (Pittsburgh), VIII, 2 (1969), 19-32.
1325.   Yusuf Jamal Husain, F. N.   "Edith Sitwell in the
        symbolist trad. , " Diss. Abstr. , XXVI (1965/6),
        5437 (Minn.).
1326.   Zardoya, Concha.   "La técnica metafórica en la
        poesía española contemp. , " Cuad. Americanos,
        XX, 116 (1961), 258-81.   (Incl. Machado, Jimé-
        nez, Guillén, Lorca.)
1327.   _____.   "J. Guillén y P. Valéry, " Comp. Lit.
        Studies, (1963), 79-89 (special advance issue).
        (Also repr. in: Asomante, XX, 1 (Enero-Marzo
        1964), 22-32.)
1328.   Zirmunskij, V. M.   "L'Evoluz. del verso russo da
        Puškin a Majakovskij, " Annali Instit. Univ. Ori-
        entale, Napoli, Sez. Slava, VIII (1965), 1-19.
1329.   Zulli, Floyd, Jr.   "T. S. Eliot and Paul Bourget, "
        Notes & Queries, XIII (1966), 415-16.

INDIVIDUAL STUDIES

BELY / BLOK / BRIUSOV

1330. Anon. "Belyj, Andrej, " Dizionario Univ. della Lett. Contemp., ed. Orlando Bernardi. Milano: 1959, I, pp. 357-9.
1331. Arseniew, N. von. "A. Belyj, " Die russ. Lit. d. Neuzeit u. Gegenwart in ihren geist. Zusammen-hängen. Mainz: 1929, pp. 256-63.
1332. Ashukin, N. S. A. Blok. Moscow: 1923.
1333. Baade, Margarete. "Die dt. Lit. kritik zu d. Poem 'Die Zwölf' von A. Blok, " Wiss. Ztschr. d. Hum-boldt-Univ. Berlin, Ges.-u. Sprachwiss. Reihe, VII (1957/8), 107-17.
1334. _____. "Zur Aufnahme von A. Bloks Poem 'Die Zwölf' in Dtschld, " Ztschr. f. Slawistik, IX (1964), I: 1920-'33, 175-95; II: 1945-'63, 551-73.
1335. _____. Zur Aufnahme d. Poems 'Die Zwölf' von A. Blok in Dtschld (1920-'64), 2 Bände. (diss.) Berlin: 1965.
1336. _____. "A. Blok: 60 Jahre dt. Rezep. geschichte, " Ztschr. f. Slawistik, XII (1967), 328-63.
1337. _____. "Grundfragen d. Ubersetzung von Dichtun-gen A. Bloks ins Deutsche, " Ztschr. f. Slawistik, XIV (1969), 1-11.
1338. Babenchikov, M. B. A. Blok i Rossiia. Moscow/Petrograd: 1923.
1339. Beketova, M. A. A. Blok. Petrograd: 1922.
1340. _____. A. Blok i Ego Mat'. Leningrad/Moscow: 1924.
1341. Bely, Andrei. "Simvolizm kak miroponimanie, " Mir Iskusstva, no. 5 (1904).
1342. _____. "Krititsizm i Simvolizm, " Vesy, no. 2 (1904).
1343. _____. "Apokalipsis v russkoi poezii, " Vesy, no. 4 (1905).

1344. _____ . "Simvolizm, " Vesy, no. 12 (1908),
1345. _____ . "Charles Baudelaire, " Vesy, no. 6 (1909),
        pp. 71-80.
1346. _____ . Simvolizm. Moscow: 1910.
1347. _____ . Poeziia Slova. Petersburg: 1922.
1348. _____ . St. Petersburg, trans. John Cournos.
        N.Y.: Grove Press, 1959. (Introd. by J. Cour-
        nos; foreword by G. Reavey.) (Reviewed: Basil
        Petron in: Russian Review, XIX, 1 (Jan. 1960),
        88.)
1349. Berberova, N. N. A. Blok et Son Temps, suivie
        d'un choix de poëmes. Paris: 1947.
1350. _____ . "A note on A. Belyj, " Russian Review,
        II (1951), 99-105.
1351. Blok, A. "O sovremennom sostojanii russkogo sim-
        volizma, " Apollon (St. Petersburg), VIII (1910),
        21-30.
1352. Blot, Jean. "A. Blok et 'Les Douze, ' " Preuves,
        CXCVI (1967), 76-7.
1353. Bonneau, Sophie. L'Univers Poétique d'A. Blok.
        Paris: 1946. (Bibliog., pp. 505-14.)
1354. _____ . Le Drame Lyrique d'A. Blok. Paris:
        1946.
1355. Bowra, C. M. "The position of A. Blok, " The Cri-
        terion (April 1932), 422-38.
1356. _____ . "A. Blok, " The Heritage of Symbolism.
        London: 1943, pp. 144-79.
1357. Briusov, V. "K istorii simvolizma, " Literaturnoe
        Nasledstvo, XXVII-VIII (1937).
1358. _____ , and A. L. Miropol'skii. Russkie simvo-
        listy. 3 vols. Moscow: 1894/5.
1359. Bümanis, Arnolds. "Beidzot ari Bloks, " Karogs
        (Riga), X (1970), 142-6.
1360. Burgi, R. T. The plays of A. Blok. (M. A.
        thesis) Columbia Univ.: 1947.
1361. Burkhart, Dagmar. "Leitmotivik u. Symbolik in A.
        Belyjs Roman 'Peterburg, ' " Die Welt der Slaven
        (Wiesbaden), IX (1964), 277-323.
1362. Christa, Boris (Baris?). "Metrical Innov. in Blok's
        lyrical verse, " Journ. Australasian Univ. Lang.
        & Lit. Assoc., no. 17 (1962), 44-52.
1363. _____ . "Sound and structure in the poetry of A.
        Bely, " Proceed. 9th Congr. Australas. Univ.
        Lang. & Lit. Assoc., (19-26 Aug. 1964), ed.
        Marion Adams. Melbourne: 1964, pp. 158-9.
1364. Chukovskii, K. A. Blok Kak Chelovek i Poet.
        Petersburg: 1924.

1365. _____ . Kniga ob A. Bloke. Berlin: 1922.
1366. Cioran, S. "In the imitation of Christ: a study of
      A. Bely's 'Zapiski Chudaka,'" Canadian Slavic
      Studies, IV (1970), 74-92.
1367. Cioran, Samuel D. "The apocalyptic symbolism of
      A. Bely," Diss. Abstr. Intern'l, XXX (1970),
      5411A (Toronto).
1368. Damiani, Enrico. "Belyj, Andrej," Grande Dizionario
      Enciclopedico, fond. par Pietro Fedele. Torino:
      1955, II, p. 302.
1369. Eihvalds, V. "A. Bloka lirika Latvija," Literatura
      un Maksla, XLVII (1969), 2-3.
1370. Ellis, A. (pseud for L. Kobylinskii). "A. Belyj,"
      Russkie Simvolisty. Moscow: 1910, pp. 207-316.
1371. Emmer, H. "Belyj, Andrej," Die Weltliteratur, ed.
      E. Frauwallner et al. Wien: 1951, p. 154.
1372. Essays by var. hands. Ob A. Bloke. Petersburg:
      1921.
1373. _____ . Pamiati A. Bloka. LXXXIII Otkrytoe
      Zasedanie Vol'noi Filos. Assos., 28 Avgust 1921.
      Petersburg: 1921. (Incl. speeches by A. Bely,
      Ivanov-Razumnik, and A. Z. Shteinberg.)
1374. Ferrari, Elena. Erifilli Stichi, ein Gedicht ist
      Belyj gewidmet. Berlin: 1923.
1375. Futrell, Michael. "A. Blok," Survey, no. 36 (1961),
      119-20.
1376. Gatto, E. Lo. "Belyj, Andrej," Enciclopedia Italiana.
      Milano/Roma: 1930, VI, pp. 587-8.
1377. Gauvain, J., and E. Bickert. A. Blok, Poète de la
      Tragédie Russe. Fribourg: 1943.
1378. Gol'tsev, V. V. "Briusov i Blok," Pechat' i Revo-
      liutsiia, nos. 4-5 (1928).
1379. Goodmann, Th. A. Block (sic), eine Studie zur
      neueren russ. Lit. gesch. Königsberg: 1936.
1380. Grossman, L. "Brjusov i francuzskie simvolisty,"
      Mastera Slova. Moscow: 1928, pp. 261-9.
1381. Guenther, J. von. A. Blok. Der Versuch e.
      Darstellung. München: 1948.
1382. Gurian, Waldemar. "The memoirs of Bely," Russian
      Review, III, 1 (1943), 95-103.
1383. Haertel, E. "Pietroburgo nella lett. russa," Riv. di
      Lett. Slave (Roma), VII, 5-6 (1932), 428-35.
      (On Bely's novel.)
1384. Hart, Pierre R. "A. Belyj's 'Petersburg,'" Diss.
      Abstr. Intern'l, XXX (1969), 2023A/24A (Wisc.).
1385. Hindley, Lily. Die Neologismen A. Belyjs. Mün-
      chen: 1966. (Forum Slavicum, 3.) (Orig.:

diss. Heidelberg: 1962).

1386. Holthusen, Johannes. "A. Belyj und Rudolf Steiner, " Festschrift für Max Vasmer zum 70. Geburtstag, Berlin: 1956.

1387. _____. "A. Bely, " Lexicon der Weltlit. im 20. Jh. Freiburg/Basel/Wien: 1960, I, pp. 146-9.

1388. _____. "Nachwirk. der Trad. in A. Bloks Bild-symbolik, " Slaw. Stud. z. V Intern'l Slaw. Kongr. in Sofia (1963), ed. M. Braun, et al. Göttingen: 1963, pp. 437-44. (Opera Slavica, 4.)

1389. _____. "A. Belyj, " Russ. Gegenwartslit. I, 1890-1940. Bern: 1963, pp. 39-45.

1390. Hönig, Anton. A. Belyjs Romane: Stil u. Gestalt. München: 1965. (Bibliog., pp. 114-24.) (Forum Slavicum, 8.)

1391. Ivanof, Alessandro. "Blok (1909): Signific. di una protesta, " Atti del R. Instit. Veneto di Scienza, Lett. ed. Arti., classe di scienza morali e lett. (Venezia), CXIX (1960/1), 25-44.

1392. Jur'eva, Zoja. " 'A. Blok: Between Image and Idea, ' " Novyj Žurnal (New York), no. 71 (1963), 276-81. (Review of book by F. D. Reeve.)

1393. Kemball, Robin. "Transl. of A. Blok's 'The Scythians, ' " Russian Review, XIV, 2 (April 1955), 117-20. (Introd., pp. 117-18.)

1394. _____. "Poems from Blok and Akhmatova, " Russian Review, XVIII, 4 (Oct. 1959), 306-12. (Transl., incl. 'To the Muse' and 'Dreams').

1395. _____. "From A. Blok's 'Songs of the Lady Beau-tiful' (transl.), " Russian Review, XVII, 1 (Jan. 1968), 56-9.

1396. _____. "A. Blok's 'Of What the Wind Sings' and Other Poems (transl. with comment.), " Russian Review, XXI, 2 (April 1962), 148-53.

1397. _____. "James B. Woodward's (ed.) Sel. Poems of A. Blok, " Russian Review, XXIX, 2 (1970), 239. (Review).

1398. _____. A. Blok: A Study in Rhythm and Metre. Hague: 1965. (Reviewed by Richard F. Gustav-son in: Russian Review, XXV, 4 (1966), 421-3.)

1399. Keuchel, Ernst. "A. Bjely u. d. russ. Symbolis-mus, " Dt. Monatsschr. f. Russland (Riga-Reval), LVI, 3 (1914), 195-202.

1400. Kisch, Sir Cecil. A. Blok: Prophet of the Revo-lution. London: 1960/N. Y.: 1961.

1401. Klotz, Volker. Die erzählte Stadt: ein Sujet als Herausforderung des Romans von Lesage bis

Döblin. München: 1969. (On Bely's St. Petersburg.)

1402. Kluge, R. D. Westeuropa u. Russland im Weltbild
A. Bloks. München: 1967.

1403. Kniazhnin, V. N. Aleksandr A. Blok. Petersburg:
1922.

1404. Kolpakova, E. P., et al. "Bibliog. A. Bloka, "
Uchënye Zapiski Vil'niusskogo Gosudarstvennogo
Pedagogicheskogo Instit., Vol. VI. n.p.: 1959.

1405. Laffitte, S. "Le symbolisme occid. et A. Blok, "
Review of English Studies (London), XXXIV (1957),
88-94. (Also in: Rev. des Etudes Slaves,
XXXIV (1957), 88-94.)

1406. _____. A. Blok: Une Etude (avec trad.) Paris:
1958.

1407. Lavrin, Janko. Aspects of Modernism: From Wilde
to Pirandello. London: 1935. (Incl. Blok.)

1408. Lednicki, Waclaw A. "Blok's 'Polish Poem,' " (on
'Retribution'). Russia, Poland, and the West.
N. Y.: 1954, pp. ?.

1409. Lettenbauer, Wilhelm. "A. Belyj, " Russ. Lit. gesch.
Frankfurt am Main/Wien: 1955, pp. 318-20.
(Later ed. Wiesbaden: 1958.)

1410. Lewitter, L. R. "The inspir. and meaning of A.
Blok's 'The Rose and the Cross,' " Slav. & East
Europ. Review, XXXV, 85 (1957), 428-43.

1411. Lidin, V., ed. "Belyj, A. " Bibliogr., Pisatelei.
Moscow: 1926, pp. 43-7.

1412. Makovskij, Sergej K. A. Blok. Paris: 1955.
(Unpubl. work.)

1413. _____. "Einige Worte über A. Belyj, " Na Parnase
Serebrjanogo Veka. München: 1962.

1414. Maksimov, D. Poezija Valerija Brjusova. Leningrad: 1940.

1415. _____. Brjusov: Poèzija i pozicija. Leningrad:
1969.

1416. Malmstad, John E. "The poetry of A. Belyj: a
variorum edn. " Diss. Abstr. Intern'l, XXX
(1969), 2031A (Princeton). (In Russian, with
English introd.)

1417. Manning, A. Clarence. "Belyj, Andrey, " Slavonic
Encyclopedia, ed. J. S. Roucek. N. Y.: 1949,
p. 95.

1418. Markovitch, Milan. "Venise dans l'oeuvre poétique
d'un symboliste russe, " Venezia nelle Lett.
Moderne, ed. Carlo Pellegrini. Venezia/Roma:
1961, pp. 212-18. (On Briusov.)

1419. Mašbic-Verov, I. Russkij Simvolizm i Put' A. Bloka.
Kujbyšev: 1969.

1420. Maslenikov, Oleg A. "Bely, Andrei," Columbia Dict.
of Mod. Europ. Lit., ed. Horatio Smith. N. Y.:
1947, pp. 12-13.

1421. _____. "A. Belyj's 'Third Symphony,' " Amer.
Slav. & East Europ. Review, VII, 1 (1948), 78.

1422. Maurina, Zenta. Auf der Schwelle zweier Welten,
2nd edn. Memmingen: 1961. (On Bely.)

1423. Medvedev, P. N. Pometki A. Bloka v Tetradiakh
Stikhov. Leningrad: 1926.

1424. _____. Dramy i Poemy A. Bloka. Leningrad:
1928.

1425. _____, ed. Pamiati Bloka. Petersburg: 1922.

1426. Miasnikov, A. S. Aleksandr A. Blok. Moscow:
1949.

1427. Michaut, Jacques. "Blok, le peuple et l'intelligentsia: étude d'une théorie à travers la prose de
Blok, " Cah. du Monde Russe et Soviétique, X
(1969), 459-77.

1428. Mirsky, D. S. (Svjatopolk-Mirskij). "A. Belyj, "
Contemp. Russian Lit.: 1881-1925. London:
1926, pp. 225-35.

1429. Močul'skij, K. V. A. Blok. Paris: 1948.

1430. _____. V. Brjusov. Paris: 1962.

1431. Møller, Peter U. "A. Blok, " Fremmede Digtere i
det 20. Arhundrede, Vol. I, ed. Sven M. Kris-
tenson. Copenhagen: 1967, pp. 439-50.

1432. Muratova, K. D., ed. "Belyj, Andrej. " Bibliogr.
Ukazatel'. Moscow/Leningrad: 1963, pp. 118-23.

1433. Nemerovskaia, O., and Ts. Vol'pe. Sud'ba Bloka.
Leningrad: 1930.

1434. Neumann, Friedrich W. "A. Bloks 'Neznakomka,' "
Die Welt der Slaven (Wiesbaden), VIII (1963),
5-17.

1435. Nikitina, E. F., ed. O Bloke. Sbornik. Moscow:
1929.

1436. _____, and S. V. Shuvalov. Poeticheskoe Iskusstvo
Bloka. Moscow: 1926.

1437. Orlov, V. N. A. Blok. Moscow: 1956.

1438. _____. "Lirika i Poemy A. Bloka, " (Preface) A.
Blok, Polnoe Sobranie Stixotvorenij. 2 vols.
Moscow: 1946, I, pp. v-xlviii.

1439. _____. "A. Blok i A. Belyi v 1907 godu, " Literaturnoe Nasledstvo, XXVII-VIII (1937).

1440. Pascal, Pierre. "Trois poètes russes à Venise au
début du XXe siècle, " Venezia nelle Lett. Moderne,

ed. Carlo Pellegrini. Venezia/Roma: 1961, pp.
219-29. (Incl. Blok.)

1441. Pertsov, P. Rannij Blok. Moscow: 1922.
1442. Pflanzl, Jutta. Weltbild u. Kunstschau d. russ.
Symbolismus in d. theoret. Gestaltung durch A.
Belyj. (Diss.) Wien: 1946.
1443. Poggioli, Renato. "Studi su Blok: 'I versi della
bellissima dama,' " Riv. di Lett. Slave, V,
(1930), 38-59.
1444. _____. "Qualis Artifex Pereo! or barbarism and
decadence," Harvard Library Bull., XIII, 1 (Winter 1959), (on Briusov's poem 'The Coming Huns.')
1445. Putnam, George. "A. Blok and the Russian intelligentsia," Slav. & East Europ. Journ., IX, 1
(Spring 1965), 29-46.
1446. Raggio, O. "Brjusov e la poesia francese," Lett.
Moderne, VI (1956), 569-82.
1447. Reeve, F. D. "Structure and symbol in Blok's 'The
Twelve,' " Amer. Slav. & East Europ. Review,
XIX, 2 (1960), 259-75(?).
1448. _____. A. Blok: Betw. Image and Idea. London/
N. Y.: 1962. (Reviewed by Robin Kemball, Russian Review, XXII, 2 (April 1963), 203-5.)
(Columbia Studies in the Humanities, 1.)
1449. _____. "A geometry of prose," Kenyon Review,
XXV (1963), 9-25. (On Bely.)
1450. Remenik, G. Poemy A. Bloka. Moscow: 1959.
1451. Rybnikova, M. A. A. Blok--Gamlet. Moscow: 1923.
1452. Sapir, Boris. "An unknown corresp. of A. Bely:
A. Bely in Berlin, 1921-3," (Nadezhda Shchupak),
Slav. & East Europ. Review, XLIX, 116 (July
1971), 450-2.
1453. Setschkareff, V. "The narrative prose of Brjusov,"
Intern'l Journ. Slav. Linguistics and Poetics, I-II
(1959), 237-65.
1454. Specovius, Günther. "Wiederentdeckung des A.
Belyj," Dt. Rundschau, LXXXVI (1960), 376-8.
1455. Steffensen, Eigil. "Symbol og vision: Om A. Belyj
og hans forfatterskab," Dansk Udsyn (Askov), L
(1970), 114-26.
1456. Stepun, Fedor. "Dem Andenken A. Belyjs," Hochland, XXXIV (Juni 1936/7), 200-15.
1457. _____. Vstrechi: Dostoevsky--Tolstoy--Bunin--
Zaitsev--Ivanov--Belyi--Leonor. Munich: 1962.
(Reviewed by Heinrich A. Stammler, Russian Review, XXIII, 3 (July 1964), 294.)
1458. _____. Mystische Weltschau: Fünf Gestalten d.

104 A Post-Symbolist Bibliography

russ. Symbolismus. München: 1964. (Incl.
Bely.)

1459. Struck, Danylo. "The great escape: principal
themes in Brjusov's poetry," Slav. & East Europ.
Journ., XII, 4 (Winter 1969), 407-23.

1460. Struve, Gleb P. "A. Bely (Boris Bugayev)," Slavonic & East Europ. Review, XIII, 37 (1934),
183-5.

1461. _____. "Bely, Andrey," Chambers Encyklopaedia.
London: 1955, II, p. 243.

1462. _____. "A. Belyj's experiments with novel technique," Stil-u. Formprobleme in der Lit., ed.
Paul Böckmann. Heidelberg: 1959, pp. 459-67.

1463. Svjatopolk-Mirskij (Mirsky, D. S.). "V. J. Brjusov,"
Sovremennye Zapiskii, XXII (1924), 418-19.

1464. Tager, Iu. A. Blok. Moscow: 1946.

1465. Taranovsky, Kiril. "Certain aspects of Blok's symbolism," Stud. in Slav. Linguistics and Poetics
in Honor of Boris O. Unbegaun, ed. R. Magidoff
et al. N.Y./London: 1968, pp. 249-60.

1466. Thompson, Ewa M. "The develop. of A. Blok as a
dramatist," Slav. & East Europ. Journ., XIV, 3
(Fall 1970), 341-51.

1467. Thomson, R. D. B. "The non-lit. sources of 'Roza
i Krest,'" Slav. & East Europ. Review, XLV,
105 (1967), 292-307. (On Blok's "The Rose and
the Cross.")

1468. Timofeev, L. I. A. Blok. Moscow: 1946.

1469. Tschižewskij, D. "A. Belyj," Versdicht. d. russ.
Symbolisten. Wiesbaden: 1959, pp. 8-14.

1470. _____. Anfänge d. russ. Futurismus. Wiesbaden:
1963. (Heidelberger slav. Texte, 7.) (Incl. Bely.)

1471. Tsingovatov, A. Aleksandr A. Blok. Moscow/Len-
ingrad: 1926.

1472. Turkov, A. A. Blok. Moscow: 1969.

1473. Vogel, Lucy. "Blok in the land of Dante," Russian
Review, XXVI (1967), 251-63.

1474. _____. "Blok and Italy," Diss. Abstr., XXX
(1969), 334A/5A (N.Y.U.).

1475. Volkov, N. A. Blok i Teatr. Moscow: 1926.

1476. Woodward, James B. "Rhythmic modul. in the
'dol'nik' trimeter of Blok," Slav. & East Europ.
Journ., XII, 3 (Fall 1968), 297-310.

1477. Zirmunskij, Viktor M. V. Brjusov i nasledie Puš-
kina. St. Petersburg: 1922.

1478. _____. Poeziia A. Bloka. Petrograd: 1922.

1479. _____. "Formprobleme in d. russ. Lit. wiss.
schaft," Ztschr. f. Slav. Phil., I (1925), 117-
52. (On Bely.)

BENN

1480. Ahl, Herbert. "Absender: G. Benn, Berlin," Literar. Porträts. München/Wien: 1962, pp. 211-
16.
1481. Allemann, B. "Statische Gedichte: Zu e. Gedicht
von G. Benn," Merkur, X (1956), 402-13. (Discusses coll. of B's poetry publ. in 1948.)
1482. _____. G. Benn: Das Problem der Geschichte.
Pfullingen: 1963.
1483. Anon. "Dokumentation zu G. Benn," Neue dt. Hefte,
XCV (1963), 56-66. (Corresp. with and concern.
G. Benn, from Lit. u. Dichtg im Dritten Reich
by Joseph Wulf.)
1484. Arbasino, A. "La doppiezza di Benn," Paragone,
XX, 228 (1969), 69-73.
1485. Asai, Masao. "Das Pathos der Distanz. Uber d.
spät. Gedichte von G. Benn," Doitsu Bungaku,
XLIII (1969), 84-90. (In Japanese, with summary in German.)
1486. Ashton, E. B., ed. G. Benn, Primal Vision. Norfolk, Conn.: 1960. (Anthology.)
1487. Balser, Hans-Dieter. Das Problem d. Nihilismus im
Werk G. Benns. (Diss.) Kiel: 1962. (Publ. as
book, Bonn: 1965; 2nd rev. edn., 1970.)
1488. Bansberg, Dieter Heinz. "Interpr. z. frühen Lyrik
G. Benns," Diss. Abstr. Intern'l, XXXI (1970/1),
1258A (Cornell)
1489. Bednarik, K. "G. Benn, zum Gedächtnis des letzten
Dichters d. dt. Expressionismus," Wort u. Wahrheit, XI (1956), 770-2.
1490. Bein, Sigfrid. "Rückblick auf Benn. Aus Anl. d.
10 Wiederkehr s. Todestages," Welt u. Wort,
XXI (1966), 219-21.
1491. Benn, Gottfried. "Phase II: Antworten auf e. Interview u. meine neuen Bücher," Merkur, IV
(1950), 23-9.
1492. _____. "Zeitfremde Verse," Welt u. Wort, VII
(1952), 153ff.

1493. _____. Ausdruckswelt: Essays u. Aphorismen.
Wiesb.: 1954. (Later ed. Frankf. /M. /Berlin:
1964.)

1494. _____. "Nihilistisch oder positiv? Uber d. Lage
des heutig. Menschen," Neue Dt. Hefte, I (1954/
5), 60-1.

1495. _____. "Soll die Dichtg d. Leben bessern?"
Neue dt. Hefte, II (1955/6), 834-47.

1496. _____. Probleme d. Lyrik (Vortr. in d. Univ.
Marburg am 21 Aug. 1951) Wiesb: 1956. (48
pp.)

1497. _____. "Zur Problematik d. Dichterischen," Der
goldene Schnitt. Grosse Essayisten der Neuen
Rundschau 1890 bis 1960. Frankf/M.: 1960,
pp. 343-53. (Orig. in: N. Rds., 1930.)

1498. Bleinagel, Bodo. Absolute Prosa. Ihre Konzep. u.
Realisation bei G. Benn. Bonn: 1969. (Zugl.
diss: Würzburg.)

1499. Blöcker, G. "G. Benn," Die neuen Wirklichkeiten.
Linien u. Profile der mod. Lit. Berlin: 1957,
pp. 149-65.

1500. Böckmann, Paul. "G. Benn u. d. Sprache d. Expressionismus," Der dt. Expressionismus. Formen u. Gestalten, ed. H. Steffen. Göttingen:
1965, pp. 63-87. [2nd ed. 1970.]

1501. Buddeberg, Else. "Probleme um G. Benn," Dt.
Vierteljahrsschrift, XXXIV (1960), 107-61.

1502. _____. "Probleme um G. Benn--II. Teil," Dt.
Vierteljahrsschrift, XXXV (1961), 433-79.

1503. _____. G. Benn. Stuttgart: 1961.

1504. _____. "Syntax u. Sinn: Eine Untersuchung zu
'September' von G. Benn (... aber heute ist der
Satzbau das Primäre)," Euphorion, LVI (1962),
104(5)-24.

1505. _____. Studien zur lyrischen Sprache G. Benns.
Düsseldorf: 1964. (Beiheft, Wirkendes Wort, 8.)

1506. Claes, A. Der lyrische Sprachstil G. Benns. (diss.)
Köln: 1956.

1507. Erckmann, Rudolf. "Jazz u. Lyrik. Erarbeitg Benn-
scher Dichtg von d. Schallplatte her," Dt.-
unterr., XVII, 4 (1965), 97-117.

1508. Erval, F. "G. Benn ou la double vie des intellec-
tuels allemandes," Temps Mod., no. 103 (1954),
2276-85.

1509. Essays by var. hands. G. Benn-Heft: Streit-Zeit-
Schrift. Frankf/M: 1964, H. 5, 1.
(Incl. W. Segebrecht, "Zu B's Lebenslauf, "; W.

Weyrauch, "Versuch über B' nachzudenken, "; H.
J. Heise, "Tendenz. im Werk G. B's, "; K. Riha,
"Wie modern ist G. B.?".)

1510. Fabri, Albrecht. "Rede auf G. Benn ('56), " Varia-
tionen: Essays. Wiesb: 1959, pp. 119-33.

1511. Fancelli, Maria. "Bibliogr. degli studi benniani in
Italia con una nota introd., " Studi Germanici,
VIII (1970), 463-74.

1512. Fick, Joseph. "G. Benn: 'Reisen, ' " Interpr. mod.
Lyrik. Frankf. M /Berlin/Bonn: 1964, pp. 86-9.

1513. Flügel, Heinz. "G. Benn. Das Laboratorium für
Worte, " Herausforderung d. dt. Wort. Stutt:
1962, pp. 54-69.

1514. Fritz, Horst. "G. Benns Anfänge, " Jahrb. d. dt.
Schiller-Gesell., XII (1968), 383-402.

1515. Gajek, Bernhard. "G. Benns 'Valse triste, ' " Mod.
Lyrik als Ausdr. relig. Erfahrg. Gött: 1964,
pp. 55-62.

1516. Garnier, Pierre. "Un demi-siècle allemand vécu
par un intellectuel, " Critique, X, 89 (1954), 847-
63.

1517. _____. G. Benn: Un demi siècle vécu par un
poète allemand. Paris: 1959.

1518. Gerth, Klaus. "Absolute Dichtg? Zu e. Begriff in
d. Poetik G. Benns, " Dt. unterr., XX, 4 (1968),
69-85.

1519. Goffin, Roger. "Die Leere u. d. gezeich. Ich. G.
Benns Gedichte, " Rev. des Langues Vivantes, XXV
(1959), 202-16.

1520. Grenzmann, Wilhelm. "G. Benn. Der Nihil. u. die
Form, " Stimmen d. Zeit, CXLIX (1951/2), 106-16.
(Repr. in: Dichtg u. Glaube. Probleme u.
Gestalten d. dt. Gegenwartslit. Bonn: 1952, pp.
70-87. (Subseq. editions: 1960, pp. 71-96;
1964, pp. 82-99; 1967, pp. 82-99.)

1521. _____. "Die Dicht G. Benns, " Universitas, X
(1955), 119-29.

1522. Grimm, Reinhold. G. Benn. Die farbliche Chiffre
in d. Dichtg. Nürnberg: 1958. (Orig. Diss.
Erlangen.)

1523. _____. "Ergriffen sein u. dennoch unbeteiligt:
Über G. Benns Verhältnis z. Geschichte, " Welt
u. Wort, XVI (1961), 269-73.

1524. _____, und W.-D. Marsch, eds. Die Kunst im
Schatten des Gottes: Für u. wider G. Benn.
Gött: 1962. (Essays by var. hands; incl.: R.

Grimm, "Bewusstsein als Verhängnis. Uber G. Benns Weg in die Kunst, " pp. 40-84.)

1525. _____. "Krit. Ergänzgn z. Benn-Lit., " Strukturen: Essays z. dt. Lit. Gött: 1963, pp. 273-352.

1526. _____. "Der Dichter G. Benn u. die geistige Situation unserer Zeit, " Universitas, XIX (1964), 33-41.

1527. _____. "Die problem. 'Probleme der Lyrik, ' " Festschr. G. Weber, ed. H. O. Burger & K. von See. Bad Homburg/Berlin/Zürich: 1967, pp. 299-328.

1528. Gsteiger, Manfred. "... doch unausdeutbar bleibt das Stundenlied, " (zu Gedichten G. Benns) Poesie u. Kritik. Betracht. über Lit. Bern/München: 1967, pp. 105-9.

1529. Gürster, E. "Das Schöne u. d. Nichts. Die Welt G. Benns, " Hochland, XLVII (1954/5), 310-21.

1530. Gürster-Steinhausen, E. "G. Benn, e. Abenteuer d. geist. Verzweiflung, " Neue Rundschau, LVIII (1947), 215-26.

1531. Haller, Elmar. Die Entwickl. d. Weltansch. G. Benns in s. frühen Werk. Die Geschichte e. Kunsttheorie (diss.) Innsbruck: 1959. (Publ. in book form--Dornbirn: 1965.)

1532. Hamburger, Michael. "G. Benn, " Reason and Energy. Stud. in German Lit. London: 1957, pp. 273-312. (Cf. Vernunft u. Rebellion. Aufs. z. Gesellschafts-kritik in d. dt. Lit. München: 1969, pp. 195-224.)

1533. Hannum, Hunter G. "G. Benn's 'Gladiolen, ' " Mod. Lang. Quart., XXII (1961), 167-80.

1534. _____. "G. Benn's Music, " German Review, XL (1965), 225-39.

1535. Hautumm, Hans-Ludwig. "G. Benn: Das mod. Ich, " Dt. unterr., XII, 3 (1960), 79-89.

1536. Heimann, Bodo. Der Süden in d. Dichtg. G. Benns. (Diss.) Freiburg i. B.: 1962.

1537. _____. "Ich-Zerfall als Thema u. Stil. Untersuch. z. dichter. Sprache G. Benns, " Germanisch-Romanische Monatsschrift, (N. F. XIV) (1964), 384-403.

1538. Heiseler, B. von. "Benn, " Ges. Essays z. alten u. neuen Lit. Bd II: Figuren 2. Feldzeichen. Formen. Stutt: 1967, pp. 85-8.

1539. Hillebrand, Bruno. "G. Benn im Spiegel der Lit.: Krit. Durchsicht des Schrifttums seit 1949, " Lit.-wiss. Jahrb. d. Görres-Gesellschaft, V (1964),

381-426. (Review article.)

1540. _____ . "G. Benn 10 Jahre nach seinem Tod, "
Neue dt. Hefte, XIII, 2 (1966), 96-
107.

1541. Hilton, Ian. "G. Benn, " German Men of Letters.
Twelve Lit. Essays, ed. Alex Natan. London:
1964, III, pp. 129-50.

1542. Hinske, Norbert. "Ars definitio hominis. Zur Fest-
stellung d. Menschen bei G. Benn, " Die Kunst im
Schatten d. Gottes, ed. R. Grimm u. W. -D.
Marsch. Gött: 1962, pp. 143-59.

1543. Hohendahl, Peter U. "Die Rezep. G. Benns in d.
Vereinigten Staaten u. Frankreich: Ein krit.
Vergleich, " Dt. Vierteljahrsschrift, XLI (1967),
233-57.

1544. Hohoff, Curt. "G. Benn, " Wort u. Wahrheit, V
(1950), 838-48.

1545. _____ . "Hyperbeln des Ausdrucks, " Geist u.
Ursprung. Zur mod. Lit. München: 1954, pp.
87-101.

1546. _____ . "Wirklichkeit u. Traum im dt. Gedicht, "
Merkur, X (1956), 703-15; 808-17. (Incl. Benn.)

1547. Holthusen, H. E. "G. Benn, " Jahresring, (1956/7),
Stuttgart: 1956, pp. 317-30.

1548. _____ . "Rede auf G. Benn, " Das Schöne u. d.
Wahre. Neue Studien z. mod. Lit. München:
1958, pp. 183-201.

1549. Homeyer, Helene. "G. Benn u. die Antike, " Ztschr.
f. dt. Philologie, LXXIX (1960), 113-24.

1550. Jens, W. "Sektion u. Vogelflug G. Benn, " Texte u.
Zeichen, III (1957), 389-407. (Also in: Statt e.
Lit. geschichte. Pfüllingen: 1958, pp. 133-57.)

1551. _____ . "Mythos u. Logos. Dichtg im 20. Jh., "
Statt e. Lit. -geschichte. Pfüllingen: 1958,
pp. 11-22.

1552. Kasack, H. "Notiz über G. Benns Lyrik, " Mosaik-
steine. Beitr. z. Lit. und Kunst. Frankf/M.:
1956, pp. 127-33. (Zuerst in Hören (1927).)

1553. Kaufmann, Erhard. "Das Fremdwort in d. Lyrik G.
Benns, " Ztschr. f. dt. Sprache, XX (1964), 33-
49; 141-77.

1554. Kerner, Dieter. "Benn, " Arzt-Dichter. Lebensbilder
aus 5 Jh. Eine Ausw. Stutt: 1967, pp. 151-72.

1555. Klemm, G. G. Benn. Wuppertal-Barmen: 1958.

1556. Koch, T. "G. Benns letzte Jahre, " Neue dt. Hefte,
III (1956/7), 652-63.

1557. Krämer-Badoni, R. "Die zeitlose Situat. d. Dichters.

Bemerkgn z. Werk G. Benns, " Lit. Dtschld, II, 9 (1951), 4.

1558. _____. "G. Benn, " Triffst du nur das Zauberwort. Stimmen von heute z. dt. Lyrik, ed. J. Petersen. Frankf. M.: 1961, pp. 231-43. (1967 ed., pp. 131-44.)

1559. _____. "G. Benn. Ein Porträt, " Vorsicht, gute Menschen von links. Aufs. u. Essays. Gütersloh: 1962, pp. 149-59. (Also: "Benn, Brecht oder Kesten, " pp. 160-4.)

1560. Kröll, Joachim. "Das Wort im dt. Gedicht (G. Benn), " Muttersprache (Lüneburg), LXIX (1959), 201-8.

1561. Krüger, H. "G. Benns schöpfer. Pessimismus, " Eckart, XXV (1955/6), 433-5.

1562. Kügler, H. "Wort u. Wirklichkeit im Frühwerk G. Benns, " Weg u. Weglosigkeit. Neun Essays z. Geschichte d. dt. Lit. im 20 Jh. Heidenheim: 1969, pp. 51-75. (Also: "Künstler u. Geschichte im Werk G. Benns, " pp. 77-104.)

1563. Kurella, Alfred. "Nun ist dies Erbe zu Ende, " Zwischendurch. Verstreute Essays, 1934-40. Berlin: 1961, pp. 133-44.

1564. Lennig, Walter. G. Benn in Selbstzeugn. u. Bilddokumenten. Hamburg: 1962, (Rowohlts Monogr., 71.) (Later ed. 1968.)

1565. Lion, Ferdinand. "Excurs über G. Benn, " Dt. Lit. im 20 Jh. Struktur u. Gestalten, ed. H. Friedemann & O. Mann. 2 Bde. Heidelberg: 1961, I, pp. 51-63. (1967 ed., pp. 45-57.)

1566. Lohner, E. "A crit. interpr. of G. Benn's poem 'Spät, ' " Monatshefte f. dt. Unterr., XLV (1953), 308-19.

1567. _____. "The Develop. of G. Benn's Idea of Expression as Value, " German Quarterly, XXVI (1953), 39-54.

1568. _____. "G. Benn: German Poet, " Western Review, XVII (1953), 177-84.

1569. _____. "G. Benn. Bibliog. 1912-'55, " Philobiblon, I (1957), 59-79.

1570. _____. G. Benn Bibliogr. 1912-1956. Wiesb: 1961.

1571. _____. Passion u. Intellekt: Die Lyrik G. Benns. Neuwied/Berlin: 1961.

1572. _____. "Traum vom Mythos. Eine Gedichtinterpr., " Die Kunst im Schatten d. Gottes, ed. R. Grimm & W.-D. Marsch. Gött: 1962, pp. 85-111. (On

B's poem 'V. Jh.'.)

1573. _____. "G. Benn," Dt. Dichter der Moderne:
Ihr Leben u. Werk, ed. Benno von Wiese. Berlin: 1965, pp. 479-99. (1969 ed., pp. 507-27.)

1574. _____, ed. G. Benn. München/Wiesb.: 1969.
(Dichter über ihre Dichtgn.)

1575. Loose, Gerhard. Die Asthetik G. Benns. Frankf.M:
1961.

1576. _____. "G. Benn and the Problem of Art in Our
Time," Criticism (Detroit), IV (1962), 340-52.

1577. Lüders, Eva M. "Das lyrische Ich u. das gezeichn.
Ich. Zur späten Lyrik G. Benns," Wirk. Wort,
XV (1965), 361-85.

1578. Märkel, F. "G. Benn u. d. europ. Nihilismus,"
Zeitwende, XXIX (1958), 308-22.

1579. _____. "Die Uberwindung d. Nihilismus durch
Kunst. Zur neueren Lit. über G. Benn," Zeitwende, XXXVI (1965), 528-34.

1580. Martini, Fritz. "G. Benn: Der Ptolemäer," Das
Wagnis d. Sprache. Interpr. dt. Prosa von
Nietzsche bis Benn. Stutt: 1954, pp. 468-517.

1581. Masini, Ferruccio. G. Benn e il Mito del Nihilismo.
Padova: 1968.

1582. Mehl, Dietrich. Mitteilung u. Monolog in der Lyrik
G. Benns. (Diss.) München: 1961.

1583. Melchinger, S. "Hybris u. Grenzen d. Gedichtes,"
Wort u. Wahr., VII (1952), 238-40.

1584. Mendelssohn, P. de. "Das Verharren vor d. Un-
vereinbaren. Versuch über G. Benn," Der Geist
in d. Despotie. Berlin: 1953, pp. 236-82.

1585. Michelsen, Peter. "Das Doppelleben u. die ästhet.
Anschauungen G. Benns," Dt. Vierteljahrsschrift,
XXXV (1961), 247-61.

1586. Milch, W. "Das Nichts u. die Form: Bemerk. z.
Werke von G. Benn," Preuss. Jahrb., CCXL, 3
(Juni 1935).

1587. Mö(ü)ller, Joachim. "Zur Thematik der Bennschen
Lyrik," Dt. unterr., XIV, 3 (1962), 60-75.

1588. Motekat, Helmut. "G. Benns 'Verlorenes Ich,'"
Wege z. Gedicht, ed. R. Hirschenauer & A.
Weber. München/Zürich: 1961, pp. 326-38.

1589. _____. "G. Benn. Das lyrische Ich im Experiment u. die Bilderfülle der Tradit.," Experiment
u. Tradit. Vom Wesen der Dichtg im 20 Jh.
Bonn/Frankf.M: 1962, pp. 237-68.

1590. Muschg, W. "Der Ptolemäer. Abschied von G.
Benn," Die Zerstörung d. dt. Lit. Bern: 1956,

pp. 47-70. (1958 ed., pp. 175-99.)

1591. _____. "Abrechnung mit G. Benn, " Welt u. Wort, XII (1957), 39-41.

1592. Naito, Michio. "Der Ausdruck d. mod. Lyrik. Uber Benns Poetik, " Doitsu Bungaku, XXIX (1962), 58-62.

1593. Nebel, G. "G. Benns Lob d. 'Ausdruckswelt, ' " Thema (München), no. 7 (Jan. 1950), 22-4.

1594. Nef, E. Das Werk G. Benns. Zürich: 1958.

1595. Paetel, K. O. "Von d. Einsamkeit u. d. Publizität. Randbemerk. z. G. Benns neuen Büchern, " Sammlung (Göttingen), VI (1951), 277-81.

1596. _____. "G. Benn im Lichte amerik. Kritik, " Neue dt. Hefte, I (1954/5), 475-8.

1597. _____. "Auslandsstimmen über G. Benn, " Eckart, XXVIII (1959), 83-6.

1598. Perlitt, Lothar. "Verborgener u. offenbarer Gott. G. Benn vor d. Gottesfrage, " Die Kunst im Schatten d. Gottes, ed. R. Grimm & W. -D. Marsch. Gött: 1962, pp. 112-42.

1599. Pesch, Ludwig. Die romant. Rebellion in der mod. Lit. u. Kunst. München: 1962. (Incl. Benn.)

1600. Pfanner, Helmut F. " 'Valse triste.' Ein Versuch G. Benns z. Uberwindung d. Nihilismus, " Dt. unterr., XXI, 2 (1969), 28-41.

1601. Raabe, Paul & Max Niedermayer, eds. G. Benn. Den Traum alleine tragen: Neue Texte, Briefe, Dokumente. Wiesb: 1966.

1602. Requadt, Paul. "G. Benn u. d. 'südliche Wort, ' " Die Bildersprache der dt. Italiendichtg von Goethe bis Benn. Bern: 1962, pp. 282-302. (Also in: Neophil., XLVI (1962), 50-66.)

1603. Rey, William H. "G. Benns Abschiedsgedicht: Hintergrund u. Struktur, " Wirk. Wort, XX (1970), 161-83.

1604. Römer, Ruth. "Benns Auffass. von der Sprache, " Muttersprache, LXXII (1962), 107-12(13).

1605. Rossek, Detlev. Tod, Verfall u. das Schöpferische bei G. Benn. (Diss.) Münster: 1969.

1606. Rothmann, Kurt K. "Zu G. Benns Drogenlyrik. Interpr. d. Gedichte 'Betäub. u. Entwurzelungen, ' " Mod. Lang. Notes, LXXXII (1967), 454-61.

1607. Rudolph, G. "G. Benn: Ein Nekrolog, " Dt. Univ. Ztg., XI (1956), nos. 13-14, 24-5.

1608. Runge, E. A. "G. Benns 'Nur zwei Dinge, ' " Monatshefte, 49 (1957), 161-78.

1609. Rychner, Max. "G. Benn: Züge s. dichter. Welt, "

Merkur, III (1949), 781-93; 872-90. (Also in:
N. Schweiz. Rds., N. F., XVII (1949/50), 148-
80.)

1610. Schaefer, O. "Der Künstler u. d. Olive," (G. Benn)
Wort u. Wahrh., VI (1951), 636-8.

1611. Schneider, Jean-Claude. "G. Benn, essayiste,"
Nouvelle Revue Française, XIV, 157 (1966), 115-
18.

1612. Schonauer, Franz. "War G. Benn ein Scharlatan?"
Augenblick, III, 2 (1958), 45-52.

1613. Schümann, K. G. Benn. Emsdetten: 1957.

1614. Schwedhelm, K. "Das metaphys. Abenteuer d. Poesie. Der Weg d. Dichters G. Benn," Dt. Rds.,
LXXVII (1951), 637-47.

1615. Schwerte, H. "G. Benn," Denker u. Deuter im
heutig. Europa, ed. H. Schwerte & W. Spengler.
2 Bde. Oldenburg/Hamburg: 1954, I, pp. 125-9.

1616. Seidler, Ingo. "Statische Montage: Zur poet. Technik im Spätwerk G. Benns," Monatshefte, LII
(1960), 321-30.

1617. Seyppel, J. H. "A renaiss. of German Poetry: G.
Benn," Mod. Lang. Forum, XXXIX (1954), 115-
25.

1618. _____. "Stilanalyse von G. Benns früher Prosa,"
Langue et Litt.: Actes du VIIIe Congrès de la
Fed. Intern'l des Langues et Litt. Mod. (Bibliot.
de la Fac. de Philos. et Lettres de l'Univ. de
Liège, fasc. CLXI.) Paris: 1961, p. 299.

1619. Snodgrass, W. D. "G. Benn: The Dissolution of
Matter," Hudson Review, XIV (1961), 118-26.
(Review article.)

1620. Sorensen, Nele Poul. Mein Vater G. Benn. Wiesb.:
1960.

1621. Steinhagen, Harald. Die Statischen Gedichte von G.
Benn. Die Vollendg s. express. Lyrik. Stutt:
1969.

1622. Tietgens, H. "G. Benn," Welt u. Wort, VI (1951),
3-5.

1623. _____. "Die Benn-izitis," Literatur (Stutt), no. 7
(1952), 3.

1624. Townson, M. R. "The Montage-Technique in G.
Benn's Lyric," Orbis Litterarum, XXI (1966),
154-80.

1625. Uhlig, H. "G. Benn," Expressionismus. Gestalten
e. lit. Bewegung, ed. H. Friedemann & O.
Mann. Heidelberg: 1956, pp. 168-81; 352-3.

1626. _____. G. Benn. Berlin: 1961.

1627. Vietta, E. "Auseinandersetzung mit Benn, " Lit.
       Echo, XXXVII, 2 (Nov. 1934), 70-3.
1628. Wallmann, Jürgen P. G. Benn. Mühlacker: 1965.
1629. _____, ed. Après aprèslude. Gedichte auf G.
       Benn. Zürich: 1967.
1630. Weinhaus, Wolf. Die Stimme hinter d. Vorhang.
       Stutt: 1967.
1631. Wellershoff, Dieter. Untersuch. über Weltanschg u.
       Sprachstil G. Benns. (Diss.) Bonn: 1952.
1632. _____. G. Benn, Phänotyp dieser Stunde. E.
       Studie über d. Problemgehalt s. Werkes. Köln/
       Berlin; 1958. (Later ed. Frankf. M/Berlin:
       1964.)
1633. _____. "G. Benn--Realitätszerfall u. Artistik, "
       Universitas, XVI (1961), 605-18.
1634. _____. "Fieberkurve d. dt. Geistes. Uber G.
       Benns Verhältnis z. Zeitgeschichte, " Die Kunst
       im Schatten d. Gottes, ed. R. Grimm & W. -D.
       Marsch. Gött: 1962, pp. 11-39.
1635. Wessels, P. B. "Sprachzertrümmerung u. Sprach-
       schöpfung in der Lyrik G. Benns, " Ztschr. f. dt.
       Philologie, LXXXVII, 3 (1968), 457-69.
1636. Widmaier, G. "Ein ästhet. Irrtum, " (Benns 'Artis-
       tik' als 'neue Transzendenz') Literatur (Stuttgart),
       no. 6 (1952), 3.
1637. Wildbolz, Rudolf. "Geschichte u. Lyrik bei G.
       Benn, " Festgabe Hans v. Greyerz. Bern: 1967,
       pp. 817-33.
1638. Wodtke, Frdr. Wilh. "Die Antike im Werk G.
       Benns, " Orbis Litt., XVI (1961), 129-238. (Book
       form--Wiesb: 1963.)
1639. _____. G. Benn. Stutt: 1962. (SM, 26) (2nd
       rev. ed., 1970.)
1640. _____. "G. Benn, " Expressionismus als Lit.:
       Ges. Studien, ed. W. Rothe. Bern: 1969,
       pp. 309-32.
1641. Wood, Frank. "G. Benn's 'Attic Triptych, ' " Ger-
       manic Review, XXXVI (1961), 298-307.
1642. Zimmermann, W. "G. Benn: 'Gehirne, ' " Dt.
       Prosa-dichtgn d. Gegenwart. Interpr. für Lehrende
       u. Lernende. 3 Bde. Düsseldorf: 1961, pp. 54-
       71. (1966 ed., I, pp. 228-43.)

BONNEFOY

1643.   Albert, Walter. "Y. B. and the Archit. of Poetry, "
        Mod. Lang. Notes, LXXXII, 5 (1967), 590-603.
1644.   _____ . "B'--'Un Rêve fait à Mantoue, ' " French
        Review, XLII (1968/9), 629-30. [Review.]
1645.   Alyn, Marc. "Y. B. près de l'accord parfait, "
        Figaro Litt., XX, 991 (15-21 avril 1965), 6.
1646.   Anon. "A Y. B. 'la Nouvelle Vague, ' " Figaro Litt.,
        XIV, 713 (19 déc. 1959), 5(?).
1647.   _____ . "Le Prix de la Nouvelle Vague à B', "
        Mercure, CCCXXXVIII (1960), 171-2.
1648.   _____ . "Transpose or translate?" Yale French
        Studies, no. 33 (1964), 120-6. (On B's transl.
        of 'Hamlet. ')
1649.   _____ . "Belgian 'Hamlet' seen in a distorting
        mirror, " N. Y. Times Book Review, LVI, 248 (Feb.
        17, 1965), p. 16. (A. M. Julien's produc. of Y. B's
        transl. at the Belgian Nat'l Theatre.)
1650.   _____ . "Oeuvres en cours, " Quinzaine Litt., no.
        14 (15-31 oct. 1966), 7.
1651.   _____ . "Miró images, " Times Lit. Suppl., no.
        3, 415 (Aug. 10, 1967), 720.
1652.   _____ . "Anglophil, " Times Lit. Suppl., no. 3,
        422 (Sept. 28, 1967), 906. (On B's 'Un Rêve....)
1653.   _____ . "Juliette quatorze ans?" Les Lettres
        Françaises, no. 1251 (2-8 Oct. 1968), 11.
1654.   _____ . "France: Y. Bonnefoy, " Poetry Intern'l
        70, no. 7 (June 1970), 30. (Incl. two transl.
        from 'Pierre Ecrite' by A. Rudolf.)
1655.   Arndt, Béatrice. La Quête Poétique d'Yves Bonne-
        foy. Zürich: 1970. (Orig. (diss.) Zürich:
        1970.)
1656.   Attal, Jean-Pierre. "La Quête d'Y. B., " Critique,
        XVI année, t. XXI, 217 (juin 1965), 535-40.
        ('Pierre Ecrite') (Also in: L'Image Métaphys.
        et autres Essais. Paris: 1969, pp. 209-16.)
1657.   Bersani, Jacques, et al. La Litt. en France Depuis
        1945. Paris: 1970.
1658.   Bigongiari, Piero. "La metamorfosi di Bonnefoy, "
        Poesia Francese del Novecento. Firenze: 1968,
        pp. 235-52.
1659.   Blanchot, Maurice. "Le grand refus, " Nouv. Rev.
        Française, VII (1959), 678-89. (On B's 'L'Im-
        probable. ')

1660. _____. "Comment découvrir l'obscur, " Nouv.
Rev. Française, XIV (1959), 867-89. (On B's
'L'Improbable.') (Variant listing: Nouv. Nouv.
Rev. Française, VII, 83 (nov. 1959), 867-79.)

1661. Boase, Alan M. "Crit. français, crit. anglais; ce
qui les divise. Réponse à Y.B., " Cah. de
l'Assoc. Intern'l des Etudes Françaises, XVI
(mars 1964), 157-65; 290-2.

1662. Bondy, François. "Intern'l Ztschriftenschau: Sprache
des Schweigens aus Polen, " Die Welt der Lit.,
II, 2 (21 Jan. 1965), 28.

1663. _____. "Die Dichtg gehört nicht zu den Kunsten.
Vergessene Dimens. der französ. Sprache, " Die
Welt der Lit., III, 16 (4 Aug. 1966), 3.

1664. Bonnefoy, Yves. "Critics, English and French, and
the Distance Betw. Them, " Encounter, XI, 1 (July
1958), 39-45.

1665. _____. "La critique anglo-saxonne et la critique
française, " Preuves, no. 95 (janv. 1959), 68-73.

1666. _____. "L'acte et le lieu de la poésie, "
L'Improbable. Paris: 1959, pp. 147-85. (Also
in: Les Lettres Nouvelles, VII, n.s., 1 (4 mars
1959), 21-7; 2 (11 mars 1959), 37-47.)

1667. _____. "Notice sur Valéry, " L'Improbable.
Paris: 1959, pp. 147-85.

1668. _____. "La décision de Rimbaud, " Preuves, no.
107 (janv. 1960), 3-16.

1669. _____, et al. "Poets on Poetry: II, " X, A Quarterly Review, I (1960), 230-41.

1670. _____. "Une Saison en Enfer, " Mercure de
France, CCCXL, 1171 (mars 1961), 385-412.

1671. _____ & Fr. Kemp. "Der Dichter in seiner Zeit,"
Der Schriftsteller u. seine Zeit.
Otzenhausen: 1963, pp. 46-55.

1672. _____. "The Feeling of Transcendency, " (Surrealism) Yale French Studies, no. 31 (1964), 135-
7. (autobiogr.)

1673. _____. "Sept Feux, " L'Ephémère, no. 2 (avril
1967), 69-77 (autobiogr.).

1674. _____. Selected Poems, trans. (with a note on
the author) Anthony Rudolf. London: 1968.
(Cape Ed., 24.) (Bibliogr., pp. 125-6.)

1675. Borel, Jacques. "D'une expérience de l'impuissance,"
Cah. du Sud, LVIII, 380 (nov.-déc. 1964), 270-
87.

1676. Bosquet, Alain. "Y.B., " Rev. de Paris, LXV, 10
(oct. 1958), 163-4. (Review of 'Hier régnant

désert.')
1677. _____ & Pierre Seghers, eds. Les Poèmes de
l'Année 1959. Paris: 1959.
1678. _____. "B' ou la fuite devant le signifiant,"
Verbe et Vertige. Paris: 1961, pp. 165-73.
1679. _____. "L'impressionnisme dans l'essai: Y.B.,
critique," Le Monde des Livres, no. 7020 (9
août 1967), I-II. (On 'Un Rêve....')
1680. Boyars, Arthur & P. Lyon, eds. Intern'l Lit. Annual, no. 3. London: 1961. (Incl.: Jean
Fanchette, "The Situation in French Poetry,
1960," pp. 154-66.)
1681. Bruch, J.-L. "Approches de la poésie," Chantiers,
XXIV, 4 (févr. 1960), 11-13.
1682. Chappuis, Pierre. "'Un Rêve fait à Mantoue,'"
Nouv. Rev. Française, XXX (1967), 697-9.
1683. Charpentreau, Jacques. "Poésie du temps," Signes
du Temps, no. 1 (janv. 1960), 29-32.
1684. Chavardès, Maurice. "Poésie et solitude," Signes
du Temps, no. 6 (juin 1961), 32-3.
1685. Clancier, G.-E. "'Hier régnant désert,'" Mercure,
CCCXXXIV (1958), 293-8.
1686. Coe, Richard N. "Coming after the gods," Stand,
V, 4 (1962), 48-51. On New French Writing,
ed. G. Borchardt.
1687. Deloffre, Fréderic. "Versific. trad. et versific.
libérée d'après un recueil d'Y.B.," Le Vers
Français au XXe Siecle: Colloque org. par le
Centre de Philol. et de Litt. Romanes de l'Univ.
de Strasbourg (du 3 mai au 6 mai 1966), ed. M.
Parent. Paris: 1967, pp. 43-64.
1688. Diéguez, Manuel de. "Y.B. et la crit. du style,"
Esprit, no. 12 (déc. 1960), 2120-8.
1689. Duits, Charles. "L'énigme poétique de Bonnefoy,"
Critique, 11e année, t. XIV, 137 (oct. 1958),
832-7.
1690. Essays by var. hands. "Postwar French Poets,"
Poetry, LXXX, 6 (Sept. 1952), 311-71. (Foreword, transl., biogr. notes by W. Fowlie.)
1691. Fowlie, Wallace. "Letter from the Midi," Poetry,
C, 4 (July 1962), 258-65.
1692. Gardair, Jean-Michel. "La poétique ininterrompue
de P. Bigongiari," Critique, no. 263 (Avril 1969),
304-11 (review).
1693. Gavronsky, Serge, comp. & transl. Poems and
Texts: An anth. of French Poems, Transl.,
and Interviews. New York: 1969.

1694.   Glissant, Edouard. "Note sur B' et le chemin de la
        vérité, " Lettres Nouvelles, VI, 65 (nov. 1958),
        583-7.
1695.   ____ . L'Intention Poétique. Paris: 1969.
1696.   Goffin, Marie-Louise. " 'Du mouvement et de l'im-
        mobilité de Douve,' " Rev. de l'Univ. de
        Bruxelles, IX (1956/7), 403-11.
1697.   Grandpré, Pierre de. "Le repatriement de la poésie,"
        Liberté, VI, 4 (juill-août 1964), 306-14.
1698.   Gros, Léon-Gabriel. "Pactes avec la mort, " Cah.
        du Sud, no. 322 (mars 1954), 471-6.
1699.   ____ . "Stylisation et Invention, " Cah. du Sud,
        XLVII, 348 (nov. 1958), 264-70. ('Pierre Gar-
        nier.')
1700.   Guibert, Armand. "Poètes et poésie, " Two Cities,
        no. 1 (15 avril 1959), 74-6; no. 4 (15 mai 1960),
        87-90.
1701.   ____ . "Lettre de Paris, " Colóquio, no. 3
        (maio 1959), 46-8; no. 8 (abril 1960), 47-8.
1702.   Hamburger, Michael. The Truth of Poetry. Ten-
        sions in Mod. Poetry from Baudelaire to the
        1960's. London: 1969.
1703.   Hartley, Anthony. "Les contemporains, " Chicago
        Tribune Book World, III, 43 (Oct. 26, 1969), p.
        8. (Review of Gavronsky's anthology.)
1704.   Henriot, Emile. "Essai d'explic. d'un poète: Y.B., "
        Le Monde, (2 juill. 1958), 8-9. (Review of
        'Hier régnant désert.')
1705.   ____ . "Rêverie, mémoire, temps, poésie, "
        Le Monde, (3 févr. 1960), 8-9.
1706.   Hubert, Renée R. " 'Pierre Ecrite,' " French Re-
        view, XL (1966/7), 174-5.
1707.   Jaccottet, Philippe. "Bonnefoy, " Nouv. Rev. Fran-
        çaise, VI, 6e année, no. 68 (août 1958), 296-
        300.
1708.   ____ . "Vers le 'vrai lieu,' " L'Entretien des
        Muses. Paris: 1968, pp. 251-7.
1709.   Jouffroy, Alain. La Fin des Alternances. Paris:
        1970.
1710.   Kanters, Robert. "B' et la présence au monde, "
        Figaro Litt., XXII, 1111 (31 juill. -6 août 1967),
        17-18.
1711.   Karaulac, Miroslav. "Le jardin essentiel. Notes
        sur B'," Bull. des jeunes romanistes, I (juin
        1960), 20-1.
1712.   Kemp, Friedhelm. "Das Übersetzen als lit. Gattung,"
        Sprache im Techn. Zeitalter, XXI (Jan. -März

1967), 45-58.

1713. Lacôte, René. "Bonnefoy, " Lettres Françaises, (4 mars 1965), 2.

1714. _____. "Notes, " Les Lettres Françaises, no. 1236 (12-18 Juin 1968), 8.

1715. Lawler, James R. "New Poetry in France, " Meanjin, XXII, 3 (no. 64?) (1963), 292-7.

1716. de Magny, O. "Bonnefoy, " Ecrivains d'Aujourd'hui. Paris: 1960, pp. 127-36.

1717. Marissel, André. "Poésies de Bonnefoy, " Poètes Vivants. Essai. Paris: 1969, pp. 37-44. (Coll. "iô. ")

1718. Maurin, M. "On B's Poetry, " Yale French Studies, XXI (Spring-Summer 1958), 16-22.

1719. Mora, Edith. "Poésie, poète, poème, " Nouvelles Litt., XLVI, 2120 (18 avril 1968), 5.

1720. Noulet, Emilie. "Chronique de la poésie, " Synthèses, XV, 179 (avril 1961), 262-74.

1721. _____. "Bonnefoy, Y.: 'Du Mouvement et de l'Immobilité de Douve, ' " Alphabet Critique, 1924-'64. T.I. Bruxelles: 1964, pp. 157-9. (Univ. Libre de Brux. Travaux de la Fac. de Philos. et Lettres, XXVI.) (Extrait de Synthèses (janv. 1955).)

1722. _____. "Bonnefoy, Y.: 'L'Improbable, ' " Alphabet Critique, 1924-'64. T.I. Bruxelles: 1964, pp. 163-9. (Extrait de Synthèses (avril 1961).)

1723. _____. "Bonnefoy, Y.: 'Hier régnant désert, ' " Alphabet Critique, 1924-'64. T.I. Bruxelles: 1964, pp. 160-2. (Extrait de Synthèses (sept. 1960).)

1724. Paris, Jean. "The New French Generation, " American Society Legion of Honor Magazine, XXXI, 1 (1960), 45-51.

1725. Picon, Gaëtan. "Les formes de l'esprit: L'expérience d'écrire, " Le Monde, no. 7216 (26 mars 1968), 11.

1726. Piroué, Georges. "B' ou l'acte de dégager la présence dans l'absence, " Mercure, CCCXXXIII (1958), 365-8.

1727. Pons, Christian. "Transposition et trad. A propos du 'Hamlet' d'Y.B., " Shakespeare en France, 1564-1964. Paris: 1964, pp. 536-48.

1728. Reda, Jacques. "B', Y.: 'Pierre Ecrite, ' " Cah. du Sud, LX, 383/4 (août-sept.-oct. 1965), 172-3.

1729. Richard, J.-P. "Y. B., entre le Nombre et la Nuit, " Critique, no. 168 (mai 1961), 387-411.

(Incl. 'Du mouvement ...'; 'Hier régnant ...';
'L'Improbable.')

1730.   _____. "Bonnefoy," Onze Etudes sur la Poésie
Moderne. Paris: 1964, pp. 207-32.

1731. Ronse, Henri. "Les parleurs obscurs," Lettres
Françaises, 1198 (7 sept.-13 sept. 1967), 15.
('L'Improbable' and 'Un Rêve').

1732. Roudaut, Jean. "Le Litt. de la Poésie," Critique,
XXIV, 21e année, no. 254 (juill. 1968), 635-47.
('Un Rêve....')

1733. Saillet, M. " 'Du mouvement...,' " Sur la Route de
Narcisse. Paris: 1958, pp. 187-97. (Déjà
publ. en '53, Lettres Nouvelles, no. 9 (nov.
1953), 1166-72.)

1734. Saint-Aubyn, F. C. "Y.B.: First Existentialist
Poet," Chicago Review, XVII, 1 (1964), 118-29.

1735. Sellin, Eric. "An alternative of despair in postwar
French poetry," College Lang. Assoc. Journal,
X, 4 (June 1967), 341-8.

1736. Tilliette, Xavier. "Poésie ininterrompue," Etudes,
CCCV, 5 (mai 1960), 222-32.

1737. Todd, Oliver. "Paris Letter," Hudson Review, XII,
4 (Winter 1959/60), 586-92.

1738. Trottier, P. "B' ou la poésie n'est pas un art,"
Liberté, II (1960), 118-24.

1739. Varga, A. Kibédi. "Situation de la poésie française
d'aujourd'-hui," Neophilologus, XLIX, 1 (1965),
11-24.

1740. Wevill, David. "Death's dream kingdom," Delos, IV
(1970), 235-41. (Review article.)

BRENNAN

1741. Bavington, Anne. "The Darkness of B's 'Lilith,' "
Meanjin, XXIII (1964), 63-9.

1742. Brennan, Christopher J. Sel. Poems, introd. A. R.
Chisholm. Sydney/San Francisco: 1966.

1743. Chaplin, Harry F. A B Collection: An Annot.
Catalogue of 1st edns., inscribed copies, letters,
ms. and assoc. items. Sydney: 1966. (Stud.
in Austral. Bibliog., 15.)

1744. Chisholm, A. R. "Le symbolisme français en Australie: Mallarmé et B'," Rev. Litt. Comparée,

XVIII (avril 1938).

1745. _____. "B' and Mallarmé, " Southerly, XXI, 4 (1961), 2-11; XXII, 1 (1962), 23-35.

1746. _____. "B', the sea, and the seasons: notes on 'Towards the Source, ' " Meanjin, XXV (1966), 192-5.

1747. _____. "C. B. and the idea of Eden, " Meanjin, XXVI (1967), 153-60.

1748. _____. "C. B., poet and scholar: a centenary assessment, " Meanjin, XXIX (1970), 277-80.

1749. Denat, Antoine. "C. B.: comparatiste australien, " Rev. Litt. Comparée, XXXVIII (1964), 431-9.

1750. French, A. L. "The verse of C. J. B., " Southerly (Sydney), XXIV (1964), 6-19.

1751. Kermode, Frank. "The European view of C. B., " Austral. Letters, III, 3 (1961), 57-63.

1752. Kirsop, Wallace. "B.: critic and scholar, " Southerly, XXIII (1963), 203-10.

1753. _____. " 'The greatest renewal, the greatest revelation': B's commentary on Mallarmé, " Meanjin, XXIX (1970), 303-11.

1754. Macainsh, Noel. "C. B. and Die Romantik, " Southerly, XXIII (1963), 150-63.

1755. McAuley, James. C. Brennan. Melbourne: 1963. (Austral. Writers and Their Work.)

1756. _____. "The erotic theme in B, ' " Quadrant, LVI (1968), 8-15.

1757. Pennington, Richard. C. Brennan. Sydney: 1970.

1758. Rhodes, H. Winston. "C. B., " Landfall, XVIII (1964), 338-48.

1759. Schulz, Joachim. "C. J. B., " Welt und Wort, XVI (1961), 6-7.

1760. Stewart, Annette. "C. B.: the disunity of 'Poems 1913, ' " Meanjin, XXIX (1970), 281-302.

1761. Sturm, T. L. "The social context of B's thought, " Southerly, XXVIII (1968), 250-71.

1762. Wilkes, G. A. "The interpr. of 'The Burden of Tyre, ' " Meanjin, XIX (1960), 71-7.

1763. _____. "B's coll. verse, " Meanjin, XIX (1960), 367-79.

1764. _____. "The 'Wisdom' sequence in B's poems, " Journ. Australasian Univ. Lang. & Lit. Assoc., no. 14 (1960), 47-51.

1765. _____. "The art of B's 'Towards the Source, ' " Southerly, XXI, 2 (1961), 28-41.

1766. _____. "B's coll. prose, " Meanjin, XXII (1963), 80-4.

1767. _____. "The uncoll. verse of C. J. B.," Southerly,
        XXIII (1963), 164-202.

DARIO

1768. Aguado-Andreut, Salvador. "La luz en el mundo
        poético de R. Darío," Saggi e Ricerche in Mem-
        oria di Ettore Li Gotti, Centro di studi filol. e
        linguis. siciliani, Boll. 6. Palermo: 1962, I,
        pp. 36-58.
1769. _____. Por el Mundo Poético de R. Darío.
        Guatemala: 1966. (Bibliog., pp. 277-90.)
        (Edit. Univ., publ. 54.)
1770. Allen, David H., Jr. "R. Darío frente a la creci-
        ente infl. de los Estados Unidos," Rev. Ibero-
        Amer., XXXIII (1967), 387-93.
1771. Alonso, Amado. R. Darío y los Escritores Es-
        pañoles de su Tiempo. Madrid: 1967.
1772. Alvaredo Sánchez, José. "R. Darío: Materia y
        quintaesencia," Letras, LXXVI/VII (1966), 69-78.
1773. Ancona Ponce, Mario. R. Darío y América. Mérida,
        Yucatan, México: 1968.
1774. Anderson Imbert, Enrique. La Orig. de R. Darío.
        Buenos Aires: 1967.
1775. Argüello, Santiago. "R. Darío: la encarnación del
        modernismo," Modernismo y Modernistas, 2 vols.
        Guatemala: 1935, II.
1776. Avilés Ramírez, Eduardo. "Defensa y explic. de R.
        Darío," Cuad. del Congr. por la Libertad de la
        Cultura, no. 78 (1963), 48-50.
1777. Avrett, Robert. "Music and melodic effects in
        'Sinfonía en gris mayor,'" Romance Notes (Univ.
        N. Carol.), I, 1 (1959), 30-2.
1778. Ballew, Hal L. "R. Darío's Lit. Personality,"
        South Cen. Bull., XXVII, 4 (1967), 58-63.
1779. Balseiro, José A. Seis Estudios sobre R. Darío.
        Madrid: 1967.
1780. Bellini, Giuseppe. "R. Darío e Italia," Rev. Ibero-
        Amer., XXXIII (1967), 367-86.
1781. Berretini, Célia. "R. Darío no Brasil," O Estado
        de São Paulo, supl. lit., VI (Julio 1968), 1.
1782. Cabezas, Juan A. R. Darío: Un Poeta y una Vida.
        Madrid: 1944. (Bibliogr., pp. 295-6.) (Coll.
        Lyke.)

Darío 123

1783. Campos, Mário Mendes. R. Darío e o Modernismo
Hisp. americano. Belo Horizonte: 1967.
1784. Cansinos-Asséns, Rafael. Poetas y Prosistas del
Novecientos. Madrid: 1919.
1785. Capdevila, Arturo. R. Darío, "un bardo rei."
Buenos Aires: 1946. (Col. Austral, 607.)
1786. Cardwell, Richard A. "Darío and 'el arte puro':
the enigma of life and the beguilement of art, "
Bull. Hisp. Studies, XLVII (1970), 37-51.
1787. Carilla, Emilio. Una Etapa Decisiva de Darío: R.
Darío en la Argentina. Madrid: 1967. (Biblioteca Románica Hispanica. Estudios y Ensayos,
99.)
1788. _____. "R. Darío y la revista 'Mundial Magazine, ' " Ibero, 1 (1969), 81-8.
1789. Carlos, Alberto J. "La cruz en el 'Responso a
Verlaine, ' " Hispania, XLVIII (1965), 226-9.
1790. Carrera Andrade, Jorge. Interpr. de R. Darío.
Managua: 1964.
1791. Carrión, Benjamin, et al. R. Darío y Ecuador.
Quito: 1968.
1792. Carter, Boyd G. "Clemente Palma en 'Prisma':
sobre Darío y el modernismo, " Rev. Iberoamer.,
XXXV (1969), 473-90.
1793. Cassou, Jean. Panorame de la Lit. Espagnole.
Paris: 1929.
1794. Cernuda, Luis. "Experimento en R. Darío, " Papeles
de Son Armadans (Mallorca), XVIII (1960), 123-
37.
1795. Cestero, Tulio. R. Darío: El Hombre y el Poeta.
La Habana: 1916.
1796. Contreras, Francisco. Les Ecrivains Contemp. de
l'Amérique Espagnole. Paris: 1920.
1797. _____. R. Darío: Su Vida y su Obra. Barcelona: 1930.
1798. Costanzo, Luigi. "Il mondo di R. Darío, " Alla
Botega (Brianza), VI, 3 (1968), 14-16.
1799. Darroch, Ann B. "R. Darío's 'Sinfonia en gris
mayor': a new interpr., " Hispania, LIII (1970),
46-52.
1800. Delgado, Washington. "Situación social de la poesía
de R. Darío, " Letras, LXXVI/VII (1966), 44-59.
1801. Del Greco, Arnold A. Repertorio Bibliogr. del
Mundo de R. Darío. N. Y.: 1969.
1802. De Ory, Eduardo. R. Darío. Cádiz: 1918.
1803. De Tommaso, Vincenzo. "R. Darío e il rinnova-
mento della poesía spagnola, " Carovana, XIV

(1964), 91-4.

1804. De Torre, Guillermo. Lit. Europeas de Vanguardia. Madrid: 1925.

1805. Díaz Arrieta, Hernán. "El sentimiento relig. en la obra de R. Darío," Mapocho, XVI (1968), 5-20.

1806. Díaz-Plaja, Guillermo. R. Darío: la Vida, la Obra.... Barcelona: 1930.

1807. Doyle, Henry G. A Bibliography of R. Darío (1867-1916). Cambridge, Mass.: 1935.

1808. Durán, Manuel. "Trad. y orig. en R. Darío," Insula, XXII (Julio-Augusto 1967), 3, 27.

1809. Durand, René L. "R. Darío et les lettres françaises," Rev. Interamer. de Bibliogr., XVII (1967), 157-64.

1810. Ellison, Fred P. "R. Darío and Brazil," Hispania, XLVII (1964), 24-35.

1811. Enríquez Ureña, Max. Rodó y R. Darío. Habana: 1918.

1812. Esquenazi-Mayo, Roberto. "El interamericanismo de Darío," Insula, XXII (Julio-Augusto 1967), 10.

1813. Essays by var. hands. R. Darío, Periodista. Homenaje del Gobierno de Nicaragua en el XLVIII Aniv. de la Muerte de R. Darío. Managua: 1964.

1814. _____. Rev. Nac. de Cultura (Caracas), XXVIII, 178 (1966), (special issue).

1815. _____. Asomante, XXIII, 1 (1967), 7-70; 2, 7-76, (special issues).

1816. _____. Cuad. Hisp. amer., LXXI (1967), 247-637, (special issue).

1817. _____. Papeles de Son Armadans (Mallorca), XLVI (1967), 115-320. (Special issue.)

1818. _____. "Homenaje a R. Darío," Torre, LV/VI (1967), 15-495. (Esp. Federico de Onís, "Bibliogr. de R. Darío," pp. 461-95.)

1819. _____. Darío. Santiago: Univ. de Chile, 1968. (Serie Conmemor.) (Includes essays by Luis Oyarzún et al.)

1820. _____. "Homenaje a R. Darío (1867-1967)." XIII Congreso Intern'l de Lit. Iberoamer., ed. Aníbal Sánchez-Reulet. Los Angeles: Univ. Calif., 1970. (Latin Amer. Studies, 16.)

1821. _____. R. Darío Centennial Studies, Dept. Span. & Port., Inst. Latin Am. Studies, Univ. Texas. Austin: 1970. (Edited by Miguel González-Gerth and George de Schade.)

1822. Fiore, Dolores A. R. Darío in Search of Inspiration: Greco-Roman Mythology in His Stories and

Poetry. N. Y.: 1963.

1823. Florit, Eugenio. "The Modernist Prefigurement in the Early Work of R. Darío, " (trans. John Wilcox.) R. Darío Centennial Studies, ed. Miguel González-Gerth and George de Schade. Austin: 1970, pp. 31-47.

1824. García-Abrines, Luis. "Una curiosa aliteración simbolista de R. Darío, " Rev. Hisp. Moderna, XXVIII (1962), 45-8.

1825. García Girón, Edmundo. "La adjetivación modernista en R. Darío, " Nueva Rev. de Filol. Hisp. (Mexico), XIII (1959), 345-51.

1826. García Nieto, José and Comes Francisco-Tomás. Poesía Hispanoamericana: De Terrazas a R. Darío. Madrid: 1964. (Coll. Nuevo Mundo.)

1827. García Prada, Carlos. Letras Hispanoamericanas: Ensayos de Simpatía, 2 vols. Madrid: 1963.

1828. Garciasol, Ramón de. Lección de R. Darío. Madrid: 1961. (Persiles, 17.)

1829. Ghiano, Juan Carlos. R. Darío. Buenos Aires: 1967. (Bibliog., pp. 60-4.) (Enciclopedia Lit., 21.)

1830. González, Manuel P. "La apoteosis de R. Darío, " Atenea, XLIII, 163 (1966), 125-38.

1831. González-Blanco, Andrés. Salvador Rueda y R. Darío. Madrid: 1909.

1832. _____. Rubén Darío. Madrid: 1910.

1833. González Olmedilla, Juan. La Ofrenda de España a R. Darío. Madrid: 1916.

1834. Guerrero, Francisco. "R. Darío y su trayectoria estilística, " Atenea, CXLIII, 292 (1961), 80-6.

1835. Guillermo, Edenia. "Darío y América, " Rev. Interamer. de Bibliogr., XVII (1967), 164-72.

1836. Gullón, Ricardo. "Machado reza por Darío, " Insula, XXII (Julio-Agosto 1967), 3.

1837. Hebblethwaite, Frank P. "Una bibliogr. de R. Darío (1945-1966), " Rev. Interamer. de Bibliogr., XVII (1967), 202-21.

1838. Huezo, Francisco. Ultimos Días de R. Darío. Madrid: 1925.

1839. Landarech, Alfonso M. Estudios Literarios. San Salvador: 1959.

1840. Ledesma, Roberto. Genio y Figura de R. Darío. Buenos Aires: 1964.

1841. Leiva, Raúl. "Cuatro calas desmitificadoras sobre R. Darío, " Univ. de la Habana, CLXXXIV/V (May-June 1967), 141-51.

1842.   Lida, Raimundo.   "Notas al criticismo de Rubén, "
        Rev. Iberoamer., XXXIII (1967), 333-58.
1843.   Lozano, Carlos.   "R. Darío in Spain, " Diss. Abstr.,
        XXIV (1964), 3751/2 (Calif.).
1844.   . R. Darío y el Modernismo en España
        (1888-1920): Ensayo de Bibliogr. Comentada.
        N. Y.: 1968.
1845.   Lugo, José Maria.   El Caballero de la Humana
        Energía: El Pensiamento Oculto en R. Darío.
        Monterrey, México: 1967.
1846.   Lugones, Leopoldo. R. Darío. Buenos Aires: 1919.
1847.   MacDonell, George N.   "R. Darío: poet of the west-
        ern world, " New Mexico Quart., XXXI (1962),
        105-12.
1848.   Mejía Sanchez, Ernesto.   Cuestiones Rubendarianas.
        Madrid: 1970. (Cimas de America.)
1849.   Melian Lafinur, A.   Algunos Poemas de R. Darío.
        Buenos Aires: 1916.
1850.   Neapes, Erwin K.   L'Infl. Française dans l'Oeuvre
        de R. Darío. Paris: 1921.
1851.   Nuñez, Estuardo.   "La imaginería oriental exotista
        en R. Darío, " Letras, LXXVI/VII (1966), 60-8.
1852.   Oliver Belmas, Antonio. Este Otro R. Darío. Bar-
        celona: 1960.
1853.   Ory, Eduardo de. R. Darío. Cádiz: 1918.
1854.   Paz, Octavio.   "El caracol y la sirena: R. Darío, "
        Cuadrivio: Darío, López Verlarde, Pessoa,
        Cernuda. México: 1965, pp. 11-65. (Serie del
        Volador.)
1855.   Pineda, Rafael.   "Darío y América, " Insula, XVI,
        170 (1962), 13.
1856.   Quintian, Andrés R.   "Cultura y lit. españoles en la
        obra de R. Darío, " Diss. Abstr. Intern'l, XXX
        (1970), 4999A (Indiana).
1857.   Reyes Huerte, Alejandro.   R. Darío en su Prosa.
        Managua: 1961.
1858.   Robles, Mireya.   "La desesperanza en R. Darío, "
        Cuad. Amer., CLXIX (1970), 184-93.
1859.   Rodó, J. Enrique.   "R. Darío, " Cinco Ensayos. Ma-
        drid: 1915, pp. 259-314.
1860.   Romero de Valle, Emilia.   "Homenaje a R. Darío en
        San Marcos, " Letras, LXXX/XI (1968), 156-61.
1861.   Rull, Enrique.   "El símbolo de Psique en la poesía
        de R. Darío, " Rev. de Lit., XXVII (1965), 33-
        50.
1862.   Saavedra Molona, Julio.   Los Hexámetros Castellanos
        y en Particular los de R. Darío. Santiago:

Univ. de Chile, 1935.

1863. Salinas, Pedro. La Poesía de R. Darío. Buenos Aires: 1948.

1864. Sequeira, Diego M. R. Darío, Criollo; o, Raíz y Médula de su Creación Poética. Buenos Aires: 1945. (Bibliog., pp. 305-9.)

1865. Silva Castro, Raúl. R. Darío a los Veinte Anos. Madrid: 1956.

1866. Silvestro, A. Letterio. Salvador Quasimodo y Otros Escritos. Messina: 1960.

1867. Skyrme, Raymond. "The meaning and function of music in R. Darío: A Comparative Approach," Diss. Abstr. Intern'l, XXXI (1970), 1812A (Mich.)

1868. Soto Hall, Máximo. Revelaciones Intimas de R. Darío. Buenos Aires: 1925.

1869. Sucre, Guillermo. "Relectura de Darío," Rev. de Occidente, VI (1968), 46-68.

1870. Torre, Guillermo de. "R. Darío (1867-1916)," Rev. de Occidente, VI (1968), 69-75.

1871. Torres Bodet, Jaime. R. Darío: Abismo y Cima. Mexico City: 1966.

1872. Torres Ríoseco, Arturo. R. Darío: Casticismo y Americanismo. Cambridge, Mass./London: 1931.

1873. Trueblood, Alan S. "R. Darío: the sea and the jungle," Comp. Lit. Stud., IV (1967), 425-56.

1874. Turner, John H. "Sobre el uso de los tiempos verbales en R. Darío," Rev. Hisp. Moderna, XXX (1964), 205-14.

1875. Urmeneta, Fermín de. "Sobre estética rubéniana," Rev. de Ideas Estéticas, XXIII (1965), 199-204.

1876. Valente, José A. "Darío o la innovación," Insula, XXII (Julio-Agosto 1967), 5, 27.

1877. Vargas Vila, J. M. R. Darío. Madrid: 1917.

1878. Woodbridge, Hensley C. "R. Darío: a crit. bibliog.," Hispania, LI (1968), 95-110. (Also: L (1967), 982-95--same title.)

1879. Ycaza Tigerino, Julio César. Los Nocturnos de R. Darío y Otros Ensayos. Madrid: 1964. (Coll. Nuevo Mundo.)

ELIOT

1880. Aiken, Conrad. "The poetic dilemma," Dial, LXXXVII, 5 (May 1927), 420-3.

1881. Ames, R. "Decadence in the art of T. S. Eliot, "
       Science and Society, XVI (1952), 193-221.
1882. Anon. On the "Four Quartets" of T. S. Eliot.
       London: 1953.
1883. Ants, Oras. The Crit. Ideas of T. S. Eliot, Acta
       et Commentationes, Univ. Tartuensis, B, Human-
       iora XXVIII, 3. Tartu, Estonia: 1932.
1884. Arrowsmith, William. "The comedy of T. S. Eliot, "
       English Stage Comedy, ed. W. K. Wimsatt, Jr.
       N. Y.: 1955, pp. 148-72.
1885. Ashraf, A. S., ed. T. S. Eliot Through Pakistani
       Eyes. Karachi: Dept. Engl., Univ. Karachi,
       1968.
1886. Barilli, Renato. Poetica e Retorica. Milano: 1969.
1887. Barnhill, Viron L. "Poetic content in the coll.
       poems (1909-1935) of T. S. Eliot: a linguistic
       investig. of poetic context, " Diss. Abstr., XXI
       (1961), 2284 (Mich.).
1888. [no entry]
1889. Beachcroft, T. O. "Mysticism as Criticism, " Sym-
       posium, (April 1931), 208-25.
1890. Bergonzi, Bernard, ed. T. S. Eliot's "Four Quar-
       tets": A Casebook. London: 1969.
1891. Bergsten, Staffan. "Illusive allusions: some reflect.
       on the crit. approach to the poetry of T. S.
       Eliot, " Orbis Litt., XIV (1959), 9-18.
1892. _____. Time and Eternity: A Study in the Struc-
       ture and Symbolism of T. S. Eliot's "Four Quar-
       tets." Stockholm; 1960. (Studia Litt. Upsalien-
       sia, 1.) (Later ed., London: 1961.)
1893. Bischoff, Dietrich. "T. S. Eliot: Die 'Vier Quar-
       tette, ' " Die Sammlung, VIII (1953), 114-31.
1894. Blackmur, R. P. "T. S. Eliot, " Hound and Horn, I,
       (March 1928), 187-213. (On "Waste Land. ")
1895. _____. "T. S. Eliot: II, " Hound and Horn,
       (June 1928), 291-319.
1896. _____. "The Whole Poet, " Poetry, (April 1937),
       48-51.
1897. Blamires, Harry. Word Unheard: A Guide Through
       Eliot's "Four Quartets." London: 1969.
1898. Blisset, W. "The argument of T. S. Eliot's 'Four
       Quartets, ' " Univ. Toronto Quart., XV (1946),
       115-26.
1899. Bodelsen, C. A. T. S. Eliot's "Four Quartets": A
       Commentary. Copenhagen: 1958.
1900. Bohnsack, Fritz. Zeit und Ewigkeit im Spätwerk
       T. S. Eliots. Versuch einer Deutung. (Diss.)

Hamburg: 1951.

1901. Bowra, C. M. "T. S. Eliot, " Aspects de la Litt.
Anglaise (1918-1945). Paris: 1947, pp. 166-87.

1902. _____. The Creative Experiment. London: 1949,
pp. 159-88. (On "Waste Land. ")

1903. Bradbrook, M. C. T. S. Eliot. London: 1950
(Rev. ed. 1955) (Bibliogr. series of suppl. to
British Book News; Writers and Their Work,
No. 8), pp. 44-54.

1904. Bradbury, J. M. " 'Four Quartets': the struc. symbolism, " Sewanee Review, LIX (1951).

1905. Brandabur, Edward. "Eliot and the myth of mute
speech, " Renascence, XXII (1970), 141-50.

1906. Braybrooke, Neville, ed. T. S. Eliot: A Symposium
for His Seventieth Birthday. N. Y. /London: 1958.

1907. _____. "Les écrits de jeunesse de T. S. Eliot:
un aperçu de ses poèmes et contes écrits à l'âge
de 16 ans, " Synthèses (Paris/Bruxelles), n. 232
(Sept. 1965), 321-6.

1908. Brombert, Victor. "T. S. Eliot and the Romantic
heresy, " Yale French Studies, XIII (Spring 1954),
3-6.

1909. Brooks, Cleanth, Jr. " 'The Waste Land': an analysis, " in Rajan (ed.), pp. 7-36.

1910. _____. " 'The Waste Land': Critique of the myth,"
in Unger (ed.), pp. 319-48.

1911. Brooks, Harold F. " 'Four Quartets': the struc. in
relat. to the themes, " in Martin (ed.), pp. 132-
47.

1912. Brotman, D. Bosley. "T. S. Eliot: 'The Music of
Ideas, ' " Univ. Toronto Quart., XVIII (Oct. 1948),
20-9. (On "East Coker" as a musical quartet.)

1913. Brown, Alec. "The lyr. impulse in the poetry of T.
S. Eliot, " Scrutinies, II. London: 1930, pp. 1-
52.

1914. Brown, Leonard. "Our contemp. poetry, " Sewanee
Review, (Jan. -March 1933), 43-63.

1915. Browne, E. Martin. "The poet and the stage, " The
Penguin New Writing (ed. John Lehmann), no. 31
(1947), 81-92.

1916. _____. "The dramatic verse of T. S. Eliot, " in
March and Tambimuttu (eds.), pp. 196-207.

1917. Cahill, Audrey F. T. S. Eliot and the Human Pre-
dicament: A Study in His Poetry. Mystic,
Conn. : 1967.

1918. Calliebe, Gisela. Das Werk T. S. Eliots und die
Trad. der Mystik. (Diss.) Berlin: 1955.

1919. Cattaui, Georges. T. S. Eliot, trans. Claire Pace
        & Jean Stewart. N.Y.: 1968.
1920. Chinol, Elio. "Poesia e trad. nel pensiero crit. di
        T. S. Eliot," Studi in Onore di V. Lugli e D.
        Valeri. Venezia: 1962, pp. 243-60.
1921. Church, Richard. "T. S. Eliot: a search for founda-
        tions," Fortnightly, (Feb. 1941), 163-70.
1922. Churchill, R. C. "The Age of T. S. Eliot," Concise
        Cambridge Hist. English Lit., 2nd ed. Cam-
        bridge: 1961, pp. 944-1030.
1923. Cleophas, M. "Notes on levels of meaning in 'Four
        Quartets,'" Renascence (A Crit. Journ. of
        Letters), II (1950).
1924. Cornwell, E. F. The Still Point. Newark, N.J.:
        1950.
1925. Cronin, Francis C. "T. S. Eliot's theory of lit.
        creation," Diss. Abstr., XXVIII (1967), 1391A
        (Pittsburgh).
1926. Curtius, Ernst R. "T. S. Eliot als Dichter," Neue
        Schweizer Rundschau, XXXII/III (1927), 349-61.
1927. _____. "T. S. Eliot and Germany," in March
        and Tambimuttu (eds.), pp. 119-25.
1928. Dahlberg, Edward and Herbert Read. Truth is More
        Sacred: A Crit. Exchange on Mod. Lit. N.Y.:
        1961.
1929. Daiches, David. Poetry and the Mod. World. Chi-
        cago: 1940, pp. 90-127.
1930. _____. "T. S. Eliot," Yale Review, XXXVIII, 3
        (March 1949), 460-70.
1931. Davie, Donald. "T. S. Eliot: the end of an era,"
        Twentieth Cen., CLIX (1956).
1932. Day, Robert. "'City Man' in 'The Waste Land,'"
        PMLA, LXXX (1965), 285-91.
1933. Desternes, Jean. "T. S. Eliot: Interview par J.
        Desternes," Combat de la Résistance à la Révo-
        lution, VII, 1, 182 (23 Avril 1948).
1934. Dobson, E. J. "'The Hollow Men' and the work of
        T. S. Eliot," Some Recent Develop. in English
        Lit., Sydney Univ. Extension Lectures. Sydney:
        1935, pp. 33-52.
1935. Drew, Elizabeth. T. S. Eliot: The Design of His
        Poetry. N.Y.: 1953 (1949).
1936. Eliot, T. S. "Reflect. on Contemp. Poetry, IV,"
        The Egoist, VI (July 1919), 39.
1937. _____. "Poet and Saint: a review of Baudelaire:
        Prose and Poetry, trans. A. Symons," Dial,
        LXXXII, 5 (May 1927), 424-31.

1938.   . "Baudelaire and the Symbolists: Five Es-
             says, by Peter Quennell: a review, " The Criteri-
             on, IX (Jan. 1930).
1939.   . "The music of poetry, " (W. P. Ker Mem-
             orial Lecture, Glasgow) Partisan Review, IX, 6 (Nov.
             1942).
1940.   . Poetry and Drama. Cambridge, Mass.:
             1951.
1941.   . "The three voices of poetry, " Atlantic
             Monthly, CXCIII, 4 (April 1954), 38-44. (Cf.
             "Die drei Stimmen der Poesie, " Dichter u.
             Dichtung: Essays. Frankf. am Main: 1958,
             pp. 424-48.)
1942.   . On Poetry and Poets. N. Y.: 1961.
             (Repr. "The three voices of poetry. ")
1943.   . To Criticize the Critic, and Other Writ-
             ings. N. Y.: 1965.
1944. Essays by var. hands. "For T. S. Eliot, " The Har-
             vard Advocate, (Dec. 1938) (special issue).
1945.   . "Poetry by T. S. Eliot, " Univ. Chicago
             Round Table, no. 659. (Broadcast Nov. 12,
             1950).
1946.   . "T. S. Eliot (1888-1965), " Sewanee Re-
             view, LXXIV, 1 (Jan. -March 1966) (Memorial
             volume, ed. Allen Tate).
1947. Farrell, William J. " 'The Waste Land' as rhetoric, "
             Renascence, XXII (1970), 127-40.
1948. Fluchère, Henri. "Un théâtre poétique intérieur, "
             Cah. du Sud, no. 359 (1961), 33-44.
1949. Forster, E. M. "T. S. Eliot and his difficulties, "
             Life and Letters, (June 1929), 417-25.
1950.   . "T. S. Eliot, " Abinger Harvest. London:
             1953, pp. 89-96.
1951. Foster, Genevieve W. "The archetypal imagery of
             T. S. Eliot, " PMLA, LX (June 1945), 567-85.
             (Jungian approach).
1952. Frank, Waldo. "The Universe of T. S. Eliot, " In
             the American Jungle. N. Y.: 1937, pp. 220-7.
             (Orig.: Adelphi, V, (Feb. 1933), 321-6.)
1953. Freed, Lewis. T. S. Eliot: Aesthetics and History.
             LaSalle, Ill.: 1962.
1954. Fry, Edith M. "The poetic work of T. S. Eliot, "
             British Annual of Lit., V (1948), 11-12.
1955. Frye, Northrop. T. S. Eliot. Edinburgh/London:
             1963. (Writers and Critics.)
1956. Funato, Hideo. "T. S. Eliot's idea of Time, "
             Rikkyo Review (Tokyo), no. 16 (1955), 19-51.

1957.   Fussell, Paul. "The gestic symbolism of T. S. Eliot," English Lit. Hist., XXII (1955).

1958.   Galinsky, Hans. Sprache u. Sprachkunstwerk in Amerika: Stud. u. Interpr. Heidelberg: 1961.

1959.   Gallup, D. C. A Bibliogr. Checklist of the Writ. of T. S. Eliot, incl. ... Transl. of His Work into Foreign Langs. New Haven: 1947.

1960.   _____. T. S. Eliot: A Bibliography, 2nd rev. ed. London: 1969. (1st ed. N. Y.: 1953.)

1961.   Gamberini, Spartaco. La Poesia di T. S. Eliot. Genova: 1954. (Publ. dell'Inst. Univ. di Magistero.)

1962.   Gardner, Helen. "The recent poetry of T. S. Eliot," New Writing and Daylight, (Summer 1942).

1963.   _____. " 'Four Quartets': a comment., " in Rajan (ed.), pp. 57-77.

1964.   _____. The Art of T. S. Eliot, 3rd rev. ed. London: 1968. (Earlier eds. 1959, 1949.)

1965.   _____. T. S. Eliot and the English Poetic Trad. Nottingham: 1966. (Byron Found. Lecture: 1965.)

1966.   Gary, Franklin. "New Bearings in English Poetry, " Symposium, (Oct. 1932), 521-34.

1967.   George, Arapura G. T. S. Eliot: His Mind and Art, 2nd rev. edn. N. Y.: 1969 (1963) (Lit. Perspec., 1).

1968.   Germer, R. T. S. Eliots "Waste Land. " Die Geschichte s. Wirkg. u. Beurteil. in d. Jahren 1922-'56 unter bes. Berücks. d. Rezep. in England, Amerika, Dtschld u. Frankreich. (diss.) Freiburg i. Br.: 1957.

1969.   _____. T. S. Eliots Anfänge als Lyriker (1905-'15). Heidelberg: 1966. (Beihefte z. Jahrb. f. Amerikastudien, 17.)

1970.   Gil, Kim Jong. "T. S. Eliot's infl. on mod. Korean poetry, " Lit., East & West, XIII (1969), 359-76.

1971.   Greenberg, Clement. "T. S. Eliot: the criticism, the poetry, " The Nation, CLXXI, 24 (Dec. 1950), 531-3.

1972.   Greene, Edward J. H. T. S. Eliot et la France. Paris: 1951. (Bibliogr., pp. 217-42. Incl. Corbière, Perse, Rimbaud.)

1973.   Grudin, Louis. Mr. Eliot Among the Nightingales. London/Paris: 1932.

1974.   Gunter, Bradley. The Merrill Guide to T. S. Eliot. Columbus, Ohio: 1970.

1975. Hall, Donald. "The art of poetry, I. T. S. Eliot
       (interview), " Paris Review, no. 21
       (Spring/Summer 1959), 47-70.

1976. Harding, D. W. "T. S. Eliot, 1925-1935, " Scrutiny,
       V, 2 (Sept. 1936), 171-6.

1977. Hasegawa, Mitsuaki. "Poet's communic. of meaning:
       an approach to T. S. Eliot, " Hiroshima Stud.
       English Lang. & Lit., IX, 1/2 (1963), 66-74.

1978. Haüsermann, Hans W. "T. S. Eliot's Concept. of
       Poetry, " Etudes de Lettres, XVI, 4 (Oct. 1942),
       165-78.

1979. Headings, Philip R. T. S. Eliot. N. Y.:
       1964.

1980. Heller, Erich. "T. S. Eliot: die Trad. u. das
       Moderne, " Gestalt u. Gedanke: Ein Jahrbuch,
       XI (1966), 98-137.

1981. Hewitt, Elizabeth K. "Struc. unity in 'The Waste
       Land, ' " Diss. Abstr. Intern'l, XXX (1969),
       2513A (SUNY, Buffalo).

1982. Hilton, C. "The poetry of T. S. Eliot, " English
       Journal, (Nov. 1931), 749-61.

1983. Hodin, J. P. "T. S. Eliot on the Condition of Poet-
       ry Today: An Interview with T. S. Eliot, "
       Horizon, XII, 68 (August 1945), 83-9.

1984. Hoskot, S. S. T. S. Eliot: his mind and personal-
       ity. (Diss.) Bombay: 1961.

1985. Howarth, Herbert. Notes on Some Figures Behind
       T. S. Eliot. Boston: 1964.

1986. Iser, Wolfgang. "T. S. Eliots 'Four Quartets': eine
       Stiluntersuchung, " Jahrb. für Amerika-studien,
       III (1958), 192-204.

1987. Jones, David E. The Plays of T. S. Eliot. Toronto/
       London: 1960. (Paperback edn. 1965.)

1988. Jones, Genesius. Approach to the Purpose: A Study
       of the Poetry of T. S. Eliot. N. Y.: 1964.

1989. Jury, C. R. T. S. Eliot's "The Waste Land":
       Some Annot. Adelaide: 1932.

1990. Kaul, R. K. "The poetry of T. S. Eliot, " Banasthali
       Patrika, IX, (1967), 10-25.

1991. Kenner, Hugh. "Eliot's Moral Dialectic, " Hudson
       Review, II (Autumn 1949/50?),

1992. _____. The Invisible Poet: T. S. Eliot. N. Y.:
       1959.

1993. _____. "Art in a closed field, " Virginia Quart.
       Rev., XXXVIII (1962), 597-613.

1994. _____, ed. T. S. Eliot: A Coll. of Crit. Essays.
       Englewood Cliffs, N. J.: 1962.

1995. Knoll, Robert E., ed. Storm over "The Waste Land."
       Chicago: 1964.
1996. Knox, George A. "Quest for the Word in Eliot's
       'Four Quartets,' " English Lit. Hist., XVIII
       (1951).
1997. Leavis, F. R. New Bearings in English Poetry.
       London: 1932, pp. 91-132. (On "The Waste
       Land.")
1998. Lehmann, John. "T. S. Eliot talks about himself
       and the drive to create, " (interview) N. Y. Times
       Book Review, LVIII, 48 (Nov. 29, 1953), p. 5,
       44.
1999. Levý, Jiří. "Synthesis of antitheses in the poetry of
       T. S. Eliot, " Essays in Crit., II (1952), 434-43.
2000. _____. "Rhythmical ambiv. in the poetry of T. S.
       Eliot, " Anglia, LXXVII (1959), 54-64.
2001. Lu, Fei-pai. T. S. Eliot: The Dialec. Structure of
       His Theory of Poetry. Chicago/London: 1966.
       (Bibliog., pp. 139-66.)
2002. Lucy, Séan. T. S. Eliot and the Idea of Trad.
       N. Y. /London: 1960.
2003. Macaulay, Rose. "The first impact of 'The Waste
       Land, ' " in Braybrooke (ed.), pp. 29-33.
2004. MacCallum, H. Reed. " 'The Waste Land' after 25
       years, " Here and Now, I (Dec. 1947), 16-24.
2005. Malawsky, Beryl Y. "T. S. Eliot: a checklist
       (1952-'64), " Bull. of Bibliog., XXV (1967), 59-
       61, 69.
2006. March, Richard and M. J. Tambimuttu, eds.
       T. S. Eliot: A Symposium From Conrad Aiken
       and Others. London: 1948; Chicago: 1949.
2007. Margolis, John D. "Towards a new beginning: the
       develop. of T. S. Eliot's thought, 1922-'39, "
       Diss. Abstr. Intern'l, XXX (1969), 1173A/74A
       (Princeton).
2008. _____. T. S. Eliot's Intellect. Development,
       1922-1939. Chicago: 1972.
2009. Martin, Graham, ed. Eliot in Perspective: A Sym-
       posium. London/N. Y. : 1970.
2010. _____. "Language and belief in Eliot's poetry, "
       in Martin (ed.), pp. 112-31.
2011. Martz, Louis L. "The wheel and the point: aspects
       of imag. and theme in Eliot's later poetry, " in
       Unger (ed.), pp. 444-62.
2012. Matthiessen, F. O. "Eliot's Quartets, " Kenyon Re-
       view, V (1943), 161-78.
2013. _____. The Achievement of T. S. Eliot: An Es-

say on the Nature of Poetry, 3rd edn.   London:
1958 (1947, 1935).

2014. Maxwell, D. E. S.   The Poetry of T. S. Eliot.
London: 1952.

2015. _____.   "After 'The Waste Land, ' "   Ibadan Stud.
in English, I (1969), 73-84.

2016. Mayer, John T. , Jr.   "The dramatic mode of T. S.
Eliot's early poetry, "   Diss. Abstr. , XXV (1964),
1918/19 (Fordham).

2017. McGreevy, Thomas.   T. S. Eliot: A Study.   London:
1931.

2018. Melchers, H. J.   T. S. Eliot: das 'Muster' und die
Wirklichkeitsprobleme der Dichtung.   (Diss.)
Köln: 1953.

2019. Melchiori, Giorgio.   The Tightrope Walkers: Studies
of Mannerism in Mod. English Lit.   N. Y. :   1936.

2020. Mesterton, Eric.   "The Waste Land": Some Com-
mentaries.   Chicago: 1943.

2021. Mirsky, D. S.   "T. S. Eliot et la fin de la poésie
bourgeoise, "   Echanges, 5 (Déc. 1931), 44-58.

2022. Montgomery, Marion.   T. S. Eliot: An Essay on the
American Magus.   Athens, Georgia: 1969.

2023. Muir, Edwin.   "The present lang. of poetry, "   London
Mercury, XXXI (1934/5), 34-9.

2024. Nelson, Armour H.   "The critics and 'The Waste
Land, ' 1922-1949, "   English Studies, XXXVI (1955),
1-15.

2025. Nicholson, Norman.   "T. S. Eliot, "   Writers of Today, ed. Denys Val Baker.   London: 1946,
pp. 139-43.

2026. Nimr, Amy.   "Introd. à la poésie de T. S. Eliot, "
Echanges, 4 (mars 1931), 37-57.

2027. O'Connor, Daniel.   T. S. Eliot's "Four Quartets":
A Commentary.   New Delhi/Mystic, Conn. :   1969.

2028. Panaro, Cleonice.   "Il problema della communicazione
nelle poesia di T. S. Eliot, "   Studi Americani
(Roma), XIV (1968), 193-245.

2029. Peacock, Ronald.   The Poet in the Theatre.   London:
1946, pp. 1-20.

2030. Pearce, T. S.   T. S. Eliot.   London: 1967.   (Lit.
in Persp.).

2031. Pearson, Gabriel.   "Eliot: an American use of symbolism, " in Martin (ed.), pp. 83-101.

2032. Peschmann, Hermann.   "The later poetry of T. S.
Eliot, "   English, V (Autumn 1945).

2033. Policardi, Silvio.   La Poesia di T. S. Eliot.   Milano/
Venezia: 1948/9.   (Ediz. Univ.)

2034.   Pound, Ezra. "T. S. Eliot, " Poetry, X (August
        1917), 264-71.
2035.   _____ . "Eliot, " Instigations. N. Y.: 1920.
2036.   _____ . "Prefatio Aut Cimicium Tumulus: Mr.
        Eliot's Solid Merits, " Polite Essays. Norfolk,
        Conn.: 1937, pp. 35-52, 98-105.
2037.   Powell, Dilys. "The poetry of T. S. Eliot, " Life &
        Letters, (Dec. 1931), 386-419.
2038.   Praz, Mario. "T. S. Eliot e il Simbolismo, " Il
        Simbolismo nella Lett. Nord-Americana: Atti del
        Symposium tenuto a Firenze, 27-29 nov. 1964.
        Pubbl. dell'Ist. di Studi Americani, U. degli
        Studi di Firenzi, 1. Firenze: 1965, pp. 1-27.
2039.   Preston, Raymond. "Four Quartets" Rehearsed. A
        Commentary on T. S. Elliot's Cycle of Poems.
        London: 1946.
2040.   _____ . "T. S. Elliot as a contemplative poet, "
        in Braybrooke (ed.), pp. 161-9.
2041.   Quennell, Peter. "Mr. T. S. Eliot, " Life & Letters,
        II, 10 (March 1929), 179-90.
2042.   Rai, Vikramaditya. "The Waste Land": A Crit.
        Study. Varanasi, India: 1965. (Eliot and orien-
        tal philosophy.)
2043.   Raine, Kathleen. "The poet of our time, " in March
        (ed.), pp. 78-81.
2044.   Rajan, B., ed. T. S. Eliot: A Study of His Writ-
        ings by Several Hands, Focus III. London: 1947.
2045.   _____ . "The unity of the quartets, " in Rajan (ed.),
        pp. 78-95.
2046.   Ransom, John Crowe. "T. S. Eliot as Dramatist, "
        Poetry (A Magazine of Verse), LIV, 5 (1939),
        264-71.
2047.   Rauber, D. F. "The notes on 'The Waste Land, ' "
        English Lang. Notes (Univ. Colo.), VII (1970),
        287-94.
2048.   Rayan, Krishna. "Suggestiveness and suggestion, "
        Essays in Crit. (Oxford), XIX (1969), 309-19.
2049.   Read, Herbert. The True Voice of Feeling: Studies
        in English Romantic Poetry. London: 1953,
        pp. 139-50.
2050.   Rees, Thomas R. "The orchestr. of meaning: a
        study of the relat. betw. form and meaning in
        T. S. Eliot's early poetry, (1910-'22), " Diss.
        Abstr., XXVII (1966), 484A/5A (Tulane).
2051.   Revol, Enrique L. "Permanencia de T. S. Eliot, "
        Torre, LXV (1969), 43-52.
2052.   Rhoads, Kenneth W. "The musical element of T. S.

Eliot's 'Four Quartets,' " Diss. Abstr. Intern'l,
XXX (1970), 5454A/55A (Mich. State).

2053. Robbins, Rossel H. The T. S. Eliot Myth. N.Y.:
1951.

2054. Roberts, Michael. "The poetry of T. S. Eliot,"
London Mercury, (May 1936), 38-44.

2055. Rosati, Salvatore. "Verso e ling. poetico nelle
opere dramm. di T. S. Eliot," Galleria, I
(Genn.-Febb. 1953), 21-4.

2056. Rousseaux, André. "Poésie et poétique de T. S.
Eliot," Figaro Litt., V (Mai 1950), 2.

2057. Sansom, Clive. The Poetry of T. S. Eliot. London:
1947.

2058. Schaeder, Grete. "T. S. Eliots 'Vier Quartette,' "
Die Sammlung, V (1950), 153-66.

2059. _____, and Hans Schaeder. Ein Weg zu T. S.
Eliot. Hameln: 1948.

2060. Smidt, Kristian. Poetry and Belief in the Work of
T. S. Eliot, rev. edn. Oslo/London: 1961 (1949).

2061. _____. "Point of view in Eliot's poetry," Orbis
Litt., XIV (1959), 38-53.

2062. Smith, Carol H. T. S. Eliot's Dramatic Theory and
Practice: From "Sweeney Agonistes" to "The
Elder Statesman." Princeton, N.J.: 1963.

2063. Smith, Grover. T. S. Eliot's Poetry and Plays: A
Study in Sources and Meaning, 2nd imprint. Chi-
cago/London: 1958 (1956) ("Notes and References," pp. 303-29).

2064. Soldo, John J. "Knowl. and exper. in the crit. of
T. S. Eliot," Journ. English Lit. Hist., XXXV
(1968), 284-308.

2065. Spencer, Theodore. "The poetry of T. S. Eliot,"
Atlantic Monthly, CLI, 1 (Jan. 1933), 60-8.

2066. Stamm, Rudolf. "Rebell. u. Trad. im Werke T. S.
Eliots," Universitas (Stuttgart), XXII (1967), 725-
42.

2067. Stephenson, E. M. T. S. Eliot and the Lay Reader,
2nd edn. London: 1946.

2068. Strömsdorfer, Ilse. Der Begriff der Zeit bei T. S.
Eliot. (Diss.) München: 1957.

2069. Tate, Allen. "The reading of mod. poetry," Purpose,
(Jan.-March 1938), 31-41.

2070. _____, ed. T. S. Eliot, the Man and His Work:
A Crit. Evaluation by 26 Distinguished Writers.
N.Y.: 1966. (Identical with Sewanee Review
special issue.)

2071. Taupin, René. "The classicism of T. S. Eliot,"

trans. Louis Zukofsky, <u>Symposium,</u> III, 1 (Jan. 1932), 64-82

2072. Thompson, Eric. <u>T. S. Eliot: A (The?) Metaphysical Perspective.</u> Carbondale: 1963. (Crosscurrents-Mod. Critiques.)

2073. Tindall, William Y. "T. S. Eliot in America: the recantation of T. S. Eliot, " <u>Amer. Scholar,</u> XVI, 4 (Autumn 1947), 432-7.

2074. Tordeur, Jean. <u>A La Rencontre de T. S. Eliot, un Classique Vivant.</u> Bruxelles: 1946.

2075. Traversi, Derek. " 'The Waste Land' revisited, " <u>Dublin Review,</u> no. 443 (1948), 106-23.

2076. Turnell, G. M. "Trad. and Mr. T. S. Eliot, " <u>Colosseum,</u> I, 2 (June 1934), 44-54.

2077. Unger, Leonard. <u>The Man in the Name. Essays on the Experience of Poetry.</u> Minneapolis: 1956.

2078. _____, ed. <u>T. S. Eliot: A Sel. Critique.</u> N. Y. / Toronto: 1966 (reissue; earlier edn. 1948).

2079. _____. <u>T. S. Eliot.</u> Minneapolis: 1961. (Univ. Minn. Pamphl. Am. Writers, 8.)

2080. _____. <u>T. S. Eliot: Moments and Patterns.</u> Minneapolis: 1966. (Contains 7 crit. essays.)

2081. Viebrock, Helmut. <u>T. S. Eliot.</u> Kevelaer, Rhld.: 1950. Berckers kleine Volksbibliothek, 29.)

2082. Weber, Alfred. <u>Der Symbolismus T. S. Eliots: Versuch einer neuen Annäherung an mod. Lyrik.</u> (Diss.) Tübingen: 1953.

2083. _____. "Ein Beitrag z. Chronol. u. Genesis der Dichtung T. S. Eliots, " <u>Jahrb. für Amerikastud.</u>, III (1958), 162-91.

2084. Weiss, Klaus. <u>Das Bild des Weges. Ein Schlüssel zum Verständ. des Zeitlichen u. Uberzeitl. bei T. S. Eliot.</u> Bonn: 1965.

2085. Weitz, M. "T. S. Eliot: time as a mode of salvation, " <u>Sewanee Review,</u> LX (1952), 48-64.

2086. Wells, Henry W. <u>New Poets From Old: A Study in Lit. Genetics.</u> N. Y.: 1940.

2087. Weston, Jessie. <u>From Ritual to Romance.</u> Cambridge, England: 1920.

2088. Wheelwright, P. "The 'Burnt Norton' Trilogy, " <u>Chimera,</u> 1 (1942), 7-18.

2089. _____. "Eliot's philos. themes, " in Rajan (ed.), pp. 96-106.

2090. Williamson, George. <u>The Talent of T. S. Eliot.</u> Seattle: 1929. (Univ. Wash. Chapbooks, 32.) (Orig.: <u>Sewanee Review,</u> XX, 3 (July-Sept. 1927), 284-95.)

2091. _____. A Reader's Guide to T. S. Eliot. N. Y.:
       1955 (1953).
2092. Williamson, Hugh R. "T. S. Eliot and his concep.
       of poetry, " Bookman, LXXIX, 474 (March 1931),
       347-50.
2093. _____. The Poetry of T. S. Eliot. London:
       1932/N. Y.: 1933.
2094. Wilson, Edmund. "T. S. Eliot, " Axël's Castle....
       N. Y.: 1931, pp. 93-131.
2095. _____. "T. S. Eliot, " in Unger (ed.), pp. 171-4
       (discusses Eliot's French sources).
2096. Wilson, Frank. Six Essays on the Develop. of T. S.
       Eliot. London: 1948.
2097. Wimsatt, W. K., Jr. "Eliot's Comedy, " Sewanee
       Review, LVIII (Autumn 1950), 666-78.
2098. Winters, Yvor. "T. S. Eliot, or the illusion of re-
       action, " The Anatomy of Nonsense. Norfolk,
       Conn.: 1943, pp. 120-67. (Reprinted in: Unger
       (ed.), pp. 75-113.)
2099. Woodward, Daniel. "Notes on the publ. hist. and
       text of 'The Waste Land, ' " Papers of the Bibli-
       og. Soc. of America, LVIII (1964), 252-69.
2100. Wynn, Dudley. "The integrity of T. S. Eliot, " Univ.
       Denver Publ., Studies in Humanities, No. 1:
       'Writers of Our Years, ' ed. A. M. I. Fiskin.
       Denver: 1950.
2101. Zabel, M. D. "T. S. Eliot in mid-career, " Poetry,
       XXXVI (May 1930), 330-7. (Review article.)

GEORGE

2102. Angelloz, J. -F. "St. George et son cénacle, "
       Mercure de France, CCCXIV (1952), 713-16.
2103. Arbogast, Hubert. Die Erneuerung der dt. Dichter-
       sprache in den Frühwerken St. Georges: Ein
       stilgeschichtliche Untersuchung. Köln/Graz:
       1967. (Orig.: Diss.--Tübingen: 1961.)
2104. _____. "Zwischen Alexandriner u. Hexameter.
       Eine Studie z. Verskunst St. Georges, "
       Dtschunterr., XVI, 6 (1964), 109-23.
2105. Asbeck-Stausberg, St. George... Warendorf: 1951.
       (Gestalt u. Werk, VI.)

2106. Bennett, Edwin K. St. George. New Haven/Cambr.:
       1954.
2107. Benrath, H. St. George. Paris: 1936.
2108. Bergenthal, F. Das Werk Georges. Breslau: 1933.
2109. Bergmann, Joachim. "Musik u. geistige Erneuung.
       Uber d. Verhältnis d. George-Kreises z. Ton-
       kunst, " St. G'. Lehrzeit u. Meisterschaft....
       Bingen: 1968, pp. 135-51.
2110. Bertram, Ernst. "St. George, " Dichtg als Zeugnis.
       Frühe Bonner Studien z. Lit. Bonn: 1967,
       pp. 160-85. (Geschr. '08.)
2111. Bianquis, G. et Claude David. "Nouv. études sur
       St. G', " Etudes Germaniques, XVI (1961), 259-
       69.
2112. Bie, R. St. George. Berlin: 1934.
2113. Binder, A. Die Sprachkunst G's in seinen Frühwerk-
       en. (Diss.) Frankft: 1933. (Teildruck).
2114. Bithell, J. "St. G'--the man, " German Life &
       Letters, N. S., IX (1955/6), 47-55.
2115. Blank, B. "St. George, " Ztschr. f. dt. Philol.,
       LXI, 2 (Juni 1936), 167-209.
2116. Bock, Claus V. "Wort-Konkord. z. Dichtg St. G's, "
       Castrum Peregrini, LXIV (1964), 26-34. (Book
       form: Amsterdam: 1964.)
2117. Bock, W. "St. G' u. s. Kreis, " Universitas, XII
       (1957), 1027-32.
2118. Böckmann, P. "Der Formanspruch in der Dichtg
       G's, " Ztschr. f. dt. Bildung, IV (1928), 308-20.
2119. Boehringer, R. Ewiger Augenblick. Aarau: 1945.
       (Coll. interviews with G.)
2120. _____. Mein Bild von St. G'. München: 1951.
       (Later ed. --Düssel/München: 1967.)
2121. _____, ed. St. George--Stiftung. Der Genius d.
       Abendlandes. Düsseldorf/München: 1970.
2122. Borchardt, R. "Die Gestalt St. G's, " Prosa, Stutt:
       1957, I, pp. 295-313. (Zuerst in: Die Horen
       (1928) u. d. T. "Der Dichter u. s. Zeit. ")
2123. Bornmann, Bianca M. "Interpr. Georghiane: 'L'Al-
       gabal' e le sue fonti storiche antiche, " Studi
       Germanici, VIII (1970), 251-68.
2124. Böschenstein, Bernard. "Die Sprache d. Entsagung
       in St. G's Dichtg, " Studien z. Dichtg d. Absolu-
       ten. Zürich: 1968, pp. 150-7. (Zuerst in:
       N. Zürcher Ztg, no. 4974 (1.12.'63).)
2125. Bowra, Cecil M. "St. George, " The Heritage of
       Symbolism. London: 1947, pp. 98-143.
2126. Brodersen, A. St. George. Berlin: 1935.

2127.   Bruneder, H. "Wandel des G'-Bildes seit 1930, "
         Dt. Vjschr., XXVIII (1954), 248-67.
2128.   Burgert, H. "Der metaphys. Sinngehalt im Sprach-
         werk G's, " Jahrb. d. österr. Leo-Gesell., Wien:
         (1934), 65-92.
2129.   Closs, August. "St. G's 'Third Humanism,' "
         Medusa's Mirror. Studies in Ger. Lit. London:
         1957, pp. 185-201.
2130.   Curtius, E. R. "Gespräche m. G', " Krit. Essays
         z. europ. Lit. Bern: 1950, pp. 138-57.
2131.   Dahmen, H. Lehren über Kunst u. Weltanschauung
         im Kreise um St. George. Marburg: 1926.
2132.   David, Claude. St. G': Son Oeuvre Poétique.
         Lyons/Paris: 1952. (Bibliot. des Etudes Ger-
         maniques, IX.)
2133.   _____. "St. George, " Universitas, XIV (1959),
         825-32.
2134.   _____. "St. G' u. d. Jugendstil, " Formkräfte d.
         dt. Dichtg vom Barock bis z. Gegenwart. Gött:
         1963, pp. 211-28. (Later ed. 1967; Kleine Van-
         denhoeck-Reihe. Sonderbd 1.)
2135.   _____. "St. G': Grandeur et Misère, " Mercure
         de France, CCCLII (1964), 522-38.
2136.   _____. St. G': Sein dichter. Werk. München:
         1967. (Lit. als Kunst.) (Trans. of French origi-
         nal.)
2137.   _____. "St. G' aujourd'hui, " Preuves, CCXIV
         (1969), 24-34.
2138.   _____, and Rainer Gruenter. "Colloque St.
         George, " Revue d'Allemagne, I (1969), 241-8.
2139.   Dessoir, M. "St. George, " Ztschr. f. Asthetik u.
         allg. Kunstwissenschaft, XXIX (1935), 289-99.
2140.   Diehl, O. G' u. das Deutschtum. (Diss.) Giessen:
         1936.
2141.   Durzak, Manfred. Die Algabal-Dichtg u. die Kunst-
         theorie des frühen St. G'. Berlin: 1963. (Diss.
         --West Berlin.)
2142.   _____. Der junge St. G': Kunsttheorie u. Dichtg.
         München: 1968. (Zur Erkenntnis der Dichtung,
         3.)
2143.   _____. "Die kunsttheoretische Ausgangsposition
         St. G's: Zur Wirkung E. A. Poes, " Arcadia, IV
         (1969), 164-78.
2144.   _____. "Epigonenlyrik. Zur Dichtg d. G'-Kreises,"
         Jahrb. d. dt. Schiller-Gesell., XIII (1969), 482-
         529.
2145.   _____. "Nachwirkgn St. G's im Expressionismus,"

German Quarterly, XLII (1969), 393-417.

2146. Duthie, E. L. L'Infl. du Symbolisme Français sur le Renouveau Poétique de l'Allemagne: Les "Blätter für die Kunst, " 1892-1900. Paris: 1933.

2147. Enright, D. J. "The Case of St. G', " Scrutiny, XV (1947/8), 242-54.

2148. Essays by var. hands. Castrum Peregrini, XXX (1956)--XXXVII (1958). (Interpr. of single poems by G'.)

2149. _____. Kein ding sei, wo das wort gebricht. St. G' z. Gedenken. Darmst: 1961. (Earlier ed. 1958.)

2150. _____. St. G': Lehrzeit u. Meisterschaft. Gedenk. u. Feierschrift z. 100 Geb. d. Dichters. Bingen: 1968.

2151. Faber du Faur, Curt von. "St. G' et le Symbolisme Français, " Comp. Lit., V, 2 (Spring 1953), 151-66. (German version in: Kein ding sei.... Darmst: 1961, pp. 25-40.)

2152. Farrel, R. G's Bezieh. z. engl. Dichtg. Berlin: 1937. (Reprinted: Nendeln/Liechtenstein: 1967.)

2153. Fehse, Willi. "St. George, " Von Goethe bis Grass. Biogr. Porträts z. Lit. Bielefeld: 1963, pp. 93-6.

2154. Franck, W. "Uber St. G', " Aufbau, II (1946), 386-95.

2155. Frels, Elisabeth. "G'-Bibliogr., " Die schöne Lit., XXVII (1926), 202-7.

2156. Frommel, Gerhard. "St. George: drei Maximen über Dichtungen, " Castrum Peregrini, LXXXIX (1970), 6-40.

2157. Fügen, Hans N. "Zur lit. Strategie u. Diffusion d. G'-Kreises, " Ruperto-Carola, XXXIX, 18 (1966), 117-24.

2158. Gerhard, Melitta. "G' u. d. dt. Lyrik d. 19 Jhs., " Preuss. Jahrb., CLXXI (1918), 205-25.

2159. _____. St. G': Dichtung u. Kündung. Bern/München: 1962.

2160. Gerhardt, H. G' u. d. dt. Dichtung. (Diss.) Giessen: 1937.

2161. Goldsmith, Ulrich K. "St. G' and the Theatre, " PMLA, LXVI (1951), 85-95.

2162. _____. St. G': A Study of His Early Work. Boulder, Colo.: 1959. (Univ. Colo. Stud. Lang. & Lit., 7.)

2163. _____. "The Growth of St. G's Reputation, 1890-1900, " German Life & Letters, XIII (1960), 241-7.

2164. _____. St. George. N.Y.: 1970. (Columbia
Essays on Mod. Writers, 50.)

2165. Gottschalk, Hilde. Wesen u. Form der 'Gespräche'
aus dem Kreise der 'Blätter f. d. Kunst.' (Diss.)
Frankfurt: 1932.

2166. Gruenter, Rainer. "Rede über St. G': Zum 100.
Geburtstag (1868-1968), " Euphorion, LXIII (1969),
146-66.

2167. Guenther, Peter W. "St. G' u. d. bildenden Künste,"
Diss. Abstr., XXIX (1969), 3611A (Texas, Austin).

2168. Gundolf, Frdr. St. George. Darmst: 1968. (Reprint of 1930 edn.)

2169. Hahn, K. J. Gemeinschaftsbild u. Gemeinschafts-
kräfte G's. Halle: 1936.

2170. _____. "St. G'--Mythos u. Wahrheit, " Hochland,
XLVI (1953/4), 461-7.

2171. Heckmann, Herbert. St. G' Heute. Darmst: 1969.

2172. Heftrich, Eckhard. St. George. Frankfurt: 1968.

2173. Heiseler, B. von. St. George. Lübeck: 1936.

2174. _____. "St. George, " Lebenswege d. Dichter.
Gütersloh: 1958, pp. 121-95.

2175. _____. "St. George, " Sammlung, XIV (1959),
225-38.

2176. Helleiner, K. F. "St. G': Poet and Prophet, "
Univ. Toronto Quart., XXI (1952), 376-86.

2177. Heuschele, Otto. "St. G' in dieser Zeit, " Neue
Schau, XXIV, 3 (1963), 77-80.

2178. Heuss, Th. "St. George, " Vor d. Bücherwand.
Skizzen z. Dichtern u. Dichtg., ed. F. Kaufman
& H. Leins. Tübingen: 1961, pp. 267-71.
(Orig. written 1933.)

2179. Heybey, Wolfgang. Glaube u. Geschichte im Werke
G's u. s. Kreises. Stuttgart: 1935.

2180. Hildebrandt, Kurt. Das Werk St. G's. Hamburg:
1960.

2181. _____. Erinnerungen an St. G' u. s. Kreis.
Bonn: 1965.

2182. Hillard, Gustav. "Neue Lit. zu St. G' u. s. Kreis,"
Imprimatur, III (1961/2), 78-81.

2183. _____. "Lit. zu St. G' u. s. Kreis, " Recht auf
Vergangenheit. Essays. Aphorismen. Glossen.
Hamburg: 1966, pp. 136-41.

2184. Hobohm, Freya. Die Bedeutg französ. Dichter im
Werk u. Weltbild G's.... Marburg: 1931.

2185. Hohoff, Curt. "St. George, " Merkur, XV (1960),
623-9.

2186.   Höllerer, Walter. "Elite u. Utopie: Zum 100. Geburtstag St. G's, " Oxford German Studies, III (1968), 145-62.

2187.   Horst, K. A. "St. G'. Gedank. über das dichter. Medium, " Agora (Darmst.), IV, 11 (1958), 23-9.

2188.   Jaeger, H. "G's französ. Gedichte u. dt. Ubertragungen, " PMLA, LI (1936), 563-93.

2189.   Jaime, Edw. St. G' u. d. Weltlit. Ulm: 1949.

2190.   Jockers, E. "Das Werk G's als Gestalt seines Wesens, " Germanic Review, IV (1929), 352-72.

2191.   Jolles, Frank. "Zur Frage d. Stils in den wissenschaftl. Schriften d. G'-Kreises, " German Life & Letters, XIX (1965/6), 287-91.

2192.   _____. "Die Entwickl. der wissenschaftl. Grundsätze des G'-Kreises, " Etudes Germaniques, XXII (1967), 346-58.

2193.   Jones, Idwal. "St. G': Poet and Hierophant, " Edda, LVI (1969), 96-105.

2194.   Jost, Dominik. St. G' u. s. Elite. Studie zur Geschichte der Eliten. Zürich: 1949. (Diss. --Fribourg.)

2195.   _____. "Kosmopolitismus u. Nationalismus im Werk von St. G', " Actes du IVe Congrès de l'Assoc. Intern'l de Litt. Comp., Hague/Paris: 1966, I, pp. 404-7.

2196.   Junker, E. W. " 'an baches ranft. ' Ein Beitr. z. Untersuchg d. Sprachform u. Werkgestalt bei St. G', " Agora (Darmstadt), IV (1958), 51-66. (Cf. "Sprachform u. Werkgestalt, " Kein ding sei.... Darmstadt: 1961, pp. 63-78.)

2197.   Just, Klaus G. Studien z. Asthetizismus bei St. G' u. s. Kreis. (Diss.) Würzburg: 1948.

2198.   Kahler, E. von. St. G'. Grösse u. Tragik. Pfüllingen: 1964.

2199.   Kamnitzer, Berta. Das Kultische bei G'. (Diss.) Frankfurt: 1927.

2200.   Kapetanakis, D. "St. G' u. die Folgen, " N. Auslese, XI (1946), 84-90. (Orig.: New Writing and Daylight. London.)

2201.   Klages, L. St. George. Berlin: 1902.

2202.   Klein, C. A. Die Sendung St. Georges: Erinnerungen. Berlin: 1935.

2203.   Klein, Johannes. "St. George, " Dt. Lit. im 20 Jh.: Struktur u. Gestalten. 2 Bde, ed. H. Friedemann & O. Mann. Heidelberg: 1961, II, pp. 7-31. (1967 ed., II, pp. 9-33.)

2204.   _____. "Die Gestalt St. G's, " Welt u. Wort,

XVIII (1963), 355-7.

2205. Klein, Margarete. St. George... Heidelberg: 1938.
2206. Klussman, Paul G. Die Deutung der Kunst und die
      Bestimmung des Dichters bei St. G'. (Diss.)
      Münster: 1955. (Book form--Bonn: 1961/2
      under title St. George.)
2207. _____. St. G': Zum Selbstverständnis der Kunst
      u. des Dichters in der Moderne. Bonn: 1961.
      (BADL, 1.) (Mit einer G'-Bibliogr.)
2208. _____. "St. George," Dt. Dichter der Moderne:
      Ihr Leben u. Werk, ed. Benno von Wiese. Ber-
      lin: 1965, pp. 132-52. (1969 ed., pp. 135-56.)
2209. Koch, H. Die lyr. Gestaltung u. die Sprachform
      G's. (Diss.) Bonn: 1929.
2210. Koch, W. St. George... Halle: 1933.
2211. Kohlmeyer, O. St. G... u. die Persönlichkeitsgestalt
      als Erziehungsziel... Magdeburg: 1930(1929).
2212. Kohlschmidt, Werner. "Zur Polemik G's u. s.
      Kreises," Formenwandel: Festschr. ... P.
      Böckmann, ed. W. Müller-Seidel & W. Preisen-
      danz. Hamburg: 1964, pp. 471-82.
2213. Kraft, Werner. "Gedichte von G'," Augenblicke der
      Dichtg. Krit. Betracht. München: 1964, pp.
      147-62.
2214. Kraus, K. "G' als Wortgestalter," Wissenschaftl.
      Beihefte z. Ztschr. d. dt. Sprachvereins, VII,
      49 (1937), 4-19.
2215. Krischak, Ernst. Der Einfluss St. G's auf d.
      österr. Lyrik. (Diss.) Wien: 1950.
2216. Lachmann, E. Die ersten Bücher G's. Berlin: 1933.
2217. Landmann, Edith. Georgika. Heidelberg: 1920.
2218. _____. Gespräche mit St. G'. Düsseld: 1963.
2219. Landmann, Georg P. St. G' u. s. Kreis: Eine
      Bibliogr. Hamburg: 1960.
2220. Landmann, Michael. "St. G': Erinn. u. Interpr.,"
      Neue Dt. Hefte, CXIX (1968), 3-32. (Variant
      listing: XV, 3.)
2221. Lang, S. "St. G', d. Mensch u. d. Dichter,"
      Schweiz. Rds., XLIX, (1949/50), 410-16; LII
      (1952/3), 272-8.
2222. _____. "Weiteres über St. G'," Schweiz. Rds.,
      LVII (1957/8), 180-5.
2223. Lehmann, Peter L. Meditationen um St. G': Sieben
      Essays. Düsseld: 1965. (Incl: "Dt. Symbolis-
      mus," pp. 19-30.)
2224. Lepsius, Sabine. St. George... Berlin: 1935.

2225. Leschnitzer, F. "G' u. d. Folgen, " Von Börne zu
       Leonhard oder Erbübel--Erbgut? Aufsätze aus
       30 Jahren z. Lit. geschichte. Rudolstadt: 1966,
       pp. 63-87.
2226. Lessing, Th. Einmal u. nie wieder. Wien: 1935,
       pp. 240-63. (Vol. 1 of his Ges. Schriften, 10
       vols.)
2227. Lieser, Paul. "Fremdsprach. Ubertrag. als Nach-
       gestaltg u. Neuschöpfg. St. G's Ubertrag. werk, "
       St. G': Lehrzeit u. Meisterschaft.... Bingen:
       1968, pp. 73-96.
2228. Linke, Hansjürgen. Das Kultische in der Dichtg St.
       G's u. s. Schule. I. Text, II. Nachweise u.
       Anmerk. München: 1960. (Also: diss. --Köln:
       1954.)
2229. L'Ormeau, F. W. Die Christologie St. G's. Am-
       sterdam: 1963. (2nd ed. of 1953 publ.) (Also
       in: Castrum Per. XV (1953), 5-137.)
2230. Lützeler, H. "Gedichtaufbau u. Welthaltung des
       Dichters (G'), " Euphorion, XXV, 2 (1934).
2231. Marache, Maurice. "Du 'Tapis de la vie' à 'L'étoile
       d'alliance.' L'évol. de la pensée de St. G' à la
       lumière de l'hist. des styles, " Etudes German-
       iques, XXI (1966), 205-24; 506-26.
2232. Marx, Olga. "St. G' in seinen Ubertrag. engl.
       Dichtgn, " Castrum Peregrini, LXXVII (1967), 5-
       35. (Book form: Amsterdam: 1967.)
2233. Meessen, H. J. "St. G's 'Algabal' u. die französ.
       Décadence, " Monatshefte f. dt. Unterr., XXXIX
       (1947), 304-21.
2234. Michels, G. Die Dante-Ubertrag. St. Georges.
       München: 1967.
2235. Mommsen, Momme. "Der Rhein u. d. Rheinland in
       d. Dichtg St. G's, " Castrum Peregrini, LXXXI
       (1968), 30-43.
2236. Morwitz, E. Die Dichtg St. G's. Berlin: 1934.
2237. _____. Kommentar z. dem Werk St. G's.
       München/Düsseld: 1960.
2238. _____. Kommentar z. den Prosa-Drama-u. Ju-
       gend-Dichtgn St. G's. München/Düsseld.: 1962.
2239. Mulot, A. "St. George, " D. dt. Dichtung uns. Zeit.
       Stuttgart: 1940.
2240. Muth, K. "St. George u. s. Apotheose durch den
       'Kreis, ' " Schöpfer u. Magier, 2nd. edn. Mün-
       chen: 1953, pp. 169-252. (Earlier edn. Leipzig:
       1935, pp. 133-95.)

2241. Nohl, J. "'G' u. s. Kreis,'" Weltlit. der Gegenwart, ed. L. Marcuse. Bd. I. Leip.: 1924.

2242. Nomura, Takuichi. "St. Georges Asthetik d. Abgeschlossenheit mit bes. Berücks. von den Zeitgedichten," Doitsu Bungaku, XLIII (1969), 52-8. (In Japanese, with summary in German.)

2243. Ockenden, R. C. "'Die lang verlassne muschel.' St. G's last poems ('Das neue Reich'), " Publ. of the English Goethe Society, XXXIV (1964), 85-121.

2244. _____. "'Komm in den totgesagten park u. schau': Some Aspects of Nature and Nature Imagery in St. G's Poetry," Oxford German Studies, II (1967), 87-109.

2245. _____. "St. G': Grundworte seiner Dichtung, " Castrum Peregrini, LXXXI (1968), 5-29.

2246. Ozgü, Melâhat. "Das Dichterbild St. G's," Alman dil ve edebiyati dergisi. Studien z. dt. Sprache u. Lit. (Univ. Istanbul), IV (1958), 48-81.

2247. _____. Die Dichtg in d. Dichtg St. G's. Ankara: 1960.

2247a. Paris, J. "St. George," Mercure de France, CCCXX (1954), 464-87.

2248. Pellegrini, A. St. George. Berlin: 1935.

2249. Perl, Walter H. "New St. G' Lit. 1960-1, " Books Abroad, XXXVI (1962), 26-9.

2250. _____. "New St. G' Lit. 1965-6, " Books Abroad, XL (1966), 418-20.

2251. Pestalozzi, Karl. Die Entstehung des lyr. Ich: Stud. z. Motiv der Erhebung in der Lyrik. Berlin: 1970.

2252. Picht, Werner. "Besinnung auf St. G'," Wort u. Wahrheit, XVIII (1963), 692-713; 771-87.

2253. _____. "Um St. G'," Neue Sammlung, III (1963), 478-82.

2254. _____. Besinnung auf St. G'. Düsseld/München: 1964.

2255. Podszus, F. "St. G' heute. Zum 25. Todestag, " Merkur, XII (1958), 1146-53.

2256. Politzer, Heinz. "'Denn dazu lieben wir zu sehr euch Brüder ...' St. G' u. Osterr.," Wort u. Wahrheit, XXIV (1969), 207-23.

2257. Ringleb, Heinrich. Das Pathos St. G's. (Diss.) Heidelberg: 1948.

2258. Roffler, Th. "St. George," Bildnisse... Fravenfeld/ Leipzig: 1933, pp. 50-82.

2259. Rosenfeld, E. "Erste Begegnung St. G's mit

148 A Post-Symbolist Bibliography

Italien, " Unterscheidung u. Bewahrung. Festschr.
... H. Kunisch. Berlin: 1961, pp. 294-303.
2260. Rössner, H. "Ende des G'-Kreises, " Volk im Wer-
den, VI (1938), 459-77.
2261. Rosteutscher, J. "George, " Das ästhet. Idol im
Werke von Winckelmann.... Bern: 1956,
pp. 195-229.
2262. Rychner, Max. "St. G'. Nachruf ('33), " Aufsätze z.
Lit., ed. W. Meier. Zürich: 1966, pp. 369-93.
2263. Salin, E. Um St. G'. Godesberg: 1948. (2nd ed.
München: 1954.) (Letters.)
2264. San Lazzaro, Clementina di. St. George. Imola:
1935.
2265. Schaeffer, A. "St. George, " Dichter u. Dichtung.
Leipzig: 1923, pp. 297-501.
2266. Scheller, W. St. George. Leip: 1918. (Later work
1935--Univ. Bibliothek.)
2267. Scherer, Anton. Einführung in die Geschichte der
donau-schwäbischen Lit. Graz: 1960. (Incl.
George.)
2268. Schlösser, M. "St. G', Dichter oder Prophet?"
Agorá, IV, 11 (1958), 9-22. (Also in: Kein
ding sei.... Darmst: 1961, pp. 11-24.)
2269. Schmidt, A. M. "St. G' ou du mythe au mythe, "
Table Ronde, no. 63 (1953), 149-57.
2270. Schmiele, Walter. "St. George, " Triffst du nur das
Zauberwort: Stimmen von heute z. dt. Lyrik,
ed. J. Petersen. Frankfurt: 1961, pp. 172-85.
2271. Schmitz, Victor A. "Werk, Weg u. Umkreis St.
G's, " Ruperto-Carola, XIX, 42 (1967), 74-7.
2272. Schneider-Hermann, Gisela. St. G' in s. Dichtg.
Zürich: 1957.
2273. Schonauer, Franz. St. G' in Selbstzeugn. u. Doku-
menten. Hamburg: 1960. (Later ed. 1961.)
2274. _____. "St. G' u. s. Kreis, " Dt. Rds., LXXXVI
(1960), 615-26.
2275. Schultz, H. Stefan. Studien z. Dichtg St. G's.
Heidelberg: 1967.
2276. _____. St. G'. Rede z. Eröffng d. St. G'-Aus-
stellg in Marbach a. N., 25. Mai '68. Heidelberg: 1968.
2277. _____. "Französ. u. Dtsches bei St. George, "
Dt. Beitr. z. geist. Uberliefg, VI (1970), 120-39.
2278. Schumacher, Horst. St. George. Mühlacker: 1968.
2279. Scott, C. Die Tragödie St. G's: Ein Erinnerungs-
bild u. e. Gang durch s. Werk. Eltville: 1952.
2280. Siebert, W. Der alte St. George. Mainz am Rhein:
1939.

2281. Sieburg, F. "St. George, " Die grossen Dt. Dt.
       Biogr., ed. H. Heimpet et al. Bde IV & V.
       Berlin: 1957, IV, pp. 277-92.
2282. _____. "St. G': Seine Dichtung u. s. Leben, "
       Universitas, XVII (1962), 1289-1306.
2283. Simons, Gabriel. Die zykl. Kunst im Jugendwerk St.
       G's. Ihre Vorraussetzgn in d. Zeit u. ihre
       allg. ästhet. Bedingungen. (Diss.) Köln: 1965.
2284. Sior, Marie-Luise. G' u. der französ Symbolismus.
       (Diss.) Giessen: 1932.
2285. Specht, R. Das Ethos des G'Kreises. Grundlagen
       u. Grenzen. (Diss.) München: 1954.
2286. Steffensen, Steffen. "St. G' u. seine Wirkungen in
       Skandinavien, " Nerthus, II (1969), 52-78.
2287. Stegmeyer, F. "Die Gestalt St. G's, " Europ. Pro-
       file: Essays. Wiesb: 1947, pp. 87-103.
2288. Steiner, H. Begegnungen mit St. G'. N.Y.: 1942.
       (Later ed. '47.)
2289. Sternbach, H. St. George. Warszawa: 1937.
2290. Stettler, Michael, ed. St. G'-Stiftg. Erinnergn an
       Frank. Ein Lebenszeugnis. Düsseld/München:
       1968.
2291. Strauss, Georg. "Entzauberg e. Kunstbewegung. St.
       G' u. s. Gefolgschaft, " Irrlichter u. Leitgestirne.
       Essays über Probleme der Kunst. Zürich: 1966,
       pp. 128-46.
2292. Strich, F. "St. George, " Ztschr. f. dt. Unterricht,
       XXXIX (1925), 542-56.
2293. Susman, Margarete. "St. George, " Gestalten u.
       Kreise. Konstanz: 1954, pp. 200-19.
2294. Thormaehlen, Ludwig. Erinn. an St. G'. Hamburg:
       1962.
2295. Unger, Jörg. Studien z. Asthetik St. G's. (Diss.)
       Wien: 1967.
2296. Urban, G. R. Kinesis and Stasis: A Study in the
       Attitude of St. G' and His Circle to the Musical
       Arts. 's-Gravenhage: 1962. (AG, 2.)
2297. Usinger, Fritz. "St. G' u. d. Gegenwart, " Welt
       ohne Klassik. Essays. Darmst: 1960, pp. 97-
       110.
2298. _____. "Fortgang d. Lebens d. dt. Zauber. St.
       G', " (ein Vortrag) Castrum Peregrini, XLIX
       (1961), 34-49.
2299. _____. "St. G' u. d. Welt d. Konkreten, "
       Gesichter u. Gesichte. Darmst: 1965, pp. 57-
       62.

2300. Vanja, Horst. Stiftung u. Einweihung im Werk St.
       G's. (Diss.) Leipzig: 1950.
2301. Vermeil, E. "La poésie allemande au temps de
       Guillaume II: St. G', " Critique, X, 86/7
       (1954), 616-35.
2302. Viereck, P. "St. G': Perilous Prophet, " Antioch
       Review, IX (1949), 111-16.
2303. Vortriede, Werner. "Direct Echoes of French Poe-
       try in St. G's Works, " Mod. Lang. Notes, LX
       (1945), 461-8.
2304. _____. "St. G's Nachleben, " Neue dt. Hefte, X,
       95 (1963), 80-97.
2305. Wandrey, Conrad. St. George.   Stras: 1911.
       (Later ed. Strasbourg: 1965.)
2306. Williege, Wilhelm. "Das Werk St. Georges, " Sam-
       mlung, XIV (1959), 586-8.
2307. _____. "The Growth of St. G's Reputation: 1890-
       1900, " German Life & Letters, XIII (1959/60),
       241-7.
2308. Winkler, Eugen G. "Uber St. G', " Dichtungen, Ges-
       talten, u. Probleme, ed. W. Warnach.   Pful-
       lingen: 1956, pp. 360-4. (Earlier ed. 1937.)
2309. Winkler, Michael. St. George.   Stuttgart: 1970.
       (SM, 90.)
2310. Wolff, Robert. "Mensch u. Drud, Erfüllg e. Prophe-
       tie. St. G' u. d. Natur, " St. G': Lehrzeit u.
       Meisterschaft.... Bingen: 1968, pp. 97-110.
2311. _____. "Japan. G'-Lit., " St. George: Lehrzeit
       u. Meisterschaft.... Bingen: 1968, pp. 153-5.
2312. Wolfskehl, Karl. "St. G' u. d. Mythos, " Ges.
       Werke. Hamburg: 1960. Bd. 2: Ubertragungen.
       Prosa. II, pp. 252-60.
2313. _____. "St. G' u. d. Welt, " Ges. Werke. Ham-
       burg: 1960. Bd. 2: Ubertragungen. Prosa. II,
       pp. 260-7.
2314. Wolters, F. St. George... Berlin: 1930.
2315. Zeller, Bernhard, ed. St. G' 1868-1968: Der Dicht-
       er u. s. Kreis. Marbach: 1968. (Sonderaus-
       stellg d. Schiller-Nat'lmusemus. Katalog Nr. 18.
       München: 1968.)
2316. Zierau, G. Zum Triumphe des grossen Lebens:
       'Der Teppich des Lebens' und die 'Lieder von
       Traum und Tod.' Dresden: 1939.
2317. Zweig, A. "Standbild u. Einsturz des St. G', " Neue
       dt. Lit., V, 11 (1957), 107-16.

GUILLEN

2318. Alonso, Amado. "J. Guillén, poeta esencial, " La
Nación (Buenos Aires) (21 Abril 1929). (Repr.
in: Materia y Forma en Poesía. Madrid: 1965,
pp. 315-21.)

2319. Alonso, Dámaso. "Pasión elemental en la poesía de
J. Guillén, " Insula, III, 26 (1948).

2320. _____. "Los impulsos elem. en la poesía de J.
Guillén, " Poetas Españoles Contemp. Madrid:
1953, pp. 235-43.

2321. Aub, Max. "Apunte de J. Guillén, con Max Aub al
fondo, por éste, " Papeles de Son Armadans
(Mallorca), XLIX (1968), 309-14.

2322. Bergamín, José. "La poética de J. Guillén, " Gaceta
Literaria (1 Enero 1929).

2323. Blecua, J. M. and Ricardo Gullón. La Poesía de J.
Guillén. Saragossa: 1949.

2324. Burnshaw, Stanley, ed. The Poem Itself. New York:
1960. (Contains comment. on "Desnudo, " "Sabor
a Vida, " "Muerte a lo Lejos, " and "Primavera
Delgada, " pp. 210-17.)

2325. Cano, José Luis. De Machado a Bousoño. Madrid:
1955.

2326. _____. "J. Guillén, " Poesía Española del Siglo
XX. Madrid: 1960, pp. 211-24.

2327. Caro Romero, Joaquín. "Viaje alrededor de J.
Guillén, " Insula, XXIII (Jan. 1968), 6-7.

2328. Carranza, Eduardo. "J. Guillén, natural de Valla-
dolid, " Bol. Cult. y Bibliogr. (Bogotá), X (1967),
618-29.

2329. Casalduero, Joaquín. Estudios de Lit. Española,
2nd ed. Madrid: 1967(1962).

2330. _____. J. Guillén y "Cántico." Buenos Aires/
Santiago: 1946. (Col. Raíz y Estrella.)

2331. _____. "Cántico" de J. Guillén. Madrid/N.Y.:
1953.

2332. Cassou, Jean. "La poésie de J. Guillén, " Revue de
Paris, (Mars 1961), 80-6.

2333. Castro, Américo. "'Cántico' de J. Guillén, " Insula
(Buenos Aires), I, 1 (1943), 14-27.

2334. Cervera Tomás, J. "La concep. del mundo en la
obra de J. Guillén, " Monteagudo, no. 2 (1953).

2335. Ciplijauskaité, Biruté. "'Clamor' a la altura de las
circunstancias, " Rev. Hisp. Moderna, XXIX
(1963), 290-7.

2336. _____. "J. Guillén, confirmándose en la afirmación, " Insula, XXIV (May 1969), 1, 14.

2337. Cirre, José F. "J. Guillén y la realidad, " Insula, XVIII, 199 (1963), 7.

2338. Couffon, Claude. Dos Encuentros con J. Guillén. Paris: 1963.

2339. Darmangeat, Pierre. J. Guillén ou le Cantique Emerveillé. Paris: 1958.

2340. Debicki, Andrew P. "El tema de la poesía en 'Homenaje' de J. Guillén, " Insula, XXIII (Sept. 1968), 1, 12.

2341. _____. "J. Guillén's 'Cántico,' " PMLA, LXXXI, 5 (1966), 439-45.

2342. Dehennin, Elsa. "Introd. à l'oeuvre poétique de J. Guillén, " Rev. de l'Univ. Bruxelles, XVII (Mai-Juill. 1965), 288-304.

2343. _____. "Cántico" de J. Guillén: Une Poésie de la Clarté. Bruxelles: 1969. (Univ. Libre de Brux., Trav. de la Fac. de Philos. et Lettres, 41.)

2344. Dumitrescu, Domnita. "J. Guillén la apogeul creatiei, " România Literară, XXVII (Feb. 1969), 21.

2345. Durán, Manuel. "J. Guillén, hoy, " Insula, XXIV (Dec. 1969), 1, 13.

2346. Enwall, Dale E. "The poetic world of J. Guillén, " Diss. Abstr. Intern'l, XXX (1969), 1166A (Stanford).

2347. Essays by var. hands. Cuadernillo--Homenaje al poeta J. Guillen. Murcia: 1956. (Contains: Francisco A. Sainz, "Con la puerta entornada"; Mariano B. Boyanes, "Tiempo y vida en el 'Cántico' de Guillén"; Juan G. Ruiz, "Adiós a J. Guillén"; Luis Garay, "Recuerdo de J. Guillén en Murcia. ")

2348. _____. "An Intern'l Symposium in Honor of J. Guillén at 75, " Books Abroad, XLII, 1 (Winter 1968), 7-60. (Esp. "A J. Guillén Bibliog., " pp. 58-9.)

2349. Ferraté, Juan. "El altavoz de J. Guillén, " Teoría del Poema. Barcelona: 1957, pp. ?.

2350. Florit, Eugenio. "Notas sobre la poesía de J. Guillén, " Rev. Hisp. Moderna, XII (1946), 267-71.

2351. Friedrich, Hugo. "J. Guillén, " Estructura de la Lírica Moderna... trans. Juan Petit. Barcelona: 1959, pp. ?.

2352. Frutos, E. "El existencialismo jubiloso de J. Guillén," Cuad. Hispanoamer., no. 18 (1950).

2353. Gil de Biedma, Jaime. "Cántico." El Mundo y la Poesía de J. Guillén. Barcelona: 1960. (Reviewed: Comp. Lit., XIII (1961), 281-3.)

2354. González Muela, Joaquín. "Sobre el 'Cántico' de J. Guillén," Bull. Hisp. Studies (Liverpool), XXXII (1955).

2355. _____. La Realidad y J. Guillén. Madrid: 1962/3. (Bibliog., pp. 225-7.)

2356. Granados, Juana. Antología Lírica, versione e introd. a cura di.... Milan/Varese: 1955. (Contains bibliogr. on Guillén.)

2357. Guillén, Jorge. Language and Poetry: Some Poets of Spain. Cambridge, Mass.: 1961. (Cf. Lenguaje y Poesía. Madrid: 1962.)

2358. _____. Affirmation: A Bilingual Anthology, 1919-'66, trans. Julian Palley. Norman, Okla.: 1968. (Contains: "Introd." by Julian Palley, pp. vii-xi; "Introd." by the author, pp. 3-24, orig. called "El argumento de la obra," in All'Insegna del Pesce d'Oro. Milan: 1961.)

2359. Gullón, Ricardo. "J. Guillén: esencial y existencial," Insula, XVIII, 205 (1963), 1, 12.

2360. _____. "J. Guillén: a la cultura de las circumstancias," Insula, XIX, 208 (1964), 1, 10.

2361. _____. "'Homenaje' con variaciones," Insula, XXIII (Sept. 1968), 1, 6, 16.

2362. _____, and José M. Blecua. La Poesía de J. Guillén. Zaragoza: 1949. ("Estudios Literarios," II.)

2363. Ivask, Ivar, and Juan Marichal. Luminous Reality: The Poetry of J. Guillén. Norman, Okla.: 1969. (Incl. crit. essays.)

2364. Kaul, Adelina Vidal de, and G. Kaul. "J. Guillén. Notas para una interpr. estilística," Homenaje a Fritz Krüger. Mendoza: 1954.

2365. Lida, Raimundo. "Sobre las décimas de J. Guillén," Cuad. Americanos, C (1958).

2366. Lind, G. R. J. Gulléns "Cántico." Frankf. am Main: 1955.

2367. López Estrada, Francisco. "La realidad y el poeta sobre glosa a una glosa sobre J. Guillén," Cuad. Hispanoamer., LVII (1964), 326-8.

2368. MacLeish, Archibald. "J. Guillén: a poet of this time," Atlantic Monthly, (Jan. 1961), 127-9.

2369. McSpadden, G. E. "New light on speech rhythms

from J. Guillén's reading of his poem 'Gran Silencio, ' " Hispanic Review, XXX (1962).

2370. Olson, Paul R. "Language and reality in J. Guillén, " Hispanic Review, XXXIV (1966), 149-54.

2371. Palley, Julian. "The metaphors of J. Guillén, " Hispania, XXXVI, 3 (1953), 321-4.

2372. _____. "J. Guillén and the poetry of commitment, " Hispania (Univ. Conn.), XLV, 4 (1962), 686-91.

2373. Paz, Octavio. "Horas situadas de J. Guillén, " Papeles de Son Armadans (Mallorca), XL (1966), 209-18.

2374. Pleak, Frances A. The Poetry of J. Guillén. Princeton, N. J.: 1942.

2375. Roselló Porcel, B. "Notas a Guillén, " Cuad. de la Fac. de Filos. y Letras. n. p. : n. d.

2376. Ruiz, Ramón F. "J. Guillén: Forlsningens dikter, " Vinduet (Oslo), XVII (1963), 142-9.

2377. Salinas, Pedro. "J. Guillén, " Lit. Española Siglo XX. Mexico: 1941, pp. 263-76.

2378. Valente, José Angel. "De la lectura a la crítica y otras metamorfosis, " Insula, XVI, clxxviii (1962), 7. (Review of J. Gil de Biedma's 'Cántico': El Mundo y la Poesía de J. Guillén.)

2379. Valverde, J. M. "Plenitud crítica de la poesía de J. Guillén, " Estud. sobre la Palabra Poética. Madrid: 1952, pp. ?.

2380. Vigée, Claude. "J. Guillén y la trad. simbolista francesa, " Cuad. del Cong. por la Libertad de la Cultura, XLV (Nov. -Dic. 1960), 53-9.

2381. _____. "Le message poétique de J. Guillén face à la trad. symboliste française, " Critique, XVI, 154 (Mars 1960), 195-221.

2382. _____. "J. Guillén et l'esthét. du symbolisme français, " Stud. in West. Lit. Jerusalem: 1962, pp. 270-92.

2383. Vivanco, Luis F. "J. Guillén, poeta de tiempo, " La Poesía Española Contemp. Madrid: 1957, pp. 88-92.

2384. Weber, Robert J. "De 'Cántico' a 'Clamor, ' " Rev. Hisp. Moderna, XXIX (1963), 109-19.

2385. Whittredge, R. "The poetic world of J. Guillén, " Romanic Review, XXXIX (1948).

2386. Xirau, Ramón. "Lectura a 'Cántico, ' " Poetas de México y España. Madrid: 1962.

2387. _____. "Lectura a 'Cánticos, ' " Cuad. Americanos, XXI, 121 (1962), 248-57. (Guillén and Valéry.)

2388. Young, Howard T. "J. Guillén and the lang. of poe-
       try, " Hispania, XLVI (1963), 66-70.
2389. Zardoya, Concha. "J. Guillén, " Poesía Española
       Contemp., Madrid: 1961, pp. 288-90.
2390. _____. "J. Guillén: teoría y prática poética, "
       Poetic Theory, Poetic Practice, ed. Robert
       Scholes. Paper pres. at the 1968 Midwest MLA
       meeting, pp. 145-52.

HOFMANNSTHAL

2391. Alewyn, R. H's Wandlung (Vortr.) Frankfurt: 1949.
2392. _____. "H' u. diese Zeit, " N. Rds., LX (1949),
       381-90.
2393. Altenhofer, Norbert. "Die H'-Forschung von 1964
       bis 1967, " H' Blätter, I (1968), 41-65.
2394. _____. "Die H'-Forschung 1968/9 (mit Nachtrag
       1964-7), " H' Blätter, II (1969), 157-78; III (1969),
       228-38.
2395. _____. "Die H'-Forschung 1969 u. 1970. Mit
       Nachtr. 1964-'68, " Hofmannsthal-Blätter, IV
       (1970), 305-15. (Part II: V (1970), 402-12.)
2396. Baschata, Wolfgang. Die Entwicklg. d. dramat.
       Technik u. Form in H's lyr. Dramen. (Diss.)
       Innsbruck: 1948.
2397. Bauer, Gerhard. Abhängigkeitsbewusstsein u. Frei-
       heitsgefühl im Werk H's. (Diss.) Marburg: 1962.
2398. Bauer, Sybelle, ed. H. v. H. Darmst: 1968.
       (Sammelbd.) (Wege der Forsch., 183.)
2399. Bednall, J. B. "From high lang. to dialect. A
       study in H's change of medium, " H' Studies in
       Commem., ed. F. Norman. London: 1963, pp.
       83-117.
2400. Berendsohn, W. A. Der Impressionismus H's als Zeit-
       erscheinung; eine stilkritische Studie. Hamburg: 1920.
2401. Berger, D. "H. v. H's Gestalt im Wandel d. Jahre, "
       Wort in d. Zeit, II, 7 (1956), 1-15.
2402. Bianquis, Geneviève. "Le Testament Moral de H, "
       Mélanges H. Lichtenberger. Paris: 1934,
       pp. 347-60.
2403. _____. "H et la France, " Rev. de Litt. Comp.,
       XXVII (1953), 301-18.
2404. Block, Haskell M. "H. v. H. and the Symbolist

Drama, " Trans. Wisconsin Acad. Sciences, Arts, and Letters, XLVIII (1959), 161-78.

2405. Borchardt, R. "H's Wirkung, " Prosa. Stuttgart: 1957, I, pp. 197-205.

2406. Brand, Olga. Traum u. Wirklichkeit bei H. (Diss.) Münster: 1932.

2407. Braun, Felix. "Das Welterlebnis H's, " Das musikal. Land: Versuch über Osterr. Landschaft u. Dichtg. Innsbruck: 1952, pp. 165-78.

2408. Brecht, W. "Grundlinien im Werk H's, " Euphorion, XXV (Ergänzungsheft 16) (1923-4), 164-79.

2409. Brinkmann, Richard. "H u. die Sprache, " Dt. Vjschrift, XXXV (1961), 69-95.

2410. Broch, H. "Der junge H: Aus e. Studie über H' u. s. Zeit, " Lit. Revue, IV (1949), 287-92.

2411. _____. "H u. s. Zeit. Eine Studie, " Essays, ed. H. Arendt. 2 Bde. Zürich: 1955, I, pp. 43-181. (Later ed. München: 1964.)

2412. Burger, Hilde. "French Infl. on H. v. H., " Comp. Lit.: Proceed. 2nd Cong. Intern'l Comp. Lit. Assoc., ed. W. Friederich. 2 vols. Chapel Hill: 1959, II, pp. 691-7. (UNCSCL, nos. 23/4.)

2413. _____. "H: Ses Relations Avec la Belgique et la Suisse, " Rev. de Litt. Comp., XXXVI, 3 (1962), 369-76.

2414. Coghlan, Brian. "Trad. Form u. eigener Stil im Spätwerk H. v. H.'s, " Stil-u. Formprobleme in d. Lit., ed. P. Böckmann. Heidelberg: 1959, pp. 492-8.

2415. Cohn, Hilde D. "Mehr als schlanke Leier: Zur Entwick. dramat. Formen in H. v. H's Dichtg, " Jb. d. dt. Schiller-Gesell., VIII (1964), 280-308.

2416. David, Claude. "Le dernier homme de lettres, " Critique, XI, 96 (1955), 387-408.

2417. _____. "Sur H, " Etudes Germaniques, XVII (1962), 58-63.

2418. _____. "H's Frankreich-Bild, " Arcadia, V (1970), 163-75.

2419. Dorungs, Werner. Form u. Weltbild d. Gedichte H. v. H's in ihrer Entwicklung. Zürich: 1960. (Also: diss. --Freiburg/Schw.)

2420. Erken, Günther. "H. v. H, " Dt. Dichter der Moderne: Ihr Leben u. Werk, ed. B. v. Wiese. Berlin: 1965, pp. 213-36. (1969 ed., pp. 217-40.)

2421. _____. H's dramat. Stil: Untersuch. z. Symbolik u. Dramaturgie. Tüb: 1967. (Hermaea,

20.) (Orig. diss. --Mchn.)

2422. Essays by var. hands. "H-Festschrift, " Eranos
(1924).

2423. _____. H. v. H., Worte des Gedenkens: Nach-
rufe aus dem Todesjahr 1929, ed. Leonhard M.
Fiedler. Heidelberg: 1969. (Esp. Hans H.
Schaeder, "Das Werk H. v. H's, " pp. 83-98.)

2424. Exner, Richard. "Problemkrise d. H-Forschung, "
Schweiz. Monatshefte, XLVI (1967), 1023-41.

2425. _____. "Der Weg über die höchste Vielfalt: Ein
Bericht über einige neue Schriften z. H-Forschung, "
German Quarterly, XL (1967), 92-123.

2426. _____. "Die Zeit d. anderen Auslegung. Ein
Bericht über Quellen u. Studien z. H-Forschung,
1966-'69, " German Quarterly, XLIII (1970), 453-
503.

2427. Fahrner, R. Dichter. Visionen menschlicher Urbilder
in H's Werk. Ankara: 1956. (Schriften f. dt.
Sprache u. Lit., 3.) (Philos. Fak. d. Univ. Ankara.)

2428. Felder, A. Das Wesen d. Dichters u. d. Dichtg bei
H. v. H. (Diss.) Berlin: 1954. (Freie Univ.)

2429. Fiechtner, H. A. "H et la France, " Culture Française, VI, 5 (déc. 1957), 32-5.

2430. _____. "H als Magnet: Die Wirkg d. Dichters
auf s. Zeitgenossen, " Forum (Wien), IX (1962),
163-5; 223-5.

2431. _____, ed. H. v. H.: Der Dichter im Spiegel
der Freunde. Bern: 1963. (Earlier ed. 1949).

2432. Foldenauer, K. H u. d. franzÖs. Lit. des 19 u. 20
Jhs. (Thèse) Tüb: 1957/8.

2433. Forster, Leonard W. "H's Art of Lyric Concentra-
tion, " Ger. Studies presented to W. H. Bruford...
London: 1962, pp. 210(?)-34.

2434. Freiwald, C. H's Landschaftserlebnis.   : 1932.

2435. Freudenberg, Günther. Die Zeit als dichter. Erfahrg
im Werke H. v. H's. (Diss.) Freiburg: 1951.

2436. Fuchs, A. "H": Thèmes et Horizons Spirituels, "
Etudes Germaniques, III (1948), 355-81.

2437. Gilbert, M. E. "Recent Trends in the Crit. of H, "
German Life & Letters, N.S., V (1951/2), 255-
68.

2438. _____. "Arbeitsbericht aus England, " H-Blätter,
II (1969), 97-101.

2439. Goff, Penrith. "H. v. H.: The Symbol as Experience, " Kentucky Foreign Lang. Quarterly, VII
(1960), 196-200.

158   A Post-Symbolist Bibliography

2440. _____. "H. v. H and the Aesthetic Experience, "
Papers on Lang. & Lit., IV (1968), 414-19.
2441. Goldschmit, Rudolf. Die Erfahrg d. Vergänglichkeit
bei H. (Diss.) München: 1952. (Studien z.
Zeitproblem in d. Dichtg.)
2442. _____. H. v. H. Velber: 1968.
2443. Gray, M. A. R. H and 19th Cen. French Symbolism. (Diss.) Dublin: 1950/1.
2444. Gruhl, H. H. v. H. Die existenziellen Grundlagen
u. d. geistesgesch. Bezüge s. Werkes. (Diss.)
Berlin: 1957. (Freie Univ.)
2445. Guddatt, Kurt H. "H. v. H: Eine Studie z. dichter.
Schaffensweise, " Diss. Abstr., XXI (1960), 1191-
2. (Ohio.)
2446. Haas, Willy. "H. v. H, " Gestalten. Essays z. Lit.
u. Gesellschaft. Berlin/Frankf. M/Wien: 1962,
pp. 190-208. (Geschr. 1929.)
2447. _____. H. v. H. Berlin: 1964.
2448. Hadamovsky, F. "H. v. H., " Grösse Osterr., X
(1957), 180-8.
2449. Hagedorn, Günther. Die Märchen-dichtgn H. v. H's.
(Diss.) Köln: 1967.
2450. Hahn, Erika. Leben, Traum u. Tod. Ihre symbol.
Gestaltg in d. Gedichten H.v.H's. (Diss.) Erlangen-Nürnberg: 1962.
2451. Hamburger, Michael. "H's Bibliothek: Ein Bericht,"
Euphorion, LV (1961), 15-67.
2452. _____. "H and England, " H. Studies in Commem-
mor., ed. F. Norman. London: 1963, pp. 11-
28.
2453. _____. H. v. H.: Zwei Studien. Gött: 1964.
(1. Die Gedichte u. kleinen Dramen. 2. Die
Dramen u. Libretti.)
2454. _____. H: Three Essays. Princeton: 1970. (Bol-
lingen Paperback, 216.) (Suppl. essay: "H's
Debt to the English-Speaking World.")
2455. Hammelmann, H. A. H. v. H. London: 1957.
2456. Hannover, Emma. Weltanschauung u. Stil: Ein stil-
psychologischer Versuch z. H's Wesen u. Werk.
(Diss.) Bonn: 1935.
2457. Heberlé, A. Beobachtungen über H's Stil. (Diss.)
Amsterdam: 1937.
2458. Hector, M. Die Wesenbestimmung d. lyrischen
Gedichtes durch H. v. H. (Diss.) Erlangen:
1954.
2459. Hederer, E. "H's Weg u. Vermächtnis, " Hochland,
XLVI (1953/4), 313-25.

2460. _____. H. v. H. Frankfurt: 1960.
2461. Hellmann, Frdr. Wilh. H u. Frankreich. Die Bedeutung Frankreichs für H's Wendg zum Sozialen. (Diss.) Freiburg i. Br.: 1959.
2462. Hennecke, H. "Neue Bücher über H, " Merkur, III (1949), 1242-7.
2463. Hestermann, O. Das myst. Element im Werke H. v. H's. (Diss.) Freiburg i. Br.: 1956.
2464. Heuschele, Otto. H. v. H.: Bildnis des Dichters. Mühlacker: 1965.
2465. Heuss, Th. "H. v. H.: Grundmotive s. Denkens u. Bekennens, " Universitas, X (1955), 1009-16.
2466. Höck, Wilhelm. Das Problem von Formen u. Form bei H. v. H. (Diss.) München: 1955.
2467. _____. " 'Das wundervollste Instrument.' H. v. H. u. d. Grenzen d. Verständigung, " Zerriebene Eitelkeiten. Kritisches z. Problemen der Sprache. München: 1965, pp. 33-45.
2468. Hofmann, Martha. "Versuch über H, " Konstellationen. Ausgew. Essays, 1945-'65. Wien: 1966, pp. 30-43.
2469. Hofmeister, K. H. Der Kritiker u. Essayist H. v. H. Die Entwickl. u. d. Wesen s. Kunst-u. Lebensanschauungen. (Diss.) Hamburg: 1953.
2470. Hoppe, Manfred. Literatentum, Magie u. Mystik im Frühwerk H. v. H's. Berlin: 1968. (Zugl. diss: Zürich.)
2471. Huber, W. Die erzählenden Werke H's. (Diss.) Zürich: 1947.
2472. Iiyoshi, Mitsuo. "Der Tod in d. Welt H's, " Doitsu Bungaku, no. 30 (1963), 126-34.
2473. Jacoby, K. "H-Bibliogr., " Imprimatur, II (1931), 241-61; III (1932), 121-51.
2474. Jens, W. "Rhetorica contra rhetoricam. H. v. H.," Von dt. Rede. München: 1969, pp. 151-79.
2475. Kayser, B. H. v. H's Beitr. z. dt. Lit. wiss. (Diss.) München: 1958.
2476. Keith-Smith, Brian. "H. v. H.," German Men of Letters: Twelve Essays, ed. A. Natan. London: 1961, pp. 253-73.
2477. Kern, Peter C. Zur Gedankenwelt d. späten H. Die Idee e. Schöpferischen Restauration. Heidelberg: 1969. (Zugl. Diss. Erlangen-Nürnberg.)
2478. Kikuchi, Takehiro. "Der Weg z. Wirklichkeit bei dem späten H, " Doitsu Bungaku, n. 26 (1961), 94-108.
2479. _____. "Der Dichter H. v. H. u. s. Lebenswerk

in d. geistigen Situation uns. Zeit, " Universitas, XX (1965), 499-506.

2480. Kindermann, Heinz. H. u. d. Schauspielkunst. Wien: 1969. (Osterr. Akad. d. Wiss. Phil. -hist. Kl. Sitzgsberichte 262, 265.)

2481. Klussmann, Paul G. "H. v. H's Lebenslied, " Ztschr. dt. Philol., LXXXII (1963), 192-210.

2482. Kobel, Erwin. Hugo von Hofmannsthal. Berlin: 1970.

2483. Koch, F. H's Leben u. Weltgefuhl. Hochstift: 1930, pp. 257-318.

2484. Kraft, Werner. "Aus H's Jugend (Frühe Gedichte), " Augenblicke d. Dicht. Krit. Betracht. München: 1964, pp. 137-46.

2485. Krämer, Eckhart. Die Metaphorik in H. v. H's Lyrik u. ihr Verhältnis z. mod. Gedicht. (Diss.) Marburg: 1963.

2486. Kuna, Franz M. "Wie modern ist H. v. H. ?" Lit. u. Kritik, IX/X (1967), 77-88.

2487. Kunisch, Hermann. "Begegnungen mit H. v. H, " Stoffe, Formen, Strukturen: Studien z. dt. Lit., ed. A. Fuchs, et al. München: 1962, pp. 487-96.

2488. _____. "H. v. H. als europ. Gestalt, " Kleine Schriften. Berlin: 1968, pp. 373-88.

2489. Lamse, Mary Jane. "Image complexes in the works of H. v. H., " Diss. Abstr., XXXI (1970/1), 1804A (Mich. '69 diss.)

2490. Laubach, J. "H's Weg von d. Magie z. Mystik. Zu s. dramat. Nachlese, " Wirk. Wort, I (1950/1), 238-45.

2491. Lewis, Hanna B. "English and American Influences on H. v. H, " Diss. Abstr., XXV (1964), 1916. (Rice).

2492. _____. "H' and America, " Studies in German..., ed. Robert L. Kahn. Houston: 1969, pp. 131-41. (Rice Univ. Studies, 55, 3.)

2493. Llewellyn, R. T. "H's Nihilism, " Mod. Lang. Review, LXI (1966), 250-9.

2494. Masui, J. "H. v. H.: le poète de la poésie, " Cah. du Sud, XLII, 333 (1956), 171-6.

2495. Mauser, W. "H-Forschung, " Riv. di lett. mod. e comp., XI (1958), 81-7.

2496. _____. "Bild u. Gebärde in d. Sprache H's, " Sitzgsberichte d. Osterr. Akad. d. Wiss. in Wien, Phil. -hist. Klasse, CCXXXVIII, 1 (1961), 14-18; 41-7. (Also in: H. v. H., ed. S. Bauer. Darmst: 1968, pp. 28-39.)

2497. _____. "Sensitive Lust u. Skepsis. Zur frühen
       Lyrik H's, " Das Nachleben d. Romantik..., ed.
       W. Paulsen. Heidelberg: 1969, pp. 116-29.
2498. Mayer, Hans. "H. u. d. Nachwelt, " in Jürgen Haupt,
       Konstellationen H. v. H's. Salzburg: 1970,
       pp. 5-44.
2499. Mennemeier, F. N. Die Gedichte H. v. H's. (Diss.)
       Münster: 1948.
2500. Metzeler, W. Ursprung u. Krise von H's Mystik.
       Mchn: 1956. (Zugl. diss. Zürich.)
2501. Moore, Sarah B. "Aspects of form in H's prose
       writings, " Diss. Abstr., XXX (1969/70), 5452A
       (Cornell '69 diss.).
2502. Müller, P. M. H's Lustspieldichtung. (Diss.)
       Basel: 1934.
2503. Nadler, J. "H. v. H. oder Welt im Traum, " Wort.
       u. Wahrheit, VII (1952), 938-43.
2504. Nägele, Rainer. "Die Sprachkrise u. ihr dicht. Aus-
       druck bei H, ' " German Quarterly, XLIII (1970),
       720-32.
2505. Naumann, Walter. "H's Verhältnis z. Trad., " Dt.
       Rds., LXXXV (1959), 612-25.
2506. _____. "H's Lyrik u. d. mod. Gedicht, " Wirk.
       Wort, IX (1959), 155-60.
2507. _____. H, d. jüngste dt. Klassiker. Darmst:
       1967.
2508. Nehring, Wolfgang. Die Tat bei H. Eine Untersuchg
       z. H's grossen Dramen. Stuttgart: 1966.
2509. Norman, F., ed. H. Studies in Commemoration.
       London: 1963. (Esp. R. Pick and A. C. Wea-
       ver, "H. v. H. in England and America: A
       Bibliography, " pp. 119-47.)
2510. Norton, Roger C. "The signif. of deeds in H's
       works, " Mod. Austrian Lit. (Journ. Intern'l A.
       Schnitzler Research Assn.) II, iii (1969), 21-3.
2511. O'Shiel, E. H's Verhältnis z. Lit. (Diss.) Wien:
       1957.
2512. Pabst, Valentin. H. v. H.'s Weg u. Wandlung vom
       Lyriker z. Dramatiker. (Diss.) Würzburg: 1952.
2513. Paris, J. "H. v. H., " Mercure de France, CCCXV
       (1952), 665-80.
2514. Perl, W. Das lyr. Jugendwerk H's. Berlin: 1936.
       (Reprint Nendeln/Liechtenstein: 1967.)
2515. Pestalozzi, Karl. Sprachskepsis u. Sprachmagie im
       Werk d. jungen H. Zürich: 1958.
2516. Pickerodt, Gerhart. H's Dramen. Kritik ihres
       histor. Gehalts. Stutt: 1968.

2517. Porter, Michael H. "The theme of consciousness in
       the poetry and early plays of H. v. H.," Diss.
       Abstr., XXXI (1970/1), 2935A (Cornell).
2518. Rang, Bernhard. H. v. H. Ein Buchverzeichn.
       Bonn/Dortmund: 1959.
2519. Requadt, Paul. "Sprachverleugnung u. Mantelsym-
       bolik im Werk H's," Dt. Vjschr., XXIX (1955),
       255-83. (Also in: H. v. H., ed. S. Bauer.
       Darmst: 1968, pp. 40-76.)
2520. Rey, William H. "Die Drohg d. Zeit in H's Früh-
       werk," H. v. H., Ed. S. Bauer. Darmst: 1968,
       pp. 165-206. (Zuerst in: Euphorion, XLVIII
       (1954), 280-310.)
2521. _____. "Gebet Zeugnis: ich war da. Die Gestalt
       H's in Bericht u. Forschg," Euphorion, III, 50
       (1956), 443-78.
2522. Rheinländer-Schmitt, Hildegard. Dekadenz u. ihre
       Überwindung bei H. (Diss.) Münster: 1936.
2523. Ritter, Frederick. H. v. H. u. Österr. Heidelberg:
       1967.
2524. Ruder, M. "H u. Frankreich," Das Buch, VII (1949),
       20-4.
2525. Ryan, Judith. "Die 'allomatische Lösung': gespaltene
       Persönlichkeit u. Konfigurationen bei H. v. H.,"
       Dt. Vierteljahrsschr. für Lit. wiss. u. Geistes-
       gesch., XLIV (1970), 189-207.
2526. Schaber, Steven C. "The Lord Chandos letter in the
       light of H's lyric decade," Germanic Review, XLV
       (1970), 52-8.
2527. Schaeder, H. H. H. v. H. u. d. geistige Welt.
       Hameln: 1947.
2528. Schmalstieg, Dieter-Olaf. "Eros u. Vogelflug. H. v.
       H. als Hermeneut alttestamentl. Weisheit," Dt.
       Vjschr., XLIII (1969), 274-88.
2529. Schmid, Martin E. Symbol u. Funktion d. Musik im
       Werk H. v. H's. Heidelberg: 1968. (Beitr. z.
       neueren Lit. geschichte, 4.) (Zugl. diss.:
       Zürich.)
2530. Schmidt, Ada. "The Limited Speaker in H's Lyric
       Poetry: A Study in Significant Form," Germanic
       Review, XXXVII (1962), 207-17.
2531. _____. "Mystic Vision and Life. Their Interrel.
       in the Writings of H. v. H.," Neophil., L (1966),
       433-6.
2532. Schüssler, Margarethe. Symbol u. Wirklichkeit bei
       H. v. H. (Diss.) Basel: 1969.
2533. Schwarz, Egon. "H and the Problem of Reality,"

Wisc. Studies Contemp. Lit., VIII (1967), 484-504. (Cf. "H's Kampf um d. Wirklichkeit, " Lit. u. Kritik, XXXIV (1969), 223-41.)

2534. Steffen, Hans. "H's Übernahme d. symbolist. Technik, " Lit. u. Geistesgeschichte: Festgabe H. O. Burger, ed. R. Grimm & C. Wiedemann. Berlin: 1968, pp. 271-79.

2535. Steinhauser, M. -L. "H et la Vie, " Bull. Fac. Lettres Strasbourg, XXX (1951), 265-76. (Le lyrisme, 1890 à 1899; de l'adolescence à la maturité.)

2536. Stern, Martin. "H's verbergendes Enthüllen, " H. v. H., ed. S. Bauer. Darmst: 1968, pp. 77-86. (Zuerst in: Dt. Vjschr., XXXIII (1959), 38-62.)

2537. Szondi, Peter. "Lyrik u. lyrische Dramatik in H's Frühwerk, " Satz u. Gegensatz: Sechs Essays. Frankfurt: 1964, pp. 58-70.

2538. Tarot, Rolf. H. v. H. Daseinsformen u. dicht. Struktur. Tübingen/Zürich: 1970.

2539. Thiemer, H. H. v. H's Ballettdichtgn. (Diss.) Greifswald: 1957.

2540. Thomése, I. A. Romantik u. Neuromantik mit bes. Berücksichtigung H. v. H's. Den Haag: 1923.

2541. Tober, Karl. "Der Begriff d. Zeit im Werk H. v. H.'s, " Germanistische Abhandlungen, ed. K. Klein & E. Thurnher. Innsbruck: 1959, pp. 247-63. (Innsbrucker Beitr. z. Kulturwissenschaft, 6.)

2542. Troppmann, W. Das Ich-Du Problem in s. Existenzbedeut. im dramat. Jugendwerk H's. (Diss.) Erlangen: 1937.

2543. Urbach, Reinhard. "Der bissige H, " Lit. u. Kritik, XX (1967), 625-7.

2544. Vanhelleputte, Michel. "Sur H, " Etudes Germaniques, XVIII (1963), 210-17. (Forschungsbericht.)

2545. _____. "Sur H, " Etudes Germaniques, XX (1965), 559-66; XXI (1966), 77-86; 572-8.

2546. _____. "H'iana (1966-7)," Etudes Germaniques, XXIV (1969), 280-5, 567-72.

2547. Waldmann, Elisabeth. H's Ethos u. Bildungswelt. (Diss.) Heidelberg: 1934.

2548. Warnach, W. "H. v. H. Sein Weg von Mythos u. Magie z. Wirklichkeit d. Geschichte, " Wort u. Wahrheit, IX (1954), 360-77. (Also in: H. v. H., ed. S. Bauer. Darmst: 1968, pp. 136-64.)

2549. Weber, Eugene M. "A Chronology of H's Poems, " Euphorion, LXIII (1969), 284-328.

2550. Weber, Horst. H. v. H.: Bibliogr. des Schriftums
      1892-1963. Berlin: 1966.
2551. Weischedel, H. H's Auffassg vom Dichter u. d.
      Dichtg. (Diss.) Tüb: 1958.
2552. _____. "H-Forschung 1945-'58, " Dt. Vjschr.,
      XXXIII (1959), 63-103.
2553. Wittmann, Lothar. Sprachthematik u. dramat. Form
      im Werke H's. Stutt/Berlin/Köln: 1966. (Zugl.
      diss.: Stutt.)
2554. Wocke, H. "H u. Italien, " Neuphil., XXV, 3 (1951),
      256-61. (Also in: Roman. Jb., IV (1951), 374-
      92.)
2555. Wolf, A. " 'Weltgeheimnis'. Reflect. on H. v. H.,"
      German Life & Letters, N. S., XI (1957/8),
      173-81.
2556. Wood, F. "H's Aesthetics," PMLA, LV, 1 (1940).
2557. Workman, J. D. "H's Use of Paradox," Ger. Quart.,
      XLII (1969), 701-17.
2558. Wunberg, Gotthart. Der frühe H: Schizophrenie als
      dichter. Struktur. Stutt: 1965. (Sprache u. Lit.,
      25.)

JIMENEZ

2559. Aguado-Andreut, Salvador. En Torno a un Poema de
      J. R. Jiménez, 2nd rev. edn. Guatemala: Univ.
      de San Carlos, 1967. (Estudio Univ., 7.)
2560. Aguirre, A. M. "Viaje de J. R. J. a la Argentina,"
      Cuad. Hisp.-americanos, CCXXI (1969), 655-73.
2561. Agullo, Mercedes. "Bibliog. de J. R. J. Su noticia
      en la prensa," La Estafeta Literaria (21 Junio
      1958.)
2562. Alfaya Bula, Javier. "J. R. J.: 'La Corriente In-
      finita, ' " Cuad. Hispanoamer., LIX (1964), 202-
      5.
2563. Anderson Imbert, Enrique. "J. R. J.," Sur (Buenos
      Aires), no. 223 (1953), 123-4.
2564. Babín, María T. "El animal en la poesía de J. R.
      J.," Asomante, XIII, 2 (Abril-Junio 1957), 72-8.
2565. Bertoli Rangel, Juan. "Una entrevista con J. R.
      J.," La Prensa (Buenos Aires), (1 Feb.
      1953).
2566. Bleiberg, Germán. "El lírico absoluto: J. R. J.,"

Clavileño, X (1951), 33-8.

2567. Bo, C. La Poesía con J. R. J., trad. Isabel de
Ambía. Madrid: 1943. (Earl. ed. Firenze:
1941.) ("Prologo" de José Alfaro.)

2568. Caballero, Agustín. "Introd., " Libros de Poesía de
J. R. J. Madrid: 1956. (Col. Premios Nobel-
Aguilar.)

2569. _____. "Prologo: J. R. desde dentro, " J. R.
J.: Libros de Poesía, 3rd ed. Madrid: Aguilar,
1967, pp. xv-lxix. ("Bibliog. , " por Francisco
Garfias, pp. 1357-1408.)

2570. Campoamor González, Antonio. "Bibliog. fund. de
J. R. J. , " Torre, XVI (1968), 177-231; XVII
(1969), 177-213; LXIV (1969), 113-45; XVII (1969),
145-79.

2571. Cole, Leo R. The Religious Instinct in the Poetry of
J. R. Jiménez. Oxford, England: 1967. (Bib-
liog., pp. 199-204.) (Orig. M. A. thesis, Univ.
London.)

2572. Contioso, Fleming. " 'Platero' como símbolo. La
cobardia de la crueldad, " Odiel (Huelva) (14 Dic.
1956).

2573. Cubiles, José A. "J. R. con la música. 'La Hora,' "
Poesía Española, LX (1956).

2574. Cyria, Sister Mary. J. R. J.'s Theory of Poetry.
Wash.: 1945. (Orig. diss., Catholic Univ. of
America, June 1944.)

2575. Díaz-Plaja, Guillermo. "Concepto del poema en J.
R. J. , " Solidaridad Nacional (Barcelona) (31 May
1958)

2576. _____. "J. R. J. , poeta de la prosa, " Arriba
(1 Junio 1958)

2577. _____. J. R. J. en su Poesía. Madrid: 1958.
(Ensayistas Hispánicas.)

2578. Diego, Gerardo. "La nueva arte poética española, "
Síntesis (Buenos Aires), II (1929).

2579. Díez Canedo, Enrique. J. R. J. en su Obra. México: 1944. (El Colegio de México.)

2580. Durán, Manuel. "J. R. J. , " Books Abroad, XLII
(1968), 391-3.

2581. Escudero, José M. "Tiempo: J. R. J. y 'Platero,' "
Arriba (5 Junio 1958)

2582. Essays by var. hands. Orto (La Habana), núm. 5
(Mayo 1939) (Homenaje a J. R. J.).

2583. _____. Espuela de Plata (La Habana) (Feb. -
Marzo 1940) (Homenaje a J. R. J.).

2584. _____. Poética (La Plata, Argentina), I, 1 (1943). (Núm. ded. a J. R. J.; incl. L. Z., "Ideario Estético de J. R. J.")

2585. _____. Los Anales de Buenos Aires, núm. XXIII (1948). (Ded. a J. R. J.)

2586. _____. Universidad, periódico infantil de la Univ. de Puerto Rico (Rio Piedra), VI, 4 (Julio 1951). (Supl. ded. a J. R. J.)

2587. _____. Poetry (Chicago), no. 4 (July 1953). (Ded. to J. R. J.)

2588. _____. "J. R. J. juzgado por sus contemp. y. discipulos," ABC (Madrid) (26 Oct. 1956).

2589. _____. Poesía Española, LX (Dic. 1956) (Num. ded. integr. a J. R. J.).

2590. _____. Clavileño, VII, 42 (Nov.-Dic. 1956). (Ded. a. J. R. J.).

2591. _____. Asomante (San Juan, Puerto Rico), XIII, 2 (Abril-Junio 1957) (Ded. íntegr. a J. R. J.).

2592. _____. Insula (Madrid), XII, 128/9 (Julio-Agosto 1957) (Homenaje a J. R. J.).

2593. _____. Mirador del Mundo (Madrid) (Oct. 1957) (Num. ded. a J. R. J.).

2594. _____. Caracola (Málaga), LX-LXI (Oct.-Nov. 1957) (Homenaje a J. R. J.).

2595. _____. La Torre, Univ. de Río Piedras (San Juan, Puerto Rico), V, 19-20 (Julio-Dic. 1957) (Más de cuatro-cientas páginas ded. a J. R. J.).

2596. Fernandez Almagro, M. "La obra de J. R. Jiménez," La Verdad (Alicante) (20 Junio 1926)

2597. Fernández Méndez, Eugenio. "J. R. J., el niñodios de los niños," La Torre, V, 19-20 (Julio-Dic. 1957), 137-49.

2598. Ferraro, Sergio. "Una nota sobre 'Platero y Yo,'" Quad. Iberoamer. (Torino), XVI (1954), 519-24.

2599. Fogelquist, Donald F. "Bibliogr. italiana de J. R. J.," Cuad. Americanos, IV (Agosto 1955), 232-6. (Volume also contains: "J. R. J. en Italia.")

2600. _____. J. R. J.: Vida y Obra, Bibliogr., Antol. (Impreso por primera vez en RHM, XXIV, 2-3 (Abril-Julio 1958.)

2601. Font, Marie T. "Espacio: Autobiogr. lírica de J. R. J.," Diss. Abstr. Intern'l, XXXI (1970), 386A (Md.).

2602. Frank, Waldo. Virgin Spain. London: 1926, pp. 290-2.

2603. Gallina, Anna M. "J. R. J. petrarchista," Annali di Ca'Foscari (Venezia), II (1963), 101-9.

2604. García Videla, Miguel. 'Platero,' personage literario. (Diss.) Buenos Aires: 1942.

2605. Garciasol, Ramón de. "Los primeros libros de
poesía de J. R. J.," Cuad. Hispanoamer., XLV
(1961), 382-97.

2606. Garfias, Francisco. "Moguer en la poesía de J. R.
J.," Cuad. de Lit., XXII-XXIV (Julio-Dic. 1950),
235-48.

2607. _____. "El paisaje de Moguer en la obra de J.
R. J.," Clavileño, VII, 42 (Nov.-Dic. 1956).

2608. _____. J. R. Jiménez. Madrid: 1961(1958).
(Bibliog., pp. 207-61.)

2609. _____. "J. R. J. en lo permanente," Cuad. Hispanoamer., CCXXXV (1969), 13-24.

2610. Gasparini, Mario. Poesía di J. R. J. Poeti Spag-
noli Contemp. Univ. de Salamanca: 1947.

2611. Gicovate, Bernardo. La Poesía de J. R. J.: Ensayo de Exégesis. San Juan de Puerto Rico:
1959.

2612. _____. "La poesía de J. R. J. en el simbolismo," Comp. Lit. Studies, IV (1967), 119-26.

2613. Gómez de la Serna, Ramón. "J. R. J.," Retratos
Contemp. (Americanos y Españoles), Primera
serie. Buenos Aires: 1941.

2614. Gouffon, Claude. "Sur J. R. J.," Figaro Litt. (Nov.
1956).

2615. Goulard, Matica. J. R. J. y la Crítica en Escandi-
navia. Madrid: 1963.

2616. Guerrero Ruiz, Juan. J. R. de Viva Voz. Madrid:
1961.

2617. Gullón, Ricardo. "El dios poéticos de J. R. J.,"
Cuad. Hispanoamer., XIV (1954), 343-9. (Repr.
in special issue of Poesía Española.)

2618. _____. "J. R. en su laberinto," Insula, XII, 128-
9 (Julio-Agosto 1957).

2619. _____. Conversac. con J. R. Jiménez. Madrid:
1958. (Diálogos, 1.)

2620. _____. Estudios sobre J. R. Jiménez. Buenos
Aires: 1960.

2621. _____, and E. F. Méndez. "J. R. J. y el
modernismo," Cuad. del Congr. por la Libertad
de la Cultura, no. 56 (1962), 3-17.

2622. Hierro, José. "J. R. comparado," Insula, XII, 128-
9 (Julio-Agosto 1957).

2623. Iniesta, Martín. "Interpr. de la 'poesía esencial'
de J. R.," Ayer, (1 Junio 1958),

2624. J. M. A. "J. R. J. y los Estados Unidos," Noticias de Actualidad (Madrid) (10 Dic. 1956).

2625. Jiménez, Juan R. "Crisis del espíritu en la poesía española," Nosotros, V, 48 (Marzo-Abril 1940), 165-82.

2626. _____. "La Corriente Infinita: Crítica y Evocacion. Madrid: 1961. (Recop., sel. y. pról. de Francisco Garfias.)

2627. _____. El Modernismo. México: 1962. (Ensayistas Hispánicos.)

2628. _____. Estética y Etica; Crítica y Complemento, ed. Francisco Garfias. Madrid: 1967. (Col. Lit.: Novelistas, Dramaturgos, Ensayistas, Poetas.)

2629. Johnson, Jerry L. "J. R. J., the critic," Diss. Abstr., XXVIII (1967), 1051A/52A (Va.).

2630. Kemmerer, Caroline R. "The creative process of J. R. J.," Diss. Abstr., XXIII (1963), 4359 (Bryn Mawr).

2631. Lacalle, Angel. "Signif. poética de J. R.," Valencia (Oct. 1956)

2632. LaOrden Miracle, Ernesto. "J. R. ya muerto en vida," Abside, XXIV (1960), 191-4.

2633. Lepera, José. J. R. J., poeta spagnolo--elogio. Napoli: 1928.

2634. Lida, Raimundo. "Sobre el estile de J. R. J.," Nosotros, III-IV (Enero-Agosto 1937), 15-29.

2635. Marías, Julián. "'Platero y yo' o la soledad communicada," La Torre, V, 19-20 (Julio-Dic. 1957), 381-95.

2636. Martín, Carlos. "J. R. J. e Hispanoamérica," El Tiempo (Bogotá), (8 Junio 1958).

2637. Molina, Ricardo. "Paralelos y signif. de J. R. J.," Córdoba (1 Junio 1958).

2638. Moncy, Agnes T. "J. R. J. y el modernismo," Torre, XI (1963), xliii, 167-74.

2639. Morales, Rafael. "J. R. J.: Notas sobre un proceso de depuración estilistica," Nuestro Tiempo (Madrid) (29 Nov. 1956).

2640. Moreno, Alfonso. Poesía Española Actual. Madrid: 1946, pp. 79-102.

2641. Muñoz Cortés, Manuel. "El silencio sonoro," Linea (30 Mayo 1958).

2642. Nadal, José. "La música en el poeta," Ayer (1 Junio 1958).

2643. Navarro Tomás, Tomás. "J. R. J. y la lírica trad.," Torre, LIX (1968), 121-45.

2644. Neddermann, Emmy. "J. R. J.: sus vivencias y

sus tendencias simbolistas, " Nosotros, I-II
(Abril-Dic. 1936), 16-25.

2645. _____. Die symbol. Stilelemente im Werke von
J. R. J., Sem. für romanische Sprachen u.
Kultur. Hamburg: 1935. (Hamb. Stud. zur
Volkstum u. Kultur des Romanen.)

2646. Olson, Paul R. "Struc. and symbol in a poem of
J. R. J., " Mod. Lang. Notes, LXXVI (1961),
636-47.

2647. _____. "Time and essence in a symbol of J. R.
J., " Mod. Lang. Notes, LXXVIII (1963), 169-93.

2648. _____. Circle of a Paradox: Time and Essence
in the Poetry of J. R. Jiménez. Baltimore:
1967.

2649. Onís, Federico de. J. R. J.: A Crit. Introd. to
"Platero y Yo." Boston: 1922.

2650. Pablos, Basilio de. El Tiempo en la Poesía de J.
R. J. Madrid: 1965. (Con un prólogo de
Pedro L. Entralgo.)

2651. Paláu de Nemes, Graciela. "J. R. J., " Books
Abroad (Norman, Okla.), (1952), 16-19.

2652. _____. Vida y Obra de J. R. J. Madrid: 1957.
(2nd edn.) (Orig.: diss., Univ. Maryland,
1952.)

2653. _____. " 'Del fondo de la vida': La noche
oscura poética de J. R. J., " Actas del Segundo
Congr. Intern'l de Hispanistas (del 20 al 25 de
agosto de 1965), ed. Sánchez Romeralo, Jaime
and Norbert Poulussen. Nijmegen, Holland:
1967, pp. 467-71.

2654. Paseyro, Ricardo. "La poesía trágica de J. R., "
Indice, XCVII (Enero 1957).

2655. Penagos, Rafael de. "Imagen fugaz de J. R. J., "
Arriba (Madrid) (25 Oct. 1956).

2656. Pesado, Mercedes. J. R. J. y su Infl. en el Grupo
de Contemp. México: 1940.

2657. Predmore, Michael. "The prose of J. R. J., "
Diss. Abstr., XXV (1965), 5939 (Wisc.).

2658. _____. La Obra en Prosa de J. R. J. Madrid:
1966 (Bibliog., pp. 271-4).

2659. _____. "The struc. of 'Platero y yo, ' " PMLA,
LXXXV (1970), 56-64.

2660. Quiñones, Fernando. "Tres notas rápidas a la
poesía de J. R. J., " Caracola, LX-LXI (Oct. -
Nov. 1957).

2661. Ramos Mimoso, Adriana. "J. R.: Enigma de un premiro, " Torre, X, 39 (1962), 143-9.

2662. Reyes, Alfonso. "J. R. y los duendes, " Dos Caminos. Madrid: 1923, pp. 63-7.

2663. Riis Owre, J. "An interview with J. R. J., " Kentucky Romance Quarterly (formerly Kentucky Foreign Lang. Quarterly), XV (for 1968), 119-20.

2664. _____. "Un cursillo de poesía con J. R. J., " Hispania, LI (1968), 320-6.

2665. Rio, Angel del, and M. J. Benardete. El Concepto Contemp. de España. Antol. de Ensayos, 1895-1931. Buenos Aires: 1946, p. 695. (Contains bibliog. on Jiménez.)

2666. Rodriguez Luis, Julio. "Los Jiménez, " Asomante, XXI (1965), iv, 37-44.

2667. Romeralo, Antonio S. "J. R. J. en su fondo de aire, " Rev. Hisp. Moderna, XXVII (1961).

2668. Sánchez-Barbudo, Antonio. La Segunda Epoca de J. R. J. (1916-1953). Madrid: 1962. (Cf. same title plus: Cincuenta Poemas Comentados. Madrid: 1963.)

2669. Schönberg, Jean-Louis. J. R. J. ou le Chant d'Orphée. Neuchâtel: 1961.

2670. Schottländer, Kirsten. "J. R. J., " Fremmede digtere i det 20 århundrede, vol. II, ed. Sven M. Kristensen. Copenhagen: 1968, pp. 185-98.

2671. Scudieri Ruggiero, Jole. "Note alla poesía di J. R. J., " Filologia e Lett., IX (1963), 393-412.

2672. Segovia, José M. "Interpr. lírica de Moguer, " Odiel (Huelva) (Nov. 1956).

2673. Segovia, Tomás. "J. R. J., ayer y hoy, " La Torre, V, 19-20 (Julio-Dic. 1957), 341-62.

2674. _____. "Actualidad de J. R., " Cuad. Americanos, XIII, 1 (1954).

2675. Senabre Sempere, Ricardo. "El proceso creador en J. R. J., " Papeles de Son Armadans (Mallorca), XXXVIII (1965), 135-46.

2676. Soubiron, Rosemary. J. R. Jiménez. (Diss.) Univ. México: 1948.

2677. Torre, Guillermo de. "J. R. J. y su estética, " Rev. Nac. de Cultura (Caracas), IX, 70 (1948), 36-47.

2678. Torrente Ballester, G. Panorama de la Lit. Española Contemp. Madrid: 1956, pp. 223-32, 569-76.

2679. Torres Ríoseco, Arturo. "La agonía de J. R. J., " Duquesne Hispanic Review, III (1964), 165-8.

2680. Trend, J. B. "J. R. J.," Bol. del Inst. de las Españas (N. Y.), núms. 5, 7-11 (1948).
2681. Uhlíř, Kamil. "K charakteristice vývojových tendencí poezia J. R. J. v leteche 1907-16 (Characteristic features of the poetry of Jiménez, 1907-'16), " Casopis pro moderní filologii, XLIV (1962), 1-7. (With a summary in Spanish.)
2682. Ulibarri, Sabine R. El Mundo Poética de Juan Ramón: Estudio Estilistico de la Lengua Poética y de los Simbolos. Madrid: c. 1962. (Bibliog., pp. 282-5.) (Estud. de lit. española.)
2683. Unamuno, Miguel de. "Carta a J. R. J.," La Torre (Puerto Rico), I (Enero-Marzo 1953).
2684. Ureña, Enrique. La Obra de J. R. J. Buenos Aires: 1919. (In "Cursos y Conferencias. ")
2685. Valbuena Prat, Angel. Hist. de la Lit. Española, tomo II. Barcelona: 1946, pp. 935-50.
2686. Valente, José A. "J. R. J., en la trad. poética del medio siglo, " Indice, XCVII (Enero 1957),
2687. Valéry, Paul. "A J. R. J., que me envió tan frescas rosas, " Poética, I (1943),
2688. Verdevoye, Paul. "Coloripoesía de J. R. J.," La Torre, V, 19-20 (Julio-Dic. 1957), 245-82.
2689. Vientós Gaston, Nilita. " 'Platero y yo,' " La Torre, V, 19-20 (Julio-Dic. 1957), 397-403.
2690. Vivanco, Luis Felipe. "La plenitud do lo real en la poesía de J. R.," Insula, XII (Enero 1957).
2691. Yndurán, Francisco. "De la sinestesia a la poesía de J. R.," Insula, XII, 128-9 (Julio-Agosto 1957).
2692. Young, Howard T. "Two poems on death by J. R. J.," Mod. Lang. Notes, LXXV (1960), 502-7.
2693. _____ . J. R. Jiménez. N. Y.: 1967 (Columbia Essays on Mod. Writers, 28.)
2694. Zardoya, Concha. "El dios deseado y deseante de J. R. J.," Poesía Española Contemp. Madrid: 1961, pp. 217-40.

LORCA

2695. Aguirre, A. M. "El sonambulismo de F. G. Lorca," Bull. Hispanic Studies, XLIV (1967).
2696. Albe. F. G. Lorca. Breda: 1960.

2697. Allen, Rupert, Jr. "Una explic. simbológica de 'Iglesia abandonada' de Lorca, " Hispano, no. 26 (1966), 33-44.

2698. _____. "An analysis of narrative and symbol in L's 'Romance Soñambulo, ' " Hispanic Review, XXXVI (1968), 338-52.

2699. Alvarez de Miranda, Angel. La Metáfora y el Mito. Madrid: 1963. (Cuad. Tauros, 49.)

2700. Aubrun, C. V. "Sur F. G. Lorca, " Iberia (Bordeaux), année III, no. 3, fasc. VIII (Mars 1948), 10-15.

2701. Babín, M. T. "Narciso y la esterilidad en la obra de G. Lorca, " Rev. Hisp. Moderna, XI (1945), 48-51.

2702. _____. El Mundo Poético de F. G. Lorca. San Juan/Madrid: 1954.

2703. _____. F. G. Lorca: Vida y Obra. N. Y.: 1955.

2704. _____. La Prosa Mágica de G. Lorca. Santander: 1962. (Orig. in: Asomante (Jan. -March 1962).)

2705. Bardi, U. "Matériaux pour une bibliogr. italienne de F. G. Lorca, " Bull. Hispanique (Burdeos), LXIII (1961), 88-97.

2706. Barea, Arturo. Lorca, the Poet and the People. N. Y.: 1949 (1958) (cf. Lorca, el Poeta y su Pueblo. Buenos Aires: 1956).

2707. _____. "Las raíces de lenguaje poético de G. L., " Bull. Spanish Studies (Liverpool), XXII (1945), 3-15.

2708. Bayón, Damián C. "G. Lorca en Francia, " Asomante, XVIII, 1 (1962), 94-101.

2709. Belamich, A. Lorca. Paris: 1962.

2710. Bellini, Giuseppe. "Lorca en Italia, " Asomante, XVIII, 1 (1962), 102-5.

2711. Berenguer-Carísomo, Arturo. Las Máscaras de F. G. Lorca. Buenos Aires: 1941. (Traces Europ. bckgd of L's work.)

2712. Bosch, Rafael. "Los poemas paralelísticos de G. Lorca, " Rev. Hisp. Moderna, XXVIII (1962), 36-44.

2713. _____. "El choque de imágenes como principio creador de G. Lorca, " Rev. Hisp. Moderna, XXX (1964), 35-44.

2714. Bowra, C. M. "F. G. Lorca: 'Romancero Gitano,' " The Creative Experiment. London: 1949, pp. 189-219.

2715. Campbell, Roy. F. G. Lorca: An Apprec. of His

Lorca   173

Poetry, 2nd edn. London: 1961. (Orig.: N.Y./
Cambridge/New Haven: 1952.)

2716. Cangiotti, Gualtiero. "F. G. Lorca, poeta del 'De-
sengaño,'" Lett. Moderne, XI (1961), 34-55.

2717. Cannon, Calvin. "Lorca's 'Llanto por Ignacio
Sánchez Mejías' and the elegiac trad.,'" Hispanic
Review, XXXI (1963), 229-38.

2718. Cano, Jose L. García Lorca. Barcelona: 1962.

2719. Cano Ballesta, J. "Una veta reveladora en la poesía
de G. Lorca (Los tiempos del verbo y sus
matices expresivos)," Romanische Forschungen,
LXXVII (1965), 75-107.

2720. Cardwell, R. A. "The persistence of Romantic
thought in Spain," Mod. Lang. Review, LXV
(1970), 803-12.

2721. Carubba, Giuseppe. "Magia nelle lirica lorchiana,"
Lucerna, XXIII, 6 (1968), 37-8.

2722. Cirre, J. F. "El caballo y el toro en la poesía de
G. L.," Cuad. Americanos, LXVI (1952), 231-
45.

2723. Cobb, Carl W. F. G. Lorca. N.Y.: 1967.
(Twayne's World Author Series, 23.)

2724. Cobelli, Enzo. García Lorca. Mantua: 1959.

2725. Comincioli, J. "F. G. Lorca. Un texto olvidado y
cuatro documentos," Cuad. Hispanoamer., no.
130 (Oct. 1960), 25-36.

2726. _____. "En torno a G. Lorca. Sugerencias,
Documentos, Bibliografía," Cuad. Hispanoamer.,
no. 139 (1961), 37-76.

2727. Correa, Gustavo. "Estudios estilisticos sobre F. G.
Lorca," Rev. de las Indias (Bogotá), XXXIV
(1949), 185-96.

2728. _____. "El simbolismo religioso en la poesía de
F. G. Lorca," Hispania, XXXIX (1956).

2729. _____. "El simbolismo de la luna en la poesía de
F. G. Lorca," PMLA, LXXII (1957).

2730. _____. "El simbolismo del sol en la poesía de
F. G. Lorca," Nueva Rev. de Filol. Hispánica
(Mexico), XIV (1960), 110-19.

2731. _____. La Poesía Mítica de F. G. Lorca. Eugene, Ore.: 1957.

2732. Couffon, Claude. Granada y G. Lorca, trans.
Bernardo Kordon. Buenos Aires: 1967. (Orig.
A Grenade. Sur les Pas de G. Lorca. Paris:
1962.)

2733. Crow, John A. "Bibliogr. hispano-americana de F.
G. Lorca," Rev. Iberoamer. (Iowa), I (1939),

469-73.

2734. _____. F. G. Lorca. Los Angeles: 1945.
2735. Devoto, Daniel. "Notas sobre el elem. trad. en la obra de G. Lorca," Filología, II (1950), 292-341.
2736. _____. "Lecturas de G. Lorca," Rev. Litt. Comparée, XXXIII (1959), 518-28.
2737. Díaz-Plaja, Guillermo. "Notas para una geografía lorquiana," Rev. de Occidente (Madrid), XXXIII (1931), 352-7. (Repr. in El Arte de Quedarse Solo.... n.p.: 1936, pp. 103-10.)
2738. _____. F. G. Lorca. Su Obra e Infl. en la Poesía Española. Buenos Aires: 1948. [3rd edn. Madrid: 1961.]
2739. _____. F. G. Lorca: Estudio Crítico. Buenos Aires/Madrid: 1954 (earlier edn. 1948).
2740. Diego, Gerardo. "'Canciones,'" Rev. de Occidente, XVII (1927), 380-4.
2741. Durán, Manuel. "G. Lorca, poeta entre dos mundos," Asomante, XVIII, 1 (1962), 70-7.
2742. _____, ed. Lorca: A Coll. of Crit. Essays. Englewood Cliffs, N.J.: 1962. (Twentieth Cen. Views.) (S-TC-14.)
2743. Eich, Christoph. F. G. Lorca: Poeta de la Intensidad, trad. Gonzalo Sobejano, 2nd rev. edn. Madrid: 1970 (1958).
2744. Essays by var. hands. F. G. Lorca (1899-1936). Vida y Obra--Bibliog.--Antol.--Obras Ineditas--Música Popular. N.Y.: Hispanic Instit. in U.S., 1941.
2745. _____. "Una encuesta de 'Insula': El teatro de G. Lorca," Insula, XV, 168 (1962), 8.
2746. Fergusson, Francis. "Don Perlimplín: Lorca's Theatre-Poetry," Kenyon Review, XVII (Spring 1955), 337-48.
2747. Flecniakoska, Jean-Louis. L'Univers Poétique de F. G. Lorca. Essai d'Exégèse. Bordeaux/Paris: 1952.
2748. Flys, Jaroslaw M. El Lenguaje Poético de F. G. Lorca. Madrid: 1955. (Biblioteca Románica Hispánica. 2. Estud. y. Ensayos, 23.)
2749. Foster, Davis W. "Lit. struc. and the study of poetic language," Hispania, LII (1969), 222-30.
2750. Franks, Gene H. "The absurd element in the plays of F. G. Lorca," Diss. Abstr., XXIX (1968), 259A (Ark.).
2751. Frattoni, Oreste. La Forma en Góngora y Otros Ensayos. Rosario: 1961.

2752. Gallejo Morell, Antonio. "El primer poema publ. por F. G. Lorca, " Bull. Hispanique, LXIX (1967), 487-92.

2753. García Lorca, Federico. Obras Completas, ed. Arturo del Hoyo, 4th ed. Madrid: Aguilar, 1960. (Contains full bibliog.) (Pról. Jorge Guillén; epíl. Vicente Aleixandre.)

2754. García-Luengo, Eusebio. "Revisión del Teatro de F. G. Lorca, " Cuad. de Política y Lit. (Madrid), num. 3 (1951).

2755. Gebser, Jean. Lorca: Poète-Dessinateur. Paris: 1949.

2756. _____. Lorca, oder das Reich der Mutter. Stuttgart: 1949.

2757. Gibson, Ian. "Los primas escritos impresos de F. G. Lorca: dos articulos más, " Bull. Hispanique, LXX (1968), 116-21.

2758. Gicovate, Bernardo. "Serenidad y conflicto en la poesía de F. G. Lorca, " Asomante, XVIII, 1 (1962), 7-13.

2759. Glasser, Doris M. "Lorca's 'Burla de Don Pedro a Caballo, ' " Hispania, XLVII (1964), 295-301.

2760. Gorman, John A. "The recep. of F. G. Lorca in Germany, 1927-'66, " Diss. Abstr., XXVIII (1967), 1818A (Johns Hopkins).

2761. Guardia, Alfredo de la. G. Lorca, Persona y Creación. Buenos Aires: 1944 [later edn. 1952].

2762. Guereña, Jacinto-Luis. "García Lorca et les lettres françaises (1936-'56), " Langues Modernes, LII (1958), 162-4.

2763. Guibert, Armand. "Lorca de soleil et d'ombre, " Preuves, CCXVIII (1969), 89-91. (Review article.)

2764. Guillén, Jorge. "F. G. Lorca, " Merkur, XVI (1962), 816-34.

2765. _____, ed. Federico in Persona: Carteggio. Milano: 1960.

2766. _____. Federico en Persona: Semblanza y Epistolario. Buenos Aires: 1959.

2767. Henry, Albert. Les Grands Poèmes Andalous de F. G. Lorca. Gante: 1958.

2768. Hierro, José. "El primer Lorca, " Cuad Hispano-amer., LXXV (1968), 437-62.

2769. Higginbotham, Virginia. "Lorca's apprenticeship in surrealism, " Romanic Review, LXI (1970), 109-22.

2770.   Honig, Edwin. "Lorca to date," Tulane Drama Re-
        view, VII, 2 (1962), 120-6.
2771.   Honig, H. G. Lorca. Norfolk, Conn.: 1963. (A
        New Dir. Paperbook, No. 102.) (Earlier ed.
        1944.)
2772.   Hoyo, Arturo Del. Estudio Prelim. a las Obras
        Completas de G. Lorca. Madrid: n.d.
2773.   Iglesias Ramirez, Manuel. F. G. Lorca: el Poeta
        Universal. Barcelona: 1963.
2774.   Jiménez, J. R. "Caricatura lírica de F. G. Lorca
        (1928)," Rev. Hisp. Moderna, I, 3 (1935), 185.
2775.   _____. "F. G. Lorca," Españoles de Tres Mun-
        dos. Buenos Aires: 1942, pp. 134-5.
2776.   Kelin, F. "On Lorca in Russian," Intern'l Lit., II.
        Moscow: 1943, pp. 50-5.
2777.   Laffranque, Marie. F. G. Lorca: Estudio sobre su
        Estética. Toulouse: 1953.
2778.   _____. "Essai de chron. de F. G. Lorca," Bull.
        Hispanique, LIX, 4 (1957), 418-29.
2779.   _____. "F. G. Lorca. Déclarations et inter-
        views retrouvés," Bull. Hispanique, LVIII (1956),
        301-43.
2780.   _____. "Conférences, déclarations et interviews
        oubliés," Bull. Hispanique, LX, 4 (1958), 508-
        45.
2781.   _____. "Expérience et conception de la condition
        du dramaturge," Le Théâtre Moderne--Hommes
        et Tendances. Paris: 1958, pp. 276-99.
2782.   _____. "Interview sur le théâtre contemp.,"
        Bull. Hispanique, LXI, 4 (1959), 437-40.
2783.   _____. "F. G. Lorca: le théâtre et la vie,"
        Réalisme et Poésie au Théâtre. Paris: 1960,
        pp. 147-71.
2784.   _____. "Pour l'étude de F. G. Lorca: Bases
        chronologiques," Bull. Hispanique, LXV, nos.
        3/4 (1963), 333-77.
2785.   _____. Lorca et la Nécessité d'Expression
        Dramatique. Paris: 1966.
2786.   _____. Les Idées Esthétiques de F. G. Lorca.
        Paris: 1967. (Bibliog., pp. 349-61.) (Thèses,
        Mémoires et travaux, 7.)
2787.   Lida, Raimundo. "Asi que pasan trienta añs: Lorca
        (1936-'66)," Mundo Nuevo (Paris), IV (1966), 81-
        3.
2788.   Lima, Robert. The Theatre of G. Lorca. N.Y.:
        1963.
2789.   Lindo, Hugo. Cuatro Grandes Poetas de América.
        Buenos Aires: 1960.

2790. López Landeira, Richard. "La zeugma, figura de dicción en la poesía de F. G. Lorca," Romance Notes (Univ. N. Carol.), XI (1969), 21-5.

2791. López-Morrillas, Juan. "G. Lorca y el primitivismo lírico: Reflex. sobre el 'Romancero Gitano,' " Intelectuales y Espirituales. Madrid: 1961, pp. 195-216.

2792. Loughran, David K. "The anchored city: a study of existence and its limits in the poetry of G. Lorca," Diss. Abstr. Intern'l, XXX (1969), 2536A (Johns Hopkins).

2793. Machado Bonet, Ofelia. F. G. Lorca: Su Producción Dramática. Montevideo: 1951.

2794. Marinello, Juan. "Du nouveau sur F. G. Lorca," Europe, nos. 437-8 (1965), 133-55.

2795. Martínez Nadal, R. "Introd., " Poems by F. G. Lorca, trans. Spender and Gli. N. Y.: 1939.

2796. Mora Guarnido, José. F. G. Lorca y su Mundo. Buenos Aires: 1958.

2797. Morby, E. S. "G. Lorca in Sweden, " Hispanic Review, XIV, 1 (Jan. 1946), 38-46.

2798. Morla Lynch, Carlos. En España con F. G. Lorca: (Páginas de un Diario Intimo, 1928-'36), rev. edn. Madrid: 1958 (1957).

2799. Neruda, P. "F. G. Lorca, " Homenaje a F. G. Lorca, Contra su Muerte. Valencia: 1937, pp. 43-9.

2800. Nims, John F. "Explic. of five Lorca poems, " The Poem Itself, ed. Stanley Burnshaw. N. Y.: 1960, pp. ?. (Incl.: 'Preciosa y el aire'; 'Despedida.')

2800a. Nourissier, François. F. G. Lorca: Dramaturge. Paris: 1955. (Les Grands Dramaturges, 3.)

2801. Ory, Carlos E. de. F. G. Lorca, trad. Jacques Deretz. Paris: 1967. (Classiques du XXe siècle, 91.)

2802. Parrot, Louis. F. G. Lorca. Paris: 1949. (Poêtes d'Aujourd'hui.)

2803. Pérez Marchand, M. L. "La inquietud existencial en la poesía de F. G. Lorca, " Asomante (Puerto Rico), V (1949), 72-86.

2804. Picciotto, Robert S. " 'La Zapatera Prodigiosa' and Lorca's poetic credo, " Hispania, XLIV (1966), 250-7.

2805. Quadri, Giancarlo. "La poesía di G. Lorca, " Cenobio, XII (1963), 365-82.

2806. Ramos-Gil, Carlos. Claves Líricas de G. Lorca: Ensayos sobre la Expresión y los Climas Poéti-

cas Lorquianos. Madrid: 1967.
2807. Riley, Edward C. "Consid. on the poetry of G.
Lorca, " Dublin Magazine, XXVII, 2 (1952), 14-22.
2808. Río, Angel del. "El poeta F. G. Lorca, " Rev. Hisp.
Moderna, I (1935), 174-84. (Also: vol. VI
(1940).)
2809. _____. Vida y Obras de F. G. Lorca. Zaragoza:
1952. (Estudios Lit., 3.)
2810. _____. "Prólogo, " Poet in New York, trans. Ben
Belitt. N. Y.: 1955. (In Spanish: Madrid:
1958.)
2811. Rizzo, G. L. "Poesía de F. G. Lorca y poesía
popular, " Clavileño, VI, 36 (1955),
2812. Roberts, Gemma. "La intuición poética del tiempo
finito en las 'Canciones' de F. G. Lorca, " Rev.
Hisp. Moderna, XXXIII (1967), 250-61.
2813. Robles, Emmanuel. G. Lorca. Algier: 1949.
2814. Rosenbaum, Sidonie C. F. G. Lorca (1899-1936).
N. Y.: Hispanic Instit. of U. S., 1941. (Contains
bibliog.)
2815. _____, and J. Guerrero Ruiz. "Bibliogr. de G.
Lorca, " Rev. Hisp. Moderna, I (1935), 186.
2816. Salinas, Pedro. "Dramatismo y teatro de F. G.
Lorca, " Lit. Española del Siglo XX, México:
1941, pp. 289-302.
2817. _____. "Lorca and the poetry of death, " Hopkins
Review, V (1951), 5-12.
2818. Sánchez, Roberto G. G. Lorca: Estudio sobre su
Teatro. Madrid: 1950.
2819. Scarpa, R. E. El Dramatismo en la Poesía de F.
G. Lorca. Santiago: Univ. de Chile, 1961.
2820. Schönberg, Jean-Louis. F. G. Lorca: l'Homme,
l'Oeuvre. Paris: 1956. (In Spanish: trans.
Aurelio Garzón del Camino. México: 1959.)
(Col. Ideas, Letras y vida.)
2821. _____. A La Recherche de Lorca. Neuchâtel:
1966. (Langages, 19.)
2822. Schweitzer, M. "Souvenirs sur F. G. Lorca, musi-
cien, " F. G. Lorca. Paris: 1949, pp. ?.
2823. Terracini, Benvenuto. "Intorno a due liriche di G.
Lorca, " Quad. Ital. di Buenos Aires, I-II (1961),
307-12.
2824. Torre, Guillermo de. "G. Lorca (1898-1936): vida
y obra, bibliografía... obras inéditas, " Rev. Hisp.
Moderna, VII (1941).
2825. _____. "F. G. Lorca, " Triptico del Sacrificio.
Buenos Aires: 1948.

2826. _____. "F. G. Lorca y sus orig. dram.,"
Clavileño, (Madrid), núm. 26 (1954), 14-18.

2827. _____. "Así que pasen veinte años. Presencia
de F. G. Lorca," El Fiel de la Balanza. Madrid: 1961, pp. 171-99.

2828. _____. La Aventura Estética de Nuestra Edad.
Barcelona: 1962.

2829. Trend, John B. F. G. Lorca. Oxford: 1951.

2830. _____. Lorca and the Span. Poetic Trad. Oxford:
1956.

2831. Trépanier, E. Le Théâtre d'Essai de Lorca (inédit).
Paris: 1957.

2832. Turcato, Bruno. "Strutt. ed evol. delle prime meta-
fore lorchaine," Quad. Iberoamer., IV, 27
(1961/2), 129-42.

2833. Umbral, Francisco. Lorca, Poeta Maldito. Madrid:
1968.

2834. Vásquez Ocaña, Fernando. G. Lorca: Vida,
Cántico y Muerte. México: 1957.

2835. Vian, Cesco. F. G. Lorca, Poeta e Drammaturgo.
Milan: 1951 (2?).

2836. Wells, C. Michael. "The natural norm in the plays
of F. G. Lorca," Hispanic Review, XXXVIII
(1970), 299-313.

2837. Williams, William Carlos. "F. G. Lorca," Kenyon
Review, I (1939), 148-55.

2838. Xiráu, Ramón. "La relac. metal-muerte en los
poemas de G. Lorca," Nueva Rev. de Filol.
Hispánica (Méjico), VII (Julio-Dic. 1957), 364-71.

2839. _____. Poesía Hispano-Americana y Española...
Mexico: 1961.

2840. Yahni, Robert. "Algunos rasgos formales en la
lírica de G. Lorca: función del paréntesis,"
Bull. Hispanique, LXVI (1964), 106-24.

2841. Zardoya, Concha. "La técnica metafórica de F. G.
Lorca," Rev. Hisp. Moderna, XX (1954), 295-
326. (Repr. in: Poesía Española Contemp.
Madrid: 1961, pp. 335-96.)

2842. Ziomek, Henryk. "El simbolismo del blanco en la
'Casa de Benarda Alba' y en la 'Dama del Alba,'"
Symposium, XXIV (1970), 81-5.

2843.   Adam, Kl.-P.   R als Ubersetzer französ Lit.   (Diss.)
        Berlin: FU, 1955.
2844.   Adolf, Helen.   "Wrestling With the Angel.   R's
        'Gazing Eye' (Der Schauende) and the Archetype, "
        Yearbook of Comp. Crit., I (1968), 29-39.
2845.   Albert-Lazard, L.   Un Image de R.   Paris: 1953.
2846.   Allemann, Beda.   Zeit u. Figur beim späten R: Ein
        Beitr. z. Poetik d. mod. Gedichtes.   Pfullingen:
        1961.
2847.   Angelloz, J.-F.   R. M. R.:   L'Evol. spirituelle du
        poète.   Paris: 1936.   (Cf. R. M. R.:   Leben u.
        Werk, übertr. aus d. französ.   von F. Kuoni.
        Zürich/Mchn: 1955.)
2848.   _____ . Rilke.   Paris: 1952.
2849.   _____ . "R-Forschungsberichte, " Mercure de
        France, CCCXIV (1952), 135-48.
2850.   _____ . "R trad. de Valéry, " Cah. Assoc.
        Intern'l Etudes Françaises, VIII (1956), 107-12.
2851.   Anon.   "The Lang. of R, " Times Lit. Suppl., XXVIII
        (July 1961), 484.
2852.   _____ . "R. M. R.--bibliogr. Aanvullingen en
        correcties, " Levende talen (Groningen), 219 (1963),
        233-5; 226 (1964), 516-17.
2853.   Barker, Orus C.   "Cosmic Play.   R. M. R.'s Un-
        derstanding of Man and the World, " Diss. Abstr.,
        XXIX (1969), 3125A (Duke).
2854.   Bartlett, James R.   "A word index to R. M. R's
        lyric poetry, with a crit. word study, " Diss.
        Abstr. Intern'l, XXX (1970), 3934A (Brigham
        Young).
2855.   Bassermann, D.   Der späte R.   München: 1947(8).
2856.   _____ . R's Vermächtnis f. uns. Zeit.   (Vortr.)
        Berlin: 1948.
2857.   _____ . Am Rande d. Unsagbaren.   Neue R-
        Ausfsätze.   Berlin: 1948.
2858.   _____ . Der andere R.   Ges. Schriften aus d.
        Nachl., ed. H. Mörchen.   Bad Homburg v. d.
        H: 1961.   (Incl.:   "R's Aufenthalt im allemani-
        schen Raum, " pp. 122-39.)
2859.   Batterby, K. A.   R and France: A Study in Poetic
        Development.   London: 1966.
2860.   Bauer, Arnold.   R. M. R.   Berlin: 1970.
2861.   Bauer, Marga.   R. M. R. u. Frankreich.   Bern:
        1931.   (Sprache u. Dichtg, 49.)

2862. Belmore, H. W.   R's Craftsmanship: An Analysis
       of His Poetic Style.   Oxford: 1954.
2863. _____.   "Sexual Elements in R's Poetry, " German
       Life & Letters, XIX (1965/6), 252-61.
2864. Berger, Hans.   "R's Weg d.   Lebensbewältigung, "
       Unterg. u. Aufgang. Vier Vortr. z. Lebenslage
       d. mod. Menschen in d. Dichtg.   Karlsruhe:
       1968, pp. 108-41.
2865. Berger, Kurt.   R's frühe Lyrik.   Entwickl. gesch.
       Analyse d. dichter. Form.   Marburg: 1931.
       (Reprint: N. Y. /London: 1968.)
2866. Betz, Maurice.   Rilke Vivant à Paris.   Paris: 1937.
       (German transl. by W. Reich.   Zürich: 1948.)
2867. Blankenagel, J. C.   "R's Striving For Inner Harmony, "
       Germanic Review, XI, 2 (April 1936), 109-21.
2868. Böhme, Marion.   R u. d. russ. Lit. Neue Beitrr.
       mit bes. Berücks. d. Rezep. R's in Russland.
       (Diss.) Wien: 1967.
2869. Bollnow, Otto F.   "Der reife R, " Doitsu Bungaku,
       no. 23 (1959), 114-26.
2870. _____. Rilke. Madrid: 1964.   (Earlier eds.:
       Stutt: 1951, 1956.)
2871. Bradley, Brigitte L.   "The Internal Unity of R's
       Cathedral Poems, " Ger. Quart., XLI (1968),
       207-21.
2872. _____. "The Tension of Contrast: R. M. R.'s
       'Neue Gedichte' as a Poetic Structure, " Diss.
       Abstr., XXVIII (1968), 4621A/22A (Columbia).
2873. Bretterbauer, R.   R. M. R.'s 'Sonette an Orpheus'
       u. 'Duineser Elegien' in d. engl. Lit.   (Diss.)
       Wien: 1956.
2874. Brewster, R. R.   "Optic and Acoustic Elements in
       the Poetic Works of R. M. R., " Summ. Doct.
       Diss., Univ. of Wisconsin, XI (1950), 364-6.
2875. _____. "Visual Expression of Musical Sound in
       R's Lyric Poetry, " Monatshefte f. dt. Unterr.,
       XLIII (1951), 395-404.
2876. Buchheit, G. R. M. R.   Zürich: 1928.   (Later ed.:
       Mengen: 1947.)
2877. Buddeberg, Else.   Kunst u. Existenz im Spätwerk
       R's. Eine Darstellung Nach s. Breifen.   Karls-
       ruhe: 1948.
2878. Butler, E. M. R. M. R.   Cambridge: 1941.
       (Later ed. 1946.)
2879. Carlsson, A. Gesang ist Dasein. R's geistiger Weg
       von Prag nach Muzot. Heidelberg: 1949.
2880. Cassirer-Solmitz, E. R. M. R.   Heidelberg: 1957.

2881.   Cleff, E.   Grundzüge dt. Wesens in d. Dichtg R's.
        (Diss.) Bonn: 1936.
2882.   Closs, August.   "The Infl. of Art on R's Poetic
        Vision, " Riv. di lett. mod., N. S., I (1951/2),
        357-61.
2883.   _____.   "R. M. R.'s Poetic Vision, " Medusa's
        Mirror: Stud. in Ger. Lit.   London: 1957,
        pp. 169-84.
2884.   Colleville, Maurice.   "R's Auffassung von d. Dichtg,"
        Lit. wissenschaftl. Jb. d. Görres-Gesell., II
        (1961), 135-44.
2885.   Comerford, Mollie J.   "R in English: 1946-'66, "
        Germanic Review, XLII (1967), 301-9.
2886.   Corcoran, M. B.   Zur Bedeut. wichtig. Wörter in d.
        frühen Schriften von R.   (Diss.) Bryn Mawr:
        1958.   (Diss. Abstr., XIX (1959), 2950/1.)
2887.   Cysarz, Herbert.   "Diesseits u. Jenseits im Werk
        R. M. R.'s, " Welträtsel im Wort. Stud. z.
        europ. Dichtg u. Phil.   Vaduz: 1948, pp. 277-
        310.
2888.   Daniel-Rops, Henry.   Rilke.   Paris(?):   1926.
2889.   _____.   "Rilke, " Où Passent des Anges.   Paris:
        1947, pp. 39-63.
2890.   _____.   "R et la France, " Revue d'Allemagne
        (janv. 1928).
2891.   David, Claude.   "Le sens de la réalité dans l'oeuvre
        de R, " Etudes Germaniques, no. 2 (oct. -nov.
        1947), 411(13)-25.
2892.   _____.   "R-Forschungsberichte, " Etudes Ger-
        maniques, VI (1951), 46-8; VII (1952), 171-4.
2893.   _____.   "La Saison Rilcéenne, " Etudes Germani-
        ques, X (1955), 36-41.
2894.   _____.   "R et l'expressionisme, " Etudes Germani-
        ques, XVII (1962), 144-57.
2895.   Dédéyan, Charles.   R et la France.   4 Tomes.
        Paris: 1964.
2896.   Dehn, F.   Rilke.   München: 1935。
2897.   Delfiner, Liselott.   R: Cet Incompris.   Paris: 1960.
2898.   Demetz, Peter.   R. M. R.'s Prager Jahre (1875-'96).
        Düsseldorf: 1953.
2899.   _____.   "Engl. Spiegelungen R. M. R.'s, " Orbis
        Litterarum, XI (1956), 18-30.   (Bei St. Spender,
        W. H. Auden u. S. Keyes.)
2900.   _____.   "Epochen d. R-Deutung, " Merkur, XI
        (1957), 985-91.
2901.   _____.   "In Sachen R, " Insel-Almanach auf das
        Jahn 1967.   Frankf. a. M.:   1966, pp. 31-41。

2902. Desgraupes, P. R. M. R.: Une Etude. Paris:
       1949. (Poètes d'Aujourd'hui, 14.)
2903. Despert, Jean. La Pensée de R. M. R. à Travers
       les Grands Thêmes de Son Oeuvre. Bruxelles:
       1962.
2904. Duruman, Safinaz. Der Wandel d. dichter. Sprach-
       form bei R. M. R. Istanbul: 1959. (Philos.
       Fak. d. Univ.)
2905. Ekner, Reidar. En Sällsam Gemenskap. Stockholm:
       1967. (Rilke in Scandinavia.)
2906. Essays by var. hands. "Reconnaissance à R, " Cah.
       du Mois (Paris) 1926.
2907. _____. Rilke et la France. Paris: 1942.
2908. _____. "Rilke, " (Gedächtnis-Nr.) Stechert-Hafner
       Book News, VI, 3 (1951), 1-18.
2909. _____. "Rilke, " Germanic Review, XXVII (1952),
       Nr. 4, 241-320.
2910. _____. "Rilke, " Les Lettres (Paris), nos. 14-16,
       IV (1952), 240 pp.
2911. Feise, E. "R's Weg zu d. Dingen, " Xenion: Themes,
       Forms, and Ideas in Ger. Lit. Baltimore: 1950,
       pp. 261-8. (Zuerst in Monatshefte f. dt. Unterr.
       (1936).)
2912. Fickert, Kurt J. "Form and Meaning in Rilke's
       Sonnets, " Kentucky Foreign Lang. Quart. , X
       (1963), 69-81.
2913. Forsting, B. R. M. R.'s Verhältnis z. Sprache.
       (Diss.) Berlin: FU, 1952.
2914. Freedman, Ralph. "Gods, Heroes, and Rilke, "
       Hereditas: Seven Essays on the Mod. Exper. of
       the Classical, ed. F. Will. Austin: 1964,
       pp. 3-30.
2915. Fuerst, N. Phases of R. Bloomington: 1958.
2916. Fülleborn, U. "Zur magischen Gebärdensprache des
       späten R, " Festgruss f. H. Pyritz.... Heidel-
       berg: 1955. (Also in: Euphorion, III, 49
       (1955)--Sonderheft.)
2917. _____. Das Strukturproblem d. späten Lyrik R's:
       Voruntersuchungen z. e. histor. R-Verständnis.
       Heidel: 1960. (Also: diss. --Hamburg: 1957.)
2918. Gebser, Jean H. R u. Spanien. Zürich: 1940(6).
2919. _____. "R. M. R. in uns. Zeit, " Das Schweiz.
       R'-Archiv (Zürich), (1952), 31-8.
2920. Goertz, Hartmann. Frankreich u. d. Erlebnis d.
       Form im Werke R. M. R.'s. Stutt: 1932.
2921. Graff, W. L. R. M. R.: Creative Anguish of a
       Mod. Poet. Princeton, N.J.: 1956.

2922. _____. R's lyr. Summen. Aus d. Engl. Übers.
Berlin: 1960.
2923. Greifenstein, Karl. Der Engel u. d. Dimensionen d.
Unsäglichen bei R. M. R. (Diss.) Heidel: 1950.
2924. Grosser, A. "R trad. du 'Cimetière Marin,' "
Etudes Germaniques, IV, 4 (oct.-déc. 1949), 373-
86.
2925. Grossmann, Dietrich. R. M. R. u. d. französ.
Symbolismus. (Diss.) Jena: 1938.
2926. Günther, H. "R u. d. mod. Welt," Welt u. Wort,
VIII (1953), 77-81.
2927. Günther, W. Weltinnenraum: d. Dichtg R's. Berlin:
1943. (Lat. ed. 1952.)
2928. Haber, Bernhard. Die Gestalt d. Dichters in d. Mod.
(Diss.) Münster: 1950.
2929. Hahn, K. J. R. M. R., e. Studie. Regensbg:
1949.
2930. _____. "D. jüngste R-deutg," Hochland, XLVIII
(1955/6), 69-78.
2931. Hajek, S. R. M. R. Wuppertal-Barmen: 1949.
2932. Halda, Bernard. R. M. R. Paris: 1961.
2933. Hamburger, Käte. "Die phänomenolog. Struktur d.
Dichtg R's," Philos. d. Dichter. Novalis.
Schiller. Rilke. Stutt: 1966, pp. 179-275.
(Excerpt in Jb. f. Asthetik u. Kunstwiss., X
(1966), 217-34.)
2934. Hamburger, Michael. "An Anatomy of Orpheus: R
Among the Critics," Encounter (London), XVIII,
103, iv (1962), 46-51.
2935. Hecht, Roger. "R in Transl.," Sewanee Review,
LXXI (1963), 513-22.
2936. Heerikhuizen, F. W. van. R. M. R.: His Life and
Work, trans. K. J. Hahn. N.Y.: 1952.
2937. Heftrich, Eckhard. Die Philos. u. R. Freiburg:
1962. (Symposium, 9.) (Cf. Zu philos. Interpr.
von R's Dichtg. (Diss.) Freib. i. Br. /Mchn:
1958.)
2938. Hell, Victor. R. M. R. Existence Humaine et
Poésie Orphique. Paris: 1965.
2939. Henkelum, H. van. 'Rühmen, das ists': Stud. z.
späten Gedichten R's. (Diss.) Würzburg: 1936.
2940. Hergershausen, Lore. "Sur quelques termes du vocab. des arts plastiques dans l'oeuvre de R. M.
R.: Les Reflets," Etudes Germaniques, XVII
(1962), 281-9.
2941. Hermann, Alfred. R's ägyptische Gesichte. Ein
Versuch wechselseitiger Erhellg von Dichtg u.

Altkultur. Darmst: 1966. (Zuerst in: Symposium, IV (1955), 367-461.)

2942. Hermann, Rosemarie. R. M. R. u. d. französ. Geist. (Diss.) Tüb: 1947.

2943. Hess, G. "R u. Frankreich," Neuphil. Zs., I, 2 (1949), 2-15.

2944. Heygrodt, R. H. Die Lyrik R. M. R.'s: Versuch e. Entwickl. gesch. Freiburg: 1921.

2945. Hoeniger, F. D. "Symbolism and Pattern in R's 'Duino Elegies,' " German Life & Letters, NS, III (1949/50), 271-83.

2946. Hohoff, Curt. "R. M. R. in s. Exegeten," Wort u. Wahrheit, VI (1951), 226-8.

2947. Holmes, Theodore. "To Be Transformed," Poetry, XCIV (1959), 59-61.

2948. Holyroyd, S. "R, the Visionary Individualist," Emergence From Chaos. London: 1957, pp. 166-90.

2949. Holthusen, H. E. R. M. Rilke... New Haven: 1952. (Stud. in mod. Europ. Lit. & Thought.)

2950. _____. "R u. d. Dichtg d. Gegenwart," Universitas, XII (1957), 1157-70.

2951. _____. "R Nach 30 Jahren," Anstösse (Hofgeismar), (1959), 147-54.

2952. _____. "R Nach 40 Jahren. Zur Geistesgesch. e. Nachruhms," Plädoyer f. d. Einzelnen. Krit. Beitr. z. lit. Diskuss. Mchn: 1967, pp. 155-62. (Zuerst in: Frankf. Allg. Ztg (22 Nov. 1966).)

2953. Huder, W. Die Dialektik in d. Dichtg R. M. R's. (Diss.) Berlin: FU, 1956.

2954. _____. "Umkehr d. Räume. Ein Beitr. z. Erkenntnis d. Spätdichtg R. M. R.'s," Welt u. Wort, XIII (1958), 203-6.

2955. Hünich, F. A. R-Bibliogr. Leipzig: 1935.

2956. Hysek, Ingeborg. Das R-bild in d. Memoirenlit. (Diss.) Wien: 1968.

2957. Isler, E. -P. "La Structure des 'Elégies de Duino,' " Langues Modernes, XXXV (avril 1937).

2958. Jaccottet, Philippe. Rilke Par Lui-Même. Paris: 1970.

2959. Jaloux, Edmond. "Le Message de R," Revue Nouvelle, (mars 1907)

2960. _____. Rilke. Paris: 1928.

2961. Jayne, Dick P. "The Symbolism of Space and Motion in the Works of R. M. R.," Diss. Abstr., XXX (1969), 1170A/71A (Berkeley).

2962. Jonas, Klaus W. "Die R-Kritik 1950-'66, " Insel-
Almanach (1967), 94-121.

2963. Kanzog, Klaus. "Wortbildwahl u. phallisches Motiv
bei R. M. R. Beitr. z. e. zukünftigen R-Wörter-
buch, " Ztschr. f. dt. Philol., LXXVI (1957),
203-28.

2964. Kaufmann, F. "Sprache als Schöpfung, " Ztschr. f.
Asthetik, XXVIII (1934), 1-54.

2965. _____ . "Vom Vermächtnis R. M. R.'s, " Monatsh.
f. dt. Unterr., XL (1948), 113-25.

2966. Kitamura, Seikichi. "Das Ding bei R, " Doitsu Bungaku, no. 30 (1963), 76-84.

2967. Klatt, F. R. M. R. Wien: 1936. (Later eds.,
1948, '49.)

2968. Koch, F. R's Kampf um die Wirklichkeit. Hochstift:
1936/40.

2969. Kohlschmidt, Werner. R-Interpr. Lahr: 1948.

2970. Kollitsch, Willibald. Allit. u. Konsonantismus in d.
Gedichten R. M. R.'s (Diss.) Wien: 1949.

2971. Koshina, Yoshio. "R. M. R.: Dichtung u. d. mod.
Ausdruckswelt, " Universitas, XXIII (1968), 713-
17.

2972. Kraft, Werner. "R in Fall u. Stand, " Augenblicke d.
Dichtg. Krit. Betrachtgn. Mchn: 1964, pp. 163-
74.

2973. Kretschmar, E. R als Dichter des Seins. Dresden:
1934.

2974. _____ . Die Weisheit R's. : 1936.

2975. Kreutz, H. R's 'Duineser Elegien.' Eine Interpr.
München: 1950.

2976. Kröger, E. P. "Rilke und die französ. Lit., " Neue
Schweizer Rundschau (Zürich), XXII (1929), 73-9.

2977. Kunisch, Hermann. R. u. d. Dinge. Köln: 1946.
(Also in: Kleine Schriften. Berlin: 1968,
pp. 389-420.)

2978. Kunz, Marcel. Narziss. Untersuch. z. Werk R. M.
Rs. Bonn: 1970 (orig.: diss. Zürich).

2979. Kyritz, Heinz-Georg. R's Auffassg von d. Kunst u.
d. Künstler vor Duino, 1896-1912. (Diss.)
McGill Univ. Montréal: 1961.

2980. Lachmann, E. "Bezauberung durch Orpheus. Zur
Verdrängg im Werk d. späten R, " Wort u. Wahr.,
IV (1949), 922-6.

2981. Lang, Renée. "R and His French Contemp., " Comp.
Lit., X, 2 (Spring 1958), 136-43.

2982. Langenfeld, L. "Nicht abreissende R Interpr., "
Bücherei u. Bildung, VIII (1956), 6-11. (1945-'54

in Germany.)
2983.   Lavrin, Janko. "R and Russia, " Russian Review,
        XXVII, 2 (1968), 149-60.
2984.   Lehnert, Herbert. "Spiel zw. Prosa u. Vers.
        Grenzsituationen. R, 'An d. sonngewohnten
        Strasse'..., " Struktur u. Sprachmagie. Zur
        Methode d. Lyrik Interpr. Stutt: 1966, pp. 107-
        36.
2985.   Leishman, J. B. "Betrachtgn e. engl. R-Ub`erset-
        zers, " Gestalt u. Gedanke, VIII (1963), 137-55.
2986.   Leschnitzer, A. "Romantik u. Mystik in d. Dichtg
        R's, " ... Ztschr. f. Volkskunde, IV (1930).
2987.   Mágr, Clara. R. M. R. u. d. Musik. Wien: 1960.
2988.   Mandel, Siegfried. R. M. R.: The Poetic Instinct.
        Carbondale: 1965. (Also: Diss. Abstr., XXVIII
        (1968), 4639A (Denver).)
2989.   Mason, Eudo C. R's Apotheosis: A Survey of Re-
        pres. Recent Publ. on the Work and Life of R.
        Oxford: 1938.
2990.   _____. Lebenshaltung u. Symbolik bei R. M. R.
        Weimar: 1939.
2991.   _____. "Stichproben: Vers. e. Morphologie d.
        R-Deutung, " Orbis Litt., VIII (1950), 104-60.
2992.   _____. R, Europe, and the English-Speaking
        World. Cambridge, Engl.: 1961.
2993.   _____. R. M. R.: Sein Leben u. Sein Werk.
        Gött: 1964. (English ed. Edinburgh/London:
        1963.)
2994.   _____. "R's Experience of Inspiration and His
        Concep. of 'ordnen, ' " Forum for Mod. Lang
        Studies, II (1966), 335-46.
2995.   Matejka, Ladislav. "R. M. R. and the Czech lan-
        guage, " Amer. Slav. & East Europ. Review,
        XIII, 4 (1954), 588ff.
2996.   Meyer, Herman. "Die Verwandlg d. Sichtbaren.
        Die Bedeutg d. mod. bild. Kunst f. R's späte
        Dichtg, " Zarte Empirie. Stud. z. Lit. gesch.
        Stutt: 1963, pp. 287-336. (Zuerst in: Dt.
        Vjschr., XXXI (1957), 465-505.)
2997.   Milch, W. "R u. England, " Universitas, II (1947),
        1463-74.
2998.   Mises, R. von. R in English: A Tentative Bibliog-
        raphy. Cambridge, Mass.: 1947.
2999.   Moore, H. T. "The Later R, " 20th Cen. Ger. Lit.
        N.Y./London: 1967, pp. 52-6.
3000.   Morse, B. J. "R. M. R. and English Lit., " Ger-
        man Life & Letters, NS, I (1947/8), 215-28.

3001. _____. "Contemp. English Poets and R, " German
       Life & Letters, NS, I (1947/8), 272-85.
3002. Motekat, Helmut. "R. M. R. Durch d. Experiment
       z. Trad., " Experiment u. Trad.: Vom Wesen d.
       Dichtg im 20 Jh. Frankf: 1962.
3003. Müller, F. W. "R u. d. französ. Dichtg, " Prisma,
       XXII (1948), 3-6.
3004. Müller, H. R. R als Mystiker. Berlin: 1935.
3005. Muret, Maurice. "La Formation de R. M. R., "
       Journ. des Débats, (23 fév. 1938)
3006. _____. "R et la Critique Française, " Journ. des
       Débats, (12 juill. 1939)
3007. Musil, R. "Discours sur R, " Nouv. Nouv. Rev.
       Française, V (1957), no. 51, 457-67.
3008. Neumann, Alfred R. "R and His Relation to Music, "
       South Central Bull., XX, iv (1960), 25-8.   (Tulsa,
       Okla. Studies by Members of the South Central
       MLA.)
3009. Neumann, Elisabeth. Die Verschiebung d. Erlebnisses
       'Wirklichkeit' im mittleren u. späteren Dichtgn
       R's. (Diss.) Münster: 1935.
3010. O'Connell, R. B. "Concepts and Symbols in the
       Poetry of R. M. R.: A Study of Their Develop-
       ment, " Diss. Abstr., XII (1952), 190-1.   (Univ.
       of Minn.)
3011. Olbrich, M. "R and the World of Feeling, " Quart.
       Rev. of Lit., II (1945), 36-44.
3012. Oliver, K. "R. M. R.'s Basic Concept of Lit. Art, "
       Monatsh. f. dt. Unterr., XL (1948), 382-90.
3013. Osann, Christiane. R. M. R. Der Weg e. Dichters.
       Zürich: 1941.
3014. Ouwehand, C. and S. Kusunoki. R in Japan: Ver-
       such e. Bibliogr. s'-Gravenhage: 1960.
3015. Pauquet, P. P. Schöpferische Angst: Versuch e.
       Angst-Kosmologie bei R. (Diss.) Bonn: 1939.
3016. Peters, Heinz F. R. M. R.: Masks and the Man.
       Seattle: 1960.
3017. Pitrou, Robert. R. M. R.: Les Thèmes Principaux
       de Son Oeuvre. Paris: 1938.
3018. Pleyer, W. "Uber d. Wirkungen R's, " Pforte, II
       (1949/50), 694-70.
3019. Pongs, H. "Rilke, " Das Bild in d. Dichtg. Marburg:
       1927/39, II, pp. 322-481.
3020. Posteuca, Vasile. "Inner Experience in R's Work, "
       Diss. Abstr., XXIV (1963), 1605/6 (Toronto).
3021. Poths, Marg. R. M. R.'s dichter. u. persönl.
       Verhältnis z. Mitmenschen. (Diss.) Frankf:
       1949.

3022. Puckett, Hugh W. "R's Beginnings, " Germanic Re-
       view, VIII (1933), 99-113.
3023. Puknat, E. M. and S. B. "American Lit. Encounters
       with R, " Monatshefte, LX (1968), 245-56.
3024. Purtscher-Wydenbruck, Nora. R, Man and Poet.
       London: 1949.
3025. Rehm, W. "Wirklichkeitsdemut u. Dingmystik, "
       Logos, XIX, 3 (1930), 297-358.
3026. Ritzer, W. R. M. R.-Bibliogr. Wien: 1951.
3027. _____. "Ein Streifzug durch d. R-Forschung, "
       Antiquariat (Wien) VIII, 13-18 (1952), 67-9.
3028. Robinet de Cléry, A. R Traducteur. Genève: 1956.
3029. _____. R. M. R., Sa Vie, Son Oeuvre, Sa Pensée.
       Paris: 1958.
3030. Rolleston, James L. "R in Transition: A Study of
       His Poetry 1896-1902, " Diss. Abstr., XXIX
       (1969), 4018A/19A (Yale).
3031. _____. Rilke in Transition. An Explor. of His
       Earliest Poetry. New Haven, Conn. /N. Y.:
       1970. (YGS, 4.)
3032. Romain, W. P. R. M. R., le Poète. Bulle: 1952.
3033. Rose, W. & G. C. Houston, eds. R: Aspects of
       His Mind and Poetry. London: 1938. [Reprinted:
       N. Y.: 1970.]
3034. Rothmann, Kurt K. "Die Stilentwicklg in R's dichter.
       Prosa, " Diss. Abstr., XXVII (1967), 3062A/63A
       (Cincinnati).
3035. Rousselot, Jean. "Le Message de R. M. R., "
       Verger, I, 1 (1947/8), 6-13.
3036. _____. "L'Univers de R. M. R., " L'Age Nouveau,
       no. 73 (1952), 22-30.
3037. Ryan, Judith. Umschlag u. Verwandl. poetische
       Struk. u. Dichtungstheorie in R. M. R's Lyrik der
       mittl. Periode (1907-'14). München: 1972.
3038. Ryan, Lawrence. "Die Krise d. Romantischen bei R.
       M. R., " Das Nachleben d. Romantik..., ed. W.
       Paulsen. Heidel: 1969, pp. 130-51.
3039. Saas, Christa. "R's Expressionism, " Diss. Abstr.,
       XXVIII (1967/8), 3683A.
3040. Salinger, H. An Index to the Poems of R. Madison:
       1942.
3041. Schelbitzki Pickle, Linda L. "R's poetic vocab. in
       the 'Duineser Elegien' and 'Sonnette an Orpheus, ' "
       Diss. Abstr., XXXI (1970/1), 398A (Colorado).
3042. Schlötermann, Heinz. R. M. R.: Versuch e. Wesen-
       deutung. Mchn. /Basel: 1966.

190   A Post-Symbolist Bibliography

3043.   Schneider, Jean-Claude.   "Le Regard de R, " Nouv.
          Rev. Française, XIV (nov. 1966), 881-7.
3044.   Schoolfield, George C.   "Reassessing R, " Journ.
          English and Germanic Philology, LXII (1963),
          336-51.   (Review article.)
3045.   Schrank, W.   Sein u.   Erziehung im Werk R's.
          Weimar: 1931.
3046.   Schroeder, A. E.   "A sel.   R bibliogr., " Stechert-
          Hafner Book News,   VI (1951),   37-41.
3047.   _____ .   "R. M. R. in America.   A Bibliogr.,
          1926-'51, " Monats. f. dt. Unterr., XLIV (1952),
          27-38.
3048.   Schwerte, H.   Studien z.   Zeitbegriff bei R. M. R.
          (Diss.) Erlangen: 1948.
3049.   Seifert, Walter.   Das epische Werk R. M. R's.
          Bonn: 1969.   [AKML, 82.]   (Zugl. diss. F. U. :
          Berlin.)
3050.   Shinichi, Hoshino.   "R u. unsere Zeit, " Doitsu Bunga-
          ku, XLIII (1969),   75-83.   (In Japanese, with sum-
          mary in German.)
3051.   Sieber, C.   René R: die Jugend R's.   Leipzig: 1932.
3052.   Sieburg, F.   "R, das Zeitsymptom, " Die Lust am
          Untergang.   Hamburg: 1954, pp. 337-64.
3053.   Sievers, Marianne.   Die biblischen Motive in d.
          Dichtg R. M. R. 's.   Berlin: 1938.   (Reprint
          Nendeln/Liechtenstein: 1967.)
3054.   Simenauer, E.   R. M. R. :   Legende u.   Mythos.
          Bern: 1953.
3055.   Simoens, Leo.   "R. M. R. -bibliogr. :   Aanvullingen
          en correcties, " Levende Talen, no. 219 (1963),
          233-5.
3056.   Smith, Peter.   "Elements of R's Creativity, " Oxford
          Ger. Stud., II (1967), 129-48.
3057.   Spender, Stephen.   "Der Einfluss R's auf d. engl.
          Dichtg, " Neue Auslese, I, 10 (1946), 21-5.
          (Aus e. BBC-Sendg--übers.)
3058.   Spenlé, Jean-Edouard.   "Les Thèmes Inspirateurs
          de la Poésie de R, " Mercure de France, CXCIV
          (15 févr. 1927),
3059.   Stahl, August.   'Vocabeln der Not' u. 'Früchte der
          Tröstung':   Studien z. Bildlichkeit im Werke R.
          M. R. 's.   Heidel: 1967.   (AUS, 8.)   (Zugl.
          diss. :   Saarbrücken.)
3060.   _____ .   "Das Sein im 'angelischen Raum':   zum
          Gebrauch d. Konjunktivs in d. Lyrik R. M. Rs, "
          Ztschr. f. dt. Philol., XCIX (1970), 481-510.
3061.   Stämpfli, G.   Die Entwickl. d. formalen Bewusstseins

in d. Gedichten R's.   (Diss.) Erlangen: 1935.
3062. Steffensen, Steffen.   "R-Forschungsberichte, " Orbis
Litt., IV (1946), 289-303.
3063. _____. "R's Kampf um die Wirklichkeit, " R u.
Skandinavien. Copenhagen: 1958, pp. 13-36.
3064. Steiner, Jacob.   "Die Thematik d. Worts im dichter.
Werk R's, " Neophiloligus, XLVI (1962), 287-308.
3065. _____. R's 'Duineser Elegien.' Bern: 1962.
(Also: Stockholmer germanistische Forschungen,
3. Stockholm: 1962.)
3066. _____, comp. "Stimmen über Rilke, " Insel-
Almanach (1967), 69-93.
3067. Stephens, Anthony.   "The Problem of Completeness
in R's Poetry 1922-6, " Oxford Ger. Studies, IV
(1969), 155-87.
3068. Storck, J. W.   "Neue R Lit., " Dt. Univ. Ztg, IX,
10 (1954), 14-17; 11, 14-17.
3069. _____. "R's Dichtg u. d. Grenzen d. Sprache, "
German Life and Letters, NS, VIII (1954/5), 192-
200.
3070. _____. "Wort-Kerne u. Dinge. R u. d. Krise d.
Sprache. Zu d. Gedichten 1906-'26, " Akzente, IV
(1957), 346-58.
3071. Strauss, Georg.   "Berichtigung über R. M. R., "
Irrlichter u. Leitgestirne. Essays über Probleme
d. Kunst. Zürich: 1966, pp. 97-107.
3072. Takayasu, Kuniyo.   "R u. d. Japaner, " Doitsu Bungaku, XXXII (1964), 5-13.
3073. Thorlby, A.   "R and the Ideal World of Poetry, "
Yale French Stud., no. 9 (1952), 132-42.
3074. Tilliette, Xavier.   "R. M. R. ou la Méditation Sur
l'Existence, " Existence et Litt. Bruges:
1962, pp. 11-45.
3075. Valéry, Paul et al. Reconnaissance à Rilke. Paris:
1926. (Cah. du Mois.)
3076. Vogt, Joachim. Studien z. Geschichtsverhältnis R.
M. R's. (Diss.) Jena: 1946.
3077. Wais, Karin. Studien z. R's Valéry-Übertr. Tüb:
1967.
3078. Wandel, Joseph.   "R u. d. Maler., " Diss. Abstr.,
XXVI (1965), 3355. (Northwestern.)
3079. Warnach, W.   "R-Forschungsberichte, " Hochland,
XLII (1950), 498-506.
3080. Webb, Karl E.   " 'Das Buch der Bilder.' A Study
of R's changing attitudes and artistry, " Diss.
Abstr., XXX (1969/70), 3029/30A (Pennsylvania).

3081. 		. "Themes in transition: Girls and love in
R's 'Buch der Bilder, ' " German Quarterly, XLIII
(1970), 406-17.
3082. 	Weigand, Hermann. "Zu R's Verskunst, " Neophilolo-
gus, XLVIII (1964), 31-51.
3083. 		. "Das Wunder im Werk R. M. R's, "
Fährten u. Funde. Aufs. z. dt. Lit., ed. L. Wil-
lson. Bern/Mchn: 1967, pp. 232-53. (Zuerst
in: Monatsh., XXI (1939), 1-21.)
3084. 	Wolfrom, Janine. "Essai Sur le Silence Dans les
Poèmes Français de R. M. R., " Rev. des
Lettres Mod., VI (1959), 1-112.
3085. 	Wood, F. H. "R and the Theater, " Monatsh. f. dt.
Unterr., XLIII (1951), 15-26.
3086. 		. R. M. R. The Ring of Forms. Minne-
apolis: 1958.
3087. 	Zeber, Ludwig. R's dichter. Seins-Entwurf u. d.
Stellenwert d. 'französ.' R. (Diss.) Köln: 1960.
3088. 	Zimmermann, Ch. Grundworte d. dichter. Denkens
im Spätwerk R. M. R.'s. (Diss.) Heidel: 1954.

STEVENS

3089. 	Adams, Richard P. " 'The Comedian as the Letter
C': A somewhat literal reading, " Tulane Stud.
in English, XVIII (1970), 95-114.
3090. 	Alexander, Charles. "The idea of Evil in W. S.'s
poetry, " Mass. Stud. in English, I (1968), 100-5.
3091. 	Baird, James. The Dome and the Rock: Structure
in the Poetry of W. S. Baltimore: 1968.
3092. 	Baker, Howard. "W. S. and other poets, " Southern
Review, I (1935), 373-89.
3093. 	Baym, Nina. "The transcendentalism of W. S., "
Emerson Society Quarterly, LVII (1969), 66-72.
3094. 	Benamou, Michel. "Le thème du héros dans la
poésie de W. S., " Etudes Anglaises, XII (1959),
222-30.
3095. 		. "W. S.: some relat. betw. poetry and
painting, " in Brown and Haller (eds.), pp. 232-
48.
3096. 		. "W. S. and the symbolist imagination, "
Journ. English Lit. Hist., XXXI (1964), 35-63.
(Repr. in Pearce (ed.), pp. 92-120.) (Cf. coll.
essays under same title. Princeton, N.J.: 1972).

3097. _____. "The struc. of W. S.'s imagination,"
       Mundus Artium, I (1967), 73-84.
3098. Benziger, James. Images of Eternity. Carbondale:
       1962, pp. 241-3. (On W. S.'s 'Not Ideas About the
       Thing.')
3099. Bevis, William W. "The arrangement of 'Harmoni-
       um,'" Journ. English Lit. Hist., XXXVII (1970),
       456-73.
3100. Bewley, Marius. "The poetry of W. S.," Partisan
       Review, XVI (Sept. 1949), 895-915. (Repr. in
       Brown & Haller (eds.), pp. 141-61.)
3101. Blackmur, R. P. "Examples of W. S.," The Double
       Agent. N. Y.: 1935, pp. 68-102. (Repr. in
       Brown & Haller (eds.), pp. 52-80(81?).)
3102. _____. Form and Value in Mod. Poetry.   Garden
       City: 1957.
3103. Blessing, Richard A. W. S.'s 'Whole Harmonium.'
       Syracuse, N. Y.: 1970. (Bibliog., pp. 173-80.)
3104. Bloom, Harold. "'Notes Toward a Supreme Fiction':
       A Comment.," in Borroff (ed.), pp. 76-95.
3105. Borroff, Marie, ed. W. S.: A Coll. of Crit. Es-
       says. Englewood Cliffs, N. J.: 1963. ("Introd."
       & "W. S.: the world and the poet," pp. 1-23.)
3106. Breit, Harvey. "Sanity that is magic," Poetry,
       LXII (1943), 48-50.
3107. Brezianu, Andrei. "Pe marginea motivului solar in
       poezia lui W. S.," Secolul XX, XII, 9 (1969),
       156-63.
3108. Brinnin, John M. "Plato, Phoebus, and the man
       from Hartford," Voices, CXXI (Spring 1945), 30-
       7.
3109. Brown, Ashley, and R. S. Haller, eds. The Achieve-
       ment of W. S... Philad.: 1962.
3110. Brown, Merle E. "Concordia Discors in the poetry
       of W. S.," Amer. Lit., XXXIV (1962), 246-9.
3111. _____. W. S.: The Poem as Act. Detroit:
       1970(71?).
3112. Bruns, Gerald L. "Poetry as reality: the Orpheus
       myth and its modern counterparts," Journ.
       English Lit. Hist., XXXVII (1970), 263-86.
3113. Bryer, J. R., and J. N. Riddel. "A checklist of
       Stevens Crit.," Twentieth Cen. Lit., VIII, 3-4
       (Oct. 1962-Jan. 1963), 124.
3114. Buhr, Marjorie C. "The essential poem: a study
       of W. S.'s ontology," Diss. Abstr. Intern'l, XXX
       (1970), 3451A (Miami).
3115. _____. "When half-gods go: S's spiritual odyssey,"

Wallace Stevens Newsl., I, 2 (1970), 9-11.
3116. Burney, William. W. Stevens. N.Y.: 1968.
3117. Burnshaw, Stanley. "W. S. and the statue," Sewanee
        Review, LXIX (Summer 1961), 355-66.
3118. Buttell, Robert W. "W. S. at Harvard: some ori-
        gins of his theme and style," Journ. English Lit.
        Hist., XXIX (March 1962), 90-119. (Repr. in
        Pearce & Miller (eds.), pp. 29-57.)
3119. _____. "Prelude to 'Harmonium': the develop.
        of style and technique in W. S.'s early poetry,"
        Diss. Abstr., XXVII (1967), 3448/49A (Columbia).
3120. _____. W. S.: The Making of Harmonium.
        Princeton, N.J.: 1967.
3121. Cunningham, J. V. "The poetry of W. S.," Poetry,
        LXXXV (Dec. 1949), 149-65.
3122. _____. Trad. and Poetic Struc.: Essays in Lit.
        Hist. and Crit. Denver, Colo.: 1960.
3123. _____. "Trad. and modernity: W. S.," in Brown
        and Haller (eds.), pp. 123-40.
3124. _____. "The styles and proced. of W. S.," Univ.
        Denver Quart., I, 1 (1966), 8-28.
3125. Davie, Donald. "Essential gaudiness: the poems of
        W. S.," Twentieth Cen., CLIII (1953), 455-62.
3126. Dietrichson, Jan W. "W. S.'s 'Sunday Morning,'"
        Edda, LXX (1970), 105-16.
3127. Doggett, Frank. "W. S.'s later poetry," Journ.
        English Lit. Hist., XXV (June 1958), 137-54.
3128. _____. "The poet of earth: W. S.," College
        English, XXII (1961), 373-80.
3129. _____. "W. S. and the world we know," English
        Journal, XLVIII (1959), 365-73.
3130. _____. "This invented world: S's 'Notes Toward
        a Supreme Fiction,'" in Pearce & Miller (eds.),
        pp. 13-28.
3131. _____. S's Poetry of Thought. Baltimore: 1966.
3132. Donoghue, Denis. "Nuances of a theme by S," in
        Pearce & Miller (eds.), pp. 224-42.
3133. Eder, Doris L. "The meaning of W. S.'s two
        themes," Critical Quart., XI (1969), 181-90.
3134. _____. "W. S.: heritage and infl.," Mosaic (A
        Journ. for the Comp. Study of Lit. & Ideas), IV,
        1 (1970), 49-61.
3135. _____. "A review of S criticism to date,"
        Twentieth Cen. Lit., XV (1969), 3-18.
3136. _____. "W. S.: the major poems," Diss. Abstr.,
        XXIX (1969), 4482A (CUNY).
3137. Ellmann, Richard. "W. S.'s 'Ice Cream,'" Kenyon

Review, XIX (Winter 1957), 89-105.
3138. Enck, John J. W. S.: Images and Judgments.
       Carbondale: 1964.
3139. Essays by var. hands. Harvard Advocate ("W. S.
       Issue"), CXXVII (Dec. 1940). (Incl. articles by
       Matthiessen, Moore, Tate, Williams, et al.)
3140. Finch, John. "North and south in S's America, "
       Harvard Advocate, CXXVII (Dec. 1940), 23-6.
3141. Ford, Charles H. "Verlaine in Hartford: has the
       mystery man of mod. poetry really another self?"
       View, I (Sept. 1940), 1, 6.
3142. Ford, N. F. "Peter Quince's orchestra, " Mod. Lang.
       Notes, LXXV (1960), 405-11.
3143. Ford, W. T. "Some notes on S's foreign bibliog., "
       W. Stevens Newsl., I, 1 (1969), 1-3.
3144. Frankenberg, Lloyd. "W. S., " Pleasure Dome: On
       Reading Mod. Poetry. Boston: 1949, pp. 197-
       267.
3145. Frye, Northrop. "The realistic (romantic?) oriole:
       a study of W. S., " Hudson Review, X (Autumn
       1957), 353-70. (Repr. in Borroff (ed.), pp. 161-
       76.)
3146. Fuchs, Daniel. The Comic Spirit of W. S. Durham,
       N. C.: 1963.
3147. Galilea, Hernán. El Mundo Impresionista de W. S.
       Cuad. del Centro Investig. de Lit. Comparada,
       Univ. Chile. Santiago: 1965.
3148. Gangewere, Robert J. "The aesthetic theory of W.
       S., " Diss. Abstr., XXVII (1967), 3453A (Conn.).
3149. Girlinghouse, Mary J. "The new romantic of W. S., "
       Diss. Abstr. Intern'l, XXXI (1970), 387A (Catho-
       lic Univ.).
3150. Gregory, Horace. "The Harmonium of W. S., " A
       Hist. of Amer. Poetry, 1900-'40. N. Y.: 1942,
       pp. 326-35.
3151. Guereschi, Edward F. "The inventive imagination:
       W. S.'s dialectic of secular grace, " Diss. Abstr.
       Intern'l, XXXI (1970), 1229A/30A (Syracuse).
3152. Hafner, John H. "One way of looking at 'Thirteen
       Ways of Looking at a Blackbird, ' " Concerning
       Poetry (West Wash. State Coll.), III, 1 (1970),
       61-5.
3153. Hammond, Mac. "On the grammar of W. S., " in
       Pearce & Miller (eds.), pp. 179-84.
3154. Harstock, Mildred E. "S's 'Bantam in Pine Woods, ' "
       The Explicator, XVIII (March 1960), item 33.
3155. Heringman, Bernard. "W. S.: one use of poetry, "

in Pearce & Miller (eds.), pp. 1-12.
3156. Honig, Edwin. "Meeting W. S.," W. Stevens Newsl.,
       I, 2 (1970), 11-12.
3157. Howe, Irving. "Another way of looking at the black-
       bird," The New Republic, CXXXVII (Nov. 4,
       1957), pp. 16-19.
3158. Huguelet, Theodore L. Checklist of W. S. (Merrill
       Checklists). Columbus, Ohio: 1970.
3159. Jarrell, Randall. "Reflect. on W. S.," Poetry and
       the Age. N.Y.: 1959 (1953), pp. 133-48.
3160. _____. "The Coll. Poems of W. S.," in Brown
       & Haller (eds.), pp. 179-92 (3?). (Review arti-
       cle.)
3161. Jumper, Will C. "The language of W. S.," Iowa
       English Yearbook, VI (Fall 1961), 23-4.
3162. Kermode, Frank. "The words of the world: on W.
       S.," Encounter, XIV (April 1960), 45-50.
3163. _____. " 'Notes Toward a Supreme Fiction': a
       comment.," Annali dell'Istit. Univ. Orientale,
       Sez. Germanica. Naples: 1961.
3164. _____. W. Stevens. Edinburgh: 1967. (Earlier
       edn., Edinburgh/London: 1960).
3165. _____. "Afterthoughts on W. S.," Continuities.
       N.Y.: 1968, pp. 77-91.
3166. Kessler, Edward L. "Controlling images of W. S.,"
       Diss. Abstr., XXVIII (1967), 2251A (Rutgers).
3167. _____. Images of W. S. New Brunswick, N.J.:
       1971/2.
3168. Lafferty, Michael. "W. S.: a man of two worlds,"
       Historical Review of Berks County, XXIV (Fall
       1959), 109-13, 130-2.
3169. Laros, Fred. "W. S. today," Bard Review, II
       (Spring 1947), 8-16.
3170. Laughlin, James. "The laureate of Hartford," Busi-
       ness Week, (April 8, 1950), p. 94.
3171. Litz, A. Walton. Introspective Voyager: The Poetic
       Develop. of W. Stevens. N.Y.: 1972(?).
3172. Lowell, Robert. "Imagination and reality," The Na-
       tion, CLXVI (April 5, 1947), pp. 400-2.
3173. Macsey, Richard A. "The old poets," Johns Hopkins
       Mag., XIX, 1 (1968), 42-8.
3174. _____. "The climates of W. S.," in Pearce &
       Miller (eds.), pp. 185-223.
3175. Martz, Louis L. "W. S.: the world as meditation,"
       Lit. and Belief: English Inst. Essays (1957), ed.
       M. H. Abrams. N.Y.: 1958, pp. 139-65.
       (Repr. in Borroff (ed.), pp. 133-50.)

3176. _____. "W. S.: the romance of the precise,"
Yale Poetry Review, II (Aug. 1946), 13-20.

3177. _____. "The world of W. S.," Mod. Amer. Poetry: Focus V, ed. B. Rajan. London: 1950,
pp. 94-109.

3178. McFadden, G. "Probings for an integration: color
symbolism in W. S.," Modern Philology, LVIII
(1961), 186-93.

3179. McGrory, Kathleen. "W. S. as romantic rebel,"
Connecticut Review, IV, 1 (1970), 59-64.

3180. McNamara, Peter L. "The multi-faceted blackbird
and W. S.'s poetic vision," College English, XXV
(Oct.-May 1963/4), 446-8.

3181. Miller, J. Hillis. "W. S.'s poetry of being," in
Pearce & Miller (eds.), pp. 143-62.

3182. Mills, Ralph J., Jr. "W. S.: the image of the
rock," in Borroff (ed.), pp. 96-110.

3183. Mitchell, Roger S. "W. S.: a checklist of crit.,"
Bull. of Bibliog., XXIII, 9-10 (Sept.-Dec. 1962),
208-11; (Jan.-April 1963), 232-3.

3184. Monroe, Harriet. "W. S.," Poets and Their Art.
N.Y.: 1926, pp. 39-45.

3185. _____. "From Mr. Yeats and the poetic drama,"
in Brown & Haller (eds.), pp. 9-21.

3186. Moore, Geoffrey. "W. S.: a hero of our time," in
Brown and Haller (eds.), pp. 249-70.

3187. Moore, Marianne. "Unanimity and fortitude," Poetry,
L (Feb. 1937), 268-72. (Review of Owl's Clover
and Ideas of Order.)

3188. _____. "Well Moused, Lion," and "The world
imagined ... Since we are poor," in Brown &
Haller (eds.), pp. 21-8 & 162-5.

3189. Morse, Samuel F. W. S.: A Prelim. Checklist of
His Publ. Writings: 1898-1954. New Haven,
Conn.: 1954.

3190. _____, et al. W. S. Checklist and Bibliog. of
Stevens Crit. Denver: 1963.

3191. _____. "The native element," in Brown & Haller
(eds.), pp. 193-210.

3192. _____. W. S.: Poetry as Life. N.Y.: 1970.

3193. Munson, Gorham B. "The dandyism of W. S.,"
Dial, LXXIX (Nov. 1925), 413-17. (Repr. in
Brown & Haller (eds.), pp. 41-5.)

3194. Mulqueen, James E. "A reading of W. S.'s 'The
Comedian as the Letter C,'" Cimarron Review
(Okla. State Univ.), XIII (1970), 35-42.

3195. _____. "W. S.: radical transcendentalist," Midwest Quart. (Pittsburg, Kan.), XI (1970), 329-40.

3196. Nassar, Eugene P. W. S.: An Anat. of Figuration. Philad.: 1965.

3197. _____. The Rape of Cinderella: Essays in Lit. Continuity. Bloomington, Ind.: 1970.

3198. Nathan, Leonard E. "W. S. and mod. poetry," Indian Lit., X, 1 (1967), 82-101.

3199. Nemerov, Howard. "The poetry of W. S.," Sewanee Review, LXV (1957), 1-14.

3200. Nichols, Lewis. "A talk with Mr. Stevens," N.Y. Times Book Review (Oct. 3, 1954), 3, 31.

3201. Nilsen, Helge N. "The quest for reality: a study in the poetry of W. S.," Americana-Norvegica. Norwegian Contrib. to Amer. Studies, Vol. II, ed. Sigmund Skard. Philad.: 1968, pp. 219-98. (Publ. of the Amer. Inst., Univ. of Oslo.)

3202. O'Connor, William van. The Shaping Spirit: A Study of W. S. Chicago: 1950. (Bibliog., pp. 141-6.)

3203. _____. "W. S.: impressionism in America," Rev. des Langues Vivantes, XXXII (1966), 66-77.

3204. Olson, Elder. "The poetry of W. S.," College English, XVI (April 1955), 395-402.

3205. Pack, Robert. W. S.: An Approach to His Poetry and Thought. New Brunswick, N.J.: 1958.

3206. Pearce, Roy H. "W. S.: the life of the imagination," PMLA, LXVI (Sept. 1951), 561-82. (Repr. in Borroff (ed.), pp. 111-32.)

3207. _____. "W. S. and the ultimate poem," The Continuity of Amer. Poetry. Princeton, N.J.: 1961, pp. 376-419.

3208. _____, and J. Hillis Miller, eds. The Act of the Mind: Essays on the Poetry of W. S. Baltimore: 1965. (Incl. Roy H. Pearce, "W. S.: the last lesson of the master," pp. 121-42.)

3209. Powell, Grosvenor E. "W. S. and the pressures of reality," Private Dealings: Eight Mod. Amer. Writers. Stockholm: 1970, pp. 32-49.

3210. Powes, Llewelyn. "The Thirteenth Way," Dial, LXXVII (1924), 45-50. (Repr. in Brown and Haller (eds.), pp. 29-34.)

3211. Quinn, Sister Mary B. "Metamorphosis in W. S.," Sewanee Review, LX (Spring 1952), 230-52. (Repr. in Borroff (ed.), pp. 54-71.)

3212. Ransom, James C. "The anecdotal imagination: a study of W. S.'s 'Harmonium,'" Diss. Abstr. Intern'l, XXXI (1970), 1288A (Yale).

3213.   Ransom, John Crowe.   "Poets without laurels," The
        World's Body.   N.Y.:   1938, pp. 55-75.

3214.   Riddel, Joseph N.   "Disguised pronunciamento: W.
        S.'s 'Sea Surfaces,' " Texas Stud. in English,
        XXXVII (1958), 177-86.

3215.   _____.   "Authorship of W.S.'s 'On Poetic Truth,' "
        Mod. Lang. Notes, LXXVI (1961), 126-9.

3216.   _____.   "The contours of S's criticism," in
        Pearce & Miller (eds.), pp. 243-76.

3217.   _____.   "W. S.'s 'Visibility of Thought,' " PMLA,
        LXXVII, 4 (Sept. 1962), 482-98.

3218.   _____.   The Clairvoyant Eye: The Poetry and
        Poetics of W. S.   Baton Rouge, La.:   1965.

3219.   Rizzardi, Alfredo.   La Condizione Americana.   Studi
        su Poeti Nord-Americani.   Bologna: 1959.

3220.   Rosenfeld, Paul.   "W. S.," Men Seen.   N.Y.:   1925,
        pp. 151-62.

3221.   Simons, Hi.   "The humanism of W. S.," Poetry,
        LXI (Nov. 1942), 448-52.

3222.   _____.   " 'The Comedian as the Letter C':   its
        sense and signif.," Southern Review, V (Winter
        1940), 453-68.   (Repr. in Brown & Haller (eds.),
        pp. 97-114.)

3223.   _____.   "The genre of W. S.," Sewanee Review,
        LIII (Autumn 1945), 566-79.   (Repr. in Borroff
        (ed.), pp. 43-53.)

3224.   Stallknecht, Newton P.   "Absence in reality: a study
        in the epistemology of the 'Blue Guitar,' " Ken-
        yon Review, XXI (Fall 1959), 545-62.

3225.   Stern, Herbert J.   "Art of uncertainty: studies in
        the early career of W. S.," Diss. Abstr., XXVI
        (1965), 2762/3 (Ind.).

3226.   _____.   W. S.:   Art of Uncertainty.   Ann Arbor,
        Mich.:   1966.   (Works cited, pp. 194-9.)

3227.   Stoenescu, Stefan.   "W. S. şi reactivarea poetică
        a umanului," Secolul XX, XII, 9 (1969), 149-55.

3228.   Sukenick, Ronald.   "A W. S. handbook: a reading
        of his maj. poems and an exposit. of his theory
        and practice," Diss. Abstr., XXIV (1963), 305/6
        (Brandeis).

3229.   _____.   W. S.:   Musing the Obscure.   N.Y.:
        1967.

3230.   Swetman, Glenn R.   "The poetics of W. S.:   an
        examin. of the basic struc. of his poetry," Diss.
        Abstr., XXVII (1967), 3473A (Tulane).

3231.   Symons, Julian.   "A short view of W. S.," Life
        and Letters Today, XXVI (Sept. 1940), 215-24.

(Repr. in Brown & Haller (eds.), pp. 114-22.)

3232. Sypher, Wylie. "Connoisseur in chaos," Partisan
       Review, XIII (1946), 83-94.

3233. Taupin, René. L'Infl. du Symbolisme Français sur
       la Poésie Américaine. Paris: 1929, pp. 275-
       8.

3234. Tindall, William Y. W. Stevens. Minneapolis,
       Minn.: 1961. (Univ. Minn. Pamphl. on Amer.
       Writers, 11.)

3235. Untermeyer, Louis. Amer. Poetry Since 1900.
       N.Y.: 1923, pp. 323-8.

3236. Vendler, Helen H. "The qualified assertions of W.
       S.," in Pearce and Miller (eds.), pp. 163-78.

3237. _____. "S's 'Like Decorations in a Nigger Ceme-
       tary,'" Massachusetts Review, VII (Spring 1966),
       136-46.

3238. _____. On Extended Wings: W. S.'s Longer
       Poems. Cambridge, Mass.: 1969. (Bibliog.
       notes, pp. 317-34.)

3239. Wagner, C. Roland. "A central poetry," in Borroff
       (ed.), pp. 71-5.

3240. Walsh, Thomas F. Concord. to the Poetry of W. S.
       Univ. Park, Penn.: 1963.

3241. Wells, Henry W. Introd. to W. S. Bloomington,
       Ind.: 1963/4.

3242. Whitaker, Thomas R. "On speaking humanly," The
       Philosopher-Critic, ed. Robert Scholes. Tulsa,
       Okla.: 1970, pp. 67-88. (Discusses the meaning
       for S of the act of speech.)

3243. Williams, William Carlos. "W. S.," Poetry, LXXXVII
       (Jan. 1956), 234-9.

3244. Winters, Yvor. "W. S., or the hedonist's progress,"
       In Defense of Reason. N.Y.: 1959(1947),
       pp. 431-59.

3245. Zabel, Morton D. "The Harmonium of W. S.,"
       Poetry, XXXIX (1931), 48-54. (Repr. in Brown
       & Haller (eds.), pp. 46-52.)

3246. _____. "W. S. and the image of man," in Borroff
       (ed.), pp. 151-60.

UNGARETTI

3247. Accrocca, E. F. Ritratti su Misura di Scrittori
       Italiani. (Notizie biogr., confessioni, bibliogr.

di poeti, narratori e critici). Venezia: 1960.
3248. _____, ed. Ungaretti-Poesia. Milano: 1964.
_____(Includes crit. comm. plus bibliog., pp. 119-24.)
3249. _____, and F. Sampoli. "U letto e commentato
da U, ' " Fiera Letteraria (15 & 22 Sett. 1963),
pp. 1-2, 1-2.
3250. Anceschi, Luciano. "Ungaretti, " Cronache Latine
(20-27 Febb. 1932).
3251. _____. "Di U' e la critica, " Galleria, XVIII, 4-6
_____(1968), 196-7.
3252. _____. Questi Giorni (Milano) (5-20 Dic. 1945)
_____(contains crit. guide to U').
3253. Angioletti, G. B. L'Italia Lett. (16 Giugno 1929)
(alcuni brani sono pubbl. su Lirici Nuovi di Anceschi) (contains interview with U').
3254. Anon. "Restoring the virginity of the world, " Times
Lit. Suppl. (Sept. 25, 1970), 1083-5. (Review
article.)
3255. Arnao, Giancarlo. "Un paziente modello, " Galleria,
XVIII, 4-6 (1968), 198-9.
3256. Assunto, Rosario. "L'antecedenza della poesia, "
Galleria, XVIII, 4-6 (1968), 200-12.
3257. Bàrberi Squarotti, Giorgio. Astrazione e Realtà.
Milano: 1960.
3258. _____. La Cultura e la Poesia Ital. d. Dopoguerra.
Bologna: 1966.
3259. Barbieri, Carlo. "U' e Napoli, " Galleria, XVIII,
4-6 (1968), 213-18.
3260. Barlozzini, Guido. "Il viaggiatore, " Galleria, XVIII,
4-6 (1968), 219-21.
3261. Berenice. "Il bastone dal pomo d'avorio, " Galleria,
XVIII, 4-6 (1968), 222-3.
3262. Betocchi, Carlo. "Il più italiano, " Galleria, XVIII,
4-6 (1968), 226-8.
3263. Bieberstreu Michael, Freiherr M. von. "Das her-
metische Tagebuch G. U's, " Akzente, XVII (1970),
436-44.
3264. Biggiaretti, Libero. "A cinquant'anni dall' 'Allegria,' "
Galleria, XVIII, 4-6 (1968), 229-30.
3265. Bigongiari, Piero. Il Senso d. Lirica Ital. Firenze:
1952.
3266. _____. "Ungaretti, " Poesia Ital. del Novecento:
Nuovi Studi Critici. Milano: 1960, pp. 133-67.
(Later edn. Firenze: 1967.)
3267. _____. "Introd., " Un Grido e Paessagi, di G. U.
2nd ed. Milano: 1962, pp. 57-84.
3268. _____. "Introd. sinottica alla poesia di U', "

L'Approdo Lett., VIII (1962), xix, 58-76.

3269. _____ . "Penultimo U', " Forum Italicum, II (1968), 185-93.

3270. Biondolillo, Francesco. D'Annunzio e Altri Saggi. Urbino: 1963.

3271. Bo, C. Otto Studi. Firenze: 1939.

3272. _____ . Riflessioni Critiche. Firenze: 1953.

3273. Bocelli, Arnaldo. "Morte di U', " Stampa (Torino) (4 Giugno 1970), 4.

3274. _____ . " 'Il taccuino del vecchio' e il 'terzo tempo' ungarettiano, " Galleria, XVIII, 4-6 (1968), 243-53.

3275. Borlenghi, A. Tra Ottocento e Novecento. Pisa: 1955.

3276. Bozzoli, Adriano. "Per l'interpr. de 'L'Allegria' di G. U., " Dialoghi, XIII, 3 (Maggio-Giugno 1965), 135-54.

3277. Cambon, Glauco. "U's poetry from evocation to invocation, " Italian Quarterly, V-VI, 20-1 (1962), 97-105.

3278. _____ . G. Ungaretti. N. Y.: 1967 (Columbia Essays on Mod. Writers, 30.)

3279. _____ . "Il deserto e dopo: U' prosatore, " Studi Ghisleriana (Pavia), II, 3 (1967), 239-56.

3280. Cary, Joseph B., Jr. Three Mod. Italian Poets: Saba, U', Montale. N. Y.: 1969. (Bibliog., pp. 343-8.)

3281. Casnati, F. Cinque Poeti. Milano: 1940.

3282. Cavalli, G. Ungaretti. Milano: 1958.

3283. Cimmino, Nicola F. Scritti d'Occasione, seconda serie. Roma: 1962.

3284. Contini, G. Eserciẑi di Lettura. Firenze: 1939.

3285. Crémieux, B. "Ungaretti, " La Nouvelle Revue Française, (Mars 1924).

3286. Cro, Stelio. Algunos Aspectos de la Poesía de G. U. Buenos Aires: 1967.

3287. Dalmati, Margarita. "G. U. (1888-1970), " Nea Hestia, LXXXVIII (1970), 874-9.

3288. Debenedetti, Giacomo. "Commento a un poema di U', " Nuovi Argomenti, XVIII (1970), 62-9. (On 'Stamani mi sono desteso. ')

3289. Del Colle, Gherardo. "G. Ungaretti, " Italia Francescana, XLIII (1968), 169-74.

3290. Demarchi, Silvano. "Aspetti formali della poesia ungarettiana, " Cristallo, X, 2 (1968), 115-24.

3291. DeMartinis, Vincenzo. "U': Uomo ferito, uomo di pena, " Civiltà Cattolica, CXXI (1970), 541-53.

3292. De Robertis, D. "Ungaretti, " Letteratura, VIII, 5
(Sett.-Ott. 1946).
3293. _____. "Prefazione, " alla Poesia Disperse, di G.
U. 4th ed. Milano: 1964.
3294. De Robertis, G. Scrittori del Novecento. Firenze:
1940.
3295. _____. Altro Novecento. Firenze: 1962/3.
(Incl. Ungaretti, pp. 1-18, 208-16.)
3296. Di Bella, Nino. "I quattro 'ventenni' di U': tra
crepuscolarismo ed ermetismo, " Parole e il
Libro, LI (1968), 215-17.
3297. _____. "Momenti esistenziali e poesia in G. U., "
Cristallo, X, 1 (1968), 179-90.
3298. _____. "L'Egitto nella poesia di U', " Cristallo,
XI, 1 (1969), 119-22.
3299. Essays by var. hands. Fiera Letteraria (1 Nov. 1953)
(special issue on U').
3300. _____. Letteratura, V, 35-6 (Sett.-Dic. 1958)
(numero speciale ded. a U').
3301. _____. Galleria, XVIII, 4-6 (1968), (special issue
devoted to U').
3302. _____. "Homage to G. Ungaretti, " Books Abroad,
XLIV (1970).
3303. _____. "G. U. Special Issue, " ed. Andrew Wylie.
Agenda, VIII, 2 (1970).
3304. Falqui, Enrico. Novecento Letterario, II. Firenze:
1960 (1954).
3305. _____. "U' e la 'Ronda, ' " Nuova Antologia, 509
(1970), 326-9.
3306. Ferrata, G. "Ungaretti, " Circoli, no. 1 (Genn.-
Febb. 1932),
3307. Fiumi, L. Parnaso Amico. Genova: 1940.
3308. Flora, F. La Poesia Ermetica. Bari: 1936.
3309. Forti, Marco. Le Proposte della Poesia: Civiltà
Lett. del Novecento, Saggi 5. Milano: 1963.
3310. Frattarolo, R. "Per una bibliogr. di U', " Dal
Volgare ai Moderni. Roma: 1962, pp. 193-
209.
3311. Frattini, Alberto. Da Tommaseo a Ungaretti.
Bologna: 1959.
3312. Gargiulo, A. "Ungaretti, " Primo Tempo, nos. 11-
12 (1923).
3313. _____. "Introd. " al Sentimento del Tempo, di
G. U., 7th ed. Milano: 1963.
3314. _____. Lett. Ital. del Novecento. Firenze: 1940.
3315. Gorlier, Claudio. "Il Blake di U', " Paragone, XVII,
196 (1966), 142-6.

204   A Post-Symbolist Bibliography

3316.   Guglielminetti, M.   Struttura e Sintassi del Romanzo
        Italiano.   Milano, 1964.
3317.   Gutia, Joan.   "La sinestesia in U'," Lett. Moderne
        (1954).
3318.   _____.   Linguaggio di U'.   Firenze: 1959.
3319.   Harder, Uffe.   "Tre italienske digerte," Fremmede
        Digtere i det 20 Arhundrede, Vol. II, ed. Sven
        M. Kristensen.   Copenhagen: 1968, pp. 527-37.
        (Incl. U', Montale, Quasimodo.)
3320.   Livi, Grazia.   "Parliamo col dolce e terribile U',"
        Epoca, XIII, 612 (1962), 80-5.
3321.   Macrì, O.   Caratt. e Figure d. Poesia Ital. Contemp.
        Firenze: 1956.
3322.   Marabini, Claudio.   "Ricordo di U'," Nuova Antologia,
        509 (1970), 319-25.
3323.   Marianni, Ariodante.   "Bibliogr. essenziale," Galleria,
        XVIII, 4-6 (1968), 336-40.
3324.   Marvardi, Umberto.   "G. U.:   Da 'Il Porto Sepolto'
        a 'Il Taccuino del Vecchio,' " L'Italia Che Scrive,
        XLIV (1961), 29-32.
3325.   _____.   "U' poeta del mistero," Studium, LXVI
        (1970), 668-77.
3326.   Mezzacappa, Carmine A.   " 'Caino' o del sentimento
        ungarettiano di noia e inquietudine," Studium,
        LXV (1969), 461-75 (repr. in: Italica, XLVII
        (1970), 183-201).
3327.   _____.   "Noia e inquietudine nella vita d'un uomo
        di G. U.," Diss. Abstr., XXIX (1969), 4011A
        (N. Y. U.).   (Publ. in book form: Padova: 1970.)
3328.   Molinaro, Julius A.   "U's 'Mattina':   Fifty years of
        crit. stud.," Cesare Barbieri Courier, IX, 2
        (1969), 3-6.
3329.   Morand, Bernadette.   "G. Ungaretti," Europe, 498
        (1970), 207-12.
3330.   Mormino, Giuseppe.   Ritratti di Autori.   Milano:
        1961.
3331.   Noferi, Adelia.   "Le poetiche crit. novecentesche
        'sub specie' Petrarchae," Approdo, XLVI (1969),
        61-89.   (Incl. Contini, De Robertis, and U'
        studies.)
3332.   Nogara, G.   "Pena d'uomo: Ungaretti," Lett.
        Italiane, II (1950), 3-26.
3333.   Nolan, David.   "Three mod. Italian poets," Studies,
        LVI (1967), 61-72.   (Incl. U', Montale, Quasi-
        modo.)
3334.   Pancrazi, P.   Scrittori Ital. d. Novecento.   Bari:
        1934.

3335. _____. Scrittori d'Oggi, I. Bari: 1946.
3336. Papatzonis, Takis. "U': the great renovator of mod.
        Italian poetry, " Books Abroad, XLIV (1970), 616-
        17.
3337. Papini, G. Ritratti Ital. Firenze: 1932.
3338. Pasolini, P. P. Passione e Ideologia. Milano:
        1960.
3339. Paulhan, Jean. "Introd., " Il Taccuino del Vecchio,
        di G. U. [Verona]: 1960, pp. 47-9.
3340. Peritore, G. A. Alcuni Studi. n. p.: 1961.
3341. Petrucciani, Mario. "Il fachir, l'angelo, il deserto, "
        Galleria, XVIII, 4-6 (1968), 279-85.
3342. _____. La Poetica dell'Ermetismo Italiano. To-
        rino: 1955.
3343. Piccioni, Leone. Lett. Leopardiana e Altri Saggi.
        Firenze: 1952.
3344. _____. Sui Contemporanei. Milano: 1956.
3345. _____. "G. Ungaretti, " Autori Vari, I. Contemp.,
        II. n. p.: 1963.
3346. _____. Lavagna Bianca. Firenze: 1964.
3347. _____. "Linguaggio poetico di U', " Galleria,
        XVIII, 4-6 (1968), 296-9.
3348. _____. Vita di un Poeta: G. U. Milano: 1970.
3349. _____, ed. Confessioni di Scrittori. Torino:
        1951.
3350. _____. Pazienza ed Impazienza: Studi e Saggi,
        1946-'66. Firenze: 1968.
3351. _____. "La poesia di U': Dal 'Deserto' alla
        'Terra Promessa, ' " Approdo... XIV (1968), 6-38.
3352. Picon, Gaëtan. "Sur la poésie de G. Ungaretti, "
        Lettres Nouvelles, IV (Févr. 1956), 247-58.
3353. Portinari, Folco. G. Ungaretti. Torino: 1967.
        (Scrittori del Secolo, 34.) (Bibliog., pp. 210-
        12.)
3354. Pozzi, G. La Poesia Ital. d. Novecento: Da Goz-
        zano Agli Ermetici. Torino: 1967(1965).
3355. Ravegnani, G. Uomini Visti, III. Milano: 1955.
3356. Rebay, Luciano. Le Origini della Poesia di G. U.
        Roma: 1962.
3357. Rispoli, G. , and Amedeo Quondam. Poesia Contemp.
        Firenze: 1968.
3358. Sait Halman, Talât. "U' and Turkish poetry, " Books
        Abroad, XLIV (1970), 615.
3359. Sanavio, Piero. "Voici mon chant intérieur, "
        Nouvelles Litt. , XXIV (Avril 1969), 1. (Inter-
        view with U'.)
3360. Sanguinetti, Edoardo. Tra Liberty e Crepuscolarismo.

Milano: 1961.
3361. Santilli, Tommaso. La Poesia del Novecento.
L'Ermetismo di G. U., E. Montale, S. Quasimodo. Spunti Critice. Pescara: 1966.
3362. Sempoux, André. "Le premier U' et la France, "
Rev. Litt. Comparée, XXXVII (1963), 360-7.
3363. Seroni, A. Ragioni Critiche. Firenze: 1944.
3364. Silori, Luigi. "Casa U', " Galleria, XVIII, 4-6 (1968),
308-17.
3365. Sobrero, Ornello. "Saggi e articoli, " Galleria,
XVIII, 4-6 (1968), 341-8.
3366. Solmi, S. Scrittori Negli Anni: Saggi e Note Sulla
Lett. Italiana del '900. Milano: 1963.
3367. Spagnoletti, G. Tre Poeti Italiani de Novecento.
Torino: 1956.
3368. _____. Saba, Ungaretti, Montale. Torino: 1967.
3369. Spezzani, P. "Ungaretti, " Ricerche Sulla Lingua
Poetica Contemp. Padova: 1966, pp. 91-160.
3370. Steiner, Carlo. "The early work of U', " Agenda,
VIII, 2 (1970), 111-21. (Trans. Marion Mashe-
der.)
3371. Tognelli, Jolse. "Oltre il sentimento del tempo, "
Galleria, XVIII, 4-6 (1968), 323-5.
3372. Tomlinson, C. "A note on translating U', " Delos,
III (1969), 132-3.
3373. Turoldo, David. "Poesia come preghiera, " Galleria,
XVIII, 4-6 (1968), 329-30.
3374. Ungaretti, G. "Riflessioni sullo stile, " Inventario,
I, 2 (1946).
3375. _____. "Ragioni di una poesia, " Inventario, II, 1
(1949).
3376. _____. "Il nostro destino di scrivere versi, "
Fiera Lett., (18 Dic. 1955) (repr. in G. Spagnoletti. Poesia Ital. Contemp. Parma: 1959).
3377. _____. Da Gongora e da Mallarmé. Verona:
1961.
3378. _____. "Dalle lezioni su Leopardi: Sul frammento
'Spento il diurno raggio in Occidente' (Canto
XXIX), " Galleria, XVIII, 4-6 (1968), 178-89.
3379. Varese, C. Cultura Lett. Contemp. Pisa: 1951.
3380. Wylie, Andrew. "U's poetry and experimental time, "
Books Abroad, XLIV (1970), 611.
3381. Zaccaro, Gianfranco. "Dramma e possibilità della
rinascita liederistica, " Galleria, XVIII, 4-6
(1968), 331-5.
3382. Zagarrio, Giuseppe. "Per G. Ungaretti, " Il Ponte,
XXVI (1970), 655-60.

3383. Adorno, Theodor W. "V's Abweichungen, " Die Neue
Rundschau, LXXI, 1 (1960), 1-38. (Also in:
Noten z. Lit. Frankf. /M.: 1961, II, pp. 42-94.
Bibliothek Suhrkamp, Bd 71.)

3384. Aigrisse, Gilberte. Psychanalyse de P. V. Paris:
1964. (Bibliog., pp. 320-1.) (Encyclopédie Univ.)

3385. Alain. "Hommage à la poésie (de P. V.)," Mercure
de France, CCC, 1008 (août 1947), 587-96.

3386. Andouard, Yves. "Recherches de P. V.," Revue de
Languedoc, no. 8 (1945), 360-72. (Also publ.
sep. as book: Albi: 1946.)

3387. Anon. Contributions to P. V.'s Bibliography; sur
Programme Soirée Guilde Intern'l des Arts.
Londres (7 août 1945).

3388. _____. "Essai de bibliogr. des oeuvres de P. V.,"
Biblio, XVII, 2 (févr. 1949), 18-24.

3389. _____. "Oeuvres de P. V., essai de bibliogr.,"
Biblio, XXXVI, 2 (févr. 1968), 17-21.

3390. Arnold, Albert J. "French-language Criticism of P.
V. from 1890 to 1927: A Critical Bibliography,"
Diss. Abstr., XXIX, 2 (Aug. 1968), 591A
(Wisconsin).

3391. _____. P. Valéry and His Critics. A Bibliog.
French-Language Crit., 1890-1927. Charlottesville: 1970. (Bibliogr. Society of Virginia.)

3392. Aron, Jean-Claude. "L'Oeuvre de P. V.," Arche,
no. 10 (Oct. 1945), 27-47.

3393. Auden, W. H. "The creation of music and poetry,"
The Mid-Century, no. 2 (Aug. 1959), 18-27.

3394. _____. "V: L'Homme d'Esprit," Hudson Review,
XXII, 3 (Autumn 1969), 425-32.

3395. Audet, Noël. V et le poème en prose. (Thèse)
Paris: 1965. (Cf. abstract: Annales de l'Univ
de Paris, XXXVI, 3 (Juillet-Sept. 1966), 385-6.)

3396. Austin, Lloyd J. "P. V. and Our Time, " Mod.
Lang., XLIV, 2 (June 1963), 59-66.

3397. _____. "The Genius of P. V.," Wingspread Lectures in the Humanities. Vol. I. Racine, Wisc.:
1966, pp. 1-60 (?).

3398. _____. "Il y a cinquante ans 'Le Cimetière
Marin,' " Le Figaro Litt., no. 1260 (13-19
Juillet 1970), 17-18.

3399. _____. "Modulation and movement in V's verse,"
Yale French Studies, no. 44 (1970), 19-38.

3400.   Barjon, L.   "Le monde du connaissable: V, " De
        Baudelaire à Mauriac.   Paris: 1962, pp. 159-83.
        (Subtitle: L'Inquiétude Contemporaine.)
3401.   Bastet, Ned.   La Symbolique des Images dans
        l'Oeuvre Poétique de V.   Aix en Provence: 1962.
        (Publ. des Annales de la Fac. des Lettres d'Aix
        en Provence.   Travaux et Mémoires, 24.)
3402.   _____.   "Oeuvre ouverte et oeuvre fermée chez
        V, " Annales de la Fac. des Lettres et Sciences
        Humaines de Nice, II, 4e trim.   (1967), 103-19.
3403.   Batterby, K. A. J.   "V and the Poetic Climax, "
        Rilke and France...   London: 1966, pp. 140-84.
3404.   Baudouy, Luce.   "Inconscient freudien et structures
        formelles de la poésie, " Revue Philos. de Lou-
        vain, LXI, 3e série, no. 71 (août 1963), 435-66.
3405.   Bémol, Maurice.   "P. V. et l'esthétique, " Revue
        d'Esthétique, I, fasc. 4 (oct.-déc. 1948), 409-28.
3406.   _____.   Paul Valéry.   Clermont-Ferrand: 1949.
3407.   _____.   "P. V. et la critique litt., " Revue
        d'Esthétique, VII, 4 (oct.-déc. 1954), 366-77.
3408.   _____.   La Parque et le Serpent: Essai sur les
        Formes et les Mythes.   Paris: 1955.   (Les
        Belles Lettres.)
3409.   _____.   "A propos du 'grand silence' valéryen, "
        Revue d'Hist. Litt. de la France, LIX, 2 (avril-
        juin 1959), 213-18.
3410.   _____.   La Méthode Critique de P. V.   Paris:
        1961.
3411.   _____.   "La représ. imagée de l'esprit et l'ex-
        press. de l'inexprimable, " Revue d'Esthétique,
        XV (1962), 139-65.
3412.   Bendz, E.   P. V. et l'Art de la Prose.   Göteborg:
        1936.
3413.   Benoist, Pierre-François.   Les Essais de P. V.
        (Poèmes et Proses) Etudiés et Commentés.
        Paris: 1964.   (Les Chefs-d'Oeuvre de la Litt.
        Expliqués.   Coll. Mellotée.)
3414.   Berger, P.-Ch.   "La poétique de V, " Ecrits de
        Paris, 184 (juill.-août 1960), 126-36.
3415.   Bergeron, Léandre.   Le Son et le Sens dans Quelques
        Poèmes de 'Charmes' de P. V.   Aix-en-Provence:
        1963.   (Publs. des Annales de la Fac. des
        Lettres d'Aix-en-Provence.   Nouv. sér., 39.)
        (Orig. (thèse) Univ. Aix. Lettres: 1961.)
3416.   Berne-Joffroy, André.   Présence de V.   Paris: 1945.
        (Coll. Présences, 5e série.)   (Later ed. 1945.)
3417.   _____.   "V et les philosophes, " Rev. de Méta-

physique et de Morale, LXIII, 1 (janv.-mars 1959), 72-95.

3418. _____. "Comment situer V?" Nouv. Rev. Française, VIII, 86 (févr. 1960), 306-12.

3419. _____. Valéry. Paris: 1960. (Bibliogr., pp. 295-305.)

3420. Bisson, L. A. "A study in 'Le Faire Valéryen,'" French Studies, X, 4 (Oct. 1956), 309-21.

3421. Blanchard, Anne. "Le Silence de P. V.," Cah. du Sud, XLVIII, 361 (juin-juill. 1961), 427-45.

3422. Blumenberg, Hans. "Sprachsituation u. immanente Poetik," Immanente Asthetik, ästhet. Reflexion, ed. W. Iser. Mchn: 1966, pp. 145-55.

3423. Bolle, Louis. P. V., ou Conscience et Poésie. (Thèse) Genève: 1944. (Available at N.Y. Public Library.)

3424. _____. Paul Valéry. Fribourg/Paris: 1944. (Bibliogr., pp. 145-8.)

3425. Bonnefoy, Yves. "V l'apostat," Lettres Nouvelles, VI, 63 (sept. 1958), 234-9.

3426. Bonneville, Georges. "P. V. et l'Europe," Synthèses, no. 168 (mai 1960), 153-7.

3427. Borges, Jorge Luis. "V as a symbol," Other Inquisitions (1937-1952), trans. Ruth L. C. Simms. Austin: 1964, pp. 73-4.

3428. Bosanquet, Theodora. Paul Valéry. London: 1933.

3429. Boudot, P. "La parole comme totalité: Valéry," Nietzsche et l'Au-Delà de la Liberté. Nietzsche et les Ecrivains Français de 1930 à 1960. Paris: 1970, pp. 27-33. (Présence et pensée, 16.)

3430. Bounoure, Gabriel. "Extrêmes et contraires chez V," Valeurs (Alexandria), no. 3 (oct. 1945), 73-7. (Also in: Erasme, (1946), 148-54.) (Variant: "Extrêmes et contours....")

3431. Bourbon-Busset, Jacques de. "Un monstre de pureté: V," La Table Ronde, no. 193 (févr. 1964), 36-47.

3432. _____. P. V. ou le Mystique Sans Dieu. Paris: 1964. (Coll. La Recherche de l'Absolu.) (Bibliogr., pp. 181-8.)

3433. Bousquet, Joë. "P. V. et l'idée fixe," Cah. du Sud, XXI (1934), 668-76.

3434. Bowra, C. M. "P. Valéry," The Heritage of Symbolism, 2nd edn. London: 1959 (1943), pp. 17-55.

3435. Brombert, Victor. "V: the dance of words," Hudson Review, XXI, 4 (Winter 1968/9), 675-86.

3436. Buck, Gunther. Das Denken P. V.'s. Heidelberg:

3437. Bürger, Peter. "Funktion u. Bedeut. d. 'orgueil' bei P. V.," Romantisches Jahrb., XVI (1965).

3438. Catherin-Nollace, Jeanne. "Actualité de P. V. ou l'exercisme du cinéisme," Le Cinéisme. Paris: 1964, pp. 75-177.

3439. Cattaui, Georges. "V illuministe néo-pythagoricien," Orphisme et Prophétie Chez les Poètes Français. Paris: 1965, pp. 153-77.

3440. Chadwick, C. "Valéry," French Lit. and Its Background, ed. J. Cruickshank. London: 1970, pp. 41-54.

3441. Charney, Hanna K. "V critique 'impressionniste' de la critique," Symposium, XI, 2 (Fall 1957), 281-9.

3442. _____. "V devant l'alternative de la création," Romanic Review, XLIX, 1 (Feb. 1958), 25-32.

3443. _____. Le Scepticisme de V. Paris: 1969. (Essais et Critiques, 7.) (Cf. Diss. Abstr., XVI (1956), 1138/9 Columbia.)

3444. Charpentier, Henry. "Les premières oeuvres de P. V.," Le Portique, no. 5 (1947), 1-18.

3445. Charpentier, John. "Du mystère à l'obscurité," Rev. de France, I (1930), 278-94; 512-35; 652-74.

3446. Charpier, J. Essai sur V. Paris: 1956. (Poètes d'Aujourd'hui, 51.) Bibliog., pp. 211-19.)

3447. _____. "Un adorateur secret du néant," Lettres Nouvelles, VI, 63 (sept. 1958), 240-4.

3448. Chauvet, Louis. La Poétique de P. V. Liège: 1966. (Série Brimborions, 143.)

3449. Chiari, Joseph. "Consciousness and poetic creation in the poetry of P. V.," Lett. Mod., III, 2 (marzo-aprile 1952), 158-67.

3450. _____. "The modern conflict betw. rationalism and imagination. V and inspiration," Realism and Imagination. London: 1960, pp. 192-210.

3451. Chisholm, A. R. "P. V. 1871-1945," Meanjin, IX, 1 (40?) (Autumn 1950), 50-3.

3452. _____. "Moods of the intellect in 'Le Cimetière Marin,'" Yale French Studies, no. 44 (1970), 72-86.

3453. Cioran, E. M. "V before his idols," Hudson Review, XXII, 3 (Autumn 1969), 411-24. (In French: Nouv. Rev. Française, XXXIV (1969), 801-19.)

3454. _____. Valéry Face à Ses Idoles. Paris: 1970.

3455. Clauzel, R. Trois Introd. à P. V. LaRochelle: 1928.

3456.   Clerc, Jeanne-Marie. "Valéry et les 'instants privi-
        légiés,' " L'Inform. Litt., XXII, 1 (Janv. -Févr.
        1970), 20-3.
3457.   Clogenson, Yves: "V devant la mystique et l'occul-
        tisme, " Entretiens sur V, ed. E. Noulet-Carner.
        Paris: 1968, pp. 229-46. (Avec une discussion,
        pp. 247-53.)
3458.   Clouard, Henri. "Une aventure de l'esprit: P. V.,
        poête et philosophe, " Rev. Universelle, (juin
        1944), 460-75.
3459.   Cocteau, Jean. "Paul Valéry, " Fontaine, no. 44
        (été 1945), 539-41. (Also: Partisan Review,
        XIII (Winter 1946), 124-5.)
3460.   Cohen, Gustave. "L'hermétisme de P. V., " Nouv.
        Relève, II, 8 (juill. -août 1943), 449-60.
3461.   _____. "V expliqué devant V, " AUMLA, no. 10
        (May 1959), 28-32.
3462.   Coléno, Alice. "V and the meaning of poetry, "
        Quarterly Review of Lit., III, 3 (1947), 276-85.
        (Trans. Catherine Coffin.)
3463.   Cornil, Lucien. "A propos du langage, " Cah. du
        Sud, nos. 276/8 (1946), 222-7.
3464.   Cosimi, J. "Le conflit mod. de la poésie et de
        l'intelligence. Deux strophes de P. V., " Rev. de
        l'Univ. de Lyon, V (1928), 453-73; III (1929),
        199-229.
3465.   Cournot, Michel. "Exigences de V, " Fontaine, no.
        44 (été 1945), 542-7.
3466.   Crow, Christine M. "V, poet of 'patiente im-
        patience,' " Forum for Mod. Lang. Stud. (Scot-
        land), III, 4 (Oct. 1967), 370-87.
3467.   _____. P. Valéry: Consciousness and Nature.
        N. Y.: 1972(?).
3468.   Curtius, Ernst R. "Valéry, " Französ. Geist im
        neuen Europa. Stuttgart: 1925, pp. 147-85.
        (Later ed. Französ. Geist im 20 Jh. Bern:
        1952.)
3469.   Daniel, V. J. "V's 'Eupalinos' and his early read-
        ing, " French Studies, XXI, 3 (July 1967), 229-
        35.
3470.   Davis, R. and R. Simonson. Bibliographie des
        Oeuvres de P. V. (1895-1925). Paris: 1927.
        (Coll. Plaisir de Bibliophile.)
3471.   Décaudin, Michel. "Etudes sur la poésie francaise
        contemporaine. II: Paul Valéry, " L'Informa-
        tion Litt., XV (nov. -déc. 1963), 198-207; XVIII,
        5 (nov. -déc. 1966), 199-205. (Title of article:

"Autour de V et de la poésie pure.")

3472. Delbouille, Paul. "P. V. et le mythe des sonorités,"
Ztschr. f. französ. Sprache u. Lit., LXX, 3-4
(Nov. 1960), 129-38.

3473. Delmas, Claude. "P. V. et l'univers spirituel,"
Amérique Française, II, 4 (1950), 17-31.

3474. Denat, Antoine. "L'art poétique après V, " AUMLA,
no. 11 (Sept. 1959), 63-81.

3475. _____. "L'art poétique après V, " Vu des Antipodes. Synthèses Critiques. Paris: 1969,
pp. 87-107.

3476. Doisy, Marcel. P. V.: Intelligence et Poésie.
Paris: 1952. (Bibliogr., pp. 224-41.)

3477. Dolembreux, Henri. "Un diner avec V', " Audace
(Brux.), XVI, 1 (1970), 146-8. (Dans le halo du
symbolisme.)

3478. Donoghue, Denis. "Poetry and the behavior of
speech, " Hudson Review, XIV (1961), 537-49.

3479. Douglas, K. N. "Translations, English, Spanish,
Italian, and German, of P. V.'s 'Le Cimetière
Marin, ' " Mod. Lang. Quart., VIII (1947), 401-7.

3480. _____. "P. V.'s mysticism, " Quart. Rev. of Lit.,
III, 3 (1947), 253-61.

3481. Downes, Gladys. P. V. en Face du Symbolisme et
du Surréalisme. (Thèse) Univ. Paris: 1953.

3482. Droin, A. P. V. et la Trad. Poétique Française.
Paris: 1924.

3483. Duchesne-Guillemin, J. "P. V. et la composition, "
Glanes, nos. 15-16 (nov. 1950-févr. 1951), 33-50.

3484. _____. "P. V. et la musique, " Revue Musicale,
no. 210 (janv. 1952), 113-21.

3485. _____. "P. V.: orgueil et transformation, "
Orbis Litt., X, 3 (1955), 321-34.

3486. _____. Etudes Pour un P. V. Neuchâtel: 1964.
(Notes bibliogr., pp. 221-4.)

3487. _____. "V au miroir: les 'Cahiers' et l'exégèse
des grands poèmes, " French Studies, XX, 4 (Oct.
1966), 348-65.

3488. _____. "Les N dimensions
de V, " Entretiens sur V, ed. E. Noulet-Carner.
Paris: 1968, pp. 9-30. (Avec une discussion,
pp. 31-43.)

3489. DuColombier, Pierre. "P. V. et les arts d'imitation, " Rev. Française de l'Elite, no. 10 (25
juill. 1948), 59-63.

3490. Duhamel, Roger. "P. Valéry: finesse et géométrie,"
L'Action Nationale, LX, 1 (sept. 1970), 75-85.

3491. Eigeldinger, Marc, ed. Poésie et Tendances. P.
       V.: Essais et Témoignages Inédits. Neuchâtel/
       Paris: 1945.
3492. Eliot, T. S. "Leçon de V, " Cah. du Sud, nos. 276-
       8 (1946), 74-82.
3493. _____ . "L'art poétique de V, " Preuves, IX, 106
       (déc. 1959), 14-22.
3494. Elsen, Claude. "P. V. et la tentation romanesque, "
       La Table Ronde, no. 40 (avril 1951), 150-3.
3495. Essays by var. hands. Hommages des Ecrivains
       Français â P. V. Paris: 1929.
3496. _____ . "Hommage à P. V., " Nouv. Litt., no.
       938 (numéro spécial) (26 juillet 1945).
3497. _____ . "Valéry, " Nea Hestia d'Athènes (numéro
       spécial) (1946) (avec une bibliogr. hellénique de
       V).
3498. _____ . "Hommage à P. V., " Eaux Vives de
       Lutèce, no. 3 (sept.-déc. 1946), 1-79.
3499. _____ . "P. V. Vivant, " Cahier du Sud (Marseille)
       276-8 (numéro spécial) (1946), 381 pp.
       (bibliogr., pp. 359-71.)
3500. _____ . Revue Française de l'Elite (numéro spé-
       cial) (25 juillet 1948).
3501. _____ . "Paul Valéry, " L'Esprit Créateur (Iowa
       City), IV, 1 (Spring 1964), 48 pp. (Incl.: James
       R. Lawler, "The serpent, the tree, and the crys-
       tal, " 34-40; E. von Richthofen, "Quelques obser-
       vations fond. de V sur le problème de la forme,
       contenues dans ses cahiers, " 28-33.)
3502. _____ . "P. Valéry, " New Haven, Conn.: 1970.
       (Special issue of Yale French Studies, no. 44
       (1970).) (Incl. Mallarmé, Breton, Gide, Reverdy,
       Apollinaire, Léautaud, et al.)
3503. Estève, L. "Autour de V, " Rev. de Métaphysique et
       de Morale, XXXV (1928), 55-105.
3504. Etiemble, René. "Note adjointe sur deux ou trois
       consonnes chez Valéry, " Poètes ou Faiseurs?
       (1936-'66). Hygiene des Lettres, IV. Paris:
       1966, pp. 251-7.
3505. Fabre, Lucien. "Le langage, l'impasse et la course
       au flambeau, " Cah. du Sud, nos. 276-8 (1946),
       160-5.
3506. _____ . "Situation de V, " Rev. de Paris, LVII
       (sept. 1950), 64-8.
3507. Fabureau, Hubert. Paul Valéry. Paris: 1937.
3508. Faivre, Jean-Luc. "P. V. et le thème de la lumi-
       ère, " Lettres Romanes, XX (1966), 299-318;

XXI (1967), 3-27, 103-22, 207-22; XXII, 1 (1
févr. 1968), 50-8; no. 2 (1 mai 1968), 133-50.

3509. Farrell, Clarence F., Jr. "V. His thought, with
an index to his non-fictional writings publ. during
his lifetime, " Diss. Abstr., XXVI (1965/6), 3333
(Pittsburgh).

3510. Felici, Noël. Regards sur V. Paris: 1951.

3511. Fernandat, R. P. V. Essai. Paris: 1927.

3512. _____. Autour de P. V.: Lignes d'Horizon.
2nd rev. ed. 1945.

3513. Ferrari, Eugène. "M. P. V., une mystique
nouvelle, " Cah. Protestants, (1932), 92-9.

3514. Fowlie, Wallace. "P. V.: the man and his work, "
New English Review, XII, 1 (Jan. 1946), 42-8.

3515. _____. "Homage to V, " Sewanee Review,
(LIV?), 2 (April-June 1946), 250-7.

3516. _____. "Paul Valéry, " Poetry, LXXVI, 5 (Aug.
1950), 279-87.

3517. Frank, Joseph. "P. V.: Masters and Friends, "
Sewanee Review, LXXV, 3 (Summer 1967), 393-
414.

3518. Fumet, Stanislas. La Poésie à Travers les Arts.
Paris: 1954. (Sagesse et Cultures.)

3519. Gelsey, Elizabeth A. de. "L'architecture du
'Cimetière Marin,' " Rev. d'Hist. Litt. de la
France, LXIII (1963), 458-64.

3520. Genette, Gérard. "V et l'axiomatique litt., " Tel
Quel, no. 23 (automne 1965), 75-82.

3521. Geoffrey, William. "P. V.: hero of the mind, "
South Atlantic Quarterly, XLV, 4 (Oct. 1946),
489-503.

3522. Gerber, Sister Aline Marie, C.S.J. "Les poèmes
de jeunesse de P. V., " Diss. Abstr., XXVIII
(1967), 1817(14?)A (U.C.L.A.).

3523. Gerlötei, E. "Méditations valéryennes: principes
de recherches conformes à la poésie classique, "
Rev. d'Esthétique, X, 1 (janv.-mars 1957), 65-
76.

3524. Germain, Gabriel. "Le mystère créateur dans l'expérience poétique de V, " Rev. de Méditerranée,
XV, 4 (juill.-août 1955), 373-87.

3525. _____. "D'un humanisme intégral: oppositions et
positions, " Cah. du Sud, XLV, 349 (1958), 417-
27.

3526. Gerstel, Eva-Maria. "P. V.: the formation of his
aesthetic ideas, " Diss. Abstr., XXVI (1965),

2750 (Rice).

3527. _____. "The creative process in two early MSS. of V's 'Fragments du Narcisse,' " Symposium, XXIII, 1 (Spring 1969), 16-37.

3528. Gheorghe, Ion. "Les idées de V' sur le langage poétique, " Rev. des Sciences Humaines (Lille), XXXV (Juill.-Sept. 1970), 423-31.

3529. Gide, André. "Paul Valéry, " New Writing and Day-light, VII (1946), 98-108. (Trans. Dorothy Bussy.)

3530. _____. "Paul Valéry, " Penguin New Writing, no. 33 (1948), 108-22. (Trans. Dorothy Bussy.)

3531. _____. "Paul Valéry, " Kenyon Review, VIII, 2 (Spring 1946), 277-90.

3532. _____. Paul Valéry. Paris: 1946. (Coll. Au Voilier.)

3533. Gilbert, Katharine. Aesthetic Studies: Architecture and Poetry. Durham: 1952.

3534. Gillet, M.-S. "P. V. et la pensée pure, " Rev. Universelle, XXVIII (1927), 424-42.

3535. Gillet, R. P. P. V. et la Métaphysique. Paris: 1946.

3536. Glissant, Edouard. "V et le double état, " Lettres Nouvelles, VI, 63 (sept. 1958), 248-53.

3537. Goffin, Marie-Louise. "P. V. selon lui-même, " Synthèses, XI, 126-7 (nov.-déc. 1956), 134-54.

3538. Goffin, Robert. "P. V. et quelques autres, " Fil d'Ariane Pour la Poésie. Paris: 1964, pp. 182-9.

3539. Grégoire, A. V Linguiste. Paris: 1937.

3540. Grubbs, Henry A. Paul Valéry. New York: 1968 (TWAS, 43) (bibliogr., pp. 143-8).

3541. Guedenet, Pierre. "La prévision en P. V., " Sur, XII, 94 (julio 1942), 59-70.

3542. Guégen, P. P. V.: Son Oeuvre. Paris: 1928.

3543. _____. "Un monde valéryen, " Cah. du Sud, nos. 276-8 (1946), 171-3.

3544. Guéhenno, Jean. "Regards sur le monde actuel de P. V., " Europe, XXVI (1931), 575-8.

3545. Guiran, Emile. P. V. et le Problème de la Créa-tion Poétique. Cordoba: 1934.

3546. Guiraud, Pierre. Langage et Versification d'Après l'Oeuvre de P. V. Etude Sur la Forme Poétique dans ses Rapports avec la Langue. Paris: 1953.

3547. _____. Index du Vocabulaire du Symbolisme. Vol. II: Index des Mots des Poésies de P. V. Paris: 1953.

3548. _____. "Le champ stylistique du mot 'ombre' et

sa genèse chez P. V. , " Orbis Litt. , XIX, 1
(1964), 12-26.

3549.   Guy-Grand, G.   "P. V. et la crise de l'esprit, "
Rev. Hebdomadaire, XI (1924), 5-17.

3550.   Halden, H.   "P. V. et l'obscurisme, " Grande Revue,
CXXVI (1928), 67-75.

3551.   Hambro, Carl.   "La création poétique selon P. V. , "
Edda, XXXVIII (1938), 211-44.

3552.   Henriot, Emile.   "Où en est V?" Maîtres d'Hier et
Contemporains.   Paris: 1955, pp. 294-324.

3553.   Henry, Albert.   "Aspects du vocabulaire poétique de
P. V. , " Mercure de France, CCCXI, 1049 (janv.
1951), 67-77.

3554.   _____ .   Langage et Poésie Chez V.   Paris: 1952
(62?) (avec un lexique des oeuvres en vers).

3555.   _____ .   "V a-t-il emprunté à Mallarmé son vocabulaire poétique?" Synthèses, nos. 258-9
(déc. 1967-janv. 1968), 73-80.

3556.   Hippolythe, Jean.   "Note sur P. V. et la crise de la
conscience, " La Vie Intellectuelle, XIV, 3 (mars
1946), 121-6.

3557.   Hofmann, Claude.   "De quelques sources à V, "
Entretiens sur V, ed. E. Noulet-Carner.   Paris:
1968, pp. 135-47.   (Avec une discussion, pp. 148-
61.)

3558.   Howald, Ernst.   "Die absolute Dichtung im 19. Jh. , "
Trivium, VI (1948), 23-52.

3559.   Howlett, Jacques.   "Sagesse de V, " Lettres Nouv. ,
VI, 63 (sept. 1958), 244-8.

3560.   Huber, Egon.   "P. V. 's Metaphorik u. d. französ.
Symbolismus, " Ztschr. f. französ. Sprache u.
Lit. , LXVII, 2 (April 1957), 168-201; LXVIII,
3-4 (Mai 1958), 165-85; LXIX, 1-2 (1959), 1-21.

3561.   Hytier, Jean.   "The refusals of V, " Yale French
Studies, II, 1 (Spring/Summer 1949), 105-36.

3562.   _____ .   "La théorie des effets dans la poésie de
V, " Romanic Review, XLII, 1 (févr. 1951), 35-
44.

3563.   _____ .   La Poétique de V.   Paris: 1953.   (Bibliogr. , pp. 301-9.) (English ed. trans. Richard
Howard.   Garden City: 1966.)

3564.   _____ .   "Formules valéryennes, " Romanic Review, XLVII, 3 (Oct. 1956), 179-97.

3565.   _____ .   "Autour d'une analogie valéryenne, " Cah.
de l'Assoc. Intern'l des Etudes Françaises, no.
17 (mars 1965), 171-89.

3566.   _____ .   "L'esthét. valéryenne du sonnet, " Austral.

Journ. French Studies (Melbourne), VI (1969), 326-36.

3567.   Ince, W. N. The Poetic Theory of P. V.: Inspiration and Technique. Leicester: 1961. (Also: (thèse) en français, Univ. de Paris. Lettres: 1955.) (Bibliogr., pp. 178-82.)

3568.   _____. "P. V. --'poésie pure' ou 'poésie cuite'?" French Studies, XVI, 4 (Oct. 1962), 348-58.

3569.   _____. "Transcendance in V or Inspiration by the Back Door," Mod. Lang. Notes, LXXX, 3 (May 1965), 373-8.

3570.   _____. "Impatience, immediacy and the pleasure principle in Valéry," Forum for Mod. Lang. Studies, II (April 1966), 180-91.

3571.   _____. "La voix du maître ou moi et style selon V," Rev. des Sciences Humaines, CXXIX (1968), 29-39.

3572.   _____. "Resonance in V," Essays in French Lit. (Nedlands, W. A.), V (1968), 38-57. (Variant: "Romance in V," Nov.)

3573.   _____. "Etre, connaître et mysticisme du réel selon V," Entretiens sur V, ed. E. Noulet-Carner. Paris: 1968, pp. 203-22. (Avec une discussion, pp. 223-8.)

3574.   Jallat, Jeannine. "V et le mécanisme. La notion de modèle et la théorie de la construction," Saggi e ricerche di lett. francese, VII (1968), 185-241.

3575.   _____. "V' and the mathem. lang. of identity and difference," Yale French Studies, no. 44 (1970), 51-64. (Trans. A. Smock.)

3576.   Johnston, H. Paul Valéry. Liège: 1936.

3577.   Jones, Henri. "L'écriture automatique et son infl. sur la poésie d'aujourd'hui," Dialogue, II, 2 (Sept. 1963), 182-90.

3578.   Jones, Rhys S. "Hegel and French Symbolism. Some observ. on the 'Hegelianism' of P. V.," French Studies, IV, 2 (April 1950), 142-50.

3579.   Julien-Cain, L. Trois Essais Sur V. Paris: 1958. (Incl.: "V et l'utilization du monde sensible"; "L'être vivant selon V"; "E. Poe et V.")

3580.   Kemp, Robert. "Le culte de V," La Nef, no. 9 (août 1945), 106-10. (Also in: La Vie des Livres. Paris: 1955, pp. 172-7.)

3581.   _____. "Tentations valéryennes," La Vie des Livres. Paris: 1955, pp. 178-85.

3582.   Kennett, W. T. E. "P. V. and the dark night of the soul," Univ. Toronto Quart., XXXIII, 2 (Jan.

1964), 178-99.

3583. Köhler, Hartmut. Poésie et Profondeur Sémantique dans 'La Jeune Parque' de P. V. Nancy/Saint-Nicolas-du-Port: 1965. (Publ. du Centre Europ. Univ.) (Coll. des Mémoires.)

3584. Labica, Georges. "Introd. à la méthode de V. Autopsie d'une esthétique," Cah. Algériens de Litt. Comparée, I, 1 (1966), 70-94.

3585. Lacarra, Marcel. "P. V. et la poésie," Le Français dans le Monde (Paris), LXXIV (Juill.-Août 1970), 24-33.

3586. Lafont, Aimé. Paul Valéry. L'Homme et L'Oeuvre. Marseille: 1943.

3587. Lafranchi, G. P. V. et l'Expérience du Moi Pur. Lausanne: 1958.

3588. Laitenberger, Hugo. Der Begriff der 'Absence' bei P. V. Wiesbaden: 1960 (bibliogr., pp. 154-8). (Untersuch. z. Sprache-u. Lit. gesch. d. roman. Völker, hrsg. Komm. für roman. Phil. der Akad. der Wissensch. u. d. Lit., Band III.)

3589. Laleau, Léon. "P. V., professeur de poétique," Conjonction (Port-au-Prince), no. 9 (avril 1947), 14-19.

3590. Lalou, René. "Héros de l'esprit," Lettres Françaises, V, 66 (28 juillet 1945).

3591. _____, and W. Weidle. "Paul Valéry," Cah. de la Quinzaine, XXI (1931), 7-76.

3592. Lannes, Roger. Appel à V [suivi de] La Poésie, Objet de la Civilization. Paris: 1947, pp. 1-52. (Also incl.: "Portrait de P. V.," par Denise Lannes, pp. 53-95.)

3593. Larbaud, Valéry. Paul Valéry. Paris: 1931.

3594. Latour, Jean de. Examen de P. V. et Bibliographie. Lettre et un Texte Inédit de P. V. Paris: 1935.

3595. Lawler, J. R. "The technique of V's 'Orphée,'" Journ. Australas. Univ. Lang. Lit. Assoc., no. 5 (1956), 54-63.

3596. _____. "The meaning of V's 'Le Vin Perdu,'" French Studies, XIV, 4 (Oct. 1960), 340-51.

3597. _____. Lecture de V: Une Etude de 'Charmes.' Paris: 1963. (Bibliogr., pp. 267-9.)

3598. _____. "The 'Shipwreck' of P. V.," Essays in French Lit., no. 3 (Nov. 1966), 38-64.

3599. _____. "V's later poetry," Australian Journ. French Studies, IV (1967), 295-322.

3600. _____. "Light in V'," Austral. Journ. French Studies, VI (1969), 348-75.

3601. _____. "V's 'pureté,' " The Language of French
Symbolism. Princeton, N.J./London: 1969,
pp. 185-217.
3602. _____. " 'L'ange frais de l'oeil nu...,' " Essays
in French Lit., no. 7 (Nov. 1970), 38-69.
3603. _____. "Saint Mallarmé," Yale French Studies,
no. 44 (1970), 185-98. (Trans. A. & R. Win-
andy.)
3604. Lechantre, Michel. "Les refuges de V' (d'après les
'Cahiers' et les 'Oeuvres,' éd. Pléiade), " La
Revue Nouvelle (15 Avril 1969), 447-55.
3605. Lefèvre, F. "La pensée de P. V., " Le Correspon-
dant, CCCI (1925), 37-61.
3606. _____. Entretiens avec P. V. Paris: 1928.
3607. Leighton, Lawrence. "V: la poésie engagée, " Kenyon Review, VIII, 2 (Spring 1946), 291-5.
3608. Lestra, André. "P. V., le poète maître du temps, "
Rev. Palladienne, no. 4 (sept.-oct. 1948), 145-8.
3609. Levaillant, J. "P. V. et la lumière, " Cah. Assoc.
Intern'l Etudes Françaises, XX (mai 1968),
179-92.
3610. Liang, Pai Tchin. P. V. et la Poésie (thèse) Univ.
Paris: 1949.
3611. Lièvre, P. Paul Valéry. Paris: 1925.
3612. Loisy, Jean. "V poète, " Points et Contrepoints, no.
78 (juin-juillet 1966), 9-15.
3613. Loranquin, Albert. "P. V. ou le refus de vivre, "
Bull. des Lettres, 20e année, no. 195 (15 févr.
1958), 49-53.
3614. _____. "P. V. et la musique, " Bull. des Lettres,
no. 259 (15 juin 1964), 241-5.
3615. _____. "V et la mort, " Bull. des Lettres, XXVI,
273 (15 déc. 1965), 417-20.
3616. Lorenz, E. "Die V-Kritik im heut. Frankreich, "
Romanistisches Jahrb., VII (1955-6), 113-32.
3617. Löwith, Karl P. "Vs Reflex. z. Sprache, " Herme-
neutik u. Dialektik: Hans G. Gadamer zum 70.
Geburtstag, ed. R. Bübner et al., 2 Bände
Tübingen: 1970, II, pp. 115-44.
3618. MacIntyre, C. F. "The ars poetica of P. V., "
Circle Nine, (1946), 27-37.
3619. Mackay, Agnes E. The Universal Self: A Study of
P. V. London: 1961.
3620. Magnery, Louis A. "P. V. et l'Italie, " Studi Francesi, XIII, 37 (1969), 89-96.
3621. Marek, Joseph C. "V et le problème de l'être, "
Rev. de l'Univ. Laval, XIV, 6 (févr. 1960),

523-35.

3622. Martin del Campo, Angeline. Les problèmes de langage chez V' d'après des 'Cahiers.' (Diss.) Univ. Montpellier: 1968.

3623. Mascagni, Pauline. Initiation à P. V. ou le Roman d'un Poète et de son Lecteur. Paris: 1946.

3624. Massis, Henri. "P. V. et sa pensée, " Au Long d'une Vie. Paris: 1967, pp. 109-15.

3625. Mathews, Jackson. "The poetics of P. V. , " Romanic Review, XLVI, 3 (Oct. 1955), 203-17.

3626. Mauge, Gilbert. "La poétique selon P. V. , " Rev. de Paris, IV (1939), 490-504.

3627. Maurer, K. Interpr. z. späteren Lyrik P. Vs. Mchn: 1954.

3628. Maurois, André. Introd. à la Méthode de P. V. Paris: 1934.

3629. Mauron, Charles. "Valéry, " Des Métaphores Ob-sédantes au Mythe Personnel. Introd. à la Psy-chocritique. Paris: 1963, pp. 81-104. (Bib-liogr. , pp. 355-64.) (Also incl. chap. on Mal-larmé.)

3630. Meyer, François. "La métaphysique de P. V. , " Cah. du Sud, XLIV, 344 (janv. 1958), 102-8.

3631. Michel, P. Paul Valéry. Paris: 1952.

3632. _____. "Un des ouvrages les plus obscurs de la langue française, 'La Jeune Parque, ' " L'Ecole, (19 janv. 1952).

3633. _____. "Paul Valéry: Du symbolisme au classi-cisme, " Littérature. C. E. L. G. Centre de Docu-mentation Univ. : 1961.

3634. Mondor, Henri. "Premières lectures de P. V. , " Poésie 45, nos. 26/7 (août-sept. 1945), 70-7. (Cf. "V commence..., " Carrefour, (27 juillet 1945, 5.)

3635. _____. Trois Discours Pour P. V. Paris: 1948.

3636. _____. Précocité de V. Paris: 1957.

3637. _____. Propos Familiers de P. V. Paris: 1957.

3638. Monod, J. P. Regard sur P. V. Lausanne: 1947.

3639. _____. "Regard sur P. V. , " Biblio, XVII, 2 (févr. 1949), 7-11.

3640. Moreau, Jacques. "Affinités valéryennes, " Les Nouvelles Littéraires, no. 1574 (7 nov. 1957), 1.

3641. Morice, Louis. "La vision de V, " Rev. de l'Univ. Laval, XVII, 1 (Sept. 1962/3), 3-31.

3642. Mortier, Alfred. "Valorisation ou Valérysation?" Grande Revue, CXLIII (1933), 53-6.

3643. Nadal, André. "Abeille spirituelle": Poème Inconnu

et Art Poétique de P. V. Nîmes: 1968. (Privately published.)

3644. Nadal, Octave. "P. V. et l'événement de 1892," Mercure de France, no. 1100 (avril 1955), 614-26.

3645. _____. "P. V. Jeunesse et création. Arithmetica universalis," Cah. du Sud, 43e année, XLIV, 340 (avril 1957), 339-47. (Also in: A Mesure Haute. Paris: 1964, pp. 181-90.)

3646. _____. "Les palettes de P. V.," Les Lettres Nouvelles, V, 54 (nov. 1957), 604-18.

3647. _____. "La création chez V," A Mesure Haute. Paris: 1964, pp. 191-223. (Also contains: "Les larmes de l'esprit," pp. 165-80; "Note sur douze poèmes inédits," pp. 225-8; "La nuit de Gênes," pp. 151-64; "Poèmes en prose," pp. 229-46.)

3648. _____. "The prose poems of P. V.," Columbia Forum, XII, 2 (Summer 1969), 37-40.

3649. Neely, Robert T. "P. V. as a critic of 19th cen. French lit.," Diss. Abstr., XXVI, 11 (May 1966), 6720 (Colorado).

3650. _____. "V on V. Hugo: a second look," French Review, XLII, 2 (Dec. 1968), 248-53.

3651. Netzner, Jacques. "Intelligence et poésie selon P. V.," Le Français dans le Monde, no. 19 (sept. 1963), 10-14.

3652. Noulet, Emilie. Paul Valéry: Etudes. Bruxelles: 1951. (Earlier ed. Paris: 1938).

3653. _____. "V triomphant," Synthèses, XIII, 149 (oct. 1958), 259-72.

3654. _____. Suite Valéryenne. Bruxelles: 1959.

3655. _____, ed. Entretiens sur P. V. Paris: 1968. (Décades du Centre Intern'l de Cerisy-la-Salle, nouv. série, 7.) (Incl.: E. Noulet, "Présentat. de la décade P. V.," pp. 7-8.)

3656. _____. "Tone in the poems of P. V.," Yale French Studies, no. 44 (1970), 39-50. (Trans. G. Bernauer.)

3657. Nugent, Ellen. "P. V. et la poésie," French Studies, VI, 1 (Jan. 1952), 41-52.

3658. O'Brien, Justin. "P. V.: 'The Art of Poetry,'" The French Lit. Horizon. New Brunswick, N.J.: 1967, pp. 369-72. (Also contains: "P. V.: 'Dialogues,'" pp. 367-8.)

3659. Onimus, Jean. "P. V., le soleil et le ciel étoilé," Annales de la Fac. des Lettres et Sciences Humaines d'Aix, XXXVI (1962), 41-61.

3660. _____. "P. V., poète de la lumière, " Annales
du Centre Univ. Méditerranéen, XVI (1962/3),
127-36.

3661. Palmiéry, René. "P. V. et les valeurs méditer-
ranéennes, " Pensée Française, XIX, 9 (sept.
1960), 22-7.

3662. Parent, Monique. "Un aspect de la rhétorique de V.
Les variations stylistiques, " Travaux de Linguistique et de Litt., (Strasbourg) VI, 1 (1968), 187-
202.

3663. _____. Cohérence et Résonance dans le
Style des "Charmes" de Valéry. Paris: 1970.
(Bibliothèque Française et Romane, C, 24.)

3664. _____. " 'Le Cimitière Marin, ' poème du dé-
passement (Recherche sur l'unité du texte), "
Trav. de Linguis. et de Litt. (Strasbourg), VIII, 2
(1970), 85-95.

3665. Parisier-Plottel, Jeanine. Les dialogues de P. V.,
(Columbia Univ. Thesis) Paris: 1960. (Bibliogr.,
pp. 101-6) (Cf. Diss. Abstr., XX, 9 (March
1960), 3751.)

3666. Paryse(ize), Jean H. Essai sur la Pensée et l'Art
de P. V. Bruxelles: 1946.

3667. Paul, David. "V' and the relentless world of the
symbol, " Southern Review, VI, 2 (April 1970),
408-15.

3668. Paulhan, Jean. "Un rhétoriqueur à l'état sauvage,
ou la litt. consid. comme un faux, " La Nef, no.
20 (juillet 1946), 3-12; no. 21 (août 1946), 55-73.

3669. Perche, Louis. V, les Limites de l'Humain. Paris:
1966.

3670. Perros, Georges. "La poésie et V, " Les Cah. du
Chemin, I (oct. 1967), 71-82.

3670a. Peyre, Henri, ed. P. Valéry: Prose et vers.
Waltham, Mass.: 1968. (Blaisdell French Lit.
Series) (Contains good introd.)

3671. Picon, Gaëtan. "Présence de V, " Mercure de
France, no. 1134 (févr. 1958), 310-15.

3672. _____. "Poétique de V, " L'Usage de la Lecture.
Tome II. Paris: 1961, pp. 123-9. (Title of
t. II: Suite Balzacienne--Suite Contemporaine.)

3673. Pieltain, Paul. "Anciens et nouveaux regards sur
P. V., " Rev. des Langues Vivantes, XXVIII, 1
(1962), 3-22.

3674. Pierre-Quint, Léon. "Regards sur le monde actuel
par P. V., " Rev. de France, VI (1931), 326-32.

3675. Pihl, Karen. "P. Vs Poetik, " Extracta, I (1968),

238-49. (Abstr.)

3676. Pire, F. "Nature et Construction Chez V (V et l'Univers Sensible), " Le Flambeau, XLVII, 3 (mai-juin 1964), 245-62.

3677. _____ . La Tentation du Sensible Chez P. V. Paris/Bruxelles: 1964. (La Lettre et l'Esprit.)

3678. Piron, Maurice. "P. V. et l'interpr. des textes, " Bull. Acad. Royale de Langue et de Litt. Françaises, XLV (1967), 297-306.

3679. Piroué, Georges. "Trois Visages de V, " La Table Ronde, no. 130 (oct. 1958), 133-8.

3680. Pistorius, Georges. "Le problème d'influence selon V, " Actes du IVe Congrès de l'Assoc. Intern'l de Litt. Comp. Paris: 1966, pp. 1036-42.

3681. Pomès, Mathilde. "P. V. collégien, " Rev. des Deux Mondes, (1 sept. 1965), 113-17.

3682. Pommier, Jean. P. V. et la Création Litt. (Leçon d'Ouverture, College de France) Paris: 1946. (Cf. J. P., Créations en Litt. Paris: 1955.)

3683. _____ . "Regards sur P. V., " Dialogues Avec le Passé: Etudes et Portraits Litt. Paris: 1967, pp. 197-220.

3684. Pontie, François. P. V. et la Poésie Pure. Paris: 1946.

3685. Porché, Fr. P. V. et la Poésie Pure. Paris: 1927.

3686. Poucel, Victor. "Les poésies de P. V. et la poésie," Etudes, CCX (1932).

3687. Poulain, Gaston. P. V., Tel Quel. Montpellier: 1955.

3688. Poulet, Georges. "Valéry, " Etudes sur le Temps Humain. Edinburgh: 1949, pp. 366-401. (Cf. G. P., Studies in Human Time, tr. Elliott Coleman. London/Baltimore: 1956.)

3689. Pratt, Bruce. V: le Triomphe de la Vie, une Synthèse Esthétique. (Thèse) Aix: 1964.

3690. Prévost, J. La Pensée de P. V. Nîmes: 1926.

3691. _____ . "Trois héros de P. V., " Terre de France, XX, 3 (3 nov. 1946), (also in: Le Point, XLI (avril 1952), 3-9.

3692. Price, Robert H. "A consid. of P. V.'s ideas concern. art and the artist, " South Cen. Bull., XXX, (Oct. 1970), 114; no. 4 (Winter 1970), 214-16.

3693. Rambaud, H. "La poésie de P. V., " Rev. Crit. des Idées et des Livres, XXXIV (1922), 518-34.

3694. Rang, Bernhard. P. V., 30 Okt. 1871-20 Juli 1945. Ein Bücherverzeichnis. Einleit., Auswahl, Biogr., u. Bibliogr. Bonn: 1961. (Dichter u.

Denker uns. Zeit, Folge 30.)
3695.	Raphaël, Max. "Anmerk. über d. Prosastil von V, "
	Deutsche-Französ. Rundschau, IV (1931), 553-63.
3696.	Rat, Maurice. "Oiseaux charmants, les rimes ...
	P. V. , " Vie et Langage, no. 137 (août 1963),
	420-4.
3697.	Rauhut, F. P. V.: Geist u. Mythos. Mchn: 1930.
3698.	Raymond, Marcel. "Le moi pur selon V, ou le refus
	d'être quoi que ce soit... , " Les Lettres (Genève),
	IV, 1 (1946), 69-82.
3699.	_____. P. V. et la Tentation de l'Esprit. Neu-
	châtel: 1964.
3700.	Read, Herbert. "Obscurity in poetry, " Nature of Lit.
	N. Y.: 1956, pp. 89-100. (Also in: Coll. Es-
	says in Lit. Criticism. London: 1951, pp. 89-
	100.)
3701.	Régis, Georges. La Poétique Comme Philosophie de
	la Création Selon P. V. (Thèse) Toulouse: 1947.
3702.	_____. "Aspect du comique chez V, " Annales
	Publiées par la Fac. des Lettres et Sciences Hu-
	maines de Toulouse, V (mars 1966).
3703.	Richthofen, Erich von. " 'Présence' u. 'absence'
	des Ichs bei P. V. , " Romanische Forschungen,
	LXVI, 1/2 (1954), 65-111.
3704.	_____. "Quelques observ. fondam. de V sur le
	problème de la forme; contours dans ses
	'Cahiers, ' " L'Esprit Créateur, IV (1964), 28-33.
3705.	Ricour, Pierre. "P. V. ou l'horreur du vide, "
	Bull. des Etudes Françaises, VI (mars 1942),
	21-32.
3706.	Rideau, E. Introd. à la Pensée de V. Paris: 1944.
3707.	Rilke, R. M. "Fragments sur V, " Cah. du Sud,
	nos. 276/8 (1946), 217-19.
3708.	Rinsler, Norma. "The defence of the self. Still-
	ness and movement in V's poetry, " Essays in
	French Lit., no. 6 (Nov. 1969), 36-56.
3709.	Robinson, Judith. "The place of lit. and artistic
	creation in V's thought, " Mod. Lang. Rev. , LVI,
	4 (Oct. 1961), 497-514.
3710.	_____. "The analysis of consciousness in V, "
	French Studies, XVI (1962), 101-23.
3711.	_____. L'Analyse de l'Esprit dans les Cahiers
	de V. Paris: 1963.
3712.	_____. "V's conception of training the mind, "
	French Studies, XVIII, 3 (July 1964), 227-35.
3713.	_____. "New light on V, " French Studies, XXII,
	1 (Jan. 1968), 40-50.

3714. Robinson, Judith. "V's view of mental activity, "
        Yale French Studies, no. 44 (1970), 3-18. (Incl.
        Mallarmé.)
3715. la Rochefoucauld, Edmée de (pseud. Mauge, Gilbert).
        Images de P. V. Strasbourg/Paris: 1949.
3716. _____. Paul Valéry. Paris: 1954. (Classiques
        de XXᵉ Siècle, 13.)
3717. _____. "P. V. et le théâtre, " Cah. du Théâtre,
        II, 4 (3/4ᵉ trim. 1965), 10-14.
3718. _____. "V et l'Italie, " Entretiens sur V, ed. E.
        Noulet-Carner. Paris: 1968, pp. 283-92 (avec
        une discussion, pp. 293-7) (cf. also: "P. V. et
        l'Italie, " Rev. de Paris, LIX (mars 1952), 94-
        104.)
3719. Roditi, Edouard. "P. V.: poetics as an exact
        science, " Kenyon Review, VI, 3 (Summer 1944),
        398-408.
3720. Romain, Willy-Paul. P. V., le Poème, la Pensée.
        Essais et Exégèses.... Paris: 1951.
3721. Roulin, Pierre. P. V., Témoin et Juge du Monde
        Moderne. Neuchâtel: 1964. (Bibliogr., pp. 221-
        65.) (Coll. Langage.)
3722. Rousseaux, André. "P. V. ou l'intelligence désolée, "
        Rev. Universelle, XLIV (1931), 293-310.
3723. Roussillon-Bartell, Simone. "P. V.: 'Lust, la
        demoiselle de cristal. ' Quelques réflexions sur
        la langue de l'oeuvre, " Le Français Moderne,
        XXXIII, 1 (janv. 1965), 37-49.
3724. Roy, Claude. "Le spectateur intéressé, " Nouvelle
        Revue Française, X, 115 (1 juillet 1962), 112-17.
3725. Rütsch, Julius. "Probleme d. V-Betrachtung, "
        Trivium, I, 4 (1943), 34-55.
3726. Rychner, Max. "P. V.: Dichtung u. Theorie d.
        Dichtung, " Merkur, XVII (1963), 1021-36.
        (Also in: Zwischen Mitte u. Rand. Zürich:
        1964, pp. 9-56.) (Add. inform. for Merkur ar-
        ticle: Heft XI, 189 (Nov. 1963); Heft XII, 190
        (Dez. 1963).)
3727. Saint-Edouard, Soeur. "La poésie pure. I: La
        doctrine de P. V. II: Interpr. critique, " Rev.
        de l'Univ. de Laval, XIX, 6 (févr. 1965), 495-
        511; no. 7 (mars 1965), 648-57.
3728. _____. "P. V. et l'émotion poétique, " Rev. de
        l'Univ. de Laval, XIX, 9 (mai 1965), 829-41.
3729. _____. "Le théâtre dans l'oeuvre de P. V., "
        Rev. de l'Univ. de Laval, XX, 2 (oct. 1965),
        135-42.

3730.   Saisselin, R. G.   "The aesthetics of the grand
        seigneur, " Journ. of Aesthetics and Art Crit.,
        XIX, 1 (Fall 1960/1), 47-52. (Cf. "P. V.:
        l'esthétique du grand seigneur, " Rev. Univ. La-
        val, XVII, 4 (déc. 1962), 305-15.)
3731.   Saurat, Denis.   "Paul Valéry, " Mod. French Lit.,
        1870-1940. N. Y.: 1946, pp. 115-61.
3732.   Sauvy, Alfred.   "Quelques réflex. sur l'harmonie
        dans la poésie (prose?) de V, " Entretiens sur V,
        ed. E. Noulet-Carner. Paris: 1968, pp. 377-
        97. (Avec une discuss., pp. 398-409.)
3733.   Scarfe, Francis. The Art of P. V.   London: 1954.
        (Subtitle: A Study in Dramatic Monologue.)
        (Bibliogr., pp. 322-33.) (Glasgow Univ. Publ.,
        97.)
3734.   Schalk, Fritz. "Uber d. Aphorismen P. Vs, " Mé-
        langes Offerts à Rita Lejeune, Prof. à l'Univ.
        de Liège. 2 vos. Gembloux: 1968, pp. 1575-
        84.
3735.   Schiffen, E.   "Zu P. Vs Poetik, " Die neueren
        Sprachen mit Phonetischen Studien, XXXVII (1929),
        289-98.
3736.   Schmitz, Alfred. V et la Tentation de l'Absolu.
        Gembloux: 1964. (Discusses 'Le Cimetière
        Marin. ')
3737.   Schön-Pietri, Nicole.   "P. V. et le réveil, " Etudes
        Françaises (Montréal), VI, 4 (Nov. 1970), 419-
        45.
3738.   Schwab, Raymond.   "Les rencontres décisives de
        P. V., " Gavroche, (26 juillet 1945).
3739.   _____.   "Le cas V, " La Vie Intellectuelle, XIII,
        7/8 (août-sept. 1945), 164-79.
3740.   Segond, M. J. "P. V., ou l'excellence de l'architec-
        ture, " Annales de la Fac. des Lettres d'Aix,
        (1936), 95-112.
3741.   No entry.
3742.   Sewell, Elizabeth. P. V.: The Mind in the Mirror.
        New Haven, Conn.: 1952. (Studies in Mod.
        Europ. Lit. and Thought.)
3743.   _____.   "Precept or example: P. V., " British
        Journ. of Aesthetics (London), II, 3 (July 1962),
        267-9.
3744.   Shattuck, Roger. "P. V.: Sportsman and Barbari-
        an, " Delos, I (1968), 96-116.
3745.   Simon, Pierre-Henri. "V ou l'esprit pur, " Témoins
        de l'Homme. Paris: 1967, pp. 63-87.

3746. Sorensen, Hans. La Poésie de P. V.: Etude Stylistique sur 'La Jeune Parque.' Kjobenhavn: 1944.

3747. Soulairol, Jean. "P. V. ou l'avancement en soi-même," Divan, no. 240 (oct.-déc. 1941), 193-204.

3748. _____. "Grandeur de V," Divan, no. 256 (oct.-déc. 1945), 161-71.

3749. _____. Paul Valéry. Paris: 1952.

3750. Spitzer, Leo. "La génèse d'une poésie de P. V.," Renaissance (New York), II/III (1944/5), 311-21. (Also in: Romanische Lit. studien, 1936-56. Tüb: 1959, pp. 343-52.)

3751. Stevens, Wallace. "Two prefaces: I-Gloire du long désir, idées; II-Chose légère, ailée, sacrée," Opus Posthumous, ed. S. F. Morse. London: 1959(57?), pp. 268-86.

3752. Stewart, William McC. "Peut-on parler d'un 'orphisme' de V'?" Cah. de l'Assoc. Intern'l des Etudes Françaises, XXII (Mai 1970), 181-95.

3753. Subramanyam, Ka Naa. "P. V.--idol of the intellect," Thought (Delhi), XXX, 28 (July 12, 1969), 15-16.

3754. Suckling, Norman. P. V. and the Civilized Mind. London/N.Y.: 1954. (Bibliogr., pp. 272-6.)

3755. Suhami, Evelyne. P. V. et la Musique. Dakar: 1966. (Univ. de Dakar; Fac. des Lettres et Sciences Humaines; Section Langues et Litt., 15.)

3756. Sutcliffe, F. E. La Pensée de P. V.: Essai. Paris: 1955.

3757. Sylvestre, G. "P. V.: Questions de Poésie," (Préface) L'Anthologie des Poètes de la N. R. F. Paris: 1958, pp. 11-21.

3758. Taladoire, B. A. "Sur l'humanité de P. V.," Cah. du Sud, no. 245 (avril 1942), 297-302.

3759. Tanji, Tsunejiro. "La marge d'intellect. Essai sur la logique imagin. de P. V.," Kwansei Gakuin Univ. Annual Studies, XVII (1968), 53-86.

3760. Tate, Allen. "A note on P. V.," Virginia Quart. Rev., XLVI, 3 (Summer 1970), 460-70.

3761. Taumann, Léon. P. V. ou le Mal de l'Art. Paris: 1969.

3762. _____. "P. V. et son infinie recherche," Austral. Journ. French Studies, VI (1969), 454-64.

3763. Tavera, F. M. "P. V.: poète de l'intelligence," Synthèses, I, 5 (août 1946), 83-93.

3764. Thibaudet, A. "La poésie de P. V.," Rev. de Paris, III (1923), 811-42.

3765. _____. Paul Valéry. Paris: 1923.
3766. Thiébaut, Marcel. "La pensée de V, " Rev. de
       Paris, LXVI, 4 (avril 1959), 154-5.
3767. Thomson, Alastair W. Valéry. Edinburgh/London:
       1965. (Writers and Critics, 45.) (Bibliogr.,
       pp. 117-19.)
3768. Tilgher, Adriano. "L'esthétique de P. V. , " Grande
       Revue, CXXXIX (1932), 601-8.
3769. Todorov, Tzvetan. "V's poetics, " Yale French
       Studies, no. 44 (1970), 65-71. (Trans. E.
       Willis.)
3770. Tortel, Jean. "II. --Décade P. V. " Cah. du Sud, LII
       385 (nov. -déc. 1965), unn. pages.
3771. Toussaint, Georges. "Présence de V, " France-Asie
       (Saïgon), VIII, 77 (oct. 1952), 739-47.
3772. Trahard, Pierre. "L'expér. poétique de V', " Le
       Mystère Poétique. Paris: 1970, pp. 145-61.
3773. Tribouillet, Paul-Henry. P. V., le Poète (Confé-
       rence). Hanoi: 1937.
3774. Trolliet, Gilbert. "Remarques sur la poésie de V, "
       Cah. du Sud, XVIII (1931), 626-7.
3775. Troy, William. "P. V. and the poetic universe, "
       Quart. Rev. of Lit. , III, 3 (1947), 232-9. (Also
       in: Mod. Lit. Crit. An Anthology, ed. I. Howe.
       Boston: 1958, pp. 320-6.)
3776. Truc, Gonzague. "Finesses et faiblesse de M. P.
       V. , " Rev. Hebdomadaire, X (1937), 34-50.
3777. Truchet, Jacques. "Une belle page de V sur la
       création litt. , " La Pensée Française, XVI, 13
       (déc. 1957), 68-70.
3778. Turnell, Martin. "Poet of contradiction, " Common-
       weal, LXVI, 22 (Aug. 30, 1957), 544-7.
3779. Usinger, Fritz. "Valéry, " Dichtg als Inform. Von
       d. Morphologie z. Kosmologie. Mainz: 1970,
       pp. 237-45. (Die Mainzer Reihe, 23.)
3780. Valensin, Auguste. "P. V. , ascète de l'intelligence,"
       Etudes, CCL, 8 (Sept. 1946), 231-40.
3781. Valéry, Agathe R. Valéry. Paris: 1966. (Conti-
       ent de nombreux extraits d'oeuvres de V; iconog-
       raphy accompanied by texts.)
3782. Valéry, Paul. Propos sur la Poésie. Paris: 1930.
       (Cf. The Art of Poetry, tr. Denise Folliot; in-
       trod. T. S. Eliot. N. Y. : 1958. Coll. works,
       7. Bollingen series, XLV, 7.)
3783. _____. Zur Theorie d. Dichtkunst. Frankf. M. :
       1962.
3784. _____. "Nécessité de la poésie, " Conférencia, I

(1938), 179-88.

3785. _____. Exposition (31 janv.-31 mars 1956). Catalogue, par Marcel Tomas et al. Préf. de Julien
Cain. Paris: Bibliothèque Nationale: 1956.

3786. _____. "The existence of symbolism, " tr. Mal-
colm Cowley, Kenyon Review, XIX, 3 (Summer
1957), 425-47.

3787. Van Tieghem, Philippe. "Les idées litt. de P. V., "
Renaissance, nos. 13/14 (août-sept. 1945), 64-72.

3788. Vaudal, Jean. "P. V. ou la Morale
en Italique, " Domaine Français: Messages
1943. Genève: 1943, pp. 401-13. (Variant
listing: Vandel, Jean.)

3789. Vellas, Pierre. "La technique poétique de P. V., "
Concorde, (30 juillet 1945),

3790. Voisins, Gilbert de. Paul Valéry. Paris: 1931.

3791. Wahl, Jean. "Sur la pensée de P. V., " Poésie,
Pensée, Perception. Paris: 1948, pp. 77-93.
(Also in: Nouv. Rev. Française, II (1933), 449-
63.)

3792. Walzer, Pierre-Olivier. "Grandeur de P. V., "
Formes et Couleurs, VII, 2 (1945).

3793. _____. "Introd. à l'érotique valéryenne, " Cah.
Assoc. Intern'l des Etudes Françaises, no. 17
(mars 1965), 217-29.

3794. _____. La Poésie de V. Genève: 1967. (Reprint of 1953 ed.) (Bibliogr., pp. 477-86.)

3795. Watts, Harold H. "V and the poet's place, " Quart.
Rev. of Lit., III, 3 (1947), 292-305.

3796. Whiting, Charles. "Femininity in V's early poetry, "
Yale French Studies, IX (1952), 74-83.

3797. Whiting, G. V Jeune Poète. Paris/New Haven:
1960.

3798. _____. " 'Profusion du Soir' and 'Le Cimetière
Marin,' " PMLA, LXXVII, 1 (March 1962), 134-
9.

3799. _____. "Préciosité in 'La Jeune Parque' and
'Charmes,' " Yale French Studies, no. 44 (1970),
119-27.

3800. Wilson, Edmund. "Paul Valéry, " Dial, LXXVIII
(1925), 491-7.

3801. _____. "Paul Valéry, " Axël's Castle. A Study
in the Imaginative Lit. of 1870-1930. London:
1961. (Fontana Library, 539L.) [Later ed.
New York: 1969, pp. 64-92.]

3802. Winkler, E. "Sprachtheorie u. V-Deutung, " Ztschr.
f. neufranzös. Sprache u. Lit., LVI (1932), 129-

3803.   Zants, Emily.   "V and the mod.   French novel, "
        L'Esprit Créateur, VII, 2 (Summer 1967), 81-90.

VALLEJO

3804.   Abril, Xavier, ed.   "Prólogo, " Antologia de C. V.
        Buenos Aires: 1942.
3805.   _____.   Vallejo.   Ensayo de Aprox.   Crítica.
        Buenos Aires: 1958.   (Col.   Ensayos: Poetas
        de Hoy y d Siempre.)
3806.   _____.   Dos Estudios: I.   Vallejo y Mallarmé.
        II.   Vigencia de Vallejo.   Buenos Aires: 1960.
3807.   _____.   C. V. o la Teoría Poética.   Madrid:
        1962.   (Incl.   "Vallejo y Mallarmé: La estética
        de 'Trilce' y 'Una jugada de dados jamás abolirá
        el acaso, ' " pp.   15-64.)
3808.   Alegría, Ciro.   "El C. V. que yo conoci, " Letras
        Peruanas (Lima), no.   8 (Oct.   1952).
3809.   Angeles Caballero, César A.   C. V., su Obra.
        Lima· 1964.   (Bibliog., pp.   241-50.)
3810.   Anon.   "C. Vallejo, " Raam, XLIV (1968), 20-1.
        (Incl.   trans.)
3811.   Arango L., Manuel A.   "C. Vallejo, " Tres Figuras
        Represent.   de Hispano-America en la Generac.
        de Vanguardia o Lit.   de Postguerra: Porfirio
        Barba Jacob, Cesar Vallejo, Alfonso Reyes.
        Bogota, Columbia: 1967, pp.   71-115.
3812.   Asturrizaga, Juan E.   C. V.:   Itinerario del Hombre.
        Lima: 1965.
3813.   Azáigara Ballón, Enrique.   Tematica de V'.   (Diss.)
        Univ.   Nac.   de Arequipa: 1945.
3814.   Baciu, Stefan.   "C. V.:   ¿ Poeta Communista, "
        Cuad.   Brasileiros, IV, 3 (1962), 95-103.
3815.   Bar-Lewaw, Itzhak.   Termas Literarios Iberoameri-
        canos.   Mexico: 1961.
3816.   Belli, Carlos Germán.   "En torno a V', " Rev.
        Iberoamer., XXXVI (1970), 159-64.
3817.   Bergamín, José.   "Prólogo, " Trilce, de C. V.   Ma-
        drid: 1930.
3818.   _____.   "V' y su libro 'Trilce, ' " Bolívar (Ma-
        drid), I (Nov.   1930), p.   5.
3819.   Bullrich, Santiago.   "Humanidad poética de C. V., "

Recreación y Realidad en Pisarello, Gelman y
Vallejo. Buenos Aires: 1963, pp. 47-66.
(Bibliog., pp. 67-9.) (Coll. Ensayos.)

3820. Campos, Jorge. "Vallejo-Abril," Insula, XVI, 170
(1962), 11. (Review article.)

3821. Castagnino, Raul H. "Dos narraciones C. V.,"
Rev. Iberoamer., XXXVI (1970), 321-39.

3822. Castros Arenas, Mario. "Algunos rasgos estilísticos
de la poesía de C. V.," Cuad. Amer., CLX
(1968), 189-212.

3823. Chatzidaki, Sophia Emm. "Perouviani poiisi: C. V.,"
Nea Hestia, LXXXVII (1970), 379-81.

3824. Cornejo Ubillús, Edmundo, ed. "Prólogo," Antologia,
C. V. Lima: 1948.

3825. Coyné, André. "C. V., hombre y poeta," Letras
Organo de la Fac. de Letras de la Univ. Nac.
Mayor de San Marcos de Lima, primer y segundo
semestres (1951).

3826. _____. "El último libro de V'," Letras Peruanas,
Rev. de Humanidades (Lima), I, 11 (Agosto
1951).

3827. _____. "Apuntes biogr. de C. V.," El Mar del
Sur (Lima), III, 8 (Nov.-Dic. 1949),
45-70.

3828. _____. C. Vallejo, rev. edn. Buenos Aires:
1968. (Earlier edn., Lima: 1958.) (Coll.
Ensayos: Arte y Estética.)

3829. _____. "V' y el surrealismo," Rev. Iberoamer.,
XXXVI (1970), 243-301.

3830. Cueto Fernandini, Carlos. "Trilce," Sphinx Rev.
del Instit. Super. de Lingüistica y Filol. de la
Univ. Mayor de San Marcos (Lima), III, 6-7
(Julio-Oct. 1939).

3831. Essays by var. hands. "Homenaje pequeño y fervo-
roso a uno de sus fundadores: C. V.," Nuestra
España, Bol. Semanal del Comité Iberoamer. para
la Defensa de la República Española (Paris), no.
70 (21 Oct. 1938). (Incl. sel. from V's works
plus critical essays by Juan Larrea, José Carlos
Mariátegui, et al.)

3832. _____. Poesía de América (Mexico), no. 5
(1954). (Special issue on Vallejo.)

3833. _____. "Homenaje en Piríapolis a Lugones y a
Vallejo," El País (Montevideo) (Marzo-Abril
1958).

3834. _____. Aula Vallejo, nos. 1-7 (1959-'67). Univ.
Nac. de Córdoba, publ. périodica del Instit. del

Nuevo Mundo, dir. Juan Larrea.

3835. _____. Revista Iberoamericana, XXXVII (1970), 159-358. (C. V. special issue.)

3836. Esteban, Claude. "C. Vallejo," Mercure de France, CCCLII (1965), 142-50.

3837. Ferrari, Americo. "C. V.: Trajectoire du poète," C. Vallejo. Paris: 1967, pp. 7-49. (Poètes d'Aujourd'hui, 168.) (Also incl. "Note sur la bibliog. de V'," pp. 186-7.)

3838. Ferrero, Mario. "C. V.: perfil de Indoamérica," Anales de la Univ. de Chile, CXX, 125 (1962), 80-90.

3839. de la Fuente, Pablo. "Record. a un amigo muerto. Cómo era C. V.," El Sol (Madrid) (25 Sett. 1938), p. 1.

3840. García Pinto, Roberto. "Actualidad de V'," Sur, no. 265 (Julio-Agosto 1960), 47-9.

3841. Ghiano, Juan Carlos. "Equívocos sobre V'," Sur, no. 312 (1968), 17-26.

3842. Gonzalez Ruano, César. "Una entrevista al poeta C. V.," El Heraldo (Enero 1930).

3843. _____. Veintidós Retratos de Escritores Hispanoamericanos. Madrid: 1952, pp. 115-17.

3844. _____. "C. V. en Madrid: 'Trilce,'" El Heraldo (27 Enero 1931), p. 16.

3845. Guereña, Jacinto-Luis. "Orillas actuales de C. V.," Quad. Iberoamer., no. 27 (1961), 165-7.

3846. Higgins, James. "El absurdo en la poesía de C. V.," Rev. Iberoamer., XXXVI (1970), 217-41.

3847. _____, ed. "Introd.," C. V.: An Anthol. of His Poetry. N.Y.: 1970, pp. 1-82.

3848. Iduarte, Andrés. "C. Vallejo," Hora de España (Barcelona), no. 19 (1938).

3849. Izquierdo Ríos, Francisco. V' y su Tierra. Lima: 1949.

3850. Larrea, Juan. "Commem. de C. V. (15 Abril 1938)," Cuad. Amer. (Mexico), D. F., II (Marzo-Abril 1942), 211.

3851. _____. C. V. o Hispanoamérica en la Cruz de su Razón. Córdoba: 1958.

3852. Lellis, Mario Jorge de. C. Vallejo. Buenos Aires: 1960.

3853. Lora Risco, Alejandro. "Introd. a la poesía de C. V.," Cuad. Amer., XIX, 111 (1960), 261-77.

3854. McDuffie, Keith A. "C. V.: profile of a poet," Proceed. Pacific Northwest Confer. on Foreign Langs., ed. Jerrold L. Mordaunt. Victoria,

B. C.: 1968, pp. 135-43.

3855. _____. "'Trilce' (I) y la función de la palabra en la poética de C. V., " Rev. Iberoamer., XXXVI (1970), 191-204.

3856. _____. "Una fracasada trad. inglesa de 'Poemas Humanos, ' " Rev. Iberoamer., XXXVI (1970), 345-52.

3857. _____. "The poetic vision of C. V. in 'Los Heraldos Negros' and 'Trilce, ' " Diss. Abstr. Intern'l, XXX (1969), 2032A (Pittsburgh).

3858. Meo Zillio, Giovanni. Stile e Poesia in C. V. Padova: 1960.

3859. Miro, César. "Prólogo, " Poesias Completas (1918-'38), de C. V. Buenos Aires: 1949.

3860. Monguió, Luis. "C. V.: Bibliog., " Rev. Hisp. Moderna, XVI, 1-4 (Enero-Dic. 1950), 1-98.

3861. _____. C. V. (1892-1938): Bibliog., Antol. N. Y.: Hispanic Instit. in U. S., 1952.

3862. _____. C. V.: Vida y Obra. Lima: 1959.

3863. More, Ernesto. "Anecdot. de C. V., " 1949 (Lima), nos. 32-48 (1949).

3864. _____. V', en la Encrucijada del Drama Peruano. Lima: 1968.

3865. Neale-Silva, Eduardo. "Poesía y sociología en un poema de 'Trilce, ' " Rev. Iberoamer., XXXVI (1970), 205-16.

3866. _____. "Esperanza y desillusión en tres poemas de C. V., " Cuad. Hispanoamer., CCXLI (1970), 149-69.

3867. _____. "The introd. poem in V's 'Trilce, ' " Hispanic Review, XXXVIII (1970), 2-16.

3868. Nooteboom, Cees, transl. "C. V.: View Gedichten," Gids, CXXXIII (1970), 23-7.

3869. Obarrio, Felipe. "Life, death, and C. V., " Américas, XX (Nov. -Dec. 1968), 45-8.

3870. Orrego, Antenor. "Los primeros versos de C. V., " La Tribuna (Lima) (30 Marzo 1958).

3871. Ortega, Julio. "Lectura de 'Trilce, ' " Rev. Iberoamer., XXXVI (1970), 165-89.

3872. Pacheco, Leon. "C. V. y la Angustia, " Tres Ensayos Apasionados: Vallejo, Unamuno, Camus. San José, Costa Rica: 1968, pp. 21-99.

3873. Paoli, Roberto. Poesia di C. V. Milano: 1964. (Contains prelim. study, bibliog., and transl.)

3874. _____. "Observ. sobre el indigenismo de C. V., " Rev. Iberoamer., XXXVI (1970), 341-4.

3875. Pinto Gamboa, Willy. C. V. en España: Perfil

Bibliográfico. Lima: 1968.
3876.   Roggiano, Alfredo. "Minima Guía Bibliog.," Rev.
        Iberoamer., XXXVI (1970), 353-8.
3877.   Samaniego, Antenor. C. Vallejo. Su Poesia. Lima:
        1954.
3878.   Sánchez, Luis Alberto. La Lit. de Perú, 2nd edn.
        Buenos Aires: 1943.
3879.   _____. "Prólogo," Articulos Olvidados, de C. V.
        Lima: 1960.
3880.   _____. "La prosa periodística de C. V.," Rev.
        Iberoamer., XXXVI (1970), 303-20.
3881.   Teresa Léon, Maria. "C. V. el gran poeta peruano;
        i ha muerto!," El Mono Azul (Madrid), no. 45
        (Mayo 1938).
3882.   Torre, Guillermo de. "Reconocimiento crít. de C.
        V.," Rev. Iberoamer., XXV (1960), 45-58.
3883.   Torres Bodet, Jaime. "Las letras hispanoamer. en
        1930," La Gaceta Literaria (Madrid) (1 Enero
        1931), p. 6 (on V's 'Trilce').
3884.   Vaifro Sabatelli, Giacomo. "C. V., poeta di antici-
        pazioni," Vita e Pensiero, LI (1968), 794-812.
3885.   Valbuena Briones, Angel. "El nuevo estilo de C.
        V.," Atenea, XLV, 162 (1968), 153-7.
3886.   Vallejo, César. "La responsabilidad del escritor,"
        El Mono Azul (Madrid), no. 4 (1939), 103-6.
3887.   _____. El Romanticismo en la Poesia Castellana.
        Lima: 1954.
3888.   Vallejo, Georgette. "Apuntes biogr. de C. V.,"
        Los Heraldos Negros, di C. V. Lima: 1959.
3889.   Villaneuva, Elsa. La Poesia de C. V. Lima: 1951.
3890.   Yurkievich, Saúl. Valoración de Vallejo. Resistencia:
        Univ. Nac. del Nordeste, 1958.

YEATS

3891.   Adams, Hazard. "Yeats scholarship and crit.: a
        review of research," Texas Stud. in Lit. & Lang.,
        III (1962), 439-51.
3892.   _____. "Yeats, dialectic and crit.," Criticism,
        X (1968), 185-99.
3893.   _____. "Criticism, politics, and history: the
        matter of Yeats," Georgia Review, XXIV (1970),
        158-82.

3894. Adkinson, R. V. "Criticizing Yeats," Rev. des
Langues Vivantes, XXXIII (1967), 423-30.
3895. A. E. "Yeats' early poems," Living Age, CCCXXVII,
4247 (Nov. 28, 1925), pp. 464-6.
3896. Agarwala, D. C. "Yeats' concept of image," Triveni
(Machilipatnam, India), (July 1967), 23-35.
3897. Allen, James L., Jr. "Yeats' bird-soul symbolism,"
Twentieth Cen. Lit., VI (1960), 117-22.
3898. _____. "Bird symbolism in the work of W. B.
Y.," Diss. Abstr., XX (1960), 3288 (Fla.).
3899. Allt, G. D. P. "Yeats and the revision of his early
verse," Hermathena, LXIV (Nov. 1944).
3900. Alspach, Russell K. "Some sources of Yeats' 'The
Wanderings of Oisin,' " PMLA, LVIII, 3 (Sept.
1943), 849-66.
3901. _____. "Yeats' first two publ. poems," Mod.
Lang. Notes, LVIII, 7 (Nov. 1943), 555-7.
('Song of the Faeries' and 'Voices.')
3902. Anon. "Yeats' inner drama," Times Lit. Suppl.,
XXXVIII, 1931 (Feb. 4, 1939), pp. 72, 74.
3903. Archer, William. "W. B. Y.," Poets of the Younger
Generation. London: 1902, pp. 531-57.
3904. Archibald, Douglas N. "Yeats' encounters: observ.
on lit. infl. and lit. hist.," New Lit. Hist.
(Univ. Va.), I (1970), 439-69.
3905. Auden, W. H. "Yeats: master of diction," Sat. Review of Lit., XXII, 7 (June 8, 1940), p. 14.
(On: Last Poems and Plays.)
3906. _____. "Yeats as an example," Kenyon Review,
X, 2 (Spring 1948), 187-95. (Repr. in Hall &
Steinmann (eds.), pp. 308-14.)
3907. Baker, Howard. "Domes of Byzantium," Southern
Review, VII, 3 (Winter 1942), 639-52.
3908. Barton, Ruth P. " 'The natural words in the natural
order': a study of W. B. Y.'s verse syntax,"
Diss. Abstr. Intern'l, XXX (1970), 5438A (Wis.).
3909. Bayley, John. The Romantic Survival. London:
1957.
3910. Bentley, Eric. "Yeats as a playwright," Kenyon
Review, X, 2 (Spring 1948), 196-208. (Repr. in
Hall & Steinmann (eds.), pp. 213-23.)
3911. Berryman, Charles. W. B. Yeats: Design of Opposites. N. Y.: 1967.
3912. Bickley, Francis. "The develop. of W. B. Y.,"
Living Age, CCLXIV, 3429 (March 26, 1910),
pp. 802-5.

3913. _____. "Yeats and the movement, " J. M. Synge
        and the Irish Dramatic Movement. London:
        1912, pp. 49-66.
3914. Blackmur, R. P. "The later poetry of W. B. Y.,"
        The Expense of Greatness. N.Y.: 1940, pp. 74-
        106. (Repr. in Hall & Steinmann (eds.), pp. 38-
        59.)
3915. _____. "Between myth and philosophy: fragments
        of W. B. Y.," Southern Review, VII, 3 (Winter
        1942), 407-25.
3916. Bloom, Harold. Yeats. N.Y.: 1971(?).
3917. Bose, Abinash Chandra. "W. B. Yeats," Three
        Mystic Poets. Kolhapur, India: 1945, pp. 1-46.
3918. Bottomly, Gordon. "His legacy to the theatre, "
        Arrow, I (Summer 1939), 11-14.
3919. Bowra, C. M. "W. B. Yeats," The Heritage of
        Symbolism. London: 1943, pp. 180-218.
3920. Boyd, E. A. "W. B. Y.: the poems, ... the plays,
        and ... prose writings," Ireland's Lit. Renais-
        sance. N.Y.: 1916, pp. 122-44, 145-65, 166-
        87 resp.
3921. Bradford, Curtis B. "Yeats' Byzantium poems: a
        study of their develop.," PMLA, LXXV (1960),
        110-25. (Repr. in Unterecker (ed.), pp. 93-
        100.)
3922. _____. Yeats at Work. Carbondale: 1965.
3923. Brenner, Rica. "W. B. Yeats," Poets of Our Time.
        N.Y.: 1941, pp. 355-411.
3924. Bronowski, J. "W. B. Yeats," The Poet's Defense.
        Cambridge: 1939, pp. 229-52.
3925. Brooks, Cleanth, Jr. "Yeats: the poet as myth-
        maker," Mod. Poetry and the Trad. Chapel
        Hill, N. C.: 1939, pp. 173-202. (Repr. in
        Hall & Steinmann (eds.), pp. 60-84) (on 'A Vi-
        sion.')
3926. Brown, Forman G. "Mr. Yeats and the supernatural,"
        Sewanee Review, XXXIII, 3 (July 1925), 323-30.
3927. Buckley, Vincent. "Yeats: the great comedian, "
        Malahat Review, V (1968), 77-89.
3928. Burke, Kenneth. "On motivation in Yeats," Southern
        Review, VII, 3 (Winter 1942), 547-61. (Repr.
        in Hall & Steinmann (eds.), pp. 224-37.)
3929. Bushrui, Suheil Badi, transl. Shai'un min Yeats:
        Shi'r, Nathr, Masrah. Lebanon: Univ. Beirut
        Dept. English: 1969. (On Yeats' poetry, prose,
        and drama; transl. into Arabic, with introds. &
        a bibliog.)

3930.   Byrd, Thomas L., Jr., and Carolyn G. Kahn. "The
        stone as a symbol in the lyric poetry of W. B.
        Y.," Xavier Univ. Stud., VIII, 3 (1969), 28-35.
3931.   Cazamian, Madeleine L. "W. B. Yeats (1865-1939),"
        Etudes Anglaises, III, 2 (Avril-Juin 1939), 127-
        31.
3932.   Chatterjee, Bhabatosh.   The Poetry of W. B. Yeats.
        Calcutta: 1962.
3933.   Cheadle, B. D. "Yeats and symbolism," English
        Stud. in Africa (Johannesburg), XII (1969), 132-
        50.
3934.   Church, Richard.   "The later Yeats," Eight for Im-
        mortality.   London: 1941, pp. 41-54.
3935.   Cornwell, Ethel F.   The Still Point.   New Brunswick,
        N. J.:   1963.
3936.   Cowell, Raymond.   W. B. Yeats.   London: 1969.
        (Lit. P.).
3937.   Daiches, David. "W. B. Yeats: I & II," Poetry
        and the Mod. World.   Chicago: 1940, pp. 128-
        55; 156-89.   (Repr. in: Hall & Steinmann (eds.),
        pp. 106-24.)
3938.   Davidson, Donald.   "Yeats and the centaur," Southern
        Review, VII, 3 (Winter 1942), 510-16.   (Repr. in
        Hall & Steinmann (eds.), pp. 250-6.)
3939.   Davis, E.   Yeats' Early Contacts With French Poe-
        try.   Pretoria, S. Africa: 1961.   (Communic.
        of the Univ. of S. Africa.)
3940.   Day, Lewis C. "A note on W. B. Y. and the aristo-
        cratic trad.," Scattering Branches, ed. Stephen
        Gwynn.   N. Y.:   1940, pp. 157-82.
3941.   Donoghue, Denis.   "Trad., poetry, and W. B. Y.,"
        Sewanee Review, LXIX (1961), 476-84.   (Review
        article.)
3942.   _____, ed.   The Integrity of Yeats.   Cork, Ire-
        land: 1964.   (Thomas Davis Lectures.)
3943.   _____, and J. R. Mulryne, eds.   An Honored
        Guest: New Essays on W. B. Yeats.   London:
        1965.
3944.   Drew, Elisabeth, and John L. Sweeney. "W. B.
        Yeats," Directions in Mod. Poetry.   N. Y.:
        1940, pp. 148-71.
3945.   Eddins, Dwight L.   "Yeats: the 19th cen. matrix,"
        Diss. Abstr., XXVIII (1968), 4123A (Vanderbilt).
3946.   Edgar, Pelham.   "The enigma of Yeats," Queen's
        Quarterly, XLVI, 4 (Nov. 1939), 411-22.
3947.   Eliot, T. S.   "The poetry of W. B. Y.," Southern
        Review, VII, 3 (Winter 1942), 442-54.   (Repr.

in Hall & Steinmann (eds.), pp. 296-307.)
3948. Ellmann, Richard. Yeats: The Man and the Masks.
N. Y. : 1948. (London: 1949.)
3949. _____ . The Identity of Yeats. London: 1954.
3950. Engelberg, Edward. "Picture and gesture in the
Yeatsian aesthetic, " Criticism, III (1961), 101-
20.
3951. _____ . The Vast Design: Patterns in W. B.
Yeats' Aesthetic. Toronto: 1964.
3952. Engsberg, Richard C. "Two by two: analogues of
form in poetry and music, " Diss. Abstr. Intern'l,
XXX (1969), 278A (N. Y. U.).
3953. Evans, B. Ifor. "W. B. Y. and the continuance of
trad. , " Trad. and Romanticism. London: 1940,
pp. 201-8.
3954. Faulkner, Peter. "Yeats as critic, " Criticism, IV,
4 (Fall 1962), 328-39. (Villiers, Maeterlinck.)
3955. Fay, W. G. "The poet and the actor, " Scattering
Branches, ed. Stephen Gwynn. N. Y. : 1940,
pp. 115-34.
3956. Figgis, Darrell. "Mr. W. B. Yeats' poetry, "
Studies and Apprec. London: 1912, pp. 119-38.
3957. Fraser, G. S. W. B. Yeats, 2nd edn. London /N. Y. :
1962 (1954). (Writers and Their Work, no. 50.)
3958. _____ . Vision and Rhetoric in Mod. Poetry.
London: 1959.
3959. _____ . "Yeats and the ballad style, " Shenandoah,
XXI, 3 (1970), 177-94.
3960. Frayne, John P. "The early crit. prose of W. B.
Y. : Forty-one reviews, ed. with an introd. and
notes, " Diss. Abstr. Intern'l, XXX (1970),
4449A /50A (Columbia).
3961. Fréchet, René. "L'Etude de Yeats: textes, juge-
ments, et éclaircissements, " Etudes Anglaises,
XIV (1961), 36-47. (Review.)
3962. Frye, Northrop. "Yeats and the language of Symbolism, " Univ. Toronto Quart. , XVII, 1 (Oct.
1947), 1-17.
3963. Gallagher, Michael P. "Yeats, syntax, and the
self, " Ariz. Quart. , XXVI (1970), 5-16.
3964. Garab, Arra M. Beyond Byzantium: The Last
Phase of Yeats' Career. DeKalb, Ill. : 1969.
3965. _____ . "The legacy of Yeats, " Journ. Mod. Lit. ,
I (1970), 137-40. (Review article.)
3966. Gerstenberger, Donna. "Yeats and the theater: a
sel. bibliog. , " Mod. Drama, VI (1963), 64-71.
3967. Gordon, D. J. , et al. W. B. Yeats: Images of a

Poet. Manchester: 1961.
3968. Green, J. T. "Symbolism in Yeats' poetry, " Fort
Hare Papers (Fort Hare Univ., S. Africa), IV,
3 (1969), 11-23.
3969. Grubb, H. T. Hunt. "W. B. Y.: his plays, poems
and sources of inspir., " Poetry Review, XXVI,
5 (Sept.-Oct. 1935), 351-66; 6 (Nov.-Dec. 1935),
455-65.
3970. Gurd, Patty. The Early Poetry of W. B. Yeats.
Lancaster, Pa.: 1916.
3971. Gwynn, Stephen, ed. Scattering Branches. London/
N. Y.: 1940. (Recoll. of Yeats.)
3972. Haerdter, Michael. "W. B. Y.: Irisches Theater
zwischen Symbolismus u. Expressionismus, "
Maske u. Kothurn (Graz, Wien), XI (1965), 30-
42.
3973. Hall, James, and Martin Steinmann, eds. The Per-
manence of Yeats. N. Y.: 1950. (Collier Books
edn.: 1961) (bibliog., pp. 349-71.)
3974. Harper, George M. Yeats' Quest for Eden. Dublin:
1966. (Yeats Centen. Papers, 1965.)
3975. _____. "'All the Instruments Agree': Some
observ. on recent Yeats crit., " Sewanee Review,
LXXIV (1966), 739-54.
3976. Harris, Daniel A. "The spreading laurel tree: Yeats
and the aristocratic trad., " Diss. Abstr. Intern'l,
XXX (1969), 1982A (Yale).
3977. Harris, Wendell. "Innocent decadence: the poetry
of the 'Savoy, ' " PMLA, LXXVII (1962), 629-36.
3978. Haydn, Hiram. "The last of the Romantics: an
introd. to the symbolism of W. B. Y., " Sewanee
Review, LV, 2 (April-June 1947), 297-323.
3979. Healy, J. V. "Yeats and his imagination, " Sewanee
Review, LIV, 4 (Autumn 1946), 650-9.
3980. Henn, T. R. "W. B. Y. and the Irish background, "
Yale Review, XLII (1953), 351-64.
3981. _____. "The accent of Yeats' Last Poems, " in
Essays and Studies, n. s., IX (1956). Coll. for
the English Assoc. by Sir George R. Hamilton.
London: 1956, pp. 56-72.
3982. _____. "Yeats' symbolism, " The Integrity of
Yeats, ed. Denis Donoghue. Cork, Ireland:
1964, pp. 33-46.
3983. _____. The Lonely Tower: Stud. in the Poetry
of W. B. Yeats, 2nd ed. London: 1965(1950).
3984. Higgins, F. R. "Yeats and poetic drama in Ireland, "
The Irish Theatre, ed. Lennox Robinson. Lon-

don: 1939, pp. 65-88.

3985. Hone, Hoseph. W. B. Yeats: The Poet in Contemp.
Ireland. London: 1915.

3986. _____. W. B. Yeats, 1865-1939, 2nd edn. Lon-
don/N.Y.: 1962 (1943).

3987. Hough, Graham. The Last Romantics. London/N. Y.:
1961. (Univ. Paperback, UP-27.) (First publ.
1947.)

3988. Hume, Martha H. "Yeats: aphorist and epigramma-
tist. A Study of the Collected Poems," Diss.
Abstr. Intern'l, XXX (1970), 4454A (Colo.).

3989. Huttemann, G. Wesen d. Dichtung u. Aufgabe d.
Dichters bei W. B. Yeats. Bonn: 1929.

3990. Jackson, Holbrook. "The discovery of the Celt,"
The Eighteen Nineties. N.Y.: 1922, pp. 147-
56.

3991. Jarrell, Randall. "The develop. of Yeats' sense of
reality," Southern Review, VII, 3 (Winter 1942),
653-66.

3992. Jeffares, A. Norman. "The Byzantine poems of
W. B. Y.," Review of English Stud., XXII, 85
(Jan. 1946), 44-52.

3993. _____. "W. B. Y. and his methods of writing
verse," Nineteenth Cen. and After, CXXXIX, 829
(March 1946), 123-8. (Repr. in Hall & Steinmann (eds.), pp. 270-6.)

3994. _____. A Poet and a Theatre. Groningen: 1946.

3995. _____. "An account of recent Yeatsiana," Hermathena, LXXII (1948), 21-43.

3996. _____. "Notes on Yeats' 'Lapis Lazuli,'" Mod.
Lang. Notes, LXV (1950), 488-91.

3997. _____. "Yeats' 'The Gyres': sources and symbolism," Huntington Library Quart., XV (1951),
89-97.

3998. _____. The Poems of W. B. Yeats. London/
Great Neck, N.Y.: 1961. (Stud. in English
Lit., 4.)

3999. _____. "Yeats' Byzantine poems and the critics,"
English Stud. in Africa (Johannesburg), V (1962),
11-28. (Incl. sel. bibliog., pp. 26-8.)

4000. _____, ed. W. B. Yeats: Sel. Criticism. London: 1964.

4001. _____, and K. G. W. Cross, eds. In Excited
Reverie: A Centen. Tribute to W. B. Yeats,
1865-1939. London/N.Y.: 1965. (Esp. K. G.
W. Cross, "The fascin. of what's difficult: a
survey of Yeats crit. and research," pp. 315-37.)

4002. _____. W. B. Yeats: Man and Poet, 2nd edn.
    N.Y.: 1966. (Earlier edn. London: 1949.)
4003. _____. A Comment. on the Coll. Poems of W.
    B. Yeats. Stanford, Calif.: 1971(?).
4004. _____. The Circus Animals: Essays on W. B.
    Yeats. Stanford, Calif.: 1970.
4005. Jerome, Judson. "Six senses of the poet," Colorado
    Quart., X (1962), 225-40.
4006. John, Brian. "Hurt into poetry: some recent Yeats
    studies," Journ. Gen'l Educ., XVIII (1967), 299-
    306.
4007. Jones, Llewellyn. "The later poetry of Mr. W. B.
    Yeats," First Impressions. N.Y.: 1925, pp. 137-
    48.
4008. Kermode, Frank. Romantic Image. London: 1957.
4009. Killew, A. M. "Some French infl. in the works of
    W. B. Y. at the end of the 19th cen.," Comp.
    Lit. Stud., VIII (1942), 1-8.
4010. Kim, Myung Whan. "Mythopoetic elements in the
    later plays of W. B. Y. and the Noh," Diss.
    Abstr. Intern'l, XXX (1970), 4949A (Ind.).
4011. _____. "The vision of the spiritual world in
    Yeats' plays and the Noh," Phoenix K (Korea
    Univ.), XIV (1970), 39-79.
4012. Kirby, Sheelah. The Yeats Country. Dublin: 1962.
4013. Klimek, Theodor. Symbol u. Wirklichkeit bei W. B.
    Yeats. Bonn: 1967. (Abhandl. z. Kunst-,
    Musik-u. Lit. wiss. schaft, 45.)
4014. Koch, Vivienne. W. B. Yeats: The Tragic Phase.
    London: 1951.
4015. Krans, H. S. W. B. Yeats and the Irish Lit. Re-
    vival. N.Y.: 1904.
4016. Leavis, F. R. New Bearings in English Poetry.
    London: 1932, pp. 27-50. (Repr. in Hall &
    Steinmann (eds.), pp. 146-59.)
4017. Levine, Bernard. "The dissolving image: a concen-
    trative analysis of Yeats' poetry," Diss. Abstr.,
    XXVI (1965), 3341/2 (Brown).
4018. _____. The Dissolving Image: The Spiritual-
    Esthetic Develop. of W. B. Yeats. Detroit:
    1970.
4019. Linebarger, James M. "Yeats' symbolist method
    and the play 'Purgatory,'" Diss. Abstr., XXIV
    (1964), 3750/1 (Emory).
4020. MacLeish, Archibald. "Public speech and private
    speech in poetry," Time to Speak. Boston:
    1940, pp. 59-70.

4021.   . Poetry and Experience. Boston/London:
          1960/1. (Also incl. Rimbaud.)
4022.   Macleod, Fiona (William Sharp). "The later work
          of Mr. W. B. Y. , " North Amer. Review, CLXXV,
          551 (Oct. 1902), 473-85.
4023.   MacNeice, Louis. The Poetry of W. B. Yeats, 3rd
          edn. London: 1969 (1967; 1941).
4024.   Mahon, Cecil M. "The fascinat. of what's difficult.
          W. B. Y. : the mask as esthetic and discipline, "
          Diss. Abstr. , XXVIII (1968), 2689A (Santa Bar-
          bara, Calif.).
4025.   Mason, H. A. "Yeats and the English trad. , "
          Scrutiny, V, 4 (March 1937), 449-51. (Concern-
          ing the Oxford Book of Mod. Verse.)
4026.   Maxwell, D. E. S. , and Suheil B. Bushrui, eds.
          W. B. Yeats, 1865-1965. Centen. Essays on the
          Art of W. B. Yeats. Ibadan: 1965. ("A sel.
          bibliog. , " pp. 227-41.)
4027.   Maynard, Theodore. "W. B. Yeats: fairies and
          fog, " Our Best Poets. N. Y. : 1922, pp. 67-83.
4028.   Melchiori, Giorgio. The Whole Mystery of Art:
          Pattern Into Poetry in the Work of W. B. Yeats.
          London: 1960.
4029.   Menon, V. K. N. The Develop. of W. B. Yeats.
          Philad. : 1961. (2nd rev. edn.) (First edn.
          Edinburgh: 1942.)
4030.   Miller, Liam, ed. The Dolmen Press Yeats Cen-
          tenary Papers. Dublin: 1968.
4031.   Mizener, Arthur. "The romanticism of W. B. Y. , "
          Southern Review, VII, 3 (Winter 1942), 601-23.
          (Repr. in Hall & Steinman (eds.), pp. 125-45.)
4032.   Monroe, Harriet. "Mr. Yeats and the poetic drama,"
          Poetry, XVI, 1 (April 1920), 32-9.
4033.   Moore, George. Hail and Farewell. 3 vols, N. Y. :
          1914, I (Ave), passim; III (Vale), pp. 170-212.
4034.   Moore, John R. "Yeats as a last Romantic, "
          Virginia Quart. Review, XXXVII (1961), 432-49.
4035.   Moore, Virginia. The Unicorn: W. B. Yeats'
          Search for Reality. N. Y. : 1954.
4036.   Muir, Edwin. "W. B. Yeats, " Aspects de la Litt.
          Anglaise, 1918-1945, ed. Kathleen Raine and Max-
          Pol Fouchet. Paris: 1947, pp. 94-105.
4037.   Munro, John H. " 'Byzantium' or the imperial
          palace?--ultimate vision or variable compro-
          mise?" Venture (Univ. Karachi), V (1969), 93-
          109.
4038.   Murry, J. Middleton. "Mr. Yeats' swan song, "

Aspects of Lit., rev. edn. London: 1934, pp. 53-
9. (On 'The Wild Swans at Coole.')

4039. Nathan, Leonard P. "W. B. Yeats experiments with
an influence, " Victorian Studies (Indiana Univ.),
VI (1962), 66-74. (Pater.)

4040. Nevinson, Henry W. "W. B. Yeats, the poet of
vision, " London Mercury, XXXIX, 233 (March
1939), 485-91.

4041. O'Connell, J. P. Sailing to Byzantium. Cambridge,
Mass.: 1939. (Harvard Honors Theses in English, no. 11.)

4042. O'Conor, Norreys J. "Yeats and his vision, "
Changing Ireland. Cambridge, Mass.: 1924,
pp. 72-82.

4043. O'Faoláin, Sean. "Yeats and the younger generation, "
Horizon, V, 25 (Jan. 1942), 43-54.

4044. Olson, Elder. " 'Sailing to Byzantium': Prolegomena
to a poetics of the lyric, " Univ. Review, VIII, 3
(Spring 1912), 209-19. (Repr. in Hall & Steinmann (eds.), pp. 257-69.)

4045. Orel, Harold. The Develop. of W. B. Yeats: 1885-
1900. Lawrence, Kan.: 1968. (Univ. Kansas
Publ., Humanistic Studies, 39.)

4046. Parkinson, Thomas F. W. B. Yeats:...Early
Verse. Berkeley(?): 1951. (Bibliog., pp. 193-
8.)

4047. _____. "Vestiges of creation, " Sewanee Review,
LXIX (1961), 80-111. (Yeats' poetic process.)

4048. _____. W. B. Yeats: The Later Poetry. Berke-
ley/Los Angeles: 1964.

4049. _____. W. B. Yeats: Self-Critic and the Later
Poetry, 2nd edn. Berkeley: 1971 (1951). (2
vols. in 1.)

4050. Parrish, Stephen M., ed. A Concord. to the Poems
of W. B. Yeats. Ithaca, N.Y.: 1963.

4051. Paul-Dubois, Louis. "M. Yeats et la (sic) mouvement poétique en Irlande--I: le poète du rêve, "
Revue des Deux Mondes, année 99, pér. 7,
vol. LIII, 3 (Oct. 1, 1929), 558-83.

4052. _____. "M. Yeats et le mouvement poétique en
Irlande--II: le philosophe et l'influence, " Revue
des Deux Mondes, année 99, pér. 7, vol. LIII,
4 (Oct. 15, 1929), 824-46.

4053. Pauly, M.-H. "W. B. Yeats et les symbolistes
français, " Revue de Litt. Comparée, XX, 1
(Janv.-Mars 1940), 13-33.

4054. Peacock, Ronald. "Yeats, " The Poet in the Theatre.

London/N. Y.: 1946, pp. 117-28.

4055.   Perloff, Marjorie. Rhyme and Meaning in the Poetry
of Yeats. The Hague: 1970.

4056.   Polletta, Gregory T. "The progress in W. B. Yeats'
theories of poetry, " Diss. Abstr., XXII (1962),
2399/2400 (Princeton).

4057.   Pollock, J. H. W. B. Yeats. Dublin: 1935.

4058.   Quivey, James R. "Yeats and the epigram: a study
of technique in the four-line poems, " Discourse
(Concordia Coll.), XIII (1970), 58-72.

4059.   Rajan, B. "W. B. Yeats and the unity of being, "
Nineteenth Cen. and After, CXLVI (Sept. 1949),
150-61. (Incl. Mallarmé.)

4060.   _____. W. B. Yeats: A Crit. Introd. London:
1965. (Bibliog., pp. 193-9.)

4061.   Ransom, John Crowe. "Yeats and his symbols, "
Kenyon Review, I, 3 (Summer 1939), 309-22.
(Repr. in Hall & Steinmann (eds.), pp. 85-96.)

4062.   _____. "The Irish, the Gaelic, the Byzantine, "
Southern Review, VII, 3 (Winter 1942), 517-46.

4063.   Read, Herbert. "The later Yeats, " A Coat of Many
Colours. London: 1945, pp. 208-12. (On The
Coll. Poems (1933), esp. 'The Sorrow of Love.')

4064.   _____. "Révolte et réaction dans la poésie
anglaise moderne, " Presence, V, 1 (avril 1946),
56.

4065.   Reid, B. L. W. B. Yeats: The Lyric of Tragedy.
Norman, Okla.: 1961.

4066.   Reid, Forrest. W. B. Yeats: A Crit. Study. London: 1915.

4067.   Rhynehart, J. G. "Wilde's comments on early works
of W. B. Yeats, " Irish Book, I (1962), 102-4.
(Bibliog. Society of Ireland.)

4068.   Richardson, Dorothy M. "Yeats of Bloomsbury, "
Life and Letters Today, XXI, 20 (April 1939),
60-6.

4069.   Robinson, Lennox. "The man and the dramatist, "
Scattering Branches, ed. Stephen Gwynn. N. Y.:
1940, pp. 55-114.

4070.   _____. "Yeats: the early poems, " Review of
English Lit. (Leeds), VI, 3 (1965), 22-33.

4071.   Rosenthal, M. L. "On Yeats and the cultural symbolism of mod. poetry, " Yale Review, XLIV
(1960), 573-83.

4072.   Rothenstein, Sir William. "Yeats as a painter saw
him, " Scattering Branches, ed. Stephen Gwynn.
N. Y.: 1940, pp. 35-54.

4073.   Rudd, M. Divided Image. London: 1953.
4074.   Rutledge, Robert C. "The develop. of the poetry of
        W. B. Yeats as reflected in his metaphors, "
        Diss. Abstr., XXVII (1966), 1836A (George Wash.
        Univ.).
4075.   Saul, George B. Prolegomena to the Study of Yeats'
        Plays. Philad.: 1958.
4076.   _____. Prolegomena to the Study of Yeats' Poems.
        Philad.: 1958.
4077.   _____. "Yeats' verse before 'Responsibilities, ' "
        Arizona Quarterly, XVI (1960), 158-67.
4078.   _____. "Coda: the verse of Yeats' last years, "
        Arizona Quarterly, XVII (1961), 63-8.
4079.   Savage, D. S. "The aestheticism of W. B. Yeats, "
        The Personal Principle. London: 1944, pp. 67-
        91. (Repr. in Hall & Steinmann (eds.), pp. 173-
        94.)
4080.   Schaup, Susanne. "W. B. Yeats: Image of a poet
        in Germany, " Southern Humanities Review, II
        (1968), 313-23.
4081.   Schrickx, W. "W. B. Yeats: Symbolist en visionair
        Dichter, " De Vlaamse Gids, XLIX (1965), 380-96.
4082.   Schweisgut, Elsbeth. Yeats Feendichtung. Darmstadt:
        1927.
4083.   Seiden, Morton I. W. B. Yeats. The Poet as Myth-
        maker... East Lansing, Mich.: 1962.
4084.   Sena, Vinod. "W. B. Yeats and English poetic
        drama, " An English Miscellany (New Delhi), no.
        2 (1963), 23-36.
4085.   Shanks, E. B. "The later poetry of W. B. Yeats, "
        First Essays on Lit. London: 1923, pp. 238-
        44.
4086.   Sitwell, Edith. "W. B. Yeats, " Aspects of Mod.
        Poetry. London: 1934, pp. 73-89.
4087.   Skelton, Robin. The Poetic Pattern. London: 1956.
4088.   _____, and A. Saddlemyer, eds. The World of
        W. B. Yeats: Essays in Perspective. A Sym-
        posium and Catalogue, rev. edn. Seattle, Wash.:
        1967. (Earlier edn. Victoria, B. C.: 1965.)
        (W. B. Yeats Centen. Festival, Univ. of Victoria
        (Feb. 14-March 16, 1965).)
4089.   Spencer, Theodore. "The later poetry of W. B.
        Yeats, " Lit. Opinion in America, ed. Morton D.
        Zabel. N. Y.: 1938, pp. 263-77. (On 'Words
        for Music Perhaps.... ')
4090.   Spender, Stephen. "Yeats as a Realist, " The Destruc-
        tive Element. London: 1935, pp. 115-32.

4091.   _____ . "La crise des symboles, " France Libre,
        VII, 39 (Jan. 15, 1944), pp. 206-10. (On 'The
        Second Coming.')
4092.   Stace, W. T. "The faery poetry of Mr. W. B.
        Yeats, " British Review, I, 1 (Jan. 1913), 117-
        30.
4093.   Stallworthy, Jon. Betw. the Lines: Yeats' Poetry
        in the Making. Oxford, England: 1963.
4094.   _____ . Vision and Revision in Yeats' 'Last
        Poems.' London: 1969.
4095.   Staub, August W. "The 'unpopular theatre' of W. B.
        Yeats, " Quart. Journ. of Speech, XLVII (1961),
        363-71.
4096.   Stauffer, Donald A. "Yeats and the medium of poe-
        try, " English Lit. Hist., XV, 3 (Sept. 1948), 227-
        46.
4097.   _____ . The Golden Nightingale. N. Y.: 1949.
4098.   Stein, Arnold. "Yeats: a study in recklessness, "
        Sewanee Review, LVII (1949), 603-26.
4099.   Stock, A. G. W. B. Yeats: His Poetry and Thought.
        Cambridge, England: 1961.
4100.   Symons, Arthur. "Mr. W. B. Yeats, " Studies in
        Prose and Verse. London/N. Y.: 1904(?),
        pp. 230-41.
4101.   Tate, Allen. "Yeats' romanticism: notes and sug-
        gestions, " On the Limits of Poetry. N. Y.:
        1948, pp. 214-24.
4102.   Tillyard, E. M. W. Poetry Direct and Oblique, rev.
        edn. London: 1945.
4103.   Tindall, William Y. "The symbolism of W. B.
        Yeats, " Accent, V, 4 (Summer 1945), 203-12.
4104.   _____ . "Transcendentalism in contemp. lit., "
        The Asian Legacy and American Life, ed. Arthur
        E. Christy. N. Y.: 1945, pp. 175-92.
4105.   _____ . Forces in Mod. Brit. Lit., 1885-1946.
        N. Y.: 1947, pp. 248-63.
4106.   _____ . The Literary Symbol. Bloomington, Ind.:
        1960.
4107.   _____ . W. B. Yeats. N. Y.: 1966. (Columbia
        Essays on Mod. Writers, 15.)
4108.   Unterecker, John. A Reader's Guide to W. B.
        Yeats. London/N. Y.: 1959. (Noonday Press
        paperback.)
4109.   _____ , ed. Yeats: A Coll. of Crit. Essays.
        Englewood Cliffs, N. J.: 1963. (Spectrum paper-
        back.)
4110.   Ure, Peter. Towards a Mythology: Stud. in the

Poetry of W. B. Yeats. Liverpool/London:
1946.

4111. _____. Yeats the Playwright. London/Edinburgh:
1963. (Writers and Critics.)

4112. _____. W. B. Yeats. N.Y.: 1964. (Evergreen
Pilot Books, 27.)

4113. Vendler, Helen H. Yeats' Vision and the Later
Plays. Cambridge, Mass.: 1963.

4114. Verhulst, Margaret M. "Myth and symbol in the
plays of W. B. Yeats," Diss. Abstr. Intern'l,
XXX (1970), 3028A (Austin, Texas).

4115. Vordtriede, Werner. "W. B. Yeats: Urbild u.
Gegenwart," Neue dt. Hefte, CXXIV (1969), 61-
80.

4116. Wade, Allen. A Bibliog. of the Writings of W. B.
Yeats, 2nd rev. edn. London: 1958.

4117. Warren, Austin. "W. B. Yeats: the religion of a
poet," Rage For Order. Chicago: 1948, pp. 66-
84. (Repr. in Hall & Steinmann (eds.), pp. 200-
12.)

4118. Watanabe, Junko. "The symbolism of W. B. Yeats:
his doctrine of the mask," Coll. Essays by the
Members of the Faculty (Kyoritsu Women's
Junior College), no. 11. Kyoritsu, Japan: 1968,
pp. ?.

4119. _____. "The symbolism of W. B. Yeats: a
study of his later poems," Coll. Essays by the
Members of the Faculty (Kyoritsu Women's Junior
College), no. 13. Kyoritsu, Japan: 1969,
pp. 41-66.

4120. Watson, Thomas. "The French reput. of W. B.
Yeats," Comp. Lit., XII (1960), 256-62.

4121. Weeks, Donald. "Image and idea in Yeats' 'The
Second Coming,' " PMLA, LXIII, 1 (March 1948),
281-92. (Part I.)

4122. Weygandt, Cornelius. "W. B. Yeats and the Irish
Lit. Renaissance," Time of Yeats. N.Y.: 1937,
pp. 167-251.

4123. Whitaker, Thomas R. "The early Yeats and the
pattern of history," PMLA, LXXV (1960), 320-8.

4124. Wilder, Amos N. "W. B. Yeats and the Christian
option," The Spiritual Aspects of the New Poetry.
N.Y.: 1940, pp. 196-204.

4125. Williams, Melvin G. "Yeats and Christ: a study in
symbolism," Renascence, XX (1968), 174-8, 222.

4126. Wilson, Edmund. "W. B. Yeats," Axël's Castle.
N.Y.: 1931.

4127. Wilson, F. A. C. W. B. Yeats and Trad. London: 1958.

4128. _____. Yeats' Iconography. N. Y. /London: 1960.

4129. Winters, Yvor. "The Poems of T. Sturge Moore, Vols. I and II, " Hound and Horn, VI, 3 (April-June 1933), 534-45.

4130. _____. "The poetry of W. B. Yeats, " Twentieth Cen. Lit., VI (1960), 3-24.

4131. _____. The Poetry of W. B. Yeats. Denver, Colo.: 1960. (The Swallow Pamphlets, 10.)

4132. Witt, Marion W. "W. B. Yeats, " English Instit. Essays, 1946. N. Y.: 1947, pp. 74-101.

4133. _____. "Yeats: 1865-1965, " PMLA, LXXX (1965), 311-20.

4134. Worth, Katherine J. "Yeats and the French drama, " Mod. Drama, VIII (1965/6), 382-91.

4135. Wrenn, C. L. W. B. Yeats: A Lit. Study. London: 1920.

4136. Yeats, W. B. "Preface, " Axël, by Villiers de l'Isle-Adam, trans. H. P. R. Finberg. London: 1925.

4137. _____. "Der dicht. Symbolismus, " (überset. u. erl. von W. Kayser). Gestaltung-Umgestaltung. Festschrift zum 75. Geburtstag von H. A. Korff, ed. Joachim Müller. Leipzig: 1957, pp. 239-48.

4138. _____. "The symbolism of poetry" and "Louis Lambert, " Essays and Introds. London: 1961.

4139. _____. Autobiographies. London: 1955. (Collier paperback edn. N. Y.: 1965.) (On Symbolism, A. Symons' transl., Mallarmé, etc.)

4140. Youngblood, Sarah. "Yeats and the Symbolists, " South Central Bull., XXVII, 3 (Oct. 1967), 82. (Abstract.)

4141. Zwerdling, Alex. Yeats and the Heroic Ideal. N. Y.: 1965. ("List of works cited, " pp. 183-90.)

INDEX TO AUTHORS

[anonymous studies and unidentified collaborative
studies have not been included in the present index]